THE CATHEDRALS OF IRELAND

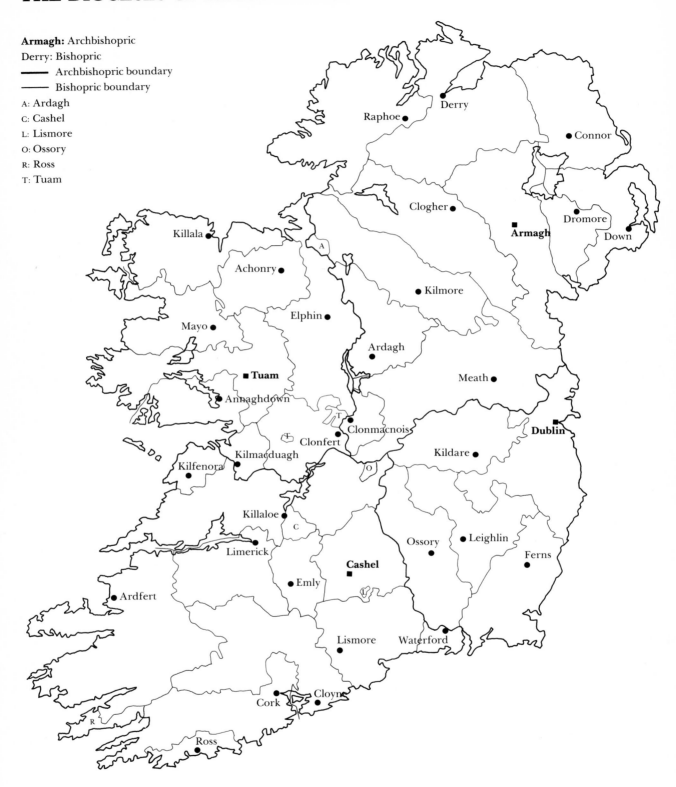

THE DIOCESES OF IRELAND c1320

Armagh: Archbishopric
Derry: Bishopric
———— Archbishopric boundary
——— Bishopric boundary
A: Ardagh
C: Cashel
L: Lismore
O: Ossory
R: Ross
T: Tuam

Derry

Raphoe

Connor

Clogher

Dromore
Down

Armagh

Killala

Achonry

Kilmore

Mayo

Elphin

Ardagh

Meath

Tuam

Annaghdown

Clonmacnois

Dublin

Clonfert

Kilmacduagh

Kildare

Kilfenora

Killaloe

Limerick

Ossory

Leighlin

Ferns

Ardfert

Emly

Cashel

Lismore

Waterford

Cork

Cloyne

Ross

Map of Dioceses, 1310

THE
CATHEDRALS
OF IRELAND

PETER GALLOWAY

Photographs by
CORMAC SIMMS

In the old grave-yard Protestants and Catholics lie together - that is, not together;

for each has a side of the ground, where they sleep, and so occupied,

do not quarrel. The sun was shining down upon the brilliant grass and I don't

think the shadows of the Protestant graves were any longer or shorter

than those of the Catholics.

William Makepeace Thackeray,
on a visit to Lismore Cathedral, c. 1841.
The Irish Sketch-Book, i, p. 96

The Institute of Irish Studies
The Queen's University of Belfast

To M.R.S.T.

For generous financial assistance towards the publication of this book we are very grateful to the Sir Alfred Beit Trust, the Esme Mitchell Trust and the Cultural Traditions Committee of the Community Relation Council which aims to encourage acceptance and understanding of cultural diversity.

Published 1992
The Institute of Irish Studies,
The Queen's University of Belfast,
Belfast

HB ISBN 0 85389 452 3

Typesetting by Textflow Services Ltd, Belfast
Printed by W. & G. Baird, Ltd., Antrim
Cover design by Rodney Miller Associates

CONTENTS

FOREWORD

by His Eminence, Cahal, Cardinal Daly, Archbishop of Armagh, and The Most Reverend Robert Eames, Archbishop of Armagh

It is our pleasure to commend this study of the cathedral churches of Ireland. The Church of Patrick has given much down through the ages to the Christian world as scholars, teachers, doctors and nurses have gone out in the name of the Gospel. Their homeland through its inheritance of the worship and practice of Celtic Christianity has so many fine cathedrals and church buildings. Each speaks of that great tradition of worship and witness. Each reflects something of the love of God so dear to the majority of Irish people. Dr Galloway has provided us with a most readable and useful book which we hope will be of great value to all who seek to understand more clearly the history of Irish Christianity and its cathedrals. We hope it will be read by many who will gain through its pages a great appreciation of these fine buildings and the message they represent.

ACKNOWLEDGEMENTS

I would like to thank the following individuals who have contributed in various ways to the appearance of this book.

The Most Revd Dermot Clifford, Archbishop of Cashel and Emly (Roman Catholic); the Most Revd Edward Daly, Bishop of Derry (Roman Catholic); the Right Revd Edward Darling, Bishop of Limerick, Ardfert, Aghadoe, Killaloe, Kilfenora, Clonfert, Kilmacduagh and Emly (Church of Ireland); the Most Revd Walton Empey, Bishop of Meath and Kildare (Church of Ireland); the Most Revd Thomas Finnegan, Bishop of Killala (Roman Catholic); the Most Revd Thomas Flynn, Bishop of Achonry (Roman Catholic);the Most Revd Michael Harty, Bishop of Killaloe (Roman Catholic); the Right Revd John Neill, Bishop of Tuam, Killala and Achonry (Church of Ireland); the Most Revd Colm O'Reilly, Bishop of Ardagh and Clonmacnoise (Roman Catholic).

The Very Revd Edward Ardis, Dean of Killala Cathedral, the Very Revd Alan Barrett, Dean of Clonmacnoise; Fr. A. Bradley, Administrator of Newry Cathedral; the Very Revd Maurice Carey, Dean of St Fin Barre's Cathedral, Cork; Fr. Sean Connolly, Administrator of St Peter's Cathedral, Belfast; the Very Revd Dr John Combe, Dean of Kilmore Cathedral; the Revd Raymond Doherty, Rector of Ennis (in charge of Kilfenora Cathedral); Fr. Patrick Duggan, Administrator of St Mary's Cathedral, Kilkenny; the Very Revd David Earl, Dean of Ferns Cathedral; the Very Revd William Grant, Dean of St Mary's Cathedral, Tuam; the Very Revd Victor Griffin, former Dean of St Patrick's Cathedral, Dublin; the Very Revd George Hilliard, Dean of Cloyne Cathedral; the Revd Samuel Jones, Rector of St Saviour's Church, Connor; the Revd Canon John McCammon, Rector of Lisburn Cathedral; the Very Reverend John McCarthy, Dean of Clogher and Rector of Enniskillen Cathedral; the Revd Canon Stuart McGee, Rector of Achonry Cathedral; the Very Revd Gilbert Mayes, former Dean of Lismore Cathedral; the Very Revd Hugh Mortimer, Dean of the Cathedral of St Mary the Virgin and St John the Baptist, Sligo, and Mrs Pauline Mortimer; Fr. William Murphy, Administrator of Killarney Cathedral; Fr. Leonard O'Brien, Adminstrator of the Cathedral of St Mary and St Anne, Cork; Fr. Peter O'Brien, Administrator of Ballina Cathedral; Fr. Nicholas O'Mahony, Administrator of Holy Trinity Cathedral, Waterford;

Mr John Barry of Emly; Sr. M. Angela Bolster, Diocesan Archivist of the Roman Catholic Dioceses of Cork and Ross; the Revd John Bond, Rector of Ballynure; Dr Bernard Brennan, Fr. Denis Dolan, Diocesan Secretary of the Roman Catholic Diocese of Clogher; Fr. Gerald Dolan, Diocesan Secretary of the Roman Catholic Diocese of Elphin; Mr Paul Drayson for the maps; Miss C. Fitzpatrick of Kilfenora Cathedral; the Revd Roger Kent; the Revd Dr Anthony Marks; Fr. Ignatius Murphy of Ennis; the Revd Timothy O'Donovan; Dr Raymond Refaussé, Librarian and Archivist of the Representative Church Body Library, Dublin; Mr Noel Ross, Honorary Secretary of the County Louth Archaeological and Historical Society; the Revd Michael Thompson; Mrs Rita Tully, the Bishop's Office, Roman Catholic Diocese of Achonry; Mr Julian C. Walton of Waterford Heritage Survey.

The photographs used to illustrate this book were taken by Cormac Simms, who also doubled as driver during a tour of Ireland's cathedrals in the summer of 1989. His knowledge of the highways and byways of Ireland enabled us to trace many of the more remote cathedrals. On two further tours in 1990 and 1991 the patient and long-suffering driver was Michael Turner.

Although some of the Irish saints from the Celtic period survive only as names and unreliable legends, their pioneering settlements were the direct ancestors of Ireland's cathedrals. In a sense their work has caused the appearance of this book in age far removed from their own.

Nathy of Achonry
Finian of Aghadoe
Brendan of Annaghdown, Ardfert and Clonfert
Mel of Ardagh
Declan of Ardmore
Macartan of Clogher
Kieran of Clonmacnoise
Finian of Clonard
Colman of Cloyne
Oengus Mac Nissi of Connor
Fin Barre of Cork
Columba of Derry
Colman of Dromore
Cianan of Duleek
Assicus of Elphin
Ailbhe of Emly
Aidan of Ferns
Kevin of Glendalough
Brigid of Kildare
Fachan of Kilfenora
Canice of Kilkenny
Muredach of Killala
Flannan of Killaloe
Colman of Kilmacduagh
Fethlimidh of Kilmore
Laserian of Leighlin
Munchin of Limerick
Carthage of Lismore
Mochta of Louth
Lurach of Maghera
Colman of Mayo
Eunan of Raphoe
Cronan of Roscrea
Fachtna of Rosscarbery
Senan of Scattery Island
Loman of Trim
Jarlath of Tuam
and
Patrick, of Armagh and of Ireland.

PREFACE

In 1894, Thomas McAll Fallow, published *The Cathedral Churches of Ireland*. His introduction began as follows:

"It is not altogether easy for a person, whose knowledge of a cathedral church has been gained by familiarity with any of the ancient cathedrals of England, to realise when standing at the door or some humble, and perhaps common-place little country church in Ireland, that the insignificant building before him may possibly possess as just a claim to the proud title of a cathedral church as any of the stateliest of the minsters, which are the glory of England, or of the continent of Europe. Yet so it is, and the insignificance of the country cathedrals of Ireland, their inaccessibility in villages remote from railway stations, and the fact that many of them are buildings of no great age in a country where nearly every parish can boast of some object of remote antiquity, have combined to contribute to the general obscurity with which most of these churches are surrounded, and we have thus an explanation of how it is that such complete ignorance prevails as to them."

Irish cathedral architecture cannot compare, and should not be compared, with the cathedrals of Britain and Europe. But it possesses many features of interest: the west door of Clonfert, the chancel arch at St Mary's, Tuam, the east windows of Killaloe, the Cistercian austerity of St Mary's, Limerick, the nave piers of Cloyne, and the ubiquitous Round Towers. Many of the cathedrals are hidden away among the hills and valleys of Ireland, but the effort needed to find them is always worthwhile. There is a quiet grace and an unostentatious beauty about these remote sites, from where prayer has risen to heaven since the 5th and 6th centuries.

Fallow, who died on 25 November 1910, was an enthusiastic antiquary and author of a number of books on Yorkshire churches. He decided that the inaccessibility of Ireland's cathedrals, and the insignificance of their size and architecture was no excuse for allowing ignorance to prevail. He travelled through in Ireland in the 1870s and 1880s, visiting many of the Church of Ireland cathedrals. But extensive as his travels were, he was unable to visit Achonry, Clogher, Elphin, Kilfenora and Killala Cathedrals, and his notes on these cathedrals were based partly on what slender printed material he could find, and partly on the study of photographs of the buildings. His book is exactly what it claims to be, a collection of "notes".

Although the construction of Roman Catholic cathedrals in Ireland was well under way at the time of his visits, they were still at the stage of historical infancy and, as an antiquary, they held little interest for him. He had no difficulty in calling his book *The Cathedral Churches of Ireland*, as though there were no others. His interest and affection lay with Ireland's small, poor and remote country cathedrals, and he wrote little about the larger and more well-known cathedrals at Cashel, Dublin, Kilkenny and Limerick. Despite these limitations, his monograph was a pioneering effort to which the present author owes much.

In 1932 John Day and Henry Patton, both bishops of the Church of Ireland, wrote another general survey. John Godfrey Fitzmaurice Day (1874–1938) was bishop of Ossory, Ferns and Leighlin 1920–1938. He was elected archbishop of Armagh on 27 April 1938 and died on 26 September in the same year. Henry Edmund Patton (1867–1943) was bishop of Killaloe, Kilfenora, Clonfert and Kilmacduagh from 1924 until his death on 2 April 1943. They produced in their words, "a series of short sketches of the cathedral churches of Ireland." They covered the greater cathedrals that Fallow had omitted, and they wrote in a more detached and lofty style. But the content is much like that of Fallow – a collection of notes. Their interest lay with the cathedrals of their own denomination, and their book was properly entitled *The Cathedrals of the Church of Ireland*. But they noted the "splendid and spacious cathedrals" of the Roman Catholic church, which were "well worthy of the attention of visitors." In 1971 a small pocket-sized illustrated guide entitled *Cathedrals of the Church of Ireland* was produced by Robert Wyse Jackson (1908–1976), Bishop of Limerick, Ardfert and Aghadoe 1963–1970. He died on 21 October 1976. Bishop Jackson's booklet was only a series of miniature portraits, although good of its kind, and added very little to the work of Day and Patton.

In the sixty years since John Day and Henry Patton wrote their book, there have been changes and developments in the story of the Church of Ireland cathedrals, especially the abandoning of Elphin Cathedral and the elevation of the church at Sligo to replace it. For some time there has been a need for a new work to update and substantially extend the work of Day and Patton.

Probably no other nation has seen such a spate of cathedral building as Ireland in the 19th century. In the years between 1793 and 1965 twenty-seven new cathedrals were built in Ireland, twenty-three of them between 1799 and 1900. With the relaxation of the penal laws and the emancipation of Catholics, the Roman Catholic Church embarked on a widespread plan of church-building, and gradually their cathedrals began to rise in the cities and towns. Two hundred years have passed since construction began at Waterford on the first post-Reformation Roman Catholic cathedral in Ireland. Twenty-five years have passed since the completion of Galway, the last such cathedral. In these ecumenical days it seems appropriate to draw together in one book all the buildings in Ireland which are, or have been, distinguished by the title of "cathedral church", and present them to a new generation.

INTRODUCTION

Christianity and the Cathedral Churches of Ireland

The First Centuries

Although Rome was aware of the existence of Ireland from the time of Julius Caesar, the country was never incorporated into the Roman Empire. An invasion was considered when Julius Agricola was governor of Britain (A.D. 78–85). Agricola claimed that he could conquer Ireland and hold it with one legion (6,000 men), but although there is some evidence of preparation for an expeditionary force, no Roman army ever landed in Ireland and the boast was never put to the test. Contact was limited to commercial expeditions and, on another level, Irish raiders frequently attacked Wales, Cumbria and Scotland. With the beginning of the withdrawal of the Romans from Britain towards the end of the 4th century, the Irish began to make permanent settlements in Wales.

It is very difficult to disentangle fact from legend in the history of Ireland before the beginning of the 5th century and to know precisely what was happening. Ireland was not one country but a collection of petty tribes and dynasties, constantly fighting against each other and striving for local supremacy. The fortunes of a particular tribe depended almost entirely on the strength and ability of its king or chieftain and there was no single individual strong enough to control the whole of Ireland. There were perhaps 150 or so petty kingdoms whose kings put themselves under the protection of a more powerful but still minor king, who in turn put himself under the protection of one of five provincial kings. One of these provincial kings would occasionally claim the title of High King, but it was seldom acknowledged throughout the whole of Ireland. If it was to be anything more than an empty title, allegiance and obedience had to be compelled by force. With the exception of a few brief years under the High Kingship of Brian Boru (1002–14), Ireland remained a fragmented state, impossible either to control or to unite. Probably not until after the civil war of 1689–91, more than six hundred years later, could there be said to be one effective rule throughout Ireland.

During the 5th century the historic four provinces of Ireland – Ulster, Leinster, Munster and Connacht – begin to appear. The word 'province' should not be taken to imply any kind of regional government at this period. Loose groupings by virtue of language, interest or activity would be a safer definition. In the north of the country was a kingdom called Ulidia (the Ulaid people) from which comes the name Ulster. In the southern half of the country were the groupings of Munster and Leinster. Munster (the place of the men of Mumha) was a collection of kingdoms mostly ruled by members of the Eoghanact dynasty, descended from Eogan, of whom nothing historical is known. The kingdom of Cashel in Co. Tipperary became the dominant kingdom in Munster.

Among the Munster kingdoms were a group of vassal peoples known as the Déisi who came to set up their own kingdom, called Dál Cais, in what is now Co. Clare. Leinster (place of broad spears) was dominated by two groups of the Laigin people.

The Arrival of Christianity

Christianity reached Ireland at an uncertain date, but there were a sufficient number of Irish Christians by the end of the 4th century to justify the dispatch of a bishop from Rome. In 431 Pope Celestine I sent a bishop named Palladius to Ireland. Nothing definite is known of him beyond his name and his papal commission. The story goes that he landed near Wexford with some companions and founded three churches, but at the end of three months, having encountered the hostility of a local ruler, he left Ireland and is supposed to have died in Scotland. Despite these late accounts, some historians maintain that he is one and the same with the great Apostle of the Irish, St Patrick.

Cormac's Chapel, Cashel. c. 1830

The history of Christianity in Ireland is inseparable from the activity of Patrick, despite the fact that little for certain is known of his life. But his ministry and that of his disciples led to the general conversion of the Irish to Christianity during the course of the 5th century. It is said that when Patrick arrived in Ireland he discovered four bishops already working there, among them St Declan of Ardmore and St Ailbhe of Emly, both places later to become the sites of cathedrals.

Patrick arrived in Ireland *c.* 432, and the foundation of his seat at Armagh (now the primatial see of Ireland in both the Roman Catholic Church and the Church of Ireland) is traditionally dated to 442. Most of his work was confined to the northern half of the island, a fact which could be explained by the presence of the existing four bishops in the south. He baptised several thousand people, introduced an episcopal form of government, appointing (it is said) 350 bishops, built perhaps fifty churches of timber, introduced monasticism, and founded several monasteries himself before his death about the year 461. Although many less reliable stories have gathered around his memory, his work was pioneering and extensive, and he is arguably the most significant figure in Irish history.

The Monasteries

The type of Christianity that developed in Ireland after the death of St Patrick *c.* 461 was almost entirely monastic. It was due to an ascetic movement that swept across Ireland in the 6th century, led by St Enda (d. 530) at Inishmore in the Aran Islands off the west coast and St Finian (*c.* 500–50) at Clonard in Co. Meath in the east. The monastic movement developed rapidly after the death of St Patrick and dominated Irish Christianity until the reforming synods of the 12th century reorganised the Irish church on the European pattern of territorial dioceses.

Monastic life in Ireland began as groups of men and women living in austere conditions in a compound of beehive-shaped huts surrounded by a wall. These early monasteries were the ancestors of the ancient diocesan sees of Ireland. With a few exceptions, the Church of Ireland cathedrals stand on the site of a 5th- or 6th-century monastery. Many monasteries were established in remote and lonely places by the more austere communities — explaining the isolated sites of many cathedrals such as Clonmacnoise, Glendalough and Kilmacduagh. Because rural Ireland is so thinly populated, the sense of remote isolation of these sites today is probably much as it was 1,500 years ago.

By A.D. 800 the monasteries had evolved into little Christian towns consisting of streets of wooden huts and halls clustering around a church, with a school for teaching religion as well as many other buildings. When Clonmacnoise was burnt in 1179, 105 houses were destroyed. In organisation these monastic communities tended to mirror the parallel political organisation. At the head was an abbot with a bishop on his staff, and the monastery enjoyed complete autonomy – there was no primate for the whole church in Ireland. The abbot or abbess held supreme authority by virtue of being the coarb (heir or successor) of the founder of the monastery; the Abbot of Armagh was styled Coarb of Patrick, and the Abbess of Kildare was the Coarb of Brigid. Some abbots nominated their successors from their own families, others were elected from those abbatial families, and gradually the office of abbot became hereditary.

Many monasteries became famous as religious centres of teaching and learning, inaugurating what has become known as the Golden Age of Ireland. The Golden Age is generally dated from *c.* 550, about a century after the arrival of St Patrick, to the time of the Viking raids on Ireland in the 9th and 10th centuries. It was a period of high artistic creativity in the areas of poetry, manuscript illumination, metalwork, jewellery, enamelling, stone-carving, woodwork and leatherwork. The Book of Kells and the Book of Durrow are the most famous examples of the beauty of illuminated manuscripts. The Ardagh Chalice (mid-8th century) is a fine example of Irish gold filigree and coloured enamelwork. The High Crosses, a series of elaborately sculptured free-standing stone crosses, a distinctively Irish art form, proliferated between the 8th and the 12th centuries.

By the 9th century the quality of Irish learning and art enjoyed the highest reputation and admiration throughout Europe, and as early as the 6th century Irish missionaries were crossing to the mainland of Europe to found monasteries there. One, St Virgilius (or Fergal) became Bishop of Salzburg; others made foundations in France and Switzerland.

'If anything held the Irish together at all, it was Christianity and culture: the abbots, bishops, priests, scholars and artists were not confined by being members of one *tuath* (tribe) or another from crossing borders and wandering freely about the whole country. Monasteries flourished in all parts, and in many instances played the composite roles of town, hostel, penitentiary, school, university, religious centre and sanctuary.'[1] All this was severely shaken by the arrival of the Vikings.

The Vikings

The Vikings were a group of peoples from Scandinavia whose technical ability had advanced far enough by the 8th century to enable them to build strong, long distance sea-going ships. Active from the 8th to the 10th centuries, they have been immortalised by history and Hollywood as hordes of savage and illiterate warriors intent only on plundering and burning. The first recorded Viking raid on Ireland took place in 795, and sporadic incursions in the form of looting and burning raids occurred in the first half of the 9th century. The monasteries, by now treasure-houses and largely defenceless, were prime targets, and several were repeatedly attacked. Many of the contents of museums on the west coast of Norway are the evidence of Viking plunder. By 841 their first fortified settlements had been established on the Louth coast near the mouth of the Liffey, to be followed by many others. Dublin, Cork, Limerick, Wicklow, Waterford and Wexford were all Viking foundations.

In the years 1002–14, Ireland saw the rule of the one monarch in its history who can be said to have been an effective and acknowleged High King – Brian Boru. Brian was king of the Dál Cais from 976 and within a few years had established himself as king of all Munster, and in 1002 he displaced the High King, Máel Sechnaill II. He decisively defeated the Vikings at the Battle of Clontarf in 1014 and effectively ended Viking power in Ireland. But his death in the same battle ended the brief existence of Ireland as a unitary state, and it relapsed into political chaos and anarchy. The Vikings were no longer a serious threat after Clontarf, but the internal political turmoil of Ireland was as much a threat to the monasteries as the Vikings had been, and the round of burning and plundering, often by the Irish themselves, continued intermittently until the 16th century.[2] In spite of this destruction, the 11th and 12th centuries saw a new renaissance of Irish craftsmanship and architecture. Illuminated manuscripts were inscribed again, poetry was written and the kings became patrons of the arts. The 12th century was a great peak in the Irish form of Romanesque architecture, and there are a number of splendid survivals that witness this fact: high on the Rock of Cashel in Co. Tipperary stands Ireland's most famous Romanesque church, Cormac's Chapel, built 1127–34 and astonishingly still intact; the great chancel arch at Tuam Cathedral (c.1152), the west doorway of Clonfert Cathedral (c.1167) and the chancel arch of the Nuns' Church at Clonmacnoise (c. 1167) are striking examples of this architectural flowering.

Reform in the 12th century

The monasteries were by now very different places from what they were in the days of their founders. The office of abbot was generally hereditary and often held by a layman, and the bishop was a subordinate official on his staff, a principle established by A.D. 700. The rigours of the monastic rule had become more relaxed, and monks were known to keep concubines and live with their families outside the monastery, treating it as a college and visiting it from time to time. More importantly, Ireland was now beginning to lag behind Europe in its development. Other European countries were founding secular universities, but the Irish felt no need to follow suit, regarding their monastic schools as sufficient centres of learning. Ireland was also unique in its maintenance of monastic bishops at a time when diocesan bishops were the rule elsewhere.

By the end of the 11th century the movement for reform was beginning to develop. Several Irish kings had made pilgrimages to Rome during the years 1028–64. They were, as one author has observed, 'the first overt symptom of a break-out from that isolation from the rest of the universal Church which has become a feature of the Irish Church in the Dark Ages'.[3] In 1101 a provincial synod was held at Cashel in Munster which began the process. Cashel, hitherto a royal fortress, was handed over by the King of Munster to the church for its exclusive use, free from any lay control; the Bishop of Cashel, styled 'the chief bishop of Munster', was appointed papal legate and was the first Irish bishop to hold that title and to establish a direct link with Rome. The synod began a programme of reform by conciliar decree. The work of the Synod of Cashel was modest, but the process of reform had begun and was virtually complete by the end of the century.

The basic flaw of the Irish Church was that it was still dominated by the anachronism of a monastic system. Monasteries such as Armagh, Clonmacnoise, Clonard, Emly, Glendalough, Kells, Lismore and others were still the focal point of ecclesiastical government, and they were ruled by powerful lay hereditary abbots with non-jurisdictional subordinate bishops. Each monastery had a bishop, whose episcopal functions were exercised on the authority of the abbot. Because of this situation, the Celtic Church cannot be said to have had cathedrals as we know them today. A cathedral church houses the cathedra, the throne of a ruling diocesan bishop, and such bishops were unknown before the reforms of the 12th century.

The Synod of Ráith Bressail, 1111

Two bishops – Celsus of Armagh and Malchus of Lismore – were the principal guides in the growing movement to reform the church. Celsus was a lay hereditary abbot who had had himself consecrated bishop. Celsus and Malchus summoned the first of the two great 12th-century synods which began the reform process. The Synod of Ráith Bressail, which met in 1111, was the first national gathering of the Irish Church. The location of Ráith Bressail is unknown, but it was probably somewhere in central Tipperary not far from Cashel. It was attended by fifty bishops (and it is likely that there were other bishops in Ireland not present), 300 priests, 3,000 clerics, the High King and many nobles. The presence of so many bishops was evidence of the loose, archaic and inefficient structure of the Irish church at the beginning of the 12th century.

Essentially Ráith Bressail brought the Irish Church into line with the European pattern by establishing a series of territorial dioceses to cover the whole island. There were to be two provincial archbishops, Armagh (an archbishopric since 1106) for the north, and Cashel for the south, and twenty four bishops, twelve for each province. Gilbert, Bishop of Limerick, papal legate in Ireland for twenty-eight years, presided at the synod and ensured that Limerick had well-defined boundaries. But the other dioceses were only vaguely defined, usually by reference to four named points. The turmoil of arguing and bargaining must have been intense because of the presence of fifty monastic bishops. Which of the monastic churches were to be the cathedral churches of the new dioceses, and which of the bishops present were to be the new diocesan bishops? It cannot have been easy for individual monasteries to subordinate their entrenched rights and dignities to the new diocesan system, and the ephemeral dioceses which appeared and rapidly disappeared in the 12th and early 13th centuries indicate areas of dispute. But Ráith Bressail was a watershed of reform from which there was no turning back. 'It was at this synod that the churches of Ireland were given up entirely to the bishops free for ever from the authority and rent of lay princes.'[4]

The work of Ráith Bressail can be summarised as follows: the power and jurisdiction of the abbot was to be limited to the cloister; the monks, like their abbots, were to abandon all worldly activities and spend their lives serving God alone and in prayer; the bishops were to become the focus of ecclesiastical government; the dioceses were to be fixed in number and territorial in extent, and the episcopate subjected to the authority of the pope.

The Synod of Kells–Mellifont, 1152

The tentative work of Ráith Bressail was completed at the second great synod in the 12th century – the Synod of Kells–Mellifont in 1152. Often referred to as the Synod of Kells, its correct conjoint name derives from the fact that its sessions were divided between the great abbeys of Kells and Mellifont in Co. Meath. The synod created several new dioceses, and the Bishops of Dublin and Tuam were given the title of archbishop. The synod was attended by Cardinal John Paparo, the papal legate, who invested all four archbishops with the pallium, a collar of lamb's wool, the emblem that directly linked them with the pope in Rome, to whose authority they were now subject. Diocesan boundaries were still undefined and remained so until about 1320.

The organisation of dioceses after Kells–Mellifont was as follows:

The Province of Armagh (Ulster)

Ardagh, Armagh, Clonard, Connor, Dair-Luis (later Kilmore), Down, Duleek, Kells, Louth (later Clogher), Maghera (later Derry) and Raphoe.

Cardinal Paparo ruled that on the deaths of the incumbents, smaller sees should be suppressed and absorbed into larger neighbours. Under this ruling (and for political reasons as well), Clonard, Duleek and Kells were amalgamated to form a diocese of Meath centred initially at Clonard and later at Trim.

The diocese of Dromore was created later in the 12th century.

The Province of Cashel (Munster)

Ardfert, Cashel, Cloyne, Cork, Emly, Kilfenora, Killaloe, Limerick, Lismore, Roscrea, Ross, Scattery Island and Waterford.

Ardmore and Mungret laid claim to diocesan status. Mungret's claim was soon quashed by Limerick, but Ardmore maintained its existence as a diocese for about fifty years. Roscrea and Scattery Island, detached from Killaloe at Ráith Bressail, were reunited with it by the end of the 12th century.

The Province of Dublin (Leinster)

Dublin, Ferns, Glendalough, Kildare, Kilkenny, Leighlin.

The Province of Tuam (Connacht)

Achonry, Clonfert, Killala, Kilmacduagh, Mayo, Roscommon (later Elphin).

The Diocese of Annaghdown was created later in the 12th century.

The ephemeral dioceses perished largely because of conflicting political interests. Ardmore, Glendalough, Scattery Island, Kells, Mayo and Roscrea barely survived into the 13th century before their episcopal status was suppressed. Generally the diocesan pattern represented the political pattern, bishops being provided for particular tribes and kingdoms, and the extension of the territory of one kingdom at the expense of a neighbouring kingdom sometimes involved the demise of a neighbouring diocese as well if its boundaries were co-terminous with the conquered kingdom.

The Former Cathedral Churches and Episcopal Sees

The former cathedrals, all now ruined and disused, are mostly in the care of public authorities. The sites covered are Annaghdown, Ardagh, Ardfert, Ardmore, Cashel, Clonmacnoise, Elphin, Glendalough, Kilmacduagh, Maghera, Roscrea, Scattery Island and Trim. The ruins at Duleek, Louth and Mayo post-date the cathedral period, but these towns were episcopal sees and are included for the sake of completeness. Aghadoe is included because it has long been styled a cathedral although it is now certain that there never was a diocese of Aghadoe. Ardmore and Roscrea were very ephemeral dioceses, but the names of bishops are known, and the remains at each site are of sufficient interest to warrant inclusion.

Ardcarn, Ardstraw, Cong, Dair-Inis, Mungret, Ratass and Roscommon are occasionally referred to as diocesan sees but have been excluded for the following reasons:

Ardcarn

Ardcarn, 6.4km east of Boyle, Co. Roscommon, was named as an alternative to Ardagh at the Synod of Ráith Bressail in 1111, but it never operated as an episcopal see. The Church of Ireland parish church stands on the site of the early monastery.

Ardstraw

Ardstraw, 6km west of Newtownstewart, Co. Tyrone, a foundation of St Patrick, was named at Ráith Bressail as the see for a diocese which corresponded with the diocese of Derry, but no names of bishops have been recorded. It was superseded by Derry at Kells–Mellifont. The remains of a medieval church and a late 17th-century church can be seen. There is no trace of the monastic episcopal foundation.

Cong

Cong, 36.8km north-west of Tuam in Co. Mayo, was designated at Ráith Bressail as the see of one of the five bishoprics for Connacht, but the diocese was not recognised at Kells–

Mellifont and no names of bishops have been recorded. The beautiful fragments the early 13th-century Cong Abbey can be seen to the south west of the village.

Dair-Inis

Dair-Inis in Co. Cavan appears in a version of Cardinal Paparo's list of dioceses in 1152, but is thought to refer to Kilmore (q.v.).

Mungret

Mungret, 4.8km south-west of Limerick, appears, with Ardmore, in Cardinal Paparo's list as a church that claimed diocesan status, but it was too close to Limerick to assert its claims. It was founded by St Nessan in the first half of the 6th century. The site includes a 12th-century church with a trabeate west door; a 13th/15th-century nave and chancel church with a square battlemented dwelling-tower at the west end, known as the 'Abbey'; and a small 13th-century chapel.

Ratass

Ratass, 1.6km east of Tralee, Co. Kerry, was named at Ráith Bressail as a see, but its position was superseded by Ardfert within six years. There is a nave-and-chancel church with antae, a trabeate west door and a simple Romanesque east window.

Roscommon

Roscommon, 32km north of Athlone, Co. Roscommon, was the site of a monastery founded by St Comman in the 6th century. It was named in Cardinal Paparo's list as a see in the province of Tuam, probably at the urging of Turlough O'Connor, King of Connacht. His death in 1156 removed its chief support, and the see moved to Elphin. A Dominican priory founded in 1253 and rebuilt in 1453 is to be seen; it has a long, narrow church with a fine west window.

The Arrival of the Anglo-Normans, 1171

In 1155–6 Pope Adrian IV issued a bull entitled *Laudabiliter*. The bull invited Henry II of England (1154–89) to 'go to the island of Ireland for the purpose of subjecting that people to the laws and to root out the weeds of vice'. The subsequent Anglo-Norman invasion of Ireland in 1171–2, for better or worse, has left an enduring legacy in Ireland.

The diocesan system, which had been so recently established at the Synod of Kells–Mellifont, and which might reasonably have been expected to settle down to a period of stability, came under pressure for largely political reasons. Not until the end of the 17th century could English control be said to extend to the whole of Ireland. In earlier centuries royal influence was limited to certain areas under direct control, and the diocesan system was used to bring the remoter areas under royal jurisdiction. Where a diocese outside Anglo-

Norman control bordered on one firmly within an Anglo-Norman sphere of influence, the practice of suppression and amalgamation was occasionally used in an attempt to extend English control. The union of the diocese of Glendalough with the diocese of Dublin in 1216 was a case in point. In 1327, in response to English pressure, Pope John XXII decreed the union of three dioceses (Achonry, Annaghdown and Kilmacduagh) with the diocese of Tuam. Lismore was united to Waterford in 1363 for much the same reason. Both these dioceses lay in Munster, which was the most difficult part of Ireland to control. By the early 14th century the majority of the bishops in the rest of Ireland were English nominees, whereas Munster's bishops were still generally Irish.

The general policy of appointing English bishops to Irish dioceses might have been an expedient way of extending English rule in Ireland, or it may have been a useful way of rewarding loyal clerics, but it was pastorally disastrous. 'Many

Kildare Cathedral in ruins, c. 1830

bishops were non-resident because they had found it pleasanter and more profitable to go as suffragans to some English bishop. About the year 1432 there were no less than four men claiming to be bishop of the poverty-stricken diocese of Dromore, and all four were residing in England. In all, we find about nine bishops of Dromore, and as many more from Annaghdown, in pre-Reformation times acting as suffragans in England and Wales. There were, besides, about four from Achonry, three from Clonfert, and three from Killala. Many an Englishman appointed to a pecunious Irish diocese never even bothered to pay it a visit.'[5]

The Reformation in Ireland

The Reformation of the 16th century and its aftermath brought considerable changes in the organisation of Irish Church. By May 1534, Henry VIII (1509–47) had instructed the Irish government in Dublin to ignore all papal provisions and appointments to Irish dioceses. The existing archbishops and bishops were to continue in office, but their successors would in future be appointed by the king instead of the pope. In 1536 the king was proclaimed 'supreme head' of the Church of Ireland and the dissolution of the Irish monasteries began. This was the first use of the title 'Church of Ireland'' which eventually became the official name of the reformed church.

The Reformation was never pursued or enforced with any vigour in Ireland because, with the still considerable power of the Irish lords, it was impossible to enforce English rule over the whole island. Consequently the great majority of the Irish people remained loyal to the pope, and for centuries afterwards the Church of Ireland suffered from being marked with the stigma of English rule in Ireland.

The reformed liturgy was introduced into all cathedral and parish churches where practicable, but uniformity remained unattainable. Ireland was as rebellious as ever, and sometimes a bishop appointed by the crown was unable to occupy his see. On the final break with Rome in 1560, separate successions of papal and royal archbishops and bishops began, and the Church of Ireland gradually assumed the shape and identity that it has today – a small minority church in possession of all the ancient places of worship in a country which is overwhelmingly Roman Catholic.

Unquiet Times

English rule in Ireland was subject to repeated rebellions in the 16th and 17th centuries, and the damage done to the Irish cathedrals was grievous. Armagh, Ferns, Lismore and Ross were burnt in the reign of Elizabeth I (1558–1603). The succeeding policy of planting English and Scottish settlers, particularly in Ulster, and the confiscation of lands belonging to those who had taken part in the rebellions, caused simmering resentment which erupted in a major rebellion in 1641 that lasted more than ten years. The difficulties between Charles I (1625–49) and the English parliament, and the imminent rebellion of Scots Presbyterians, prevented a swift and effective response from London to what was probably the most united and most serious Irish revolt since the arrival of Henry II.

The rebels, principally Irish Catholics defending their religious, political and property rights, met in alliance in October 1642 at what became known as the Confederation of Kilkenny. The king, engaged in a civil war with parliament, was prepared to negotiate with the rebels and grant them almost anything in return for an army of 10,000 men. Preliminary discussions resulted in a treaty in 1646 which removed various Catholic disabilities. It was widely accepted by the Confederation until sabotaged by the intransigence of Archbishop Giovanni Battista Rinuccini, the papal nuncio, who threatened with excommunication those who accepted any terms which did less than confirm the supreme authority of Rome. The treaty virtually disappeared.

The success of the rebellion was only guaranteed while events in England were sufficiently distracting; and with the execution of the King in January 1649, it was only a matter of time

before Oliver Cromwell turned his attention to Ireland. He landed in August 1649, and in May 1652 Galway, the last town in rebel hands, surrendered. The rebellion had been a ferocious affair, with something like 10,000 people losing their lives; one particularly bloody massacre occurred within the walls of Cashel Cathedral which never fully recovered from the horror. Cromwell's Puritan regime had no time for episcopacy, which was simply suppressed in the Church of Ireland. The underground succession of Roman Catholic bishops continued.

At the Restoration of Charles II in 1660 the Church of Ireland tried to re-establish itself as best it could. Many of its bishops had died or were in exile, and many of its cathedrals, badly damaged during the rebellion and the Confederate war, remained in ruins. In January 1661 at a great ceremony in St Patrick's Cathedral, Dublin, two archbishops and ten bishops were consecrated to fill the vacant sees, but the situation was not promising. There were many problems: the small size of the reformed church; a lengthy gap in episcopal jurisdiction; many ruined cathedrals and parish churches; and considerable discrepancy in size of revenue among the dioceses. In 1668 the Archbishop of Armagh received £3,500 per annum, the Bishop of Clonfert £400, and the Bishop of Kildare only £200. The clergy were far worse off, those in Connacht receiving stipends of 16s–40s per annum. 'Ill-paid, scattered, loosely organised and depressed, those clergy had to encounter the highly organised Roman Church, which after the arrival of Archbishop Oliver Plunkett . . . became a disciplined church.'[6]

Oliver Plunkett (1629–81) was born in Co. Meath of a noble family. After study in Rome he was ordained in 1654 and for some years acted as the representative of the Irish bishops in Rome. In 1669 he was appointed Archbishop of Armagh. Consecrated in Ghent, he returned to Ireland, where he administered his diocese energetically in the face of constant hardship. He was caught up in the aftermath of the Titus Oates Plot, arrested in 1679, and executed at Tyburn on 1 July 1681. He was canonised in 1975.

Penal Times for the Roman Catholic Church

After his flight from England in November 1688 James II (1685–8) took refuge in Ireland and raised an army with the intention of recovering his throne. The result was a civil war in Ireland from 1689 to 1691 during which James, England's last Catholic monarch, fought with his Protestant son-in-law and joint successor William III (1689–1702). The victory of William, which is commemorated to this day in parts of Ireland, led to the imposition of severe penal legislation on Roman Catholics. 'The animosity engendered by the massacres of the seventeenth century, and the endless plots and frequent rebellions, came home to roost. Instead of enjoying relief and concessions, they were oppressed with severe restrictions aimed at ensuring their absolute social and civic impotence.'[7] The Roman Catholic bishops were ordered to leave Ireland by 1 May 1698, and the members of all religious orders were expelled. Catholic secular priests were allowed to remain, but had to register, giving their age, abode, parochial jurisdiction, and particulars of ordination. These draconian regulations were enforced, though never with complete effectiveness, in a country with a population of two million of whom about three-quarters were Roman Catholic.

The intention was not to suppress the Roman Catholic Church, only to reduce it to political impotence. The decision to expel the Catholic archbishops and bishops was due to the fact that successive popes after 1688 continued to allow vacant Irish Catholic bishoprics to be filled by nominees of the exiled James II, who lived in France until his death in 1701. The practice was allowed to continue under his son and successor, styled James III, until his death in 1766. Between 1687 and 1765, James II and James III between them nominated 129 bishops to Irish Catholic dioceses. After the death of James III, neither of his two sons, styled Charles III (1766–88) and Henry IX (1788–1807), were recognised by Rome as kings in exile, and neither were granted rights of nomination in the provision to Irish sees.

The Roman Catholic Church continued a somewhat furtive existence in this state of severe restriction, but because of the loyalty of the majority of the population, it survived. The sheer tenacity of the church was an impressive testimony to many of its adherents who could so easily have conformed to the Church of Ireland and made life easier for themselves. Gradually Roman Catholic bishops returned to Ireland and took up residence in their dioceses, but after more than fifty years of persecution they were cautious. John Thomas Troy, Bishop of Ossory 1776–1786 and Archbishop of Dublin 1786–1823, was typical of the bishops of the time: 'old and simple-minded recluses of austere piety, and with spirits humbled by the operation of the popery laws'. He had two convictions: 'He believed that it was wicked to seek, by agitation, to make the people discontented with their political or social lot, for it tended, in his opinion, to weaken the influence of the Church and the stability of the State; and, ignorant as he necessarily was of the power of a people's will . . . he believed that the extension of religious freedom could only be attained by placating the government.'[8]

By the middle of the 18th century the penal legislation was no longer so strictly enforced. Memories of the 17th century had faded, a new generation of educated English settlers had grown up, and there was a growing feeling that the injustice of Catholic suffering was morally indefensible in the Age of Enlightenment. The refusal of papal recognition to 'Charles III' and 'Henry IX' removed a significant objection to the easing of restrictions on the activities of the Catholic hierarchy.

A few discreet and humble-looking Catholic churches were built, and construction increased as the 18th century pro-gressed. Gardener's Relief Act of 1782 allowed Catholics to open schools and acquire leasehold property. The first of the new Catholic cathedrals was built at Waterford between 1793 and 1796. In 1795 the Irish parliament sanctioned the opening of a college to train Catholic priests in Ireland, at Maynooth, Co. Kildare, and awarded it an annual grant of £8,000 which continued after the Union, and in 1815 work began on the construction of the Pro-Cathedral in Dublin.

The Church of Ireland in the Nineteenth and Twentieth Centuries

The Established Church of Ireland in the early nineteenth century was small, but had endowments and influence out of proportion to its size. It was over-endowed with bishops whose duties were very light when compared with those of their fellow-bishops in England. The diocese of Raphoe had twenty-five benefices, and the diocese of Killala had twenty. The diocese of Lincoln in England contained as many benefices as all twenty-two Irish dioceses put together.

In 1832 the government of Earl Grey decided to embark on a programme of ecclesiastical reform in Ireland, viewing it as a waste of money to maintain four archbishops, eighteen bishops and 1,400 clergy to minister to only 800,000 people, less than 10 per cent of the population. By the Church Temporalities (Ireland) Act, 1833, two of the archbishoprics and eight of the bishoprics were to be amalgamated with neighbouring dioceses at the next vacancy. The stipends of these dioceses were removed, and those of other remaining dioceses were reduced. No doubt because of complex historical, legal and financial problems, the act left the cathedral establishments untouched. Although there were now only ten bishops and two archbishops, there were still thirty corporations of deans and chapters in charge of thirty cathedrals.

The act of 1833 was a dramatic step towards recognising the reality of the situation, and the obvious step of disestablishment was now only a matter of time. After years of growing agitation the Irish Church Act, 1869 disestablished and partially disendowed the Church of Ireland from 1 January 1871. A preliminary report in 1868 proposed to reduce further the number of bishoprics to eight and remedy the omission of the 1833 legislation by similarly reducing the number of cathedrals to eight. The report, chaired by the Earl of Meath, proposed that there should be only eight cathedrals: Armagh, Cork, Downpatrick, Derry, Dublin (St Patrick's), Kilkenny, Limerick and Tuam. All other cathedrals would be reduced to the status of parish churches. It further proposed that as soon as a cathedral should be built in Belfast, Downpatrick should also be reduced to parish church status.

The recommendations of the 1868 report were not incorporated into disestablishment legislation. The act provided that those cathedrals still used by the Church of Ireland were to remain in its possession; the same provision applied to parish churches and glebe houses. The ruined and disused cathedrals, Ardfert, Ardmore, Cashel, Clonmacnoise, Glendalough, Kilmacduagh and others, still nominally owned by the Church of Ireland, were given into the care of the state.

Although disestablishment came as a shock to the Church of Ireland, it was not without benefits. For the first time the church was thrown back on its own resources and the care of its flock. Absenteeism was ended, and congregations became deeply involved in the management and the care of the churches and cathedrals. The stories of the maintenance of Downpatrick Cathedral and the rebuilding of Kildare Cathedral are among many accounts of determined efforts by parishioners to secure the future of their cathedrals and churches in the years after 1871.

The 20th century has brought its own problems and challenges. The partition of Ireland in 1920 did not disrupt the structure of either the Church of Ireland or the Roman Catholic Church. Both churches continue to maintain the traditional diocesan boundaries. Consequently the dioceses of Armagh, Clogher, Down and Raphoe, straddle the border between the two parts of Ireland. In the twenty-six southern counties which formed the Irish Free State, later the Republic of Ireland, the sharply declining membership of the Church of Ireland has imposed new strains on the care of churches and cathedrals. Very small congregations have been faced with the overwhelming task of trying to maintain historic structures on very slender resources. Achonry Cathedral was considered for closure in 1989, but has been spared for the time being; Clonfert Cathedral only has monthly services in the summer; Kildare, Kilfenora and Killala Cathedrals, and St Mary's Cathedral at Tuam, have loyal but small congregations.

Many Church of Ireland cathedrals are also parish churches, and the dean is not always the rector of the parish. Deans are often parish priests whose cure extends to several parishes besides the cathedral; in certain cases, e.g. Clonfert, Cloyne and Kildare, the cathedral congregation is smaller than other parishes in the group, and the dean resides elsewhere. In the case of Connor, the dean is not the parish priest of the cathedral at the time of writing. Non-residence of members of cathedral chapters is normal. The dignitaries and prebendaries are normally parish priests in the diocese, and even by the time of Disestablishment in 1871 most reported that they no functions to perform in relation to their cathedral church. The numerical decline of the Church of Ireland in the more remote parts of Ireland has now left many canonries vacant, and plurality among the titular cathedral dignitaries is common. The most sweeping rationalisation can be seen in the united dioceses of Limerick, Ardfert, Aghadoe, Killaloe, Kilfenora, Clonfert, Kilmacduagh and Emly, where a single joint chapter functions for all four surviving cathedrals.

The picture is not altogether gloomy. Many of the southern cathedrals are holding their own: St Fin Barre's Cathedral in Cork, St Canice's Cathedral in Kilkenny, St Mary's Cathedral in Limerick, Christ Church Cathedral in Waterford; and Cashel, Ferns, Killaloe, Leighlin, Lismore, Rosscarbery and Trim Cathedrals. St Patrick's Cathedral and Christ Church Cathedral in Dublin have sizeable congregations. Among Northern cathedrals, Armagh, St Ann's Belfast, Derry, Enniskillen and Lisburn are flourishing. Substantial restoration programmes have recently been undertaken at Kildare, Downpatrick and Limerick.

The Church of Ireland Cathedrals

In accordance with the provision of the Irish Church Act of 1869, all cathedrals and churches still in use by the Church of Ireland were to remain in its possession; all disused historic buildings passed into the care of the state in 1871. Both categories are treated in this section, since there are often close architectural and ecclesiological links.

For many people, the word 'cathedral' evokes an image of medieval Gothic splendour, or at least a building of extensive architectural grandeur. It needs to be said that the visitor to Ireland's cathedrals should erase all such images from his mind and not expect to see anything approaching the glories of Lincoln, Wells and York in England. Most of the contemporary medieval Irish cathedrals are small and simple in comparison; scarcely approaching the size of market-town parish churches in England. Ireland was the very western outpost of Europe, and the poverty and violence which have been recurring themes throughout its history are largely responsible for the modest size and much-reconstructed appearance of the ancient buildings which are dignified by the title of 'cathedral church'. The two cathedrals closest in appearance to the image of an English cathedral are those geographically closest to England – St Patrick's and Christ Church in Dublin. The smaller and more remote cathedrals, such as Achonry, Clogher, Clonfert, Kilfenora, Killala, Raphoe and Rosscarbery, often have little more than the bishop's cathedra, the essential prerequisite before the title of cathedral church can be used, and stalls for the prebendaries and chapter dignitaries. Snide dismissiveness about the size and decoration of these cathedrals comes easily enough, but like all cathedrals they represent the changing styles of Ireland's architecture and reflect the vicissitudes of Ireland's history. The signs are there to be read by those willing to take the trouble of making the journey.

But it is important for the visitor not to arrive in Ireland expecting to see buildings resembling the splendours of Salisbury and Wells or Rheims and Chartres. Ireland's cathedrals cannot and should not be compared with their more famous namesakes to the east. They have a style which is authentically Irish, and they are worthy representatives of a nation with limited resources. Basing an excursion on these premises, the visitor will discover that Ireland's cathedrals have much of interest and intrinsic charm, and they will repay an effort to find them and to understand their history.

The earliest church buildings were of timber, and building in wood was still regarded as the traditional Irish method in the 12th century. The cathedrals were at the heart of small settlements and were surrounded by a constellation of smaller churches or chapels; those at Clonmacnoise and Glendalough are the best-known examples, but smaller groups can be seen at Ardfert, Kilmacduagh and Scattery Island. These settlements grew around the memories, and increasingly exaggerated legends, of Christian saints, most of whose names survive today in the dedications of cathedrals.

The first cathedrals were plain rectangular single-chamber structures, such as those at Glendalough (early 9th century, with an 11th/12th-century chancel) and Scattery Island (9th/ 10th-century with 13th/14th-century alterations). Trinity and Reefert churches at Glendalough were two-chamber churches from the beginning, but the chancel was more usually a later addition. Aghadoe has a mid-12th century nave with a 13th-century chancel. Ardmore is a reversal of the usual pattern and has a 12th-century chancel and a 13th-century nave, but contains portions of a much earlier church. These early cathedrals are very difficult to date with precision because of their simple construction and lack of any datable feature or inscription.

Some cathedrals of much later date incorporate earlier features. Maghera has a Romanesque nave with later alterations, but has an Early Christian trabeate door lintel. Clonmacnoise is an 11th-century structure substantially rebuilt in the 14th century but containing a 10th-century west doorway. Ardfert (13th century) has a Romanesque west doorway. The 12th-century cathedral of St Mary at Limerick was much altered in the 14th and 15th centuries, but has the fragment of Romanesque doorway in its west wall. Killaloe (13th century) has a Romanesque doorway which now serves as a window in the south wall of the nave. Kilmacduagh was much altered in the 14th and 15th centuries but it retains a blocked 10th-century doorway in its 11th- or 12th-century west wall. Annaghdown (15th century) has a carved Romanesque east window. Killala (17th century) has a blocked Gothic doorway in its south wall. Raphoe is largely an 18th/ 19th-century rebuilding but contains medieval fragments, notably a piscina and sedilia. Kilmore (19th century) has a Romanesque doorway in its north wall. Enniskillen was rebuilt in the 19th century, but retains its 17th-century tower. Trim was similarly rebuilt in the 19th century, but the 15th-century tower and the ruin of the 15th-century chancel remain. The 19th-century Christ Church Cathedral at Dublin was carefully constructed around a 12th-century nave arcade. At St Mary's Cathedral, Tuam, the great 12th-century sanctuary arch can be seen set between the two 14th- and 19th-century cathedrals.

Two-chamber structures, consisting of nave and chancel, became common in the 12th century, and decoration began to be lavished on doorways and chancel arches; the sanctuary arch at Tuam Cathedral (c.1152) and the west doorway at Clonfert Cathedral (c.1167) are the best examples of the style known as Hiberno-Romanesque. It reached a peak in the building known as Cormac's Chapel (1127–34) adjacent to the ruined 13th-century cathedral at Cashel. A more English style can be seen in part of the nave of Christ Church Cathedral in Dublin, which is also late 12th century. The rest of Christ Church is a partly conjectural 19th-century reconstruction of the outline and style of the 12th-century cathedral. Leighlin Cathedral and St Mary's Cathedral at Limerick also date from the late 12th century, although the original simple outline at Limerick was obscured by additions in the 14th and 15th centuries.

The size and appearance of the cathedrals depended much on location and the availability of finance, craftsmanship and materials. The considerable difference in size, workmanship and decoration between the two 13th-century cathedrals of St Patrick in Dublin and St Fachan in Kilfenora is representative of the two extremes – the wealth and importance of Dublin and the poverty and remoteness of Co. Clare.

The 13th century saw a great period of church-building in Ireland, and the displacement of Romanesque by Gothic, with its characteristic pointed arches and aisleless cruciform style. The mid-13th-century Ardfert Cathedral represents the last stage of pre-cruciform architecture, and a south transept had been added before the end of the century. Cashel, Kildare, Killaloe and Lismore are typical examples of the fully cruciform but aisleless 13th-century style, and although Kildare and Lismore are much reconstructed, their original outline remains. Cloyne and St Canice's Cathedral at Kilkenny are also 13th century but have aisles. The 13th-century cathedral of St Patrick in Dublin was heavily restored in the 19th century, and its style owes much to the influence of English Gothic. Transepts began to appear later in the 13th century, but more usually in the 14th century. Kilmacduagh acquired its transepts in the 15th century.

The only major works of the 14th century were the construction of the new chancels for Tuam Cathedral and Christ Church Cathedral in Dublin. Regrettably it was felt necessary to demolish the mid-14th-century choir of Christ Church in the rebuilding of that cathedral in the 19th century.

Few of the cathedrals escaped destruction or some form of damage in the 12th – 15th centuries, but the strife of the 16th and 17th centuries was especially disastrous. Having adopted the reformed liturgy, they were more closely identified with English rule and became victims of the periodic civil disturbances which regularly punctuated Irish life at the time. Many of the buildings, particularly those in Ulster, were so badly damaged that very little of the present structures pre-date the 17th century. The cathedrals of Ardagh, Armagh, Ardfert, Cashel, Connor, Derry, Downpatrick, Dromore, Elphin, Kildare, Kilkenny, Killala, Kilmacduagh,

Lisburn, Lismore, Rosscarbery and Trim were all burnt. Most were later rebuilt, but Ardagh, Ardfert (except for the south aisle which was re-roofed) and Kilmacduagh, remained in ruins; the rebuilt church at Connor was denied cathedral status.

The 17th century saw much construction and reconstruction. St Columb's Cathedral at Derry was built in the style known as Planter's Gothic in 1629–33; Enniskillen Cathedral, a contemporary of St Columb's, was built c.1627, but was almost entirely rebuilt in 1841–2. Dromore was rebuilt in the 1660s, but two enlargements in the 19th century substantially altered the outline and removed much of the 17th-century work. A tower was added to the medieval cathedral of St Fin Barre at Cork between 1671 and 1676. Killala Cathedral (1671–80) is a plain hall-type church with a tower and spire at the west end, and is uninteresting except for a unique external battery below the east window. An unsightly and architecturally unsympathetic hall was constructed on the site of the chancel of the ruined Kildare Cathedral in 1686; it was removed in the 19th-century reconstruction. The reformed liturgy required no more of a church than that it be suitable auditorium to enable a congregation to see and hear the preacher. Many parish churches built during the 18th and early 19th centuries are architectural expressions of this principle.

The 18th century saw the complete rebuilding of Lisburn Cathedral in the style of a hall in 1708. The medieval cathedral of St Fin Barre at Cork was demolished and replaced in 1735 with a Classical Revival hall; it was universally disliked by the time of its demolition in 1865. Clogher Cathedral, built 1740–44, indicated the beginning of a move away from the hall style of Killala and Lisburn and a reversion to the medieval cruciform shape which was to reach its full flowering in the Gothic Revival of the 19th century. But the cruciformity of Clogher is only notional, the transepts being little more than shallow recesses in the north and south walls of a typical 'hall' church.

The demolitions at Clogher and Cork were followed by the demolition of the medieval church at Kells later in the 18th century. But the unroofing and abandonment of Cashel Cathedral in 1749 and the demolition of Waterford Cathedral in 1773 are the two most remembered losses of 18th-century Ireland. A number of rumours surround the losses of Cashel and Waterford: inaccessibility, structural instability, changing architectural fashion, capitular laziness, episcopal whim, etc. Probably elements of each might be discerned behind the formal decisions to abandon Cashel and demolish Waterford. Their successors are fine buildings of their kind, and typical of the light and airy classical box-style architecture in vogue at the time; a style which was suspicious of the darkness and mystery of the many rooms and hidden corners of the unfashionable and unfavoured Gothic. Cashel has an elegant exterior and a disappointing interior; the reverse is true of Waterford.

The 18th century was an age of elegance, confidence and enlightenment, and renewed interest in the classical style. The classical cathedrals of Cashel, Clogher, Cork (later demolished) and Waterford were the most visible relics of that age, but the effects were wider. Classical refurnishing or reordering work was undertaken at the cathedrals at Cloyne, Derry, Ferns, Kilkenny and Limerick. Some of Ireland's finest episcopal palaces date from the Classical Revival: Armagh (1770), Cashel (1730–32), Clogher (1819–23), Dromore (begun 1781, demolished), Ferns (begun 1785, demolished), Kilkenny (c.1740), Killaloe (Clarisford, 1774–8), Kilmore (1834, but Classical in style), Meath (Ardbraccan, begun c.1734), Raphoe (begun 1635, remodelled late 18th century, now ruined)), Tuam (1716–41), and Waterford (begun 1741). With the exception of Kilkenny and Kilmore, all the other palaces have been sold.

The 19th century witnessed a renewed period of demolition and rebuilding which reached a frenzy at the time of Disestablishment. A large number of Church of Ireland parish churches were either demolished or simply abandoned in the first two decades of the 19th century. The cause was a major building programme funded by grants or loans from the Board of First-Fruits, which disbursed more than £1,000,000 for building churches in the years 1801–22.

Achonry, Emly and Cork were the only cathedral churches to be completely demolished during the 19th century, but several former cathedrals, long reduced to parish church status, were abandoned in favour of new buildings close by; they included Ardagh, Ardmore, Duleek, Maghera and Mayo. Clonard was completely demolished and Connor was rebuilt on the same site incorporating the foundations of the old cathedral. When the medieval cathedral at Achonry was demolished in 1823, its east wall was allowed to remain standing.

Among the 19th-century demolitions was the curious little cathedral at Emly in the early 1820s, which was probably a loss, and the Classical 18th-century cathedral at Cork in 1865, which was not. Ferns Cathedral was reconstructed in 1816–1817, and the nave of Elphin Cathedral was rebuilt in 1823. New cathedrals grew progressively more elaborate as the century moved on. The line began with the modest little hall and steeple at Achonry in 1823, the only example at cathedral level of First-Fruits Gothic; then followed the small example of cruciform Gothic Revival at Emly (1827), which was quite unnecessarily demolished in 1877 in a fit of sectarian bitterness; then the more elaborate Gothic at Kilmore (1858–60); and finally there came the full flowering of high French Gothic at Cork (1865–79), the epitome of the supreme confidence felt by the disestablished church. Major restoration work, sometimes involving substantial rebuilding, took place at Downpatrick, Armagh, St Patrick's and Christ Church in Dublin, Kildare and Kilkenny.

The 20th century will be remembered for the construction of the massive Cathedral Church of St Anne in Belfast. It was begun in 1899 and its completion in 1981 almost certainly marked the end of cathedral building in Ireland on such a massive scale.

The Roman Catholic Church and its Cathedrals

The nomenclature of Catholic dioceses is identical with the names used by the Church of Ireland. With two exceptions, the Roman Catholic Church uses the names of the historic Irish dioceses. The exceptions are the diocese of Galway, which may be taken as the representative of the ancient diocese of Annaghdown, and the diocese of Kerry, which uses the ancient name of the diocese of Ardfert and Aghadoe. For every diocese from Achonry to Waterford there is a Church of Ireland bishop and a Roman Catholic bishop, and their joint use requires a brief explanation.

In the confused and confusing years of the 16th century it was not always clear whether the loyalty of a diocesan bishop was to the pope or to the crown. In the figure of Archbishop Miler Magrath of Cashel there is the example of one who tried for a while to ride both horses at once. Because of the weakness of English rule in Ireland, the principles of the Reformation were difficult to enforce in large parts of the country. Gradually, separate lines of bishops, royal and papal, began to emerge. Bishops appointed by the crown were not always able to obtain immediate possession of their dioceses, especially if they were situated in areas remote from royal control. Bishops appointed by the pope were, for some years at least, able to function openly as diocesan bishops. A similar picture emerges with regard to the religious orders. The monasteries were officially supressed in Ireland between 1536 and 1547, but the decrees of Henry VIII were only made effective in those parts of Ireland directly under the authority of the crown. Some monasteries were able to function openly until well into the reign of Elizabeth I, and a few even into the 17th century.

Because of this confusion in the 16th century, both the Church of Ireland and the Roman Catholic Church derive their lines of bishops from the undivided pre-Reformation church, and both lines of bishops use the names of the ancient sees. Perhaps in these ecumenical days this situation no longer causes the hostility that it once did in the early 18th century when the Roman Catholic Church was virtually reduced to a furtive existence and, no churches being available, mass was often said in the open air.

In the early part of the 18th century mass was said secretly in private houses. The surfacing of the Roman Catholic Church in Ireland began from the middle of the 18th century. After a tragedy in 1744, when many people were killed or injured in the collapse of a decrepit house in Dublin where mass was being said in secret, permission was granted in 1745 to open chapels in the capital and later in other towns.[9] Bishops began to take up residence in their dioceses from the middle of the century, and the small chapels were gradually replaced by larger churches which were styled 'pro-cathedrals'.

Since the Church of Ireland had possession of the ancient cathedrals, the Roman Catholic Church, emerging from the shadows in the late 18th century, had to look elsewhere to build its new cathedrals. At Armagh, Cork, Derry, Dublin, Limerick, Tuam and Waterford a suitable site was found within the boundaries of the town. In all other dioceses, particularly where the ancient see was a small and remote village such as Achonry, Clonfert, Kilfenora, Killaloe or Leighlin, the Roman Catholic cathedral is not in the historic see from which the diocese is named, but is generally in a town elsewhere within the diocese; for example the Bishop of Achonry has his cathedral at Ballaghaderreen, the Bishop of Clonfert's cathedral is at Loughrea, the cathedral of the Archbishop of Cashel is at Thurles, and that of the Bishop of Cloyne is at Cóbh. Usually, though not always, the Church of Ireland cathedral is to be found at the site of the monastic foundation after which the diocese is named, while the Roman Catholic cathedral is to be found in a neighbouring urban area.

In the early 19th century the Classical style was preferred, either because of the tastes of Catholics educated abroad or to emphasise Ireland's links with Catholic Europe. The cathedrals at Waterford (1793–6), Dublin (1815–25), Skibbereen (1824–6), Longford (1840–93) and Cavan (1936–42) are all

Interior of church of the Carmelite Friary, Dublin, c. 1830

of this style. The pre-Emancipation cathedral at Skibbereen is a modest and externally discreet structure with a very pretty sanctuary. The post-Emancipation cathedral at Longford was a clear indication that modesty and discretion had been utterly forsaken for triumphalism. Cavan was an interesting resurrection of a style that had long been thought unfashionable.

The Classical style of the 18th century was entirely superseded from about 1840 by Gothic Revival, a 19th-century craze which romanticised the later Middle Ages and regarded the churches of the period as the ideal form for Christian architecture. Classical forms were swept aside by a new fascination for chancels, transepts and stained glass. Eighteen Roman Catholic cathedrals are products of this period, some more notable than others. The phase began with the Strawberry Hill Gothick of Carlow, and the simple, inexpensive and almost experimental west-coast Gothic of Ballina and Ennis. The styles of Early English, Decorated and Perpendicular are all represented and the period reached its zenith with the florid French Gothic of the great hillside cathedral at Cóbh. Decorated was thought to be the purest form of Gothic by ecclesiologists and tends to predominate.

The architect Dominic Madden was responsible for starting the long series of 19th-century Gothic Revival cathedrals. He designed those at Ballina (1828–92), Ennis (1828–43) and Tuam (1827–37) before abandoning a career in Irish architecture for the life of an engineer in South America. A curious feature of his cathedrals is the absence of a plinth or podium which gives them a rather squat appearance.[10] Tuam was the first and finest; the square west tower with nine crocketed pinnacles, and the heavy pasta-like tracery of the Decorated east window are notable features, but the truncated chancel is unfortunate. The cathedrals at Ballina and Ennis are commonplace. Had Madden stayed in Ireland, it is unlikely that his style would have survived the inexorable juggernaut of Pugin and McCarthy.

Augustus Welby Northmore Pugin (1812–1852) firmly stamped his style of Gothic on 19th-century architecture and influenced the architects who followed him for a generation or more. He became a Roman Catholic in 1834, more, it was said, as a result of architectural rather than theological considerations. Although he denied this, it appeared that he could never think of Christianity without thinking of Gothic architecture. He was inclined to be dismissive of Ireland; "I see no progress of ecclesiastical ideas in Ireland. I think if possible they grow worse. It is quite useless to attempt to build true churches, for the clergy have not the least idea of using them properly."[11] Pugin designed two Irish cathedrals: the steep and cramped site at Enniscorthy (1843–9) produced the design of a long but narrow building, while the level ground at Killarney (1842–55) allowed him to produce a cathedral of magnificent soaring precision. He died, insane, in 1852.

Although Pugin's son Edward played an initial role in the design of Cóbh Cathedral (1868–1914), it was J.J. McCarthy who took up the cause of Pugin in Ireland. James Joseph McCarthy (1817–82), nicknamed 'the Irish Pugin', was the most famous of the neo-Gothic Irish architects and was certainly Pugin's most fervent disciple in Ireland. He adopted Pugin's ideas about Gothic architecture and the proper design and decoration of churches 'and promoted them with skill and determination at a time when ecclesiastical architecture in Ireland was about to enter an extremely prolific period'.[12] He designed the cathedrals at Armagh (1840–73), Derry (1851–73), Monaghan (1861–92) and Thurles, the tower and spire at Ennis (after the departure of Madden), and he supervised work on Killarney after the death of Pugin.

There were two brave and splendid exceptions in the 19th century to this craving for Gothic: George Goldie's cathedral at Sligo (1869–74) is an interesting and successful attempt to produce a stylised form of Romanesque; and McCarthy's cathedral at Thurles (1865–1872) is a startling but delightful architectural hybrid of Lombardic and Romanesque.

With the completion of Letterkenny Cathedral (1891–1901) and Loughrea Cathedral (1897–1902), the period of construction of cathedrals for the Roman Catholic Church in Ireland was almost complete. The building of Letterkenny and Loughrea, the completion of Cóbh in 1914, and the contemporaneous passing of the 19th century marked the end of the Gothic Revival as the normative cathedral style. But then there were by this stage very few dioceses left without cathedrals.

Three cathedrals were built in the 20th century, and all showed that Gothic was a spent force. Mullingar (1933–6) has an exterior with more than a nod in the direction of imperial India but with an opulent Renaissance basilical interior. Cavan (1936–42), was a reversion to the Classical style; Galway (1957–65) is in a category of its own but has elements of Romanesque. It was unfortunately completed as the Second Vatican Council (1962–5) was drawing to a close, and its cruciform design became anachronistic before the cathedral was finished.

The Roman Catholic church in the twentieth century

Without doubt the most significant event in the history of Roman Catholicism in the twentieth century was the summoning of the Second Vatican Council by Pope John XXIII in 1962. The reordering of churches and cathedrals in line with the decrees of the Second Vatican Council has caused significant architectural changes to substantial buildings constructed for a very different liturgy. Galway was probably the first cathedral to be affected by the liturgical decrees of the Council. In the years since the closing of the Council in 1965 most Roman Catholic cathedrals have undergone substantial internal alteration. Simplicity, visibility and the corporate nature of worship – allowing the active participation of the faithful – were the guiding principles, and in the succeeding twenty years the cathedrals (as well as the parish churches) were 'reordered' to adapt to the requirements of the new liturgy. The emphasis on the individual priest saying a daily mass was superseded by concelebration by all priests present, and there was no longer any need for large numbers of altars and side chapels. The cruciform plan, once considered the norm of ecclesiastical architectural, was rendered redundant overnight. Long chancels, rood-screens and distant and elaborate high altars fixed to the east wall were obstacles to the new liturgy; an atmosphere of remote mystery was no longer required. So altars were discarded, ignored or moved further to the west, screens were dismantled, and chancels turned into retrochoirs, as at Armagh, Enniscorthy and Galway. Assessment of the liturgical decrees of the Council is a matter for the liturgist and not within the scope of this book. Where criticism appears, it is made on the grounds of architecture and decoration.

Reorderings of chancels, sanctuaries and their furnishings divide broadly into three categories. The first is best described as the radical category. In these cases the reordering has been so extensive that little or nothing remains of the former arrangement. The new furnishings are generally of a design so different from that of the cathedral that surrounds them that the architectural harmony of the building has been greatly affected. In almost every case the chief loss was the ornate marble high altar with its equally ornate and towering reredos, and in some cases the lectern and pulpit. The results have generally been visually disastrous. Armagh and Monaghan Cathedrals are examples of radical and unsuccessful designs which required the removal of all sanctuary furnishings in a complete and total break with the past. Their replacements, almost gawkish in their simplicity, rarely succeed in filling the yawning gaps left by the removal of their elegant and beautiful predecessors. Killarney Cathedral is perhaps the only success story of the radical category. The major restoration and reordering in 1972–3 virtually obliterated the high Victorian designs of Pugin and turned the cathedral into a building of almost Cistercian austerity. But the design is bold and imaginative, and it works.

The second category is perhaps best described as the temporary category. Here the high altar remains in position but ceases to be used. It is supplanted by a new altar of simpler design, located further to the west, to enable mass to be said facing the people. Examples of this category can be seen at Enniscorthy, Kilkenny, Loughrea and Skibbereen. The high altars at Enniscorthy and Kilkenny have a somewhat forlorn and neglected look, and it is a matter for debate whether it would not have been better to remove them entirely. The altars at Loughrea and Skibbereen are still dominating eyecatchers. The reordering at Sligo, with the use of a brass fretwork screen to separate and shield and yet enhance the dignity of the high altar, is an ingenious and successful marriage of the old and the new.

A third, more subtle category is provided by those high altars which have simply been moved further to the west to allow a priest to say mass facing the people. This has at least preserved some fine altars, but the very ornateness of their design can give them an awkward and isolated appearance when removed from the backcloth of the stylistically similar reredos. The (perhaps temporary) arrangements at the Pro-Cathedral in Dublin are a good example. The most successful reorderings in this category can be seen at Letterkenny,

Mullingar and Newry where the visitor before and after will scarcely notice the difference.

It is, of course, possible to dismiss this categorisation as a crude oversimplification. Many of the reordering schemes in the radical category are interesting designs and have intrinsic merit; in other settings that merit could be better displayed and better appreciated.

Many reordering schemes have caused the disappearance of many 19th-century furnishings; the altar, the reredos, the pulpit, the lectern, the communion rail, and even the bishop's throne, have been the principal victims. It would be quite valid to argue in response that a church should never be regarded as a museum of furniture, and that furnishings valid for the celebration of the liturgy of another age should not be regarded as sacrosanct. But the total removal of these items in the cause of architectural freedom is questionable. The savage destruction at Armagh, Cork and Monaghan, compared with the subtlety of the work at Letterkenny, Mullingar and Newry, raises questions about the wisdom of allowing the wholesale disposal of original furnishings, and whether the decrees of the Second Vatican Council either required or envisaged such fierce implementation.

References

1 Peter and F. S. Fry, *A history of Ireland* (London, 1988), p.1

2 See A.T. Lucas, "The plundering and burning of churches in Ireland 7th to the 16th centuries" in Etienne Rynne (ed.) *North Munster studies*, (Limerick, 1967).

3 John Watt, *The church in medieval Ireland* (Dublin, 1972), p. 1.

4 Ibid., p.13.

5 Canice Mooney, "The Church in Gaelic Ireland" in *A history of Irish Catholicism*, ed. P. J. Corish, ii, 5, (Dublin, 1969), p. 55.

6 Margaret MacCurtain, *Tudor and Stuart Ireland* (Dublin, 1972). p. 167.

7 Brian De Breffny and George Mott, *The churches and abbeys of Ireland* (London, 1976), p. 126.

8 Michael MacDonagh, *Bishop Doyle 'J.K.L.' a biographical and historical study* (London & Dublin, 1896), pp 11–12.

9 D. S. Richardson, *Gothic Revival architecture in Ireland* (New York, 1983), ii, p. 210.

10 T. P. Kennedy, "Church Building" in *A history of Irish Catholicism*, ed. P.J. Corish, v, 8 (Dublin, 1970), p. 7.

11 B. F. L. Clarke, *Church builders of the nineteenth century* (London, 1938), p. 103.

12 Jeanne Sheehy, *J. J. McCarthy and the Gothic Revival in Ireland* (Dublin, 1977), p. 5.

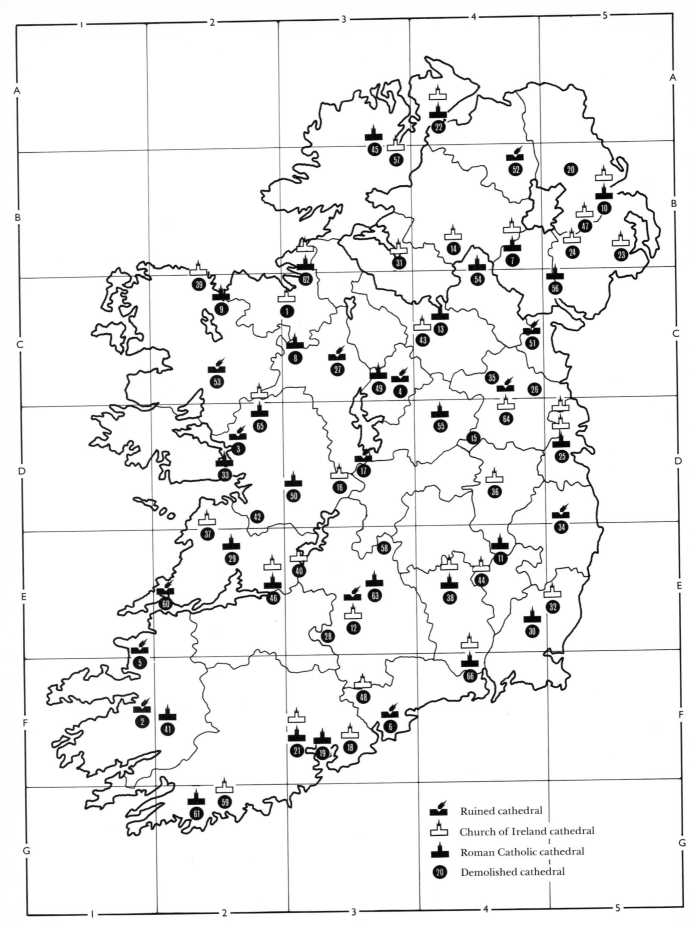

Ruined cathedral

Church of Ireland cathedral

Roman Catholic cathedral

20 Demolished cathedral

Key to the Cathedral Sites of Ireland

1 **Achonry** C3
The Cathedral Church of St. Crumnathy

2 **Aghadoe** F1
Aghadoe Cathedral

3 **Annaghdown** D2
The Cathedral Church of St. Brendan

4 **Ardagh** C3
The Cathedral Church of St. Mel

5 **Ardfert** F1
The Cathedral Church of St. Brendan

6 **Ardmore** F3
Ardmore Cathedral

7 **Armagh** B4
The Cathedral Church of St. Patrick
The Cathedral Church of St. Patrick

8 **Ballaghadereen** C3
The Cathedral Church of the Annunciation
of the Blessed Virgin Mary, and St. Nathy

9 **Ballina** C2
The Cathedral Church of St. Muredach

10 **Belfast** B5
The Cathedral Church of St. Anne
The Cathedral Church of St. Peter

11 **Carlow** E4
The Cathedral Church of the Assumption

12 **Cashel** E3
The Cathedral Church of St. Patrick
The Cathedral Church of St. Patrick's Rock
and St. John the Baptist

13 **Cavan** C4
The Cathedral Church of St. Patrick and St.
Felim

14 **Clogher** B4
The Cathedral Church of St. Macartan

15 **Clonard** D4

16 **Clonfert** D3
The Cathedral Church of St. Brendan

17 **Clonmacnoise** D3
The Cathedral Church of St. Ciaran

18 **Cloyne** F3
The Cathedral Church of St. Colman

19 **Cobh** F3
The Cathedral Church of St. Colman

20 **Connor** B5
The Cathedral Church of St. Saviour

21 **Cork** F3
The Cathedral Church of St. Fin Barre
The Cathedral Church of St. Mary and St.
Anne

22 **Derry** A4
The Cathedral Church of St. Columb
The Cathedral Church of St. Eugene

23 **Downpatrick** B5
The Cathedral Church of the Holy and
Undivided Trinity

24 **Dromore** B5
The Cathedral Church of Christ the
Redeemer

25 **Dublin** D5
The Cathedral Church of the Holy Trinity
(commonly called Christ Church)
The National Cathedral and Collegiate
Church of St. Patrick
The Pro-Cathedral of the Immaculate
Conception

26 **Duleek** C4

27 **Elphin** C3
The Cathedral Church of St. Mary the Virgin

28 **Emly** E3
The Cathedral Church of St. Alibeus

29 **Ennis** E2
The Pro-Cathedral of St. Peter and St. Paul

30 **Enniscorthy** E4
The Cathedral Church of St. Aidan

31 **Enniskillen** B3
The Cathedral Church of St. Macartin

32 **Ferns** E5
The Cathedral Church of St. Edán

33 **Galway** D2
The Cathedral Church of Our Lady Assumed
Into Heaven, and St. Nicholas

34 **Glendalough** E5
The Cathedral Church of St. Peter and St.
Paul

35 **Kells** C4

36 **Kildare** D4
The Cathedral Church of St. Brigid

37 **Kilfenora** D1
The Cathedral Church of St. Fachan

38 **Kilkenny** E4
The Cathedral Church of St. Canice
The Cathedral Church of the Assumption of
the Blessed Virgin Mary
(commonly called St. Mary's

39 **Killala** C2
The Cathedral Church of St. Patrick

40 **Killaloe** E2
The Cathedral Church of St. Flannan

41 **Killarney** F2
The Cathedral Church of St. Mary

42 **Kilmacduagh** D2
The Cathedral Church of St. Colman

43 **Kilmore** C4
The Cathedral Church of St. Fethlimidh

44 **Leighlin** E4
The Cathedral Church of St. Laserian

45 **Letterkenny** A3
The Cathedral Church of St. Eunan

46 **Limerick** E2
The Cathedral Church of St. Mary
The Cathedral Church of St. John the Baptist

47 **Lisburn** B5
The Cathedral of Christ Church

48 **Lismore** F3
The Cathedral Church of St. Carthage

49 **Longford** C4
The Cathedral Church of St. Mel

50 **Loughrea** D3
The Cathedral Church of St. Brendan

51 **Lough**
The Cathedral Church of St. Mary

52 **Maghera** B4
The Cathedral Church of the Blessed Virgin
Mary

53 **Mayo** C2
The Cathedral Church of St. Michael

54 **Monaghan** B4
The Cathedral Church of St. Macartan

55 **Mullingar** D4
The Cathedral Church of Christ the King

56 **Newry** B5
The Cathedral Church of St. Patrick and St.
Colman

57 **Raphoe** A3
The Cathedral Church of St. Eunan

58 **Roscrea** D3

59 **Rosscarbery** G2
The Cathedral Church of St. Fachtna

60 **Scattery Island**

61 **Skibbereen** G2
The Cathedral Church of St. Patrick

62 **Sligo** B3
The Cathedral Church of St. Mary the Virgin
and St. John the Baptist
The Cathedral Church of the Immaculate
Conception

63 **Thurles** E3
The Cathedral Church of the Assumption

64 **Trim** D4
The Cathedral Church of St. Peter and St.
Paul
The Cathedral Church of St. Patrick

65 **Tuam** C2
The Cathedral Church of St. Mary
The Cathedral Church of the Assumption

66 **Waterford** F4
The Cathedral Church of the Holy Trinity
(commonly called Christ Church)
The Cathedral Church of the Holy Trinity

An Explanatory Note on the Use of the Terms 'Cathedral' and 'Pro-Cathedral'

Cathedral

The word 'cathedral' is commonly used as a noun and a building is described as or referred to as 'a cathedral'. It is also an adjective and the correct title of such a building is 'the cathedral church'.

'Cathedral' derives from the Greek *kathedra* (Latin *cathedra*) meaning a chair or throne, and a cathedral church is a church in which the bishop of the surrounding diocese has his throne. The throne is the oldest and one of the most important symbols of the bishop's authority. When a bishop takes possession of his diocese he is formally 'enthroned' in his cathedral church. A bishop may set up a temporary throne in any church in his diocese but only one is designated for the establishment of a permanent cathedra. Co-cathedrals are permitted in very rare and exceptional circumstances in the Roman Catholic Church but there are no examples in Ireland. In the Church of Ireland there are two instances of co-cathedrals. The diocese of Clogher has two cathedrals – at Clogher and at Enniskillen. The dioceses of Down, Dromore and Connor, each having its own cathedral, also share the use of the Cathedral Church of St Anne in Belfast.

In the Early Christian period the bishop's throne was in the centre of the apse behind the high altar. In the Middle Ages it was placed on one side of the chancel, close to the altar rails. It is only the bishop's throne that transforms a church into a cathedral church. The size and architecture of the building are irrelevant. A cathedral church does not have to be a large, elaborate or well-appointed building, though many are, and the simplest of churches can be raised to cathedral status by the presence of the bishop's throne. This is made clear in Ireland by the modest size and appearance of many cathedral churches. There is a sharp contrast between the simple, plain and inexpensively constructed Church of St Crumnathy at Achonry and the opulent basilical splendour of the Church of Christ the King at Mullingar, yet both contain the thrones of bishops and therefore both are cathedral churches.

Pro-Cathedral

This title is peculiar to the Roman Catholic Church. A pro-cathedral is a church temporarily used as a cathedral by a bishop until a more suitable structure can be built or acquired. At present there are two remaining pro-cathedrals in Ireland – Dublin (for the diocese of Dublin) and Ennis (for the diocese of Killaloe).

ACHONRY

The Cathedral Church of St Crumnathy

Diocese of Achonry (Church of Ireland)

ACHONRY (*Achadh Conaire* – Conaire's field) is a small and obscure village on the River Moy in Co. Mayo about 27km south-west of Sligo and 4.8km north east of Tobercurry. Achonry was given to St Finian of Clonard by the chieftain of Luigne at some date in the 6th century. Finian founded a monastery here and and gave charge of it to St Nathy, one of his disciples. Nathy was also known as Cruimthir, and a conflation of the two names, Crumnathy, survives in the dedication of the Church of Ireland cathedral at Achonry. St Nathy died *c.* 610, and his feast-day is on 9 August. Nothing further is known of Achonry until the 12th century.

The diocese of Achonry was established at the Synod of Kells–Mellifont in 1152, and the first recorded bishop is Máel Ruanaid Ua Ruadáin (1152–70). Achonry is a small diocese, and its survival was probably always in question. A bull of Pope John XXII on 31 July 1327 decreed that Achonry, together with Annaghdown and Kilmacduagh, should be united with the diocese of Tuam. The union was to take place on the deaths of the then bishops of the dioceses.

The union of Achonry with Tuam should have taken place on the death of Bishop David I in 1344, but in 1346 the Chapter of Achonry, with the agreement of the Archbishop and Chapter of Tuam, petitioned Pope Clement VI to dissolve the union. The petition was apparently successful, since no more was heard of the union and Achonry retained a succession of bishops until the 16th century.

The last separate Bishop of Achonry in the Church of Ireland succession was Cormac O'Coyne, 1556–1561. After his death the see was vacant until 1591. It was held by the Bishop of Killala 1591–1607 and by the Archbishop of Cashel 1607–1622, and was united to the diocese of Killala in 1622. Both dioceses were united to the diocese of Tuam in 1834. The small Roman Catholic diocese of Achonry continues to maintain a separate existence; its cathedral is at Ballaghaderreen.

Nothing of any consequence remains of the medieval and earlier cathedral churches which must have occupied the site. The cathedral suffered during the troubles of the 16th century, whether from attack or neglect, and it was in ruins in 1615 when the Irish parliament considered the question of rebuilding. Since the disreputable Archbishop Miler Magrath of Cashel was additionally Bishop of Achonry 1607–1622, it is unlikely that very much work was done at the time. We can presume that some restoration work must have been undertaken at some date, since the building was in use until the early years of the 19th century.

The east wall of the medieval cathedral stands about 9m to the east of the present cathedral. It is a solid construction about 1m thick and now heavily veiled with ivy. Since the tracery and mouldings of its window have long since disappeared, there is no indication of a date, though 15th century might be a reasonable guess. What may be a surviving portion of the north wall, about 7–10m long and 1.5m high, is so thickly covered with ivy that it is difficult to decide whether it is part of the medieval cathedral or a later boundary wall.

Achonry from the north-west

The present cathedral is a simple and inexpensive structure built in 1823 at a total cost of £1,500, with the help of a loan of £1,066 from the Board of First-Fruits. The style, a plain hall with west tower and spire and small vestry-turned-chancel at the east, might be described as late First-Fruits Gothic. The architect may have been John Bowden, who was principal architect to the board in 1813, although by 1830 the board had separate architects for each province and Joseph Welland was the architect for the province of Tuam.

The sole entrance is set in the south wall of the tower. Inside, a spiral staircase leads up to a doorway at first-floor level, which gives access to the west gallery of the cathedral. The tower itself is empty apart from a bell.

Achonry Cathedral has possibly the plainest and simplest interior of all the cathedrals of the Church of Ireland. T. M. Fallow, who produced a short general survey of the history and architecture of Ireland's cathedrals in 1894, was very dismissive of Achonry; a drawing accompanying his text makes his comments a little easier to accept. The drawing shows a plain, unplastered, flat-ceilinged room, devoid of decoration. There is a shallow round-arched recess at the east end, containing an altar placed a little to the south to give access to a square-headed doorway leading to a vestry attached to the east end. In front of both doorway and altar is a small semi-circular communion rail. The door and altar are supported on the south side by a very high pulpit and on the north by a reading-desk. On the south side is a canopy, surmounted by a mitre, but with no bishop's throne below. Fallow also noted that there were canopies for chapter stalls along the west wall, though the seats themselves had been removed.

The presence of a vestry or vestries in the traditional position of a chancel is a curious but not unique arrangement. Emly Cathedral (demolished in 1877) had a vestry in the place of a chancel, and Ennis Cathedral likewise, though the Gothic architecture of both adds more interest. The double presence of the vestry door and altar in the 'sanctuary' at Achonry gives rise to some doubt as to which of them was meant to command the attention of the worshipper.

'Such', wrote Fallow, 'is the conception formed of what was fitting for a cathedral church in Ireland seventy years ago. It is, in fact, a complete burlesque of a cathedral church, and it is impossible to think of it beside the glories of York, or Canterbury, without a smile. In the case of Achonry the conception of a cathedral church has fallen to the lowest level it could possibly reach. The only wonder (as it is too the only point of interest) is that in such a building any recollection of its cathedral dignity should be found at all, and it is really curious to meet with the traditional arrangement of the stalls and throne.'[1]

The present internal appearance of the cathedral has changed since Fallow's withering comment in 1894. A visit in 1989 revealed that the vestry had been opened up to form a small square chancel, with the altar placed against the east wall. In the north wall of this chancel is a doorway which appears to lead nowhere, since it is immovably fixed, and there is no trace of a matching door on the external wall. It was probably intended to be the entrance to a replacement vestry which was never built. There is a chancel arch and a painted border above. A projecting polished wooden dais with two steps leads into the chancel, and the altar is placed one step higher. The east wall has a simple stained-glass window depicting the Star of David. On either side of the window are painted in gold the texts '**Christ our Passover is sacrificed for us**' (north side) and '**Therefore let us keep the feast**' (south side). Both mottoes have small decorated painted arches above. Above the altar but below the window are painted the words '**This do in remembrance of me**'.

The cathedral is arranged like a choir, with canopied return stalls for the chapter along the west wall beneath a gallery. This unusual arrangement was designed to suit a building that was both a cathedral church and also a parish church. Such cathedrals had to be arranged to suit the worshipping needs of the laity. Church of Ireland cathedrals are often parish churches, and the dean of the cathedral is also the rector of the parish. But there was no sense in providing a substantial area of seating in the chancel for a chapter whose members were usually non-resident and rarely attended cathedral services. The solution was to arrange the entire cathedral, usually a single-chamber building, as a 'choir'. The chapter stalls were placed, in return position, under a west gallery or pulpitum, which would have contained the organ or choir. The laity were accommodated in stalls between the chapter and the officiating minister. A more or less similar arrangement of stalls and pews can be seen at Cashel, Cloyne, Downpatrick, Killala, Leighlin and Rosscarbery Cathedrals.

The 'choir' arrangement at Achonry is of the simplest form. The word 'stall' is a generous description of the chapter stalls at Achonry Cathedral; they are of the most functional construction, being hard, narrow and uncomfortable wooden benches subdivided into 'stalls' by the addition of vertical strips of wood linked by simple arches which symbolize 'canopies'.

On the north side outside the chancel is a reading-desk given in 1915 in memory of Robert Reid of Court Abbey, and on the south side is a pulpit given in memory of Thomas Allen, Dean of Achonry 1916–27. The altar was presented to the cathedral in 1915 by Gordon Walker, Dean of Achonry, and his wife. The bishop's throne stands against the centre of the south wall beneath a canopy and bears an inscription in Irish recording that it was given to the Cathedral of St Nathy (sic) in 1916 by the clergy of the diocese. The dates of the reading desk, the altar and the bishop's throne tend to suggest that a refurbishment of the cathedral took place c.1915–16, which probably included the conversion of the vestry into a chancel.

For all its poverty of architecture and decoration, Achonry Cathedral has charm. True, the interior is plain and the furnishings simple, but it is neat and looks well-cared for, and is brightly lit by virtue of its clear glass windows and a recent redecoration in white and cream. The charm of this cathedral lies in its simple dignity set in the beauty of its rural surroundings. Achonry Cathedral stands on low-lying ground amid a grove of trees surrounded by rough grazing pasture with the meandering River Moy skirting it a short distance to the south. Viewed from the higher ground of the graveyard on the north side and framed by an arch of trees with cows grazing in the fields beyond, it presents a scene worthy of Constable.

The future of Achonry Cathedral was under consideration early in 1989. Its proximity to St George's Church at Tobercurry, only 4.8km distant, and the lack of any historical or architectural interest were cited as reasons for closure; but for the present Achonry Cathedral has been spared.

References

1 T. M. Fallow, *The cathedral churches of Ireland* (London, 1894), p .78.

AGHADOE

Aghadoe Cathedral

AGHADOE (*Achadh dá eo* – field of two yews) is 4.75km north-west of Killarney in Co. Kerry. It possesses a little church, ruined for centuries, which has long been known as 'Aghadoe Cathedral'.

The inclusion of Aghadoe Cathedral in a book about the cathedrals of Ireland is anomalous, since it is quite certain that there was never a diocese of Aghadoe. References in 13th-century papal letters, almost certainly mistaken, support the belief; and the common use of the title 'Diocese of Ardfert and Aghadoe' in the Church of Ireland since the 16th century has confirmed the mistaken assumption that there was at one time a separate diocese of Aghadoe. In fact Aghadoe was no more than a deanery within the diocese of Ardfert, and 'Aghadoe Cathedral' was the chief church of the deanery. There was also a mediaeval archdeaconry of Aghadoe which survived in the Church of Ireland until 1922 and is now united with the archdeaconry of Ardfert, but there was no diocese of that name.

The monastery at Aghadoe was founded in the 7th century by St Finian (Fionán Cam or Fionán Lobar) the Leper, a disciple of St Columba. At the Synod of Mag Léne which met in 630 to consider the date of the problem of Easter, Finian was the spokesman of the recalcitrant traditionalists against St Laserian of Leighlin. He died *c.* 635 and his feast-day is on 21 October.

Aghadoe: the resurrection tablet

An interesting event in the mid-12th century indicates the importance of Aghadoe at the time, and the degree of tribal rivalry which followed the introduction of territorial dioceses at the Synod of Ráith Bressail in 1111; it may partially explain the use of the title 'Ardfert and Aghadoe'. The diocese of Ardfert was established at Ráith Bressail as the diocese for the kingdom of Ciarraige (Kerry). But the new diocese also included the territories of Corco Duibne and Eoganacht Locha Léin, whose king, Amlaíb Mór Ua Donnchada (O'Donoghue), seems to have tried forcibly to move the see from Ardfert to Aghadoe in 1158; he was defeated and killed by the forces of the King of Thomond.

A further indication of the importance of the site lies in the fact that Richard O'Connell, the 17th-century Roman Catholic Bishop of Kerry, is buried at Aghadoe.

The question is now largely of academic interest. In the Church of Ireland, Aghadoe has been subsumed since 1976 in the united dioceses of Limerick, Ardfert, Aghadoe, Killaloe, Kilfenora, Clonfert, Kilmacduagh and Emly. In the Roman Catholic Church, the title of 'Diocese of Kerry' is used instead of 'Diocese of Ardfert and Aghadoe'.

There is a reference to the existence of a church at Aghadoe in 992, and a stone church is mentioned in 1044; parts of the present building survive from that time. The cathedral is a small roofless two-chamber structure. The chambers are referred to here as the nave and the chancel, but whether they originally fulfilled these functions in the accepted sense is open to debate, because of the dividing wall which shows no trace of a chancel arch and only a small blocked connecting doorway set towards the north side. Windele records, without naming his source, that the nave was dedicated to St Finian, and the chancel to the Holy Trinity.

The nave was finished in 1158 by Amláib Mór Ua Donnchada who was buried here in 1166. It measures 11m in length and 7m in width and is entered by a fine sandstone Romanesque west doorway of three orders with the remains of a fourth. It shows signs of reconstruction, and some of the stones have been wrongly reset. The arches display geometric patterns. The shaft of the second order has interesting cut-away designs and its arch has dog-tooth carving. The south wall of the nave has been partly demolished; one window survives in the remaining portion, and there is a matching but much smaller window opposite in the north wall. There is a single lancet window in the cross wall which is not bonded in with the side walls and a now blocked doorway to the left. It has been suggested that the wall is a later addition to provide accommodation for a priest in one of the chambers. Windele records that the doorway was closed up 'long before the dereliction of the building'.[1]

The Gothic chancel, a 13th-century addition, has two narrow lancet windows in the east wall with a head and a flower at the intersection. The lancets are 2.8m high and 15cm wide. Only two low sections of the south chancel wall remain; on one rests an Ogham stone bearing the inscription BRRUANANN, on the other a weathered red sandstone carving depicting the crucified Christ with the Blessed Virgin Mary and a cherub. The chancel measures 13.6m long by 7m wide. The continued use of both nave and chancel for burials has raised the internal floor level, which is now much higher than when the cathedral was built.

Whatever history Aghadoe Cathedral may have had has been lost in the mists of time. Whether it was reduced to its present ruined state by the religious strife of the 16th century, or, as seems more likely, much earlier, the only indication is a statement in Smith's *History of Kerry* of 1756, where the author states: 'The cathedral church of Aghadoe has been in ruins time out of mind'.[2]

About 27m to the north-west is the featureless remnant of a sandstone Round Tower. It has been heavily restored and reconstructed and is only about 5m high with an internal diameter of a little more than 2m. The tower probably belongs to the earliest group of its kind, but its date, like that of most Round Towers, is difficult to fix. It could be anywhere from the mid-7th to the 10th centuries.

Some 80m to the south, further down the hill, beyond the graveyard is a small but solid 13th-century round castle of unknown history. Its walls of boulder stones and rubble masonry are nearly 2m thick and have a very slight batter at the base; the diameter is 6.4m. The cathedral, the Round Tower and the castle are pleasantly situated on high ground overlooking Lough Leane, largest of the lakes of the Killarney region, to the south.

References

1   John Windele, *Historical and descriptive notices of the city of Cork and its vicinity; Gougaun Barra, Glengarrif and Killarney* (Dublin, 1840), p. 336.
2   Charles Smith, *The antient and present state of the county of Kerry* (Dublin, 1756), p. 68.

ANNAGHDOWN

The Cathedral Church of St Brendan

ANNAGHDOWN (*Eanach dúin* – marsh of the fort) is about 19.2km north of Galway on the east shore of the southern part of Lough Corrib. A monastery and a nunnery were founded here in mid-6th century by St Brendan of Clonfert, who was given the site by the King of Connacht.

St Brendan (*c.* 486 – *c.* 575 or *c.* 583) enjoys a widespread fame in Ireland, not far short of that of St Patrick. He was born on the Fenit peninsula in Co. Kerry, later becoming a disciple of St Finian of Clonard. He founded a number of monasteries of which the best known is Clonfert. Brendan has been immortalised as the archetypal voyager. He is said to have reached the American continent, and legends of his journey to discover the Isles of the Blessed were popular throughout Europe in the Middle Ages. He is said to have died at the age of ninety-four, at Annaghdown, in the house of his sister Briga, whom he had appointed head of the nunnery that he founded there. His remains were interred at Clonfert; and his feast is kept on 16 May.

The diocese of Annaghdown was probably created at the provincial synod of Clonfert in 1179, convened by St Laurence O'Toole as papal legate. Small and ill-defined it was in-tended to represent the O'Flaherty territory in Iarchonnacht (West Connacht).

Annaghdown was well enough established for its bishop to be present at the coronation of King Richard I in 1189, but it had a brief existence as a diocese. It was created at the expense of the territory of the Archbishop of Tuam, and successive arch-bishops cast covetous eyes on their possessions. In 1252 the archbishop petitioned Henry III against the continued exist-ence of Annaghdown as a separate diocese, and the king as-signed the temporalities of Annaghdown to the archbishop. But subsequent records show that Annaghdown put up strong resistance. A royal licence was granted on 12 September 1263 to elect a successor on the death of a Bishop Thomas, but there is no record of any further action. In 1283 John de Ufford, who had been Archdeacon of Annaghdown, went to Rome as bishop-elect to seek confirmation of his appointment. He spent some years pleading his cause in Rome, but withdrew when Archishop William de Bermingham of Tuam (1289–1312) persuaded him to accept the post of Archdeacon of Tuam. At some date before 1297 the archbishop forced the dean and canons of Annaghdown to resign and ordered the destruction of the staff, sandals, ring, mitre and *liber pontificalis* of the Bishop of Annaghdown.

Nothing daunted, the Dean of Annaghdown arrived in Rome in 1303 to complain to the pope. 'Dionysius, Dean of

Annaghdown from the north-west

Annaghdown, has complained that Archbishop William, in spite of the confirmation of the election of John de Ufford, Archdeacon of Annaghdown [as bishop], seized the bishopric by force and detains it and endeavours by every means to prevent the filling of the church.'[1] In *c.* 1306 a Friar Minor by the name of Gilbert Ó Tigernaig, was elected and consecrated Bishop of Annaghdown and was confirmed as such by the Vicar General of Armagh. Despite the opposition of the archbishop, Bishop Gilbert was able to maintain his position by virtue of strong local influence.

On 31 July 1327 Pope John XXII formally decreed the union of the Dioceses of Annaghdown, Kilmacduagh and Achonry with the Diocese of Tuam. But in spite of this decree, the same pope formally approved the appointment of one Albertus as Bishop of Annaghdown in 1328. Papal decrees relating to so distant a part of Christendom as Ireland were seldom swiftly obeyed. Dogged adherence to former customs and ancient loyalties encouraged the employment of many tactics from delay to outright disobedience. We can be certain that the pope and his curia had only a partial and imperfect understanding of the conditions prevailing in the west of Ireland. In *c.* 1330 one Tomás Ó Mellaig went to Avignon to appeal to the pope for recognition as bishop, but failed.

The Chapter of Annaghdown appealed for the dissolution of this union to Pope Clement VI in 1350 and again to Pope Innocent VI in 1359/60, but without success, and successive Archbishops of Tuam continued to hold Annaghdown. Nevertheless, strong local feeling may have been behind the continued maintenance of a full cathedral establishment, including a dean and archdeacon, together with vicars choral, at Annaghdown. Papal records list a number of appointments in the 15th century, but they were usually absentees, suffragan bishops in English dioceses using Annaghdown as a title but having no other connection with the see. The last substantive Bishop of Annaghdown was James O'Kearney (1323–4). The last papal appointment was Henry Burke (1540–?), and the last royal appointment was John O'More (*c.*1539–53).

In 1555 it was reported that Annaghdown 'had a small cathedral under the invocation of St Brendan, and some canons who, however, do not reside there. The cathedral itself is quite abandoned and only one mass is offered there on festival days. There is also a tower with a cemetery, one chalice and vestment. The Diocese is very small and situated amongst wild and evil men.'[2] The strife of the 16th century appears to have ended the last attempts of Annaghdown to mainain some degreee of independence, and the cathedral has been ruined since that date. After 1555 the diocese was held by Archbishop Christopher Bodkin of Tuam, and the union envisaged in 1327 became a permanent reality on 17 October 1560, when Nicholas Skerrett was made archbishop.

The extant ruins at Annaghdown are those of the cathedral, a Premonstratensian abbey and an Augustinian church and priory.

1. *The Cathedral*

Near the southern end of the graveyard is the plain roofless ruin of the 15th-century cathedral. It is said to have been rebuilt by Hugh Mór O'Flaherty *c.* 1400, but has a fine carved Late Romanesque–Transitional east window, possibly purloined from another church. Whether it was transferred from an earlier church on this site or from the Augustinian priory is uncertain. Carved in blue-grey limestone, the window has chevrons biting into the long body of a monster. Its hind legs are at the base of the right-hand jamb, while its head on the other side devours a bundle of serpents The west wall has no windows but a small square bell-turret surmounting the gable. The north wall has two large pointed arch windows devoid of tracery, with a large external buttress between them. It is possible to discern the outline of what may have been a chancel arch on this wall. The cathedral is entered from the south by a doorway whose eastern capital shows some traces of carving. Also in the south wall is a large shapeless aperture, presumably once a window.

Annaghdown Cathedral is little more than a small barn, and quite forgettable apart from its east window. The surrounding flat terrain has an initial appeal which soon evaporates. 'Though promising, as part of the far-flaunting and beautiful lough's shores, to possess much fine scenery, it is totally destitute of character, and tires the mind by alternations of tameness and of flat and broken sterility.'[3]

2. *The 'Nunnery'*

To the north of the cathedral are the foundations of an early church which has later additions. It is the oldest building on the site and may be of the 11th or 12th century. It had a chamber on the north side and a tower at the north-east corner.

3. *The Premonstratensian Abbey*

Further still to the north are the remains of the Premonstratensian Abbey of St John the Baptist, de Cella Parva. It began life as a priory *c.* 1223 and was raised to the status of an abbey before *c.* 1236. Thomas O'Malley was either the first or second abbot and is alleged to have been the son of a bishop and a nun. He became Bishop of Annaghdown *c.* 1242, but in 1247 was stated to have procured his election to the see by unlawful means. He died in 1250. There are no records of abbots after 1480, and it has been suggested that the abbey was impoverished and in a state of decline. It survived until *c.*1542.

Little remains of the building. It was a nave and chancel structure, but the east, west and south walls are virtually gone, apart from small sections of the east and south walls.

Half the north wall remains. It has an altered doorway at the west end, and beyond a small vestibule lit by two windows. The upper window is square, the lower is a lancet. Adjacent to the chancel arch are the remains of a window with an inner splay.

4. *The Augustinian Priory*

Ninety metres to the west of the cathedral, and reached by a lane to the south of it, are the remains of the Priory of St Mary de Portu Patrum. It was granted to Augustinian nuns in 1195 who took over the monastery originally founded by Brendan for his sister. The surviving remains are mostly those of a 15th-century monastery. The church on the north side of the cloister garth is of at least three periods; the small chancel is Transitional. There is some Romanesque carving in the church, including a north window in the chancel. To the south was a cloister, of which some of the surrounding buildings remain. Fragments of a Romanesque chancel arch are built into the south-west corner.

References

1 H. T. Knox, *Notes on the early history of the dioceses of Tuam, Killala and Achonry* (Dublin, 1904), p. 150.
2 Jerome Fahey, 'The Diocese of Annaghdown' in *Journal of the Galway, Archaeological and Historical Society*, iii (1903–04), p. 134.
3 *The Parliamentary Gazeteer of Ireland* (Dublin, 1844–6), i, p. 35.

ARDAGH

The Cathedral Church of St Mel

*A*RDAGH (*Ard-achadh* – high field) is a small, neat and attractive village in Co. Roscommon which, unusually for Ireland, boasts a village green. It is 4.8km south west of Edgeworthstown, and the site of a monastery allegedly founded by St Patrick. However, the origin of the church at Ardagh is inseparable from the name of St Mel. Tradition holds Mel to have been one of the four nephews of St Patrick, sons of Darerca his sister. It is also stated the he and his brothers accompanied St Patrick to Ireland as missionaries, and that he received the profession of St Brigid as a nun. But the evidence concerning him and his brothers is hopelessly entangled and conflicting. His name is Roman rather than Gaelic, and it is possible that he came from Roman Britain to Ireland *c.* 450. He died *c.* 490, and his feast-day is 6 February.

Ardagh and Ardcarn (*Ard-carna* – high cairn) were named as alternative sees for an east Connacht diocese at the Synod of Ráith Bressail in 1111; Ardagh was chosen. At the Synod of Kells–Mellifont in 1152 a greatly expanded kingdom of Breifne was incorporated into the new diocese of Kells, while the territory of the Conmaicne was formed into an independent diocese with its see at Ardagh. Kells–Mellifont placed the diocese of Ardagh in the province of Armagh, but the Connacht origins of both Uí Briúin Breifne and Conmaicne led to claims by the Archbishops of Tuam that the diocese of Ardagh rightly belonged in that province. The dispute between Tuam and Armagh began in 1177 and resulted in a schism within the diocese of Ardagh in 1224. Pope Honorius III decided in favour of Armagh in 1216, and his decision was confirmed by Pope Gregory IX in 1235. A final settlement was made in 1326.

The first named bishop is Mac Raith Ua Móráin (1152–66), and a continuous succession of bishops is recorded until Lysach O'Ferrall (1583 until after 1601). In the Church of Ireland succession the diocese of Ardagh was held with Kilmore in the periods 1604–33, 1661–92, 1693–1742, and since 1839; and with Tuam 1742–1839. It had two independent bishops in the 17th century: John Richardson (1633–54) and Ulysses Burgh for a short period in 1692.

This chapter is headed 'The Cathedral Church of St Mel'. But there is something of a problem in establishing whether one or both of the two ruined churches at Ardagh can lay claim to the title. Further confusion is caused by the fact that the existing Church of Ireland parish church is dedicated to St Patrick.

In the south-east corner of the grounds of St Patrick's Church is the ruin of a small 8th- or possibly 9th-century rectangular stone church with antae, measuring 12m by 4.5m. The building has been given the name 'St Mel's Cathedral', but it postdates the saint by at least three hundred years. Excavations on the site in the 1960s revealed the remains of an earlier wooden church on the site, as well as some early gravestones. The west doorway has a great horizontal lintel stone and inclined jambs. In the 19th century an ancient crozier was discovered at the site. Inevitably it acquired the name 'St Mel's Crozier', and can be seen in St Mel's Diocesan Museum at Longford. Although this little church may well have been the cathedral church of Ardagh at some stage in its history, it is unlikely that its size allowed it to suffice as the cathedral church of a diocese far into the Middle Ages. Give the general rebuilding of churches and cathedrals in the medieval period, it would be reasonable to assume that a new and larger cathedral was constructed at some later date.

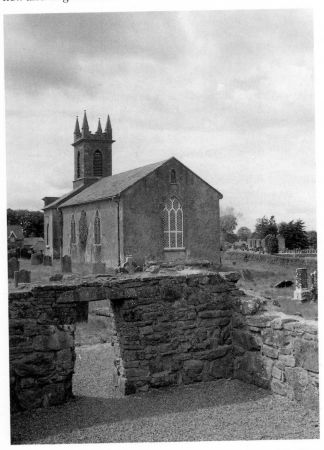

Ardagh: the 19th century Church of Ireland church with St Mel's Cathedral in the foreground

This theory is not helped by the fact that there is very little descriptive evidence of the medieval churches at Ardagh. There are a few references to Ardagh in the medieval period. Certainly more than one church existed on the site in 1167, when the town — 'both houses and churches' — was burnt. In 1230 the cathedral tower was destroyed during a fight between the supporters of rival claimants to the bishopric.

This would indicate the existence of a medieval building, since the 8th/9th-century church would not have had a tower. The cathedral was wrecked in 1496 during a bout of tribal feuding between rival branches of the O'Ferrall family. The O'Ferralls were a local family of semi-chieftain status who provided seven bishops for Ardagh in the 14th and 15th centuries. A report to Rome records that the cathedral was left without sacristy, bell-tower or bell, and with only one altar open to the sky in a roofless church.

So the cathedral remained throughout the 16th century. When Bishop William O'Ferrall died in 1516, Ardagh was said to consist of only four wooden houses and the ruined cathedral 'of which hardly the walls are left'. In 1568 a charge was laid against Bishop Patrick MacMahon (1553–72) to the effect that although the cathedral was in a ruinous condition, he had done nothing to repair it. A royal visitation in 1615 confirmed the situation: 'Ecclesia cathedralis penitus diruta et prostrata' (The cathedral church is internally destroyed and overthrown).[1]

Given its desolate state, the diocese of Ardagh was held *in commendam* by the Bishops of Kilmore after 1604. William Bedell (Bishop of Kilmore and Ardagh 1629–42) visited Ardagh and described what he saw to Archbishop William Laud of Canterbury in a letter dated 1 March 1630: 'I have not been unmindful of your Lordship's commands, to advertise to you, as my experience should inform me, of the state of the Church, which I shall now the better do, because I have been about my Dioceses, and can set down, out of knowledge and view, what I shall relate: and shortly to speak much ill matter in a few words, it is very miserable. The Cathedral Church of Ardagh, one of the most ancient in Ireland . . . together with the Bishop's House there, down to the ground.'[2]

It is difficult to decide whether Bishop Bedell's description refers to 'St Mel's Cathedral' or to the other ruined church which stands in an overgrown graveyard in the centre of the village. The latter is a single-chamber rectangle with west doorway and east window, three windows in the north wall and three in the south. There is a blocked doorway with horizontal lintel in the graveyard wall, only visible from inside the graveyard. The church is covered with ivy and lacks any architectural detail which would indicate a date. It is possible that it was a cathedral constructed at some date to replace the older smaller building, and abandoned after the opening of the present parish church in 1809; but this would not explain the withholding of cathedral status from its successor.

The building was certainly standing in 1615 and in good repair. One source refers to it as a parochial church, the revenues of which went to the dean. In the absence of more substantial evidence to the contrary, it is tempting to suppose this building to be the ruin of the medieval cathedral found by Bishop Bedell in 1630. But again, the bishop speaks of Ardagh Cathedral as 'one of the most ancient in Ireland', raising the possibility that he was referring to the 8th/9th-century church.

The small Church of Ireland parish church, dedicated to St Patrick, was erected in 1809 with a loan of 830 15s 4^1/$_2$d from the Board of First-Fruits. It is a plain hall and tower church of the First-Fruits Gothic style. Several of the bishops of the united dioceses were at one time enthroned in the neighbouring and more important parish church at Longford, but the cathedral at Sligo has served as the cathedral church for the dioceses of Elphin and Ardagh since 1961.

The Roman Catholic parish church, dedicated to St Brigid, was built in 1878–81. The architect was William Hague, who was a pupil of J.J. McCarthy, and who also designed the cathedral at Letterkenny.

References

1 J. J. MacNamee, *History of the diocese of Ardagh* (Dublin, 1954), p. 554.
2 T. M. Fallow, *The cathedral churches of Ireland* (London, 1894), pp 19–20.

ARDFERT

The Cathedral Church of St Brendan

ARDFERT (*Ard-fearta* – high grave) is a village 9.6km south-east of Ballyheige and 8km north-west of Tralee in Co. Kerry. A monastic foundation was established here by St Brendan of Clonfert in the 6th century (see ANNAGHDOWN for details of Brendan's life). But nothing certain is known about Ardfert until a stone church on the site was wrecked by lightning in 1046.

The Synod of Ráith Bressail in 1111 designated the obscure site of Ratass (Ráith Maige Deiscirt), close to Ardfert, as the see for the kingdom of Ciarraige (Kerry), probably because Ardfert had suffered severe damage in fighting between warring factions not long before the meeting of the synod. It seems that Ratass was at most a temporary see, and the first bishop, Anmchad Ua hAnmchada (?–1117), was styled 'Bishop of Ardfert' at the time of his death. The choice of Ardfert was confirmed by the Synod of Kells–Mellifont in 1152.

The site contains the cathedral, the fragment of a much older building to the north-west, and two small churches.

1. The Cathedral

The imposing red and grey stone ruin of the long and lofty aisleless cathedral church stands on the east side of the village, surrounded by a graveyard. The cathedral was originally a simple rectangle, 41.75m long by 7.62m wide, with a short aisle at the south west. Its present shape dates partly from a rebuilding in the middle of the 13th century. The west wall, with its Romanesque doorway and blind arcading, and the middle section of the north wall of the nave date from the 12th century or earlier. The rest of the nave and chancel is 13th century, dating from a rebuilding in the years 1252–6 during the episcopate Bishop Christian, a Dominican from the priory at Tralee. The heavy battlements that crown the main walls were probaby constructed *c.* 1400 for the purpose of defence; access was obtained by a staircase built into the west gable.

A large south transept and a north-east chapter house or sacristy were added in the 14th or 15th centuries. The transept has a small east chapel with a window whose remarkable state of preservation suggests that it may be no earlier than the 19th century. The section of its west wall which adjoined the now vanished south nave aisle is a 17th-century rebuilding from the restoration of the transept as the parish church for Ardfert.

The Romanesque doorway and blind arcade in the west wall are the only remaining fragments of the predecessor of the present cathedral, though it is possible that the two small square, niches in the north-eastern corner of the church may also be Romanesque. There is an effigy of a bishop in the north-east corner, while another less clear and more weatherbeaten effigy of a bishop stands in the matching niche at the south-east; both are dated to *c.* 1300. The remains of a triple sedilia can be seen in the south wall, but what little remains has been disfigured by the insertion of stone blocks to support a shaft of the lancets above. The western shaft of the sedilia has gone and been replaced by stone blocks. But part of the springing of the arches survives on both sides. Remarkably, the gutter drainage pipes (69 on the north wall and 52 on the south) are still more or less intact.

The nave has a few small windows and must have been very dark compared with the brilliantly lit chancel, which has a range of nine slender trefoil-headed lancet windows on the south side; their moulded arches and banded pier-shafts make a continuous arcade. The east wall has the characteristic triple lancet windows of which the centre light is nearly 9m high.

The heavy battlements have undoubtedly weakened the walls, and the south wall of the chancel leans out of the perpendicular at an alarming angle. The wall is supported by a massive external buttress and four metal ties connecting the north and south walls of the chancel just below roof level. The buttress and ties are of recent date and do not appear in a photograph of 1870. The south wall has a small gable with an arched opening which may once have contained a bell.

Ardfert from the south-east

2. *Teampall-na-Hoe (Church of the Virgin)*

Teampall-na-Hoe is a late 12th-century nave-and-chancel church with a small square window high in the west gable. It contains some late Romanesque carving and the unusual feature of external three-quarter columns with carved capitals at each corner of the nave. The south window has floral decoration on the interior side. There is a window in the north wall at the west end. The chancel has long since disappeared.

3. *Teampall-na-Griffin (Church of the Griffin)*

Teampall-na-Griffin is a late 15th-century single-chamber church with double-light east windows, two windows in the south wall and one in the north. Its name derives from the two intertwined griffins carved on the jamb of the north wall window.

4. *The Round Tower*

A Round Tower formerly stood opposite the west doorway of the, cathedral, 'but being neglected, it unfortunately fell to the ground in the year 1771'.[1] An eye-witness thought it 'near an hundred feet high, built mostly of a dark kind of marble; which is the first I have met with that was not composed of freestone'.[2] There is no surviving trace.

5. *The Friary*

The remains of a Franciscan friary stand 275m to the east of the cathedral. It was founded c. 1253 by Thomas FitzMaurice, 1st Baron of Kerry. The long church appears to have been influenced by the design of the cathedral; it has no division between nave and chancel and nine lancet windows in the south wall of the chancel. There is a south transept of 1453 which has a fine south window and tomb niches. Two sides of the 15th-century cloister and part of the refectory survive. There is also a 15th-century tower at the west end which was used as a barracks in the reign of Elizabeth I. The friary was built for Franciscans of the Conventual rule, but became Observant in 1518.

The last bishop to reside at Ardfert was James FitzMaurice who was appointed in 1536 at the age of twenty-five. He was expelled by soldiers of Elizabeth I in 1579, and from that point the cathedral began to fall into disrepair. In 1611 it was described as 'ruined, but to be rebuilt'.[3] Whether or not it was rebuilt Ardfert Cathedral never recovered from the final blow, an accidental burning during the rising of 1641. The nave and chancel have remained roofless since that date. The end of the cathedral and the end of the diocese were virtually simultaneous: Thomas Fulwar, Bishop of Ardfert from 1641, was translated to Cashel in 1661 and Ardfert was united to Limerick.

The south transept of the cathedral was restored and used as the parish church of Ardfert until 1871. The Irish Church Act of 1869, which came into operation on 1 January 1871, provided that all historic churches no longer in use should pass into the care of the state. A new parish church was built elsewhere in the village; the roof of the transept was then removed, and the transept was allowed to decay with the rest of the cathedral.

Ardfert Cathedral is not shown to advantage by its rather flat and uninteresting site which mercilessly exposes it as a large and sadly neglected ruin. Set it high on a rock such as Cashel, and its dignity would be doubled. As it is, the cathedral appears over-large and slightly clumsy against the modest dwellings of Ardfert.

References

1 Nicholas Carlisle, *A topographical dictionary of Ireland* (London, 1810), p. 30.
2 Charles Smith, *The antient and present state of the county of Kerry* (Dublin, 1756), p. 203.
3 J. McKenna et al., *St Mary's Cathedral, Killarney* (Tralee, 1973), p. 11.

ARDMORE

Ardmore Cathedral

ARDMORE (*Ard mór* – great height) is a small seaside resort on the south coast of Ireland in Co. Waterford about 22.4km south-west of Dungarvan and 9.6km east of Youghal. The cathedral church is a very ancient structure, though much altered and restored, occupying a commanding site on a hillside overlooking the sea.

A monastery is said to have been founded here in the 5th century by St Declan (feast-day 24 July), who was one of the four bishops already working in Ireland before the arrival of St Patrick (the others were St Ailbhe (or Alibeus) of Emly, St Ibar of Beg-Eri, and St Kieran of Saigher). Tradition has it that Declan had a bell that worked miracles, and that this bell came to him from heaven while he was celebrating mass. The legend continues with Declan leading a party of Irish monks on a visit to Wales, at the end of which they left without the bell. In response to Declan's prayer, the stone or boulder on which they left the bell floated out to them as they waited in their boat.

Ardmore enjoyed a brief existence as the seat of a bishop in the late 12th and early 13th centuries. It claimed episcopal status at the Synod of Kells–Mellifont in 1152, but the synod deferred judgement. As the principal church of St Declan, patron of the Déise, it was difficult to discount its claims, and

Ardmore maintained its status as a see for some fifty years. The first recorded bishop is one Eugenius, who is mentioned as Bishop of Ardmore in 1153 and later appears in England as a suffragan to the Bishop of Lichfield. No further names of bishops are known and the last reference to the diocese occurs in a list of suffragan sees to Cashel confirmed by Pope Innocent III on 6 April 1210. It was incorporated into the diocese of Lismore.

The oldest parts of the present cathedral are to be seen in the north and south walls of the chancel. For about three-quarters of their length, eastwards from the chancel arch, their construction is of the large and roughly coursed masonry characteristic of pre-Romanesque Irish buildings. These sections are certainly earlier than the 12th century and may perhaps be the remains of a single-chamber church dating from the 9th or 10th centuries. At some stage towards the end of the 12th century a nave and chancel arch were added. The north capital of the arch is decorated with fleur-de-lys in low relief under canopies of bolder leaves, and the south capital has a more ornamental design bordered at the top with a row of leaves.

Ardmore: the Round Tower and the west front of the cathedral

Before 1203 the nave and chancel were both extended and the chancel arch was reconstructed. The nave was made twice as long, and the west door was abandoned in favour of two matching doors in the north and south walls; it is possible that the present north door may be the original west door. The chancel was extended eastwards by 3.6m and given two new windows and a south door. The extensions were made under the supervision of the archpriest Máel Étain Ua Duib Rátha, who died in 1203, and may have been undertaken to emphasise the upgrading of the church to cathedral status.

The most remarkable feature is the collection of weathered naïve sculptures set within arcades on the west gable. They were probably reset from an older building, or else moved during the 13th-century alterations. The lower sculptures within wide arches depict Adam and Eve, the Judgement of Solomon, the Dedication of the Temple, the Adoration of the Magi, and the conversion of a pagan prince by St Declan.

The sculptures in the thirteen bays of the upper arcade are less clear and the following list was compiled in 1903: (1) blank; (2) blank; (3) a defaced figure; (4) a robed ecclesiastic laying his hand on the head of a kneeling figure; (5) two long-robed ecclesiastics; (6) a bishop with crozier; (7) a large robed standing figure, with a smaller one to the left holding a chalice, and an object like an animal in the top left hand corner; (8) a bishop (this carving was found in the cathedral by the Board of Works and placed here); (9) three bending figures on small slabs, and over them three small figures nearly prostrate, and above all was a carving alleged to be a bird but indistinguishable by 1903; (10) a pair of scales with a large ring on the handle, and a small prostrate figure holding on below (thought to represent the Archangel Michael weighing souls); (11) a seated king or bishop before whom a small figure holds aloft a rod or long tablet: (12) totally defaced; (13) blank.[1]

The nave has four round-arched windows and two doorways; the one in the south wall is blocked, and the other is much altered. There is a narrow lancet high in the west wall. The north wall has two round-arched niches which may have been wall tombs, and two blind arcades.

The chancel arch is of three orders springing from large single shafts with foliated capitals which stand on large square plinths. The arch leans towards the nave at a dangerous angle, and its supporting walls are held by massive buttresses. The chancel has four round-arched windows (two each on the north and south walls) and a blocked doorway in the south wall. An Ogham stone stands in the doorway. What looks like a doorway in the east wall was an east window now blocked. The cathedral is full of tombs and surrounded by a graveyard, and the ground level both inside and outside is much higher than originally. The blocking of doors and windows may well have been part of this process. On the south side of the cathedral the ground level has risen to the height of the base of the nave windows.

The cathedral was in use as a parish church for many centuries and was repaired in 1630, when the massive buttresses were added to the external east wall of the chancel, the west side of the chancel arch and the external north-west corner of the nave. The chancel was roofed and still in use as the Church of Ireland parish church as late as 1810; it had ceased to be used by 1838, when a new church had been constructed further down the hill towards the village. This church is of no special interest except for its 15th-century font which probably came from the cathedral. It has octagonal sides measuring 68cm face to face and a circular basin with a diameter of 53cm.

Ardmore: the sculptures on the west front

There are two Ogham stones in the cathedral. One has two inscriptions: (1) LUGUDECCAS MAQI [ ]COI NETA-SEGAMONAS ('a stone commemorating Lugaid, son or grandson of Nia-Segmon'); and (2) DOLATI BIGA ISGOB. The other stone simply reads AMADU ('the loved one').

Standing to the east of the cathedral is the small much-restored 8th-century oratory of St Declan with a small blocked west door and a small east window. The slate roof was added in 1716 by order of Thomas Mills, Bishop of Waterford (1708–40). A hollow in the south east corner is the reputed grave site of St Declan. The LUGUDECCAS Ogham stone was found in the gable and placed in the cathedral for safety; it might be safer in the locked oratory.

There is also a 29m high 12th-century Round Tower built of hard reddish sandstone that has weathered to a fine grey colour. The cap was reset with the original stones in 1875–76 and given a cross to replace one which had been believed previously to exist. The tower is unique in having external circular banding at each of its three floors and a noticeable batter. The wall is slightly inset at each band, making the top incongruously narrow. The doorway, 4m from the ground, has a regular arch of nine stones. On the internal wall there are some unusual corbels consisting of grotesque carved heads. It may be the most recent of the Irish Round Towers. Ardmore tower was last besieged in 1642 when a Confederate army was hiding in the cathedral and the tower. When they surrendered, 117 out of 154 were hanged on the spot. The tower held forty men, so its floors must have been intact at that date. Floors and ladders were fitted in the 1840s and were repaired in 1875–6; they had gone by 1903.

There are no remains of the monastic buildings which lay across the road to the west of the cathedral.

References

1   Description by T. J. Westropp in *Journal of the Royal Society of Antiquaries of Ireland* (1903).

ARMAGH

The Cathedral Church of St Patrick

Diocese of Armagh (Church of Ireland)

ARMAGH, a town of about 13,000 inhabitants, 64km south-west of Belfast, has been the ecclesiastical capital of Ireland from the days of St Patrick, and the seat of both the Church of Ireland and the Roman Catholic primates. Its name (from *Ard Macha* — Macha's height) derives from a legendary 4th-century Irish queen. She it was who made Emain Macha, 3.2km to the west of the present city, the capital of Ulster.

Whatever the legendary stories of Macha, Armagh enjoyed sufficient prestige to encourage St Patrick to found a monastery here *c*.445, and in 447 he ruled that Armagh should have pre-eminence over all other churches in Ireland. How far this rule was accepted in the 5th century is uncertain, but Armagh has for centuries enjoyed the status of being the primatial see of Ireland. There has been an unbroken succession of Bishops and (from 1106) Archbishops of Armagh since Patrick's time. But until the reforms of the 12th century no territorial jurisdiction accompanied the episcopal office. From the middle of the 8th century the *Comarbai Pátraic* (heirs of Patrick) exercised jurisdiction as abbots of the monastery to whom the Bishops of Armagh were subordinate. From 996 the office of abbot was virtually hereditary and the *comarba*, usually married and unordained, was selected from Clann Sínaigh. This remained so until Archbishops Celsus amd St Malachy restored episcopal government in the 12th century. Celsus was the last lay hereditary Abbot of Armagh but determined to conform to the practice of the western church and end the long-standing scandal of lay control of important church appointments. He took holy orders and became Bishop of Armagh and played a leading role in restoring Armagh as the primatial see. As his death approached in 1129 he sent his crozier to St Malachy, naming him as his successor.

St Patrick built his first church on a hill called Druimsalech (ridge of sallows), given to him by a chieftain named Daire, whose fortress stood on the site of the present cathedral church. Being impressed with the saint's exemplary bearing, Daire offered Patrick this site of greater prominence on the Hill of Armagh. The new church built by Saint Patrick *c*.445 was an oblong structure 42.6m in length and divided internally into two portions roughly corresponding to a nave and chancel. There is some doubt as to whether it was constructed of wood or stone, but it was probably destroyed about the middle of the 9th century during one of the many Viking raids. Probably because it was the principal centre of Irish Christianity, no other town and cathedral suffered so much destruction. Twenty-six burnings or plunderings are recorded between 670 and 1642.

In 995 the cathedral was partly burnt in a fire caused by lightning and remained roofless until 1125, when Archbishop Gilla Meic Liac or Gelasius (1137–74) gave it a roof of shingles. More burnings followed until the cathedral was effectively rebuilt by Archbishop Máel Pátraic Ó Scannail (1261–79). His successor, Archbishop Nicholas Mac Máel Isu (1280–1303), bestowed an endowment of 20 marks on the cathedral in 1283 to be spent on the fabric of the church; he also gave books, vestments and other articles.

The nave and aisles were rebuilt by Archbishop Milo Sweteman (1361–80) in 1365, and, after a serious fire in 1428 the cathedral was restored by Archbishop John Swayne (1418–39). In 1561 Lord Deputy Sussex turned the cathedral into a fortress in his war against the O'Neills, thereby inviting its burning by Shane O'Neill in 1566. It was partly repaired and used again as a fortress by Lord Deputy Russell in 1596, but a viceregal visitation in 1605 found it in ruins.

These few facts are all that is known of the development of Armagh Cathedral from its first construction by St Patrick in 444 until its burning by Shane O'Neil in 1566. From the beginning of the 17th century we begin to know much more.

In 1613 Archbishop Christopher Hampton (1613–25) repaired the cathedral. He 'restored the steeple which had been demolished, beautified the north and south walls of the church with fair windows, roofed the south and north aisles (transepts), and made platforms on both sides of the church. He also cast the great bell.'[1]

His work was short-lived, since yet again the cathedral was burnt down, on this occasion by Sir Phelim O'Neill in 1642. Restoration was begun by Archbishop John Bramhall (1661–3) and continued by his successor Archbishop James Margetson (1663–78). At his own expense, Margetson conserved the ruins of the mediaeval cathedral, and these con-

Armagh: the Church of Ireland Cathedral from the south-west

tinue to form the nucleus of the present church. Further restoration took place under Archbishop Richard Robinson (1765–94). He presented a Snetzler organ to the cathedral c.1765, and in 1782 began the erection at the crossing of a tower based on that of Magdalen College, Oxford. The piers of the old cathedral proved unable to sustain the weight, and the scheme had to be abandoned. The tower was intended to be 30.7m high, but when its height had reached 18.2m signs of collapse started to appear. 'Precautions were instantly taken, but after due deliberation the Primate was induced by the fear of some old ladies, whose alarms prevented them from continuing to attend divine service, to have the whole taken down, and he gave directions to have the tower rebuilt as nearly as possible like the original.'[2] A further scheme to erect such a tower at the west end was never implemented.

of decay as to be 'unworthy of any considerable expenditure towards its improvement'.[3] The original intention of building a new cathedral was opposed by Edward Stopford (Archdeacon of Armagh 1825–42) and others and was not adopted by the primate, who instead supervised the total restoration of the building in the years 1834–7 at a cost of £34,000. Archbishop Lord John George Beresford (1822–62) contributed £24,000 out of his own pocket.

The architect for the restoration was Lewis Nichols Cottingham (1787–1847). There is no doubt that his restoration was thorough and effective and saved the building from demolition. But his work involved the virtual rebuilding of the cathedral and the obliteration of what remained above ground of Archbishop Ó Scannail's cathedral. Cottingham

Interior of Armagh Cathedral

A very poor restoration took place in 1802 at the beginning of the archiepiscopate of William Stuart (1800–22). The altar was re-positioned at the west end of the nave, and a gallery for choristers was erected, together with a canopied pulpit. The chancel was furnished as a cathedral choir for weekday services and the crossing was used as a vestry.

By 1834 Armagh Cathedral was reported to be in such a state

opened the clerestory which had been blocked in the 18th century; enlarged the windows in the choir, which he copied from the Lady Chapel of St Alban's Abbey; erected a choir screen between the easternmost piers of the nave arcade, copied from the Abbots's Door in the south ambulatory of St Alban's; erected beneath the east window a stone altar with a reredos of canopied niches copied from the pulpitum at St Alban's; waggon-vaulted the nave in lath and plaster with bosses, copied from the medieval wooden ceiling of St Mary Overie in Southwark; and removed the wooden spire from the tower. The walls of the nave which had declined from the perpendicular were drawn back into place by a very clever device. 'They were raised by heating iron rods – the contracting of the iron in course of cooling having force enough to raise them two inches at a time; which was repeated three times a day till they were straight.'[4]

Further work was done in 1887–8. Cottingham's choir screen was removed and now stands in the south transept between the Regimental Chapel of the Royal Irish Fusiliers and the choir vestry. The sedilia, chapter and choir stalls and the new archbishop's throne were erected at this time.

Further alterations were made in 1903 when the tower arches between nave and chancel were raised by 4m and the chancel walls were raised by 2.4m and faced with stone instead of lath and plaster. The choir and chancel ceilings were also replaced in oak. The stained glass in the east window, a memorial to members of the Beresford family, was inserted at the same time.

The only remaining parts of the ancient cathedral to be seen today are the west wall of the south transept, the tower stair in the thickness of the same wall, and the 13th century crypt beneath the eastern arm of the building. Apart from these few survivals, the cathedral as it appears is effectively of the 19th century.

St Patrick's Cathedral is cruciform and is constructed of native limestone; the facing of red sandstone was part of the Cottingham restoration. It has an aisled nave of five bays, with a tower at the crossing rising to 30.48m. The internal length is 56.08m and the width 36.2m. The nave is lit by five windows in each aisle and four clerestory windows above. At the west end of the north aisle is the fragment of an 11th-century High Cross, which formerly stood in Market Street on the eastern slope of Cathedral Hill. It was damaged in 1813, and after lying in pieces in the churchyard, it was brought into the cathedral in 1916. The font, designed by Cottingham, is a copy of a carved octagonal stone found seven feet below the west door in 1805. The octagonal stone pulpit, with colonettes of red and green marble was added in 1890. The cathedral is immensely rich in 18th- and 19th-century memorial statuary including the work of Rysbrack, Roubiliac, Nollekens, Chantrey and Marochetti.

The north transept is now used as the Chapter House and contains some carved stonework from the medieval cathedral as well as some stonework dating from the Iron Age. The south transept contains the Regimental Chapel of the Royal Irish Fusiliers (designed by George Pace and dedicated in 1950); the screen dividing the choir from the south transept was added in 1950 as a memorial to Archbishop D'Arcy (1920–38). The tower contains a peal of eight bells, six

presented by Archbishop Lindsay in 1721 and a further two by Archbishop Beresford in 1842. The organ is a Walker instrument of 1849. (The Snetzler organ of 1765 was dismantled at the time of the restoration and subsequently sold to Donegall Street Methodist Church where it was destroyed by fire in 1849.) The organ has been enlarged and rebuilt on a number of occasions, the last time being in 1955. Armagh is one of the few Church of Ireland cathedrals still to boast a choral service. Though the Choir School was closed in the 1950s and the lay vicars are no longer paid, the valiant efforts of successive organists have ensured the continuation of the choral tradition.

The chancel has three bays. The wooden roof replaced the plaster vault removed with the heightening of the eastern crossing arch. The north and south walls have blind arcading. The present appearance of the east end dates from 1913 when the altar was brought back to the second bay of the chancel and backed by a fine Fellows-Prynne reredos of Corsham stone, with an opus sectile representation of the Last Supper flanked by canopied niches containing statues of the four Archangels and the four Evangelists.

On either side of the altar are gates giving access to the Lady Chapel in the eastern bay of the chancel. The chapel contains Cottingham's original main altar, backed by a reredos, copied from part of the rood-screen at St Alban's Abbey in Hertfordshire. There is also a memorial brass to Archbishop Beresford, who is shown wearing rochet, chimere, jewelled mitre and the badge of the Prelate of the Order of St Patrick, and bearing a metropolitan cross.

When Thackeray visited the cathedral in the 1840s he remarked; 'The cathedral is quite too complete. It is of the twelfth century, but not the least venerable. It is neat and trim as a lady's drawing room. It wants a hundred years at least to cool the raw colour of the stones, and to dull the brightness of the gilding; all which benefits, no doubt, time will bring to pass, and future Cockneys setting off from London-bridge after breakfast in an aerial machine, may come to hear the morning service here, and not remark the faults which have struck a too susceptible tourist of the nineteenth century.'[5]

One hundred and fifty years after Thackeray's visit, although a certain amount of weathering has taken place, the tendency is to agree with his observation. The site is impressive, though the cathedral itself is walled and shrouded by trees, and several circumnavigations of Cathedral Hill may be necessary before the visitor discovers the way to the top. The reddish-orange exterior looks interesting, but the interior, certainly very fine, is perhaps at first a little disappointing. Something is lacking, and it probably is a sense of antiquity as Thackeray suggests.

For many years Thackeray's criticisms have held good and the Cottingham–Beresford restoration has been decried as lacking in sensitivity; certainly the masking of much ancient fabric is to be regretted. But Armagh represents the transition from an older Gothicism to the romantic Gothic Revival. Cottingham's work may be alien to Armagh, but is antiquarian in inspiration. He bridges the gap between Strawberry Hill Gothick and the romantic revival. He was on the list of architects condemned by *The Ecclesiologist*, but his restoration represents an old-fashioned pre-Tractarian High Church tradition that has an integrity of its own.

The former palace of the Archbishops of Armagh is a plain and dignified late 18th-century house, nine bays wide, four bays deep and originally two storeys high. It was built in 1770 by Archbishop Robinson; a third storey was subsequently added. It is among the more beautiful surviving 18th-century episcopal residences in Ireland, and the domestic chapel with its superb stucco and exquisite stalls is second to none in these islands. It is a matter of great regret that the proposal to remove the additional storey and reconstitute the house as an episcopal residence was not followed. Now the building is in the care of Armagh County Council, and the chapel, although sensitively restored, has, under the covenant of sale, been secularised and cannot be used for worship. A new house for the archbishop was built in the precincts of the cathedral on the site of the Precentor's House, c.1978.

References

1   T. M. Fallow, *The cathedral churches of Ireland* (London, 1894), p. 5.
2   Edward Rogers, *Memoir of the Armagh Cathedral with an account of the ancient city* (Belfast, 1881), p. 107.
3   Fallow, *Cathedral churches of Ireland*, p. 6.
4   James Stuart, *Historical memoirs of the city of Armagh* (revised ed. by Ambrose Coleman, Dublin, 1900), p. 426.
5   W. M. Thackeray, *The Irish sketch-book* (London, 1843), ii, 216–17.

ARMAGH

The Cathedral Church of St Patrick

Diocese of Armagh (Roman Catholic)

THE primatial cathedral of the Roman Catholic Church is one of the most impressively sited cathedrals in Ireland. The twin-spired cathedral stands at the head of a flight of 200 steps which links seven terraces. The approach was formerly covered with bushes and trees, and the flight of steps had hedges on either side. These have been cleared away, allowing a more impressive view and approach to the cathedral. Statues of the two archbishops under whom the cathedral was started and finished can be seen on the upper terrace. The climb is tiring, but the imposing west front draws the visitor upwards and feelings of tiredness are forgotten at the sight of the interior.

After Catholic Emancipation in 1829 the Roman Catholic Archbishop resumed residence in Armagh, and the construction of a cathedral church was soon under discussion. Archbishop William Crolly (1835–49) began negotiations with the Earl of Dartrey for the lease of the site, and Thomas Duff of Newry was appointed architect. His design envisaged a cathedral in Perpendicular Gothic (a style he had used in his cathedral at Newry) with three low towers 39m high. The foundation stone was laid on St Patrick's Day 1840, and construction proceeded until 1848, when the effects of the Great Famine forced the suspension of work. Archbishop Crolly died in 1849, and his remains were interred in the unfinished cathedral on Easter Day (8 April).

Building was resumed in 1854 on the initiative of Archbishop Joseph Dixon (1852–66)and inaugurated by a Pontifical High Mass celebrated on Easter Monday in the still roofless cathedral. The weather being inclement, tarpaulins were stretched across from wall to wall to shelter the congregation. 'A dreadful storm raged during the Mass and sermon, and showers of pitiless hail came down on the heads of the congregation, in places where the covering above had been rent by the force of the wind. Just after the Elevation, a gust of wind swept through the whole cathedral and extinguished the candles on the altar.'[1]

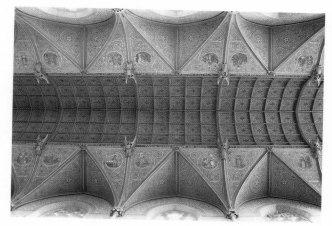

Armagh: The nave roof of the Roman Catholic Cathedral

By this time Thomas Duff was dead, and the cathedral committee chose J. J. McCarthy as his successor. James Joseph McCarthy (1817–82), nicknamed 'the Irish Pugin' was the most famous of the neo-Gothic Irish architects. As well as Armagh, he also designed the Roman Catholic cathedrals at Derry, Monaghan and Thurles, and the tower and spire at Ennis. He changed Duff's architectural style from Perpendicular to the earlier Decorated, the style considered in ecclesiological circles to be the acme of medieval Gothic. Duff's proposed three towers were abandoned in favour of two west towers surmounted by spires with lucarnes 64m high.

St Patrick's Roman Catholic Cathedral, Armagh: the west front

A great bazaar lasting one week was held in 1865 to raise funds to complete the cathedral. Prizes were donated by the pope, the Emperor of Austria and the Emperor of France (who gave two Sèvres vases). It was a successful and memorable occasion and raised £7,000.

No work was done during the episcopate of Archbishop Michael Kieran (1866–9), a sick and elderly man who took no interest in the cathedral and left it as it was. His successor,

Archbishop Daniel McGettigan (1870–87), made a determined effort to finish the structure, and the completed cathedral was dedicated on 24 August 1873 in the presence of a congregation of 20,000 from all over Ireland. On the uppermost terrace in front of the cathedral stand marble statues of two primates: Archbishop William Crolly, who began the work in 1840, is shown holding the plans, and Archbishop Daniel McGettigan, who completed it thirty-three years later, is standing beside a model of the cathedral.

St Patrick's Roman Catholic Cathedral, Armagh: the south nave arcade

The statues are by Professor Pietro Lazzerini of Carrara, whose work is also to be seen in front of the cathedrals at Monaghan and Thurles.

The Archbishop's House, 'Ara Coeli' was completed in 1877 (reconstructed in 1928), and the Sexton's Lodge (at the entrance gates) was finished in 1887.

Between 1894 and 1897 Archbishop Michael Logue (1887–1924) built a sacristy, library, synod hall and muniment room connected to the cathedral by a circular cloister at a cost of £7,828. The final step was taken in in 1898 when the freehold of the ground on which the cathedral was built, on lease since 1840, was secured from the Earl of Dartrey for £919 6s.

The cathedral is built chiefly of Armagh limestone quarried close to Navan Fort (the ancient fortress of Emain Macha) near Armagh. Dungannon freestone was used for the nave piers and arcades, and Bath stone for the groining of the aisles. The cathedral is 64.5m long, 21.9m wide at the nave and aisles, and 36.5m wide at the transepts. The height from the floor of the nave to the ridge is 33.5m, and the two western spires are 64m high. Nine-light brass electroliers hang from the nave arcades.

With the structural work complete, attention was turned to the interior decoration, and between 1887 and 1904 every inch of wall and ceiling space was covered with mosaic or marble; its completion was due only to another great bazaar in 1900 which brought in the sum of £30,000. Italian marble was used and an Italian artist, Oreste Amici of Rome, was brought in to cover the ceiling with oil paintings depicting scenes from the lives of Irish saints from St Patrick to St Laurence O'Toole. The walls of the nave are decorated with mosaic medallions depicting romantic portraits of twenty Irish saints made from designs by John Early, a Dublin artist; above are the arms of the Irish dioceses. The stained glass was ordered from Meyer & Co. of Munich. The cathedral was consecrated on 27 July 1904.

Before describing the sanctuary as it now is, the following account of the arrangement finished in 1904, is included for the purposes of record. The pulpit was designed by Medici of Rome with a base made from a variety of Italian marbles. The high altar, which stood against the rood-screen at the east side of the crossing, was of statuary marble carrying on the front a representation of Leonardo da Vinci's Last Supper by the Roman sculptor Cesare Aureli. It was moved to St Patrick's Church, Kilmore, near Armagh. The archbishop's throne and the screens which divided the crossing from the transepts were of marble. The stalls of the cathedral chapter were of Austrian oak. Behind the rood-screen was the Lady Chapel, whose reredos of Caen stone is the sole remnant of the pre-Vatican II arrangements. The nine niches are separated by columns of marble from Armagh and Down. To the south of the Lady Chapel were the Chapels of St Brigid and St Joseph. In the south transept was the Chapel of the Sacred Heart.

All this has now gone. The single greatest event in the history of 20th-century Roman Catholicism was the Second Vatican Council (1962–5) which in many ways changed the face of the church. Among its decrees was one on the sacred liturgy, calling for the redesigning of sanctuaries to make the liturgy more visible to the people. This provided an opportunity for a major restructuring of the cathedral's internal arrangements. The result is unfortunate, to say the least. With the principle of greater visibility in mind, all the submitted designs envisaged the removal of the 1904 screens dividing the transepts and chancel from the crossing. The successful design was by Liam McCormick of Derry. McCormick's design called for the removal of the screens, the high altar and the pulpit. The rededication of the cathedral took place on 13 June 1982.

The new altar, pulpit and tabernacle are of Wicklow granite and are quite out of place in this great Decorated Gothic building. The altar is a small bowl-shaped edifice standing on an even smaller plinth, and the tabernacle is wedged between two vertical curved pieces of granite that might be the bones of a prehistoric creature. The pieces are certainly imaginative in their design and would fit well into a contemporary and more sympathetic setting; here they invite strong and adverse criticism. There can of course have been neither intention nor attempt to secure architectural harmony. These contemporary designs, which do have an integrity of their own, cannot be introduced into this setting without a horrible clash of styles. The new furnishings are simplistic in their angularity and look very clumsy against the background of this intricately decorated cathedral. Of course, it may be that the clash was both intended and designed to convey a stark contrast between the old and new liturgies. If so, then the aim of the design has been achieved.

Ignoring the work at the crossing, which now has an empty feeling, this great cruciform cathedral has much beauty. Entering it for the first time is a breathtaking experience. The great height, the exquisite perfection of architectural detail, and the caring decoration of every surface of the walls, which is neither garish nor overdone, uplifts the heart and mind. The unstained clerestory windows give a wonderful high-level brightness, and although the building has a soaring loftiness, there is not a trace of gloom. This is Gothic Revival at its very best.

References

1 James Stuart, *Historical memoirs of the city of Armagh* (revised ed. by Ambrose Coleman, Dublin, 1900), p. 445.

BALLAGHADERREEN

The Cathedral Church of the Annunciation of the Blessed Virgin Mary and St Nathy

Diocese of Achonry (Roman Catholic)

BALLAGHADERREEN (*Bealach an doirín* – way of the little oak woods) is a market town in Co. Roscommon, 40km north-west of Roscommon, and 14km west of Frenchpark. It is the see town of the small Roman Catholic diocese of Achonry. Here, the *Dublin Builder* reported in in 1860 'our readers will be interested and probably somewhat surprised to learn that during the last four or five years a large cathedral church ... has been growing up in this remote locality, out of the line of railways and midst a wide extent of bogs and sterile country.'[1]

Bishop Patrick Durcan (1852–75) was the instigator of the plan to build a cathedral for his Diocese of Achonry. Ballaghaderreen Cathedral was begun in 1855 and dedicated on 11 November 1860. The cathedral was designed by a firm of English architects, Hadfield & Goldie. Matthew Ellison Hadfield (1812–85) set up an architectural practice in Sheffield in 1837 with J. G. Weightman; they were joined in 1850 by George Goldie (1828–87). The commission to design the cathedral was given to Weightman, Hadfield and Goldie in 1855. Weightman left the firm in 1858, and the deisgn of the cathedral is generally ascribed to Hadfield and Goldie. How the commission came to go to Sheffield is unknown. Matthew Hadfield may have been the principal architect; he corresponded with A. W. N. Pugin in 1849–50, and Pugin, as the designer of the cathedrals at Enniscorthy and Killarney, would have had knowledge of the Irish architectural scene. George Goldie left the firm in 1860 to work alone in London, and was later commissioned to design the Cathedral of the Immaculate Conception in Sligo.

Although Ballaghaderreen Cathedral was substantially complete in 1860, the addition of a spire, the building of new

Ballaghaderreen: the west front

sacristies and the installation of a carillon of bells in the tower was delayed until 1912; the architect was W. H. Byrne of Dublin.

The cathedral, an unsatisfactory mixture of styles, has been dismissed by other writers as 'mediocre' and 'of dubious aesthetic merit.' It is built of grey limestone and is 45.72m long, 17.9m wide, and 20.4m high to the apex of the nave; the height to the tip of the spire is 56.9m It has a nave of seven bays with clerestory and lean-to aisles. The aisled chancel is short, and its roof is lower than that of the nave. The tower has straggling buttresses to the base of the spire. There are small transepts or sacristies leading off the north and south sides of the chancel. The south transept roof has a small bell-turret.

The cathedral is something of a medley of Gothic forms.

The nave and transept roofs have decorative fretwork rails along their ridges which give a feel of 14th-century French Gothic. A classification of Early English Gothic is indicated by the small twin lancets in each bay of the nave and clerestory, but these are framed internally by deep reveals with oddly flattened arches which cramp the lancets and prevent the full effect. The large east and west windows with Decorated tracery add to the confusing mix.

The original plan envisaged internal fan-vaulting of wood and plaster, but this was abandoned owing to cost and was replaced by the present timber roof, the trusses resting on corbels of carved angel heads in the clerestory. The chancel roof is attractively painted and depicts angels with verses from the *Benedicite*.

The nave has a wainscoting of lightly varnished pine. The impressive high arcades which divide the nave from the aisles are of Scottish sandstone and rest on plain cylindrical granite piers with simple capitals, also of Scottish sandstone. The bases and shafts of the piers are of local blue limestone. Lighting is provided by good brass electroliers. The pine gallery at the west end contains an organ with continental pipework built in 1925 by Chesnutt of Waterford. The pipes have been carefully grouped in two cases at the north and south sides of the gallery to allow a full view of both the west window and a painting of the Transfiguration on the west wall above the arched entry into the tower. The Stations of the Cross are oil paintings in oak Gothic frames.

On the south side of the west door is the former baptistery, donated by Lydia, Viscountess Dillon (d.1876) in memory of her husband, the 14th Viscount Dillon, who died on 18 November 1865. The baptistery has a polychromatic tiled floor with a limestone plinth where the font used to stand; it is divided from the south nave aisle by a painted iron fretwork screen. A reconciliation room occupies the corresponding position on the north side of the west door.

The chancel arch, which rests on clustered columns, is very high and frames the Decorated east window. It is flanked by representaions of the Annunciation and St Nathy, painted in 1989 by Michael Gallagher. The communion rail, of white marble with onyx colonettes, is divided into four sections which span the width of the cathedral in the easternmost bay of the nave. The chancel floor and steps are of white marble. The former high altar, with canopied and statued reredos of Caen stone, is of white marble with colonettes of marble and onyx; it is made by Henry Lane of Dublin. It is fronted by a new marble altar, introduced when the sanctuary was reordered in 1972.

The former Chapel of the Blessed Virgin Mary on the south side of the sanctuary has a mosaic floor and contains a memorial window to Charles Strickland, the agent for Viscount Dillon. Strickland was associated with the building of the neighbouring town of Charlestown and its church. The

window was erected by the Bishop of Achonry and others 'to commemorate their respect and esteem for Charles Strickland and his wife Maria of Loughlynn and their zealous assistance in the erection of this Cathedral Church in 1860'. The altar is of white Carrara marble with colonettes of brown veined marble. The chapel is now used as the baptistery; the font is of white painted stone with panels and colonettes of marble.

The chapel on the north side of the sanctuary contains commemorative plaques to former Bishops of Achonry.

Ballaghadereen Cathedral is a solid-looking structure, but its proportions are not altogether successful. Viewed from the west, the tower and spire are too lofty and appear as uncomfortable additions to the cathedral. The low lean-to aisles only add to the disproportionate height of the tower. The mixture of Gothic styles has already been discussed. But style and proportion are of little importance here. Ballaghaderreen is a functional cathedral designed to seat as many people as possible, and this is echoed by the large, practical and no doubt very necessary car parks which sweep up to its south and west walls, giving it the appearance of a ship in dry dock. Gardens, hedges and trees were removed in 1970 to make way for the carparks, and their disappearance before the inexorable advance of the interal combustion engine is to be regretted. The landscaped gardens that surround Monaghan Cathedral, if repeated here, might help to soften the architecture of Ballaghaderreen Cathedral, which suffers from the reflected hardness of the surrounding fields of tarmac.

References

1 *Dublin Builder*, 1 Sept. 1860, p. 327.

BALLINA

The Cathedral Church of St Muredach

Diocese of Killala (Roman Catholic)

Ballina (*Beal atha an fheadha* – river mouth of the wooded ford) is 59km south-west of Sligo, 16km north of Foxford, and the largest town in Co. Mayo. It was founded by Lord Tyrawley who established a cotton factory here in 1729, and quickly developed into an important commercial centre and seaport. Standing on the banks of the River Moy near the north-east shore of Lough Conn, it has become a centre for fishing on the river and its tributaries. Historically, the Moy marked the boundary between two towns, Ballina on the left bank, and Ardnaree on the right bank, but the two have long been taken together as the town of Ballina.

An old thatched church in Chapel Lane, Ardnaree, behind the present cathedral, served as the pro-cathedral of the Roman Catholic Bishops of Killala. 'Miserably small and squalid',[1] it was built *c.* 1740 of undressed stone and mortar, probably by the parishioners themselves, and measured approximately 39.6m by 9.1m. Two aisles were added *c.*1770, but the building never had the capacity to hold the large Catholic population of the town. Bishop Peter Waldron (1815–34) had long thought of replacing the unsatisfactory chapel with a cathedral church worthy of the title, but the poverty and deprivation of the region were daunting opponents. In 1820 the Bishop adopted the usual procedure of the time, by calling a public meeting to discuss the future of the building. The meeting took the decision to build a new and larger church.

Ballina from the south-west

Little appears to have been done until John MacHale arrived at Ballina in 1825 as Coadjutor to Bishop Waldron. MacHale was a well-known figure in his day. Born in obscurity on a Mayo farm, he was a fluent Irish speaker, publishing an Irish version of the Illiad in six volumes, and translating the first six books of the Bible into Irish. He retained a memory from his childhood days of the priest who baptised him being hanged from a tree on the charge of treason; for the rest of his life he was an ardent nationalist, and became a close friend of Daniel O'Connell.

MacHale, only thirty-four at the time of his appointment as coadjutor, gave the cathedral plan high priority. Though there was no doubt about the need for such a building, he saw that it could exert a wider influence in the diocese. 'I applied myself first of all to rear a cathedral that might contribute to the majesty and splendour of religion in the town in which I reside; and that should also serve as a model and incite the clergy to undertake the building of like edifices in their respective parishes.'[2] He was faced with a daunting task, since the area was very poor; a large proportion of the subscriptions had to come from Irish emigrants resident in England. 'I was compelled to seek for means on every side. Not only did I go myself through all the parishes of the diocese, but I, moreover, begged for alms outside the diocese, both in person and by letter. God happily crowned the undertaking.'[3]

The first site considered was Barrack Hill. This huge slope dominated the approaches to the town on the Sligo side of the river. There are conflicting stories about acquisition and abandonment of the Barrack Hill site. One version relates that the asking price was too high for the limited means of the cathedral committee; the other version says that the site was actually purchased on behalf of the Committee, but when the prospective use of the site became known, the thought of a Catholic cathedral on the most prominent site in the town proved too much for certain influential figures, and pressure was brought to halt the sale.

The present site was eventually offered free by Colonel Knox Gore. The low-lying site close to the river was marshy and had to be filled with tree trunks and other suitable materials before construction could begin. The chosen architect was Dominic Madden, appointed apparently on the strength of his recent design of the Catholic cathedral at Tuam. Ballina is based on his design for Tuam, but because of financial difficulties, the design was repeatedly modified. Oral tradition states that Madden waited for a period, after the construction of the foundations, to allow for settlement. The entire site sank 30cm and then settled. About 100 years after the construction of the cathedral, excavations on an adjoining site revealed the existence of a solid limestone ridge below the marshy surface.

The cathedral fund stood at £1,800 by the spring of 1827, and the records of the cathedral committee reveal the generosity of many Protestant inhabitants of the town in funding the building of the cathedral. The foundation stone was laid on Ascension Day 1827, but completion was delayed for many years because of lack of funds. The memorial plaque over the main door, which gives the date as 1828, is incorrect. Similarly, it gives the completion date as 1893 whereas it was in fact 1892.

The cathedral dedication was changed in its earliest period, for reasons now lost. The initial dedication was to St Patrick. In a speech following the laying of the corner stone, Bishop MacHale declared 'Our Church is dedicated to the memory of St Patrick';[4] a local newspaper, reporting the event, confirmed this statement by reporting that the Archbishop of Tuam 'descended to the foundation and consecrated the stone, on which was a brass plate containing a Latin inscription, signifying that the Cathedral was dedicated to St Patrick.'[5] The reason for the change to St Muredach, and the date of the change, are unknown. The earliest reference to the cathedral being dedicated to St Muredach is a Book of Marriages for 1868.

The first mass was said in the interior of the incomplete cathedral in 1831. Although the building was roofed, it was little more than a shell; there was no ceiling; the walls and pillars were unplastered; the windows were unglazed; the spire was unfinished; and since the floor had not been laid, the congregation gathered on a floor of clay. Bishop MacHale lamented the delay in completing the cathedral but was fully aware of the reasons for the lack of funds and critical of the compulsory payment of tithes to the Church of Ireland. 'Surely the cathedral is, as yet, scarcely fit for the purposes of divine worship . . . the means of our people, after the contributions which they are rigorously compelled to pay each year to the Protestant parsons, are so exhausted that we are unable either to adorn the structure of even to complete it.'[6]

Bishop MacHale visited Rome between November 1831 and September 1832, and there received a letter from one Kenelm Henry Digby, an English Catholic author: 'During your residence in Rome there will be, no doubt, many opportunities offered for procuring objects of art, which might contribute to the adornment or service of your cathedral at Ballina, and it would be a great source of pleasure to me if I could furnish any means to assist your Lordship in taking advantage.'[7] The bishop gratefully accepted the £200 that was offered and arranged for an Italian marble sculptor to make an altar for the cathedral. The marble altar with trefoil designs that he commissioned is still the centre of the new sanctuary arrangements.

Bishop Waldron died on 20 May 1834 at the age of eighty-two. As coadjutor, Bishop MacHale had automatic right of succession; but his tenure as Bishop of Killala lasted only a few weeks. On 31 August 1834 he was appointed Archbishop of Tuam where he remained until his death in 1881 at the age of 90. He left Ballina praising the clergy for their help in the construction of the cathedral: 'Let it be recollected that, besides the aid I received from a generous public, I was mainly assisted by your zeal and large pecuniary contributions and that, besides the faithful of Kilmoremoy, whose exertions are beyond praise, the cathedral is a proud monu-

ment to the ardent zeal and generosity of the clergy and people of Killala.'[8]

Archbishop MacHale was faced with the same problem of a half-completed cathedral at Tuam. Also designed by Madden and also begun in 1827, it was finished and dedicated in 1834.

Ballina Cathedral was not completed with such swiftness. No work was done during the brief and troubled episcopate of the autocratic Bishop Francis O'Finan (1835–7)[9]; and was only resumed in the period 1841–6, after the succession of Bishop Thomas Feeny (Apostolic Administrator 1839–48; Bishop 1848–73). Bishop Feeny had collected sufficient funds to plaster the rough hewn interior. The timber and stucco vaulting and ribbing was completed in this phase. The design,

The west front of the Augustinian priory adjoining the cathedral

by Marcus Murray, is said to have been based on the the ceiling of Santa Maria sopra Minerva, the only Gothic church in Rome. Although the two buildings have the same slightly flattened vaulting, the similarity probably ends there since the ceiling of Santa Maria was restored to its original mediae-val appearance in 1847, after the completion of the ceiling at Ballina.

As with the cathedrals at Armagh, Ennis, Killarney and Long-ford this phase of construction was halted by the onset of the Great Famine. All available resources had to be used in the alleviation of hunger. The cathedral was substantially fin-ished and usable by this date although the spire was unbuilt, and certain internal improvements were still needed.

The next phase of building occurred in 1853–4 with the construction of the spire. An appeal to the Irish of Liverpool helped to raise sufficent funds. It was built by Arthur Can-ning to a design by Sir John Benson, City Architect of Cork. As Madden has based his design of Ballina of his Catholic Cathedral at Tuam, it seems likely that rather than Benson's broach spire, Madden envisaged no more than a square pinnacled tower like that at Tuam.

The organ was installed in 1872 in a specially built gallery at the west end of the nave, and the marble altar rails and broze gates were added in 1879. The last building phase in 1891–2 saw the construction of the sacristies, which nestle in the angles formed by the chancel aisles and transepts, the con-struction of the porches, and the tiling of the sanctuary. After many years of pro-cathedral status, and repairs and restoration in 1912 by W. H. Byrne and Son of Dublin, St Muredach's Cathedral was formally raised to the status of the Cathedral Church of the Diocese of Killala on 11 July 1913.

The cathedral is built of grey Moyne limestone. The plan is cruciform with an aisled nave and sanctuary, and a tower and broach spire with lucarnes, attached to the west end. The tower has emerging crenellated turrets at the north-west and south-west corners. The bronze cross at the apex of the spire was added in 1979 to replace the original rusted iron cross. The aisle walls are buttressed, the buttresses rising to pinna-cles above the crenellated parapet, giving the exterior a hint of the fanciful Gothick of Strawberry Hill, linking Ballina with its contemporaries at Carlow and Tuam.

The interior has a marked similarity to Madden's Cathedral Church of the Assumption at Tuam. It has an aisled nave of four bays with fluted columns, and an elaborate rib-vaulted ceiling with bosses and carved heads. The columns and ceiling were decorated in the rather startling colours of red and cream during the reordering in 1970. The walls are covered with a plain cream mosaic, added in 1930; a simple cross-pattern design forms a dado. The Stations of the Cross are good medium quality oil paintings commissioned by Bishop MacHale on his visit to Rome in 1831–2; the artist is unknown. The north and south aisles contain four carved pine confessional boxes with brass commemorative plates. They were donated in 1899 by Mrs William Flynn in memory of her husband.

The crossing is very broad and has a feeling of great spacious-ness; the four great piers give the impression that they should be supporting a great central tower. The pulpit of 1874, by Neal and Pearse of Dublin, was removed in the reordering of 1970, as were the marble altar rails and three sets of bronze gates bequeathed by Bishop Hugh Conway (1873–1893). The chancel is aisled and quite shallow. Kenelm Digby's high altar has been brought forward to the crossing in the reordering in 1970. The east window is disproportionately large, and low pitch of the roof has caused the window to be set low in the wall. The glass is by Meyer & Co. of Munich and was inserted in memory of Bishop Thomas Feeny (1839–73) who bequeathed the sum of 200 for the purpose. The cathedra and its canopy are at the north-east of the crossing. It was presented by the clergy of the diocese to mark the Golden Jubilee of the ordina-tion of Bishop Hugh Conway (1873–93) in 1892. Removed and put in store in the reordering of 1970, it was replaced in the sanctuary by Bishop Thomas Finnegan (1987–).

The north chancel aisle was formerly the Chapel of the Blessed Virgin Mary; it now houses the Victorian font, which formerly stood on an elaborately decorated mosaic base surrounded by grills, underneath the organ gallery on the north side; the mosaic base can still be seen, but the grills have gone. The south chancel aisle is now the Chapel of the Blessed Sacra-ment and uses the tabernacle from the High Altar.

Ballina Cathedral is adjoined by the remains of an Augustin-ian friary founded some time before 1401 by the O'Dowdas, chieftains of Ui Fiachrach. By 1410 the buildings had par-tially collapsed and what remained was threatened with ruin. Tadhg Riabhach O'Dowda is mentioned as the founder and may have been responsible for a rebuilding in the years 1417–27. The friars are believed to have remained at Ballina until as late as 1577–82.

Between the friary and the cathedral is a small burial ground, purchased in 1879 and laid out as a cemetery in 1897; a number of Bishops of Killala, and priests connected with the cathedral are buried here.

References

1   Bernard O'Reilly, *Life of John MacHale, Archbishop of Tuam* (New York, 1890), i, 113.
2   Ibid., p.114.
3   Ibid.
4   James McGuire, *Steeple and people: Ballina and its cathedral* (Ballina, 1991), p.70.
5   Ibid., p.71.
6   Ibid.
7   Ibid., p.194.
8   McGuire, *Steeple and people*, p. 43.
9   O'Finan remained nominal Bishop of Killala until his death in 1847, but lived in Rome and took no further part in the administration of the diocese.

BELFAST

The Cathedral Church of St Anne

*Dioceses of Down and Dromore and Connor
(Church of Ireland)*

BELFAST (*Béal feirste* – ford of the sandbank) is the capital city of Northern Ireland. It lies at the mouth of the River Lagan and the head of Belfast Lough. The city is 161.6km north of Dublin and 118.4km south-east of Derry. The site of Belfast was certainly occupied in both the Stone and Bronze Ages, and the remains of more than two dozen Iron Age forts (500 B.C. – A.D. 500) can be traced on the hill slopes within a few kilometres of the city centre.

In 1613 it was incorporated by royal charter of James I with the right of sending two members to parliament. With the coming of the industrial revolution in the late 18th century, the population of Belfast grew rapidly. Standing at 8,550 in 1757, it had risen to 20,000 in 1800, 37,000 in 1821, 70,000 in 1841, 121,000 in 1861, 208,000 in 1881, and 400,000 in 1925. Much of its architecture is a product of the Industrial Revolution and its aftermath. Little now survives of the late Georgian period. The lack of good building stone and the abundance of clay has produced a city built almost entirely of red brick.

Belfast was incorporated as a borough in 1842, and raised to the status of a city in 1888; the title of Lord Mayor was conferred in 1892. By the Government of Ireland Act, 1920, it became the seat of the government of Northern Ireland.

The above introduction to Belfast should be read with the fact that, despite its (recent) growth and prominence, there is no diocese of Belfast of which the city is the see. Belfast is divided between the diocese of Connor and the diocese of Down. St Anne's, the ancient parish church of Belfast, is in the diocese of Connor (whose cathedral church is at Lisburn), but a considerable part of the present city lies in the diocese of Down (whose cathedral church is at Downpatrick).

The simplest solutions to the geographical problem of this burgeoning city, a civic unity that inconveniently sprawled itself across an ecclesiastical divide, would have been either to alter diocesan boundaries so that the entire city was contained within one or other of the dioceses of Connor or Down, or to create a new single diocese of Belfast. Because of the significance of the city and the distance of the two existing cathedral churches at Lisburn and Downpatrick, it was appropriate that Belfast should be the centre of a new diocese. It is likely, however, that neither possibility was seriously considered, the former perhaps because either Connor or Down would be substantially enlarged and enriched at the expense of the other, and the latter possibly because it was considered undesirable to create a large populous diocese of Belfast, leaving two small and truncated dio-

ceses of Connor and Down. But something had to be done, since Belfast was now an important industrial and political entity. The solution was what some have seen as 'a last paroxysm of Imperial pride; others, a symbol of continuity and stability'.[1]

The idea of a cathedral for Belfast was proposed long before it became a reality. In 1860 the Dean and Chapter of Connor resolved that 'It would be highly conducive to the interests of the United Church of England and Ireland, in the Diocese of Connor generally, and of this chapter in particular, if a cathedral could be erected in the immediate vicinity of Belfast, and that we deem the present a suitable time for carrying out this important object.'[2] The commencement of construction of the Roman Catholic Pro-Cathedral of St Peter in the Falls Road area of the city may have contributed to the resolution.

In 1894 Henry Stewart O'Hara (Bishop of Cashel, Emly, Waterford and Lismore 1900-19) was appointed Rector of Belfast and he conceived the slightly illogical scheme of erecting a cathedral church for the city which would not supersede the two existing cathedrals but link them together. The concept made more sense in 1894 than it does now because the dioceses of Connor and Down and Dromore were then united and the whole city of Belfast was under the jurisdiction of a single bishop. In 1944 the diocese of Connor was separated from Down and Dromore and given its own bishop because of an increase in population, and the city is now divided between two Church of Ireland dioceses.

The scheme to provide a cathedral for Belfast was presented to the Diocesan Council by Thomas Welland (Bishop of Down, Dromore and Connor 1892–1907) on 7 March 1894. There were the inevitable objections, doubts and forebodings about cost and necessity, but the plan was approved, and the foundation stone was laid by the Countess of Shaftesbury on 6 September 1899 in the presence of the Archbishops of Armagh and Dublin. A publicity brochure lauded the proposed cathedral as a means of exerting 'a wholesome moral influence on a district whose present condition is by no means satisfactory'.[3]

The chosen site was occupied by the parish church of St Anne, and the walls of the new cathedral church were constructed around the parish church, which was used for public worship until 31 December 1903. St Anne's was a typical Classical church, built in 1776. It was a rectangle with a pedimented portico supported by four Corinthian columns. Behind the pediment rose a tower of four storeys with double pilasters at each corner, ending in a domed cupola.
The chosen architect for the new cathedral was Sir Thomas Drew (1838–1910), whose original plan called for a very orthodox 13th-century Gothic design with a large rose window at the west end, a square tower at the crossing, and a ribbed stone roof. After publication of the prospectus he revised his drawings and moved to a simplified Romanesque design with a wooden ceiling, adopting the style of a basilica.

The reason given was that the Romanesque plan would be less expensive and could more easily be built in sections as funds became available.

Drew's design envisaged a nave of six bays with side aisles, a crossing surmounted by a massive central tower, north and south transepts, and an aisled apse with an eastern chapel beyond. The nave was to be 36.88m long, 25.9m high and 25.9m wide. The crossing, transepts and apses were each to be 12m square. The design also provided for a west front of three portals, surmounted by a large triple window, and a baptistery and a chapel opening off the south and north sides respectively of the westernmost bay of the nave.

The nave was the first part of the cathedral to be finished and was consecrated by Bishop Welland on 2 June 1904. Those parts of the nave floor occupied by chairs were floored in Canadian maple, while the aisles were paved with a variety of Irish marbles: black from Kilkenny and Galway; white from Recess, Dunlewy and Clifden, and red from Cork. Immediately inside the west door is a patterned circle composed of thirty-two pieces of marble, representing the thirty-two counties of Ireland. The only tomb in the cathedral, that of Lord Carson, is in the south nave aisle. Carson, who died in 1935, is best remembered as the leader of the Ulster Unionists during the troubled years of the Home Rule controversy 1911–21.

The next phase of building began in 1917 with work on the four great piers of the crossing. Spiralling costs and a succession of different architects ensured frequent alterations to the original plan. After the death of Drew in 1910 and his successor, William Henry Lynn, in 1915, the job was given to Peter Macgregor Chalmers of Glasgow, who himself died in 1917 shortly before the beginning of the construction of the crossing. Chalmers's plans were implemented by his successor, Richard Mills Close, and the crossing was completed in 1924.

The baptistery on the south side of the nave was built on the site indicated by Drew, designed by William Henry Lynn, and decorated by Sir Charles Nicholson; it was built in the years 1922–8. The baptistery is a semi-circular building with a semi-domed roof and a patterned floor of Portland stone and various Irish marbles. The font, of Portland stone inlaid

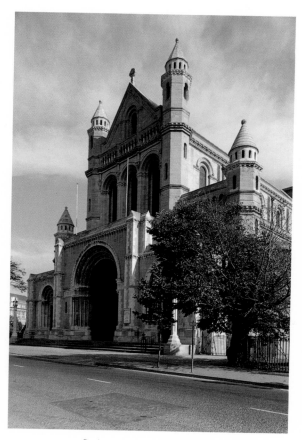

St Anne's Cathedral, Belfast

with white alabaster, is supported by columns of red marble on a base of black marble. The mosaic roof, the work of Gertrude and Margaret Martin, is made up of 150,000 pieces of glass, each one individually placed by hand. The work has representations of Fire, Air, Earth and Water and symbolises Creation, over which the hand of the Creator is raised in blessing. The Bath stone string courses were carved with children's heads by Rosamond Praeger. The baptistery was dedicated on 2 June 1928.

Before the completion of the baptistery the Cathedral Board decided to proceed with the completion of the west front, the rough brickwork of which had become shabby and unsightly with the passage of time. The chosen architect was Sir Charles Nicholson, who succeeded Close as architect for the cathedral in 1924. The work began with the laying of a foundation stone by the Duke of Abercorn (Governor of Northern Ireland 1922–45) on 2 June 1925. Exactly two years later, the completed west front was dedicated by Henry Grierson (Bishop of Down, Dromore and Connor 1919–34). It employs almost every idiom known to Gothic and Romanesque, including Corinthian pilasters. The carvings in the tympana are by Edmund Burton. Those above the north door represent the Crucifixion, those above the south door the Resurrection, and above the centre door, Christ in Glory. Burton also carved the label stops of the upper portion of the west gable with representations of the four ruling passions of Industry, Strife, Love and Avarice. The bronze gates were designed by Nicholson and made by the Tudor Art Company of London c.1929.

On the north side of the nave, opposite the baptistery, is the Chapel of the Holy Spirit, consecrated on 5 June 1932 to commemorate the 1,500th anniversary of the coming of St Patrick to Ireland. The chapel is rectangular, and the chamber above is the cathedral's muniment room. A mosaic of St Patrick in the bow of a ship, passing the Mourne Mountains, can be seen above the entrance arches. The altar is of oak inlaid with mahogany, walnut, holly and ebony. The step at the communion rail is of Hopton Wood brown stone, and the rail itself is of Portland stone, inset with green Connemara marble.

The ten capitals of the nave piers are carved with a variety of themes representing the work of men and women; the four responds, to the east and west ends, represent the four cardinal virtues; above each capital is a corbel carved with some great worthy of the Irish Church; at each corner of the nave are the four archangels, Michael, Gabriel, Uriel and Raphael. Each of the capitals and corbels has a theme. On the north side from west to east: Courage (a Celtic chieftain armed with a sword); Science (Archimedes, Roger Bacon, Sir Isaac Newton, Lord Kelvin and Bishop George Berkeley of Cloyne (1734–53)); Commerce (designed with reference to the linen industry, illustrating phases from the field to the market place, with the corbel depicts Henry O'Hara, first Dean of St Anne's, holding a model of the cathedral); Heal-ing (depicting Biblical scenes, and St Luke, the Beloved Physician, writing his gospel, with the corbel depicting William King, Dean of St Patrick's Cathedral in Dublin, who welcomed King William III in 1690); Agriculture (scenes of ploughing, sowing, reaping and threshing, with the corbel depicting George Salmon (1819–1904), Dean of Trinity College, Dublin); Music (angels playing instruments and a verse from Psalm 150, with the corbel depicting Bishop Jeremy Taylor, Down, Dromore and Connor (1661–7); and Justice (Moses holding the Book of the Law).

On the south side from east to west: Temperance; Theology (St Athanasius, St Augustine, Thomas Cranmer, Richard Hooker, James Ussher, with the corbel depicting James Ussher, Archbishop of Armagh (1625–56); Shipbuilding (the Ark of Noah, a Norse galley, a wooden sailing ship, an oil-burning ship; also miniature busts of David Lloyd George and Henry Asquith, two former Prime Ministers, with the corbel depicting Thomas Percy Bishop of Dromore (1782–1811)); Freemasonry (emblems of the various 'degrees' of this organisation, with the corbel depicting William Bedell Bishop of Kilmore (1621–42); Art (Sir Christopher Wren, Michaelangelo, Sir Joshua Reynolds, William Shakespeare, William Alexander Archbishop of Armagh (1896–1911)); Women's Work (teaching, home life, nursing and motherhood, with the corbel depicting Mrs Cecil Frances Alexander, wife of Archbishop Alexander and a noted hymn writer); and Wisdom (King Solomon). They were mostly carved between 1925 and 1937 by Morris Harding under the direction of Nicholson. The exceptions are Courage and Agriculture, which were designed by Chalmers, and Justice, designed by Nicholson but carved by Rosamond Praeger.

Sir Charles Nicholson died on 4 March 1949 at the age of eighty-one and was succeeded as supervising architect by his partner, Thomas J. Rushton, until 1963. Nicholson and Rushton together had designed the eastern apse and ambulatory c.1947. Rushton's proposal for a long eastern chapel and a great off-set eastern tower with a chapter house on the ground floor was abandoned. Work began in 1955 and the completed apse and ambulatory were dedicated on 17 April 1959. The east window behind the altar is a link with the old St Anne's Church, where it was erected in 1887.

The present pulpit was erected in 1967 to replace a Victorian pulpit of 1858 designed by Sir George Gilbert Scott for Westminster Abbey to commemorate the special Sunday evening services; the capitals of this earlier pulpit were carved by Harry Hemms. It was removed from the Abbey in 1902 for the coronation of Edward VII and presented by the Dean and Chapter to St Anne's Cathedral in 1904. It was removed in 1967 on the slightly dubious grounds that its style 'would not be in harmony with the completed cathedral'. It was destroyed by fire in a Belfast store while *en route* to the Church of the Incarnation in Dallas, Texas.

Rushton was followed by John McGeagh (architect 1963–

St Anne's Cathedral, Belfast looking east

THE CATHEDRALS OF IRELAND

79), who designed the south transept c.1964 and the north transept c.1968. Work began on the transepts in 1969, and the south transept was completed and consecrated on 20 June 1974. It contains the Chapel of Unity. For the first few years of the cathedral's existence the organ of the St Anne's Church was used. It was built in 1781 by Johann Snetzler and rebuilt by William Hill & Son of London in 1875. It was removed in August 1907 to the Church of Ireland Young Men's Society at Clarence Place Hall and sold for scrap in the 1950s. In its place a new three-manual organ was built by Harrison & Harrison of Durham and installed temporarily in the south aisle. With the completion of the south transept, the organ, which had occupied a temporary position in the easternmost bay of the south aisle, was dismantled in 1967 and re-erected in the new south transept in 1975.

Work on the north transept stopped in August 1974 in the light of reports that the cathedral was in financial difficulties. The sum of 500,000 was still needed, but appeals for money failed in Northern Ireland because industrialists deemed it unwise to finance a possible bomb target. For several years the transept remained unfinished, and its girders resembled a dark skeleton against the sky. As a result of the efforts of Samuel Crooks (Dean 1970–85), the north transept was completed, and it was consecrated on 2 June 1981. By that date McGeagh had been succeeded by Robert McKinstry (architect 1979–86), eighth and final architect of the construction period, who completed the transept to McGeagh's designs. Internally, the transept is quite shallow, owing to the unusual huge Celtic cross in the external gable which now dominates the surrounding area. The cross is an astonishing sight, but it sits a little unhappily in a Romanesque building. The Transept contains the Chapel of the Royal Irish Rangers, dedicated a few days after the consecration of the transept.

The completion of the north transept was deemed to mark the 'completion' of the cathedral, which was dedicated in the presence of the Archbishop of Canterbury on 2 June 1981. But, despite the cost, it might have been better to adhere closely to the original plans. Nowhere is the incompleteness of St Anne's more apparent than at the crossing. There is an obvious need for a tower or spire here to 'crown' the cathedral. Drew's plan for a great central tower was abandoned, as was McKinstry's design for a tall flèche. Hopefully a future generation will raise funds for the construction of Drew's tower. But, for the foreseeable future the fabric of the building is likely to remain unaltered.

St Anne's Cathedral is undoubtedly a very impressive building and a fine addition to the architecture of Belfast, but there is a faint whiff of civic pride about its origins. The reason behind the erection of such a building in Ireland's second city is quite understandable – the provision of a large and impressive church for civic and municipal occasions — but its status and style as a cathedral church is as much an anomaly as Enniskillen Cathedral. The dioceses of Down and Connor had and still have cathedral churches, and the provision of a third was (a) unnecessary (b) confusing, and (c) perpetuates the myth that a cathedral is no more than a big church. Its size would have given it all the status it needed to become a religious focal point for the city. But St Anne's is an impressive building, and its anomalous position could perhaps be rectified by returning Lisburn Cathedral to parish church status and making St Anne's the cathedral church of the diocese of Connor, while retaining the link with the diocese of Down.

Despite the criticisms, ecclesiological or architectural, that could be levelled against St Anne's Cathedral, it has an important cross-community, civic and religious role today. St Anne's is often used for services with a national, international or interdenominational character. Without bias or prejudice, it could play the role of a national cathedral for Northern Ireland, reflecting the work of St Patrick's Cathedral in Dublin. Among its activities in recent years is the famous 'sit-out', by which the cathedral has raised more than £300,000 in the past eleven years for charity. It was started by Dean Crooks, who spent a period before Christmas each year sitting outside the cathedral with a collecting box. This act of generosity on the part of the cathedral towards local charities has earned the dean and his successors the sobriquet of "the Black Santa."

Broad, spacious, massive and dignified, the cathedral is a great tribute to the enormous energy and enthusiasm of the minds who conceived it; to the several architects who have left their mark on it; and to the faith that has made St Anne's so much a part of the life of Belfast.

References

1   Brian de Breffny and George Mott, *The churches and abbeys of Ireland* (London, 1976), p. 194.
2   *Irish Ecclesiastical Gazette*, 14 Nov. 1860.
3   De Breffny and Mott, *Churches and abbeys of Ireland*, p. 194.

BELFAST

The Cathedral Church of St Peter

Dioceses of Down and Connor (Roman Catholic)

THE site for this Gothic Revival cathedral was acquired by Bernard Hughes, proprietor of the Railways and Model Bakeries in 1858 from its owner, who was resident in Co. Carlow. Hughes subsequently transferred his tenure of the land to Bishop Patrick Dorrian of Down and Connor (coadjutor 1860–5; diocesan 1865–85) at a 'peppercorn' rent.

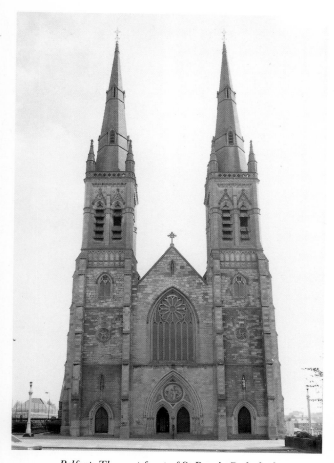

Belfast: The west front of St Peter's Cathedral

Two architects were employed on the building. The plans were drawn up by Fr Jeremiah Ryan McAuley, a native Belfast priest who had qualified and practised as an architect before ordination in 1858. Construction began in 1860. McAuley left Belfast in 1862 for the Irish College at Salamanca in Spain; he was succeeded by John O'Neill, also a Belfast architect, under whose supervision the building was mostly finished by 1866. O'Neill also designed the presbytery at the rear of the cathedral.

The new church was dedicated on Sunday 14 October 1866 in the presence of the Archbishops of Dublin and Birmingham. Generous donations were received from the large number of Protestants who attended the ceremony, and the collection amounted to 2,260. The cathedral is 54.8m long and 21.3m wide. The two west towers were built only to a height of 18.2m because of lack of funds. They were roofed and surmounted by a decorative parapet. The present slender tapering spires were completed in 1885 under the supervision of the architect Mortimer Thompson. A carillon of ten bells was installed with the completion of the spires, and the harmonium first in use was replaced by a pipe organ in 1883. The total cost of the church, including organ and bells, was £35,900.

There are three entrance doors in the west front; the tympanum above shows the release of St Peter from prison. Above the tympanum is a large traceried window. Two further doorways, one at the centre-point of each aisle, were enlarged by Pádraic Gregory in 1948–50 to provide wider entrances. One doorway served as a mortuary chapel and the other as a baptistery until the most recent renovations in 1986. The former north porch now contains a shrine of the Immaculate Conception. The south porch now houses the Reserved Sacrament.

The cathedral, which measures 54.8m by 21.3m, is built of Scrabo sandstone with Scottish stone dressings. The plan is an aisled and clerestoried nave of seven bays, with a chancel of one bay ending in an apse. Each aisle is lit by six triple-light windows, and the clerestory above is lit by eight similar windows. The apse is lit by five triple-light windows with geometrical Decorated tracery. The cylindrical nave piers have unfortunately been painted a dark blue; the spandrels contains cartouches of Irish saints. The aisles have simple mosaic floors. The Stations of the Cross are painted plaster in carved pine frames. The supports of the lean-to aisles contain a form of fretwork.

There are no transepts, and the aisles end in chapels which flank the apse. The Chapel of the Blessed Virgin Mary on the north side of the sanctuary is walled with mosaic and has a stone altar, backed by blind arcading, resting on a plinth of black marble. On the south side is the Chapel of the Sacred Heart, whose altar similarly rests on a black marble plinth.

There is a good hammer-beam roof with corbels resting on carved stone heads. The section over the chancel has been attractively painted in blue with simplistic representations of angels. The former high altar has a 10m high baldachino of Caen stone surmounted by a cross and resting on six columns. Wooden partitions now project from the north and south walls of the chancel to screen the rest of the apse, leaving only the high altar and baldachino visible.

St Peter's Cathedral Belfast looking east

St Peter's was long known as 'the Pro-Cathedral', although there is no record of any official grant of the title. But nearly all the official ceremonies appropriate to the cathedral church of a diocese took place at St Peter's, and the title was probably simply assumed by common usage in much the same way as the Pro-Cathedral in Dublin. After his installation as Bishop of Down and Connor in 1967 Bishop Cahal Daly announced his intention to have St Peter's declared the Cathedral Church of Down and Connor. Permission was sought from the Vatican, and a reordering took place, mainly involving the extension of the sanctuary area with the removal of seven rows of seats. The reordering was planned by Raymond Carroll, and the architect was Laurence McConville. The new altar, lectern, ambo and font are of mahogany; the altar has inlay depicting the Lamb of God resting on the Crossed Keys of St Peter. The font, set in front of the former Sacred Heart altar, has inlaid designs in oak and beech and rests on an octagonal base; the basin is of slate.

With the completion of the re-ordering, St Peter's was formally dedicated a cathedral church on 29 June 1986.

The cathedral is situated in the heart of the Roman Catholic Falls Road area of Belfast and is hemmed in by flats and houses which prevent a good view of the building. The architecture is not especially remarkable, nor is the interior strikingly beautiful. There is no polished intricacy of decoration or beauty of finish; no lavish and expensive decoration in marble and mosaic; and no exquisite paintings by imported Italian artists. But these absences, which are shortcomings or deficiencies in the eyes of many, are not to be counted against St Peter's Cathedral. The simple roughness of its style and decoration complements the powerful sense of its being a citadel of prayer and faith in an otherwise depressing neighbourhood. The visitor is left with the strong feeling that here is a cathedral which, for all that it may be deemed to have architectural limitations, is well used and very much at the heart of a thriving local community.

CARLOW

The Cathedral Church of the Assumption

Dioceses of Kildare and Leighlin (Roman Catholic)

CARLOW (*Ceatharlach* – four lakes), with a population of 11,000, is a marketing centre and manufacturing town on the east bank of the River Barrow in Co. Carlow. It is 79km south-west of Dublin on the main road down to Kilkenny and Waterford.

Carlow stood on the edge of the Pale, the area of effective English control in Ireland during the Middle Ages, and was of strategic importance. There were many clashes between the English and the Irish from the 14th to the 17th centuries. A castle was built here *c.*1180 by Hugh de Lacy and replaced by a stronger fortress in the early 12th century; only a fragment of the keep remains.

The Roman Catholic dioceses of Kildare and Leighlin were reduced to extreme poverty by the confiscation of church property and were placed under the jurisdiction of the same bishop in 1678. Between 1678 and 1751 a succession of seven Catholic Bishops of Kildare and Leighlin are recorded. None of them had cathedral church or episcopal residence, and their places of death and burial are unknown. Communication with their flock was difficult in the penal days of the early 18th century, and they concluded their letters with the words *Datum est refugii nostri* (Given from our place of concealment).

James O'Keeffe was consecrated Bishop of Kildare and Leighlin in 1752 and took up residence in Carlow and used the church there as his pro-cathedral. From that date Carlow became the prospective episcopal see of the Catholic dioceses of Kildare and Leighlin. The pro-cathedral was 'a low and unpretentious edifice, built of rough undressed stone, and without steeple or cross ... Inside, the plastered and whitewashed walls of the chapel were hung with rude coloured prints of the Way of the Cross, and of St Patrick and the Blessed Virgin; and its uneven earthen floor contained only a few rough forms for the accommodation of the well-to-do portion of the congregation.'[1]

In 1819 James Doyle became Bishop of Kildare and Leighlin. The life, work and writings of this remarkable bishop form an important part of the ecclesiastical and civil history of Ireland in the first half of the 19th century. His reputation was of such standing that he was invited to London in March 1825 to give evidence before a joint committee of Lords and Commons on the state of Ireland. He made a profound impression by his 'self-possession, clearness of judgement, and dignity of character', and Gladstone later referred to him as 'the Prelate who, more than any other, represented his Church and influenced the mind of England in favour of

Carlow: the interior looking east

concession at the time of Emancipation'. Bishop Doyle returned to Ireland in May to the warm congratulations of his clergy.

In 1827 the bishop put into effect his long-cherished scheme of building a cathedral for the two dioceses to replace the existing church at Carlow. The chosen architect was Joseph Lynch, who designed an oblong nave and chancel church. The foundation stone was laid on 18 March (Easter Monday) 1828, but, for unknown reasons, Lynch's design was abandoned one year later. Thomas Cobden. a Carlow architect, was appointed to succeed Lynch. He kept the design of the nave and chancel, but added transepts and conceived the striking octagonal west tower.

Initial problems were encountered with the periodic flooding of the site by water from the surrounding quarries. Cobden supervised the blocking of the inlets from the quarries and the pumping of water from the foundations. Large oak piles were driven deep into the bed of the foundations and were tied together with iron bolts. The cathedral was built around the old parochial church, and parts of its transept walls were incorporated into the new transepts as an economy measure. An earlier square-headed doorway with Doric pilasters can be seen beside the south transept. Rubble masonry of uncut stones of irregular size and shape can be seen in the end walls of the north and south transepts. The tower and west front are built of white granite ashlar from Graiguenaspidogue, and the body of the church is of dark greyish-blue limestone. The windows have simple granite dressings.

The limitation of funds which led to the retention of the transept walls of the old pro-cathedral also left a sparsely furnished interior. The floors of the nave and sanctuary were boarded except for the passageways between the benches which were paved with granite slabs. The wooden altars from the old building were used in the new cathedral, the communion rail was of wood, and benches were provided for seating. All the windows of the cathedral were timber-mullioned and glazed with plain glass. Some of them remain to this day.

The cathedral was completed in the autumn of 1833 and dedicated by Bishop Doyle on 1 December. It was the bishop's first and last solemn occasion in the cathedral. After a lingering illness he died on 15 June 1834. A tribute to his memory was seen in the size of the attendance at his funeral; the procession was two miles long and numbered some 20,000 mourners.[2] An impressive monument to his memory can be seen in the cathedral. It was carved by John Hogan (1800–58) and depicts 'J.K.L.' (James Kildare and Leighlin), as he was affectionately known, in cassock, surplice, cape and pectoral cross gazing upwards and with his right arm raised; at his feet is the weary kneeling allegorical personification of Ireland with traditional harp carved with a wolfhound's head and olive branches. It was installed in the nave at the junction of the south transept in 1840 when Hogan returned to Ireland from Rome. The statue was later moved to the north transept, where it stands on a limestone plinth. The cathedral was solemnly consecrated by Bishop Cullen a little more than a century later on 3 December 1933.

William Makepeace Thackeray visited Carlow in the 1840s and was unimpressed by the internally incomplete cathedral. 'I do not fancy a professional man would find much to praise in it: it seems to me overloaded with ornaments, nor were its innumerable spires and pinnacles the more pleasing to the eye because some of them were quite off the perpendicular. The interior is quite plain, not to say bare and unfinished . . . A wide large floor, some confession boxes against the blank walls here and there, with some humble pictures at the "Stations" and the statue, under a mean canopy of red woollen stuff, were the chief furniture of the cathedral.'[3]

The cathedral is a cruciform Gothic Revival structure which might loosely be described as Early English, except for its west front, which is dominated by a splendid lantern tower. This magnificent 46m Perpendicular Gothic tower, which cuts the gable, is square at the base and octagonal above the gable with four pinnacles. The top stage is a lantern with delicate tracery, topped by crenellations surmounted by pinnacles. It is said to be modelled on the belfry in the Grand Place at Bruges, but there is also a striking resemblance to the tower of St Botolph's Church at Boston in Lincolnshire. The tower is flanked by enclosed porches with simple chamfered arches; the date 1833 is carved over the south door. The lantern tower is echoed by slender, octagonal, castellated turrets at each corner of the roof.

The interior is a little disappointing, but its very wide nave gives a feeling of great spaciousness, and this open-plan design has meant that minimal changes were needed to bring the chancel arrangements into line with the requirements of the new liturgy. With an aisleless three-bay nave and a two-bay chancel, and transepts of three bays each entered through high pointed arches resting on tall, slender, clustered, granite columns, the cathedral is virtually square, and ninety per cent of the interior is visible from any given point. The roof, a remarkable piece of construction, has diagonal rib-vaulting with stuccoed bosses and ribs. The east wall and transepts have triple lancets, but the visual effect of those in the east wall is substantially reduced by the very length of the wall itself. At the west end is a short gallery with lattice decoration supported by clustered columns.

The decoration and furnishing of the interior and the glaz-

ing of the windows, were done as funds became available. The wooden transept altars were replaced by Caen stone altars in 1873, and the high altar of Sicilian marble was erected in 1890. It has a lofty pillared and spired canopy above the cross and was made by Samuel Daly & Sons of Cork. Some of the 19th-century stained glass is by Meyer & Co. of Munich. The magnificent Flemish pulpit, over 6m high, is of rose-cushioned oak and depicts the figures of St Victor, St Condleath and St Laserian; the panels above show Biblical scenes in high relief. It was made at Bruges and installed in the cathedral in 1899. The marble font dates from 1902. The Caen stone flanking altars were replaced by marble altars in 1903–4, and a long marble altar rail sweeps across transepts and nave at the broadest the width of the cathedral. The wrought iron balustrades between the transepts and the nave were added in 1905 to replace timber predecessors. The bishop's throne was made in Bruges and erected in 1906. The sacristy, furnished in polished Austrian oak, was constructed in 1913–14. There are two simple oval stoups of black Kilkenny marble in the porch inscribed 'The gift of Dinis Byrne, Stonecutter'.

The mosaic chancel floor is now partly covered by a large dais which supports the wooden altar. There is a Gothic-style frieze around the lower part of the chancel walls. There is some bland 1960s stained glass, typical of its date. The modern confessional boxes are eminently practical, but unharmonious, additions. The Stations of the Cross are paintings depicting the figures of the Passion in strong dark colours against misty pastel backgrounds.

The exterior of Carlow Cathedral has more than a passing resemblance to Strawberry Hill Gothick, and there are some similarities with the contemporary cathedral at Newry. It sits archly in the centre of Carlow and is difficult to view from any distance, with the exception of its attractive lantern tower.

References

1 Michael MacDonagh, Bishop Doyle, 'J.K.L.': a biographical and historical study (London & Dublin, 1896), pp 22–3.
2 W. M. Thackeray, The Irish sketch-book (London, 1843), i, 63.
3 MacDonagh, Bishop Doyle, p. 215.

CASHEL

The Cathedral Church of St Patrick's Rock

ASHEL is a small market town at the junction of the roads from Thurles (20.8km north), Urlingford (32km north-east), Fethard (16km west), Clonmel (24km south-west), Cahir (17.6km south) and Tipperary (19.2km west). It was formerly the ecclesiastical capital of Munster and the seat of an archbishop. There are two cathedrals at Cashel, one in ruins, the other still in use. But the ruined cathedral, set high on a rock above the surrounding plain, is the one that commands immediate attention.

The Rock of Cashel, a massive limestone outcrop rising out of the plain of Tipperary, is high among the list of most famous and impressive sites in Ireland. One author has described it as having 'a magnetizing presence, quickening the heart of the traveller'.[1] Poetry aside, the Rock conveys an air of majesty and power, whether viewed as the royal fortress that it was, the House of God that it became, or the proud ruin that it now is.

Rising abruptly to a height of about 30m above the plain, the Rock owes its origin, according to one legend, to the Devil who, in some great hurry to cross the mountains to the north, bit out a high block and spat it onto the plain below. Another says that the Devil bit it out in a rage at losing a soul he was carrying off to hell. Measurements taken of the gap in the Devil's Bit Mountain correspond exactly, it is said, to the dimensions of the Rock!

The name of the Rock derives from the Irish *caiseal*, (stone fort), and Cashel was the capital of the Kings of Munster from *c.* 370 to 1101, when an O'Brien king gave it to the church. It remained in the possession of the church until after the disestablishment of the Church of Ireland in 1871. Tradition relates that here in the 5th century St Patrick baptised Aengus, the young King of Munster, on the site where the Cross now stands. During the ceremony Patrick inadvertently drove the sharp-pointed staff on which he was leaning into the king's foot. Afterwards he noticed the wound and asked Aengus why he had not complained; the king replied that he thought it was part of the ritual.

At the Synod of Ráith Bressail in 1111, when Ireland was first divided into territorial dioceses, Cashel was the natural site for the southern archbishopric, the northern site being Armagh. When the number of archbishoprics was increased to four at the Synod of Kells – Mellifont in 1152, Cashel became the primatial see of the province of Munster. In the Church of Ireland hierarchy Cashel remained an archiepiscopal see until the death of Archbishop Richard Laurence on 28 December 1838, when it was reduced to the rank of a bishopric and its metropolitan rights annexed to the archbishopric of Dublin. It now forms part of the united dioceses of Cashel,

Waterford, Lismore, Ossory, Ferns and Leighlin. In the Roman Catholic hierarchy Cashel remains an archiepiscopal see, united to Emly since 1718, and the cathedral is at Thurles, 20.8km to the north of Cashel.

After the transfer of the Rock to the church a cathedral and Round Tower were built early in the 12th century and rebuilt in 1169 by Domnall Mór O'Brien. There are no surviving remains of this cathedral, which was demolished in the 13th century and replaced by the present building. It was built during the time of Archbishops Marianus O'Brien (1224–37), David MacKelly (1239–53) and David MacCarwill (1255–89) and is a simple aisleless cruciform structure consisting of a very short nave, transepts and chancel, with a squat 14th-century tower at the crossing; the total length is 51.8m.

The chancel was built by Archbishop O'Brien *c.* 1230. The walls are 12m high and lit by groups of narrow lancets in the north and south walls with wide inward splays and small quatrefoil windows between. The great east window was lit by triple lancets, but fell at an early date; a visitor at the end of the 18th century found it lying 'prostrate; but so broken, that any traces of its origins form or richness no longer exist'.[2] On the south side is the recumbent effigy of the notorious pluralist Miler Magrath (1522–1622), an extraordinary 'Vicar of Bray' individual who by astute behaviour, managed to achieve the distinction of being concurrently both a Church of Ireland bishop and a Roman Catholic bishop. He began his career as a Franciscan friar, spending some time in Rome. Appointed Bishop of Down and Connor by Pope Pius IV in 1565 he returned to Ireland and almost immediately quarrelled with Archbishop Creagh of Armagh. Magrath promptly transferred his loyalties to the Church of Ireland, and after a visit to England in 1567 he was made Bishop of Clogher by Queen Elizabeth I in 1570. In 1571 he was promoted to be Archbishop of Cashel and Bishop of Emly and remained so until his death; he was additionally Bishop of Waterford and Lismore (1582–9 and 1592–1608) and Bishop of Killala and Achonry (1613–22) and held seventy-seven livings. He managed to retain his Roman Catholic bishopric of Down and Connor until deprived by Pope Gregory XIII in 1580. He died in 1622 at the age of 100, having married twice and acquired enormous wealth for his family. He is thought to have returned to the Roman Catholic Church before he died. According to Lord Cecil, one of his contemporaries, 'he kept his church like a hogsty'.[3]

The most beautiful feature of the cathedral is the crossing, which retains its vaulting and the 14th-century tower above supported by four great pointed arches springing from massive piers. The south transept was added by Archbishop MacKelly, and the north transept, crossing and nave by Archbishop MacCarwill *c.*1260. Both transepts have triple lancets, and those in the north transept are surmounted by a small rose window. Small turrets at the junction of the nave and transepts give access to the tower and the battlements at the top of the walls.

The nave is the most curious aspect of the cathedral because it is so short, being half the length of the chancel. It originally extended to the west wall of the Archbishop's Palace and was shortened to allow its construction. The palace is basically a fortified tower, 24m high, and was built during the rule of Archbishop Richard O'Hedian (1406–40). The south wall collapsed in 1847 during a great storm.

The cathedral has not been well treated during its history. It was first burnt in 1494 by the Earl of Kildare (Lord Deputy of Ireland, 1479–1513), who was summoned to London to explain his outrageous behaviour to King Henry VII. The earl replied that his action was based on a belief that the archbishop was inside. The candour of this reply so pleased the king that he reappointed the earl as Lord Deputy.

Cashel was burnt by a parliamentary army and commanded by Lord Inchiquin on 13 September 1647 during the course of the Confederate war. The inhabitants from the town below had taken refuge on the Rock, and some 800 people lost their lives in the massacre that took place. Many of the buildings on the Rock were damaged in the fighting and remained ruined. The cathedral was used for a further century but it never recovered from the effects of the battle.

The chancel was repaired in 1667, and the tower was re-roofed in 1674, but the nave and transepts remained roofless. Cormac's Chapel was used as the Chapter House, its upper storey housing a school. Archbishop Theophilus Bolton (1730–44) attempted some restoration in 1730, but the days of the Rock as the Cathedral Church of Cashel were almost over.

In 1748 the Dean and Chapter sought permission from the Lords Justices and the Privy Council to discontinue the use of the cathedral. The request was successful, and in the following year, Archbishop Arthur Price (1744–52) ordered that the cathedral should be abandoned and the roof removed. In spite of this, his successor, Archbishop John Whitcombe (1752–3) was enthroned in both the old and the new cathedrals. A story circulated to the effect that Archbishop Price was annoyed that his carriage and horses found difficulty in climbing the steep road up to the Rock. This may have been a malicious rumour to discredit the archbishop, but the 18th century was an age that disliked Gothic architecture and rejoiced in the classical style; a similar and much worse act of vandalism was perpetrated in 1773 with the demolition of Waterford Cathedral. Cashel was at least spared that fate. Perhaps there is some truth in the story of the

The Rock of Cashel

archbishop's carriage, otherwise an 18th-century building might be seen crowning the Rock today.

After 1749 the buildings were abandoned and left to decay. By the provisions of the Irish Church Act of 1869, the Rock was handed over to the care of the state in 1874. Efforts by the Roman Catholic Church to acquire the Rock were unsuccessful. The ruins were repaired and stabilised in 1874–6, but there was no question of restoring a building which had been roofless for more than a century, and it is now in a sorry state of ruin. 'More impressive than any individual feature is its atmosphere, one of overwhelming sorrow. Other Irish ruins are softened by the landscapes about them; here, because of the elevated site, there is nothing to see from the inside the cathedral but the sky, which remorselessly emphasises its ruined state.'[4]

There are three other buildings of interest on the Rock: Cormac's Chapel, the Hall of the Vicars Choral, and the Round Tower.

1. Cormac's Chapel (Teampall Mór Chormaic)

Cormac's Chapel stands at a strange angle of alignment between the chancel and the south transept of the cathedral. This is explained by the fact that its construction pre-dated the cathedral by about a hundred years and was possibly in alignment with the former cathedral. The chapel was built between 1127 and 1134 by Cormac MacCarthy, King of Desmond, and is generally considered to be the finest and most sophisticated example of Irish Romanesque architecture. The steeply pitched roof derives from the beehive huts and oratories of Early Christian Ireland. It has a nave and chancel and twin square towers on either side of the junction. The north tower is 20m high to the top of its pyramidal roof. The south tower, which is slightly higher, has lost its roof and has been finished by a battlemented coping. The south entrance has a carved stone tympanum depicting a huge beast. The west door giving access to the cathedral has been blocked. The main entrance on the north side is now obstructed by the cathedral, but it has a tympanum showing a centaur shooting a lion and elaborate arch mouldings. The interior is dank and dark and contains a broken mid-12th-century Hiberno-Viking stone sarcophagus ornamented with interlaced serpents.

2. The Hall of the Vicars Choral

This mid-15th-century building on the south side of the Rock housed the vicars choral, a corporation of men, usually lay but sometimes clerical, appointed to assist in singing at cathedral services. There were originally eight vicars choral; the number was later reduced to five. Alterations to the building were made in the 17th century. The hall is a two-storey building with a fireplace in the main room and a dormitory at the eastern end. It was thoroughly restored in

1975 as part of Ireland's contribution to the European Architectural Heritage Year and is now used as a visitors' centre.

3. The Round Tower

Built of irregularly coursed sandstone with some limestone, the tower is plain but complete and well built; the cap was reset in 1875–6. Since Round Towers are invariably to be found at the sites of churches, the tower can be dated to the period after 1101. It stands at the north-east corner of the north transept of the cathedral.

References

1. William Anderson and Clive Hicks, *Cathedrals in Britain and Ireland* (London, 1979), p. 147.
2 St L. Hunt, *Cashel and its abbeys* (Dublin, 1952), p. 11.
3 George Holmes, *Sketches of some of the southern counties of Ireland, collected during a tour in the autumn of 1797, in a series of letters* (London, 1801), p. 24.
4 Anderson and Hicks, *Cathedrals in Britain and Ireland*, p. 149.

CASHEL

The Cathedral Church of St John the Baptist and St Patrick's Rock

Diocese of Cashel (Church of Ireland)

ON 10 June 1749 the Privy Council issued an Order constituting the Parish Church of St John the Baptist in the town of Cashel as the new cathedral for the diocese, to be known as the Cathedral and Parochial Church of St Patrick's Rock and St John Baptist, Cashel.

Nothing remains of this temporary cathedral, which was demolished to allow the construction of the present cathedral. Archbishop Price intended to erect a new cathedral on the site, but the foundation stone was not laid until 1763, and the building was only completed in 1788 as a result of the efforts of Archbishop Charles Agar (1779–1801). The addition of a spire in 1812 gave the building its present appearance. The cathedral is an elegant Classical structure with a mottled grey stone exterior and banding linking Corinthian pilasters. The three-storey porch has a triangular pediment above which is a two-storey square tower with round-arched louvred windows and Corinthian pilasters on each face. Above is a small rotunda with four windows similar to those on the storey below alternating with four blind windows; the structure is crowned by a small spire.

The interior presents no coherence of style whatever, being an accumulation of bits and pieces added over many years. The building is rectangular, with a wide and high chancel arch. The walls have painted wooden panelling, and the nave ceiling is also panelled in pine, the panels being laid in a chevron pattern; in fact the ceiling resembles a parquet floor. The nave is lit by eight standard electroliers, installed in 1969. The east window has stained glass, but the eight windows in the nave are clear. The two-bay chancel has Romanesque arches resting on marble piers, and a polychromatic tiled floor. The ceiling has stencilled decoration.

The body of the cathedral was at first arranged in the style of a choir with return stalls for the Dean and Chapter below the front of the west gallery; the rest of the area forming the narthex. These stalls were superseded during the incumbency of J. C. MacDonnell as dean (1862–73), when a bishop's throne and new stalls of pine were erected in the chancel. Cashel therefore enjoys the distinction of being a cathedral church with two sets of chapter stalls. The 18th-century chapter stalls at the west end of the nave are of grained wood and classical style; Ionic columns divide the seats.

During Dean MacDonnell's reorganization most of the 18th-century interior, including the carved stalls which lined the nave, the canopied pulpit and the box pews, was removed. The work was a disaster, since it began the process of substantially altering the interior of a Georgian church in the direction of Gothic or even Romanesque.

Given the long history and ruined beauty of the great Gothic cathedral on the rock above the town, it would be tempting to despise its successor as an unworthy usurper. One visitor within ten years of its completion thought it 'a new, plain, but very well furnished building internally' and 'the music and singing delightfull'.[1] Another late 18th-century traveller thought it was 'a magnificent structure of Grecian architecture; yet, notwithstanding its beauty and freshness, I cannot reflect on the venerable rock, without commisserating in its forlorn and neglected situation.'[2] Perhaps it would be gentler to say that Cashel Cathedral represents the general desire of its day for lightness and elegance, and that it is typical of its date. Future generations may think of it more kindly.

The former diocesan library, now called the GPA – Bolton Library, after a sensitive restoration in 1986, is housed in the precincts of the cathedral in a building of 1835. The library was founded by Archbishop Bolton and has a fine collection of 16th- and 17th-century books.

Cashel Palace, designed by Sir Edward Lovet Pearce and built in 1730–32 by Archbishop Bolton, is two storeys high and seven bays wide, and is reckoned to be one of the finest houses of its period in Ireland. A visitor to the palace in the early 19th century was enchanted by its gardens: 'All that can delight the senses is here. Parterres of lovely flowers and rare shrubs; velvet lawns; secluded walks, rich in odours; and, above the fine screen of holly and laburnum, and lilac, and copper beech, and laurel, tower the Rock and the magnificent ruins that cover it.'[3] In view of the 18th-century elegance of Cashel Palace surrounded by such gardens, one can begin to see why Archbishop Price wanted a cathedral to match. The palace was damaged in the 1798 rebellion and restored early in the 19th century. After the union of Cashel to Waterford in 1839, part of the palace was occupied by the dean until the early 1950s. It was sold to Lord Brocket in 1960, restored, and has been the Cashel Palace Hotel since 1962.

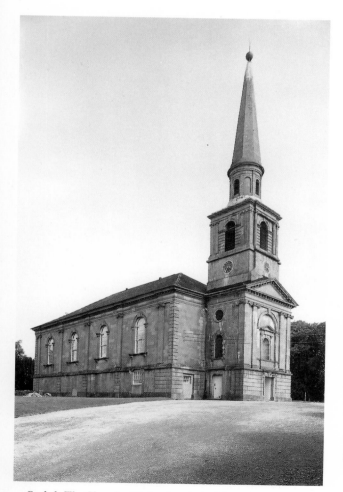

Cashel: The Church of Ireland cathedral from the north-west

References

1   Michael Quane, 'Tour in Ireland by John Harden in 1797' in *Journal of the Cork Historical and Archaeological Society*, lviii, no. 187 (1953), p. 30.
2   George Holmes, *Sketches of some of the southern counties of Ireland, collected during a tour in the autumn of 1797, in a series of letters* (London, 1801), p. 21.
3   *The Parliamentary Gazetteer of Ireland*, i, 345.

CAVAN

The Cathedral Church of St Patrick and St Felim

Diocese of Kilmore (Roman Catholic)

CAVAN (*Cabhán* – hollow place), with a population of about 3,500 inhabitants, is the county town of Co. Cavan and lies on the main Dublin to Enniskillen road. Dublin is 114km to the south-east, and Enniskillen 67.2km to the north-west.

The town grew up around a Franciscan friary founded about 1300 by Giolla Íosa Rua O'Reilly, Lord of East Breifne. Nothing remains of the friary or of any other antiquity since the destruction of the town in 1690 during the war between the armies of King James II and King William III.

The first Catholic church was built at Cavan in the middle of the 18th century. It was a small thatched building with a clay floor and no seating, and it served the Catholic population until 1823. In that year a new slated church was built on the site, and in 1862 Bishop James Browne (1829–65) had it enlarged and dedicated to St Patrick and made it the cathedral church for the diocese of Kilmore; and so it remained until 1942.

In 1936 Bishop Patrick Finegan (1910–37) initiated the project to build a new cathedral and was responsible for much of the fund-raising; his successor, Bishop Patrick Lyons, carried the scheme through to completion. The new cathedral was designed by William H. Byrne, and the cornerstone, part of an old mass rock, was laid on 10 September 1939. The official opening by Bishop Lyons took place on 8 June 1942, and the cathedral was dedicated on 27 September that year by Cardinal Joseph MacRory, Archbishop of Armagh, in the presence of the papal nuncio and the bishops of the province of Armagh. For a short while the old Gothic cathedral and its Classical successor stood side by side, but the old cathedral was eventually demolished and part of its stonework was used in the construction of the new church at Castletara.

The choice of the Classical style was an interesting move away from Gothic and a reversion to a style that many had long thought extinct. No Roman Catholic cathedral in Ireland had been designed in this style since Longford in 1840; with the exceptions of Thurles and Sligo, the second half of the 19th century was marked by solid loyalty to the Gothic Revival.

Byrne's neo-Classical cathedral is built of Wicklow granite, Portland stone and some limestone. The west front, probably the most successful part of the exterior, was inspired by Francis Johnston's (now closed) St George's Church in Hardwicke Place, Dublin (constructed 1802–13). The portico and the tower and spire above are close copies of Johnston's work, but the rest of the front, including the twin Corinthian pilasters at either end and the two small domes flanking the tower and spire, are improvements on Johnston's design. The impressive portico has four Corinthian columns with richly carved capitals supporting a tympanum, the work of George Smith, the Dublin sculptor, bearing the sculpted figures of St Patrick and St Felim on either side of Christ. The square tower with round windows rises to an octagonal tower with louvred round-arched windows and then a fluted spire above. The spire is surmounted by a 3.5m bronze cross, making a total height of 64.5m.

Cavan Cathedral from the south-west

The cathedral is cruciform in plan, and the interior arrangement is that of a basilica with a narthex, aisled nave, clerestory and apse. The nave is seven bays long and divided from the aisles by magnificent columns of grey and white Paronasetto marble from Santa Pietra, with Corinthian capitals, ox-blood marble bases and black marble plinths. The pulpit on the south side is of the same marble arrangement. The walls are of textured concrete and have a slightly unfinished appearance. The pilasters are covered with sirapite plaster. The nave ceiling has three deeply recessed roundels and a cornice of moulded swags. The Stations of the Cross are pristine grisaille panels by George Collie.

The dome over the crossing is supported by four marble columns, and the crossing and aisle pavements have mosaic work. The transepts, which end in apses, have coved and coffered ceilings with octagonal recesses enclosing flower heads. The organ is in the south transept and blocks the windows. The communion rails are of white Carrara marble. The high altar is made from green Connemara marble and pink Middleton marble. The wall of the apse has a mural of the Risen Christ surrounded by native saints and was executed in the 1960s by George Collie. Above the mural are twelve small, closely placed windows showing the heads of the Twelve Apostles. The apse has disused side chapels, two on the north and two on the south. The north chapel closest to the sanctuary has a Pietà; the other is unused. The south chapel closest to the altar now houses the Blessed Sacrament. The adjacent chapel was formerly the Mortuary Chapel and is decorated with grey and black marble; it has mosaic floor with the monogram RIP in the centre.

The interior of Cavan Cathedral is a fine basilical design, and the combination of coloured marbles for the nave columns is especially striking and unusual. The Stations of the Cross are beautiful pieces of work, but the apse mural is a mistake. The crossing has been successfully re-ordered by bringing the altar forward, but it now competes with the mural for the attention of the worshipper or visitor. The mural is a good piece of work in harmony with the Classical design of the cathedral, but it is in the wrong place. The apse was already adequately filled by the altar, and the plain wall was a perfect backdrop.

CLOGHER

The Cathedral Church of St Macartan

Diocese of Clogher (Church of Ireland)

CLOGHER is a small village in Co. Tyrone on the Dungannon–Enniskillen road, 36.8km east of Enniskillen and 32km west of Dungannon. A row of houses lines the road as it begins to climb a hill dominated by the stern Classical cathedral. Early authorities, taking their cue from the early mists of legend, long thought that its name was derived from cloch óir (golden stone). The stone was one on which the devil sat giving obscure answers to questions, much in the manner of the oracle at Delphi. A stone, said to be the original cloch óir, is preserved at the cathedral. However, it is now generally agreed that the name has a much more mundane origin, being derived simply from clochar (stone building).

The origin of Clogher lies sometime in the late 5th century. The story goes that St Patrick was being carried across a stream by his disciple and companion, St Macartan, who groaned and complained of being old and infirm, 'and all my early companions in mission work you have settled down in their respective churches, while I am still upon my travels'. Patrick replied: 'Found a church, then, that shall not be too near us for familiarity, nor too far from us for intercourse.'[1]

Macartan founded his monastery at Clogher c. 493 and died in c. 505; his feast-day is 24 March. Nothing further is known until the beginning of the 12th century when Clogher was the centre of the Airgiallan kingdom of Uí Chremthainn. When the Synod of Ráith Bressail established the diocese of Clogher in 1111, its boundaries roughly corresponded with those of the kingdom. In c. 1140 the diocese was enlarged to include the territories now comprising Co. Louth and Co. Monaghan and the see was move from Clogher to Louth (q.v.). The Synod of Kells–Mellifont in 1152 assigned the whole of the Airgialla over-kingdom ruled by Donnchad Ua Cerbaill (O'Carroll) (d.1168) to the diocese, and c.1197 the see was moved from Louth back to Clogher.

The cathedral lies within a large Celtic hill-fort, probably of the 4th/5th centuries; the site of the fort's earthen ramparts and external ditch can still be traced. Several crosses remain from an early period, one, dating from the 9th or 10th century and reconstructed in 1912, is situated 3.25m west of the cathedral; and there is a 7th-century carved stone in the north porch. The cathedral itself has been rebuilt on several occasions, and nothing remains from the 12th century. It was rebuilt c.1183 and dedicated again to St Macartan and rebuilt again c.1295. In 1395 and again in April 1396 the site was ravaged by disastrous fires which consumed the monastery, two chapels, the bishop's residence and about thirty houses. The bishop at the time, Arthur MacCawell (1390–1432), is reported to have 'applied himself with unwearied diligence to the rebuilding of his cathedral and palace.'[2]

The history of Clogher during the 16th and 17th centuries is one of total and continuous devastation and explains why so little survives from the medieval period. The monastery was burned in 1507, and Clogher was raided in 1508, 1511 and 1516. When Bishop Patrick Cullean was appointed in 1517, Clogher had been ruined by wars and the see was reported to be worth 'not more than 80 ducats a year'. The town is described in a contemporary Vatican document as a city of forty houses and the cathedral as 'square-shaped, built of natural stone, roofed partly with wood, partly with straw'.[3] Another description speaks of Clogher in the early 16th century as a walled city, and north Tyrone as a country of forests, lakes and swamps 'where the dominium of England ceases and a native count reigns'.[4]

In 1621 James Spottiswood was appointed Bishop of Clogher and found a depressing situation awaiting him: 'The Cathedral Church altogether ruynous. The walls of an Abbey Church standeth by, which will beare noe roofe.'[5] The new bishop did his best to restore the fortunes of the see: 'which was of old an auntient city decored with twoo Churches and a great number of inhabitants but in the late warres was utterlie ruyned. The Bishop therefore sett alltogether to buyld a house for himself, to repaire the Churches, to buyld an Inn, Stables, Barnes, Keill, Mill and the like and to encourage others to buyld with him.'[6] A map of 1609 shows a crude representation of the church crowned by a typically 15th-century slim battlemented tower.

Unfortunately there was still no peace for Clogher, as the area was badly affected by the rising in 1641 and the Confederate war, and in 1654 it was reported that 'all Castles, Churches and Mills were burnt and demolished and continue soe as yet'.[7] In 1697 another author spoke of "a wild enough country to Clogher ... This is a Burrough, but a most miserable one, having not above 3 or 4 houses in it and not even the remains of any one, tho' 'tis certainly a very antient See.'[8]

The dawning of the 18th century at last brought peace to Clogher. Whatever remained of the old cathedral after so long a period of devastation was swept away when the present cathedral was built in 1740–44 during the episcopate of Bishop John Stearne (1717–45) and largely at his own expense. The architect was James Martin, who is said to have designed the cathedral 'in the ancient style of English architecture'. This cannot be presumed to mean, as some have suggested, that Clogher was an early 18th-century example of Gothic Revival; there is no evidence of the cathedral ever having had a Gothic appearance. The only explanation seems to be the cruciform plan, which was a notable move away from the hall-and-tower type of church of standard design in the late 17th century, and the large plain square tower rising out of the west end of the nave, so typical of 15th-century Franciscan houses and to be seen at Clonfert Cathedral. Apart from these two features, the cathedral is clearly an 18th-century building.

In 1816–18 Dean Richard Bagwell (1805–26) reordered the cathedral 'in the Grecian style', but the meaning of this phrase and the extent of his alteration of the fabric and architecture is by no means clear. The phrases used to describe Martin's design and Bagwell's alterations have passed into the folklore history of Clogher Cathedral without being seriously challenged, and it seems likely that Bagwell's work was not the extensive remodelling of Martin's design that later chroniclers have thought.

The only external feature of Bagwell's 'remodelling' was the construction of an open stonework balustrade with obelisk finials around the top of the massive square tower. The tower has string courses and sits saddleback on a triangular pediment at the west end. Internal alterations included the provision of stalls for the chapter, a west gallery resting on Ionic columns, and transept galleries which were removed in 1865. The organ, previously housed in the south transept, was moved to the west gallery in 1873.

Clogher Cathedral has a nominally cruciform plan and measures 34.7m by 10.9m. The narthex consists of a porch and two rooms; the porch contains a 7th- or 8th-century carved cross and the so-called 'wart stone', which may have been a font or the capital of a pillar. The rooms beyond are used as a chapter house and as a vestry. The narthex was panelled in deal in 1885 for the Countess of Enniskillen and houses a portrait gallery of the Bishops of Clogher from the 16th century.

The interior of the cathedral has a modillion cornice and a flat plastered ceiling. The walls have a dado of grey grained wooden panelling. The seating was installed c.1865. The baptistery is at the west end on the north side below the organ gallery and contains an unusual 18th-century oval-shaped polished black marble font with a fluted basin on a gadrooned baluster base. It would look a little peculiar in a Gothic Revival church; here it fits perfectly.

There are three windows on each side of the nave and one in each transept. The windows are round-headed, Tuscan on the outside and Scamozzian Ionic on the inside. They contain stained glass by artists of the An Túr Gloine studio of Dublin (see LOUGHREA). The Venetian east window has three lights separated by Ionic columns and framed by Ionic pilasters. It has glass commemorating Lord John George Beresford, Bishop of Clogher 1819–20 and (with Armagh) 1850–62.

The nominal cruciformity of the cathedral is apparent when the transepts are seen to be only shallow recesses on the north and south sides of an oblong building entered by very wide semicircular archways. There is no real 'crossing' as such, the pews coming to within a metre of the sanctuary, and the sanctuary is merely the east end of this oblong. The chapter stalls are along the north and south walls of the sanctuary. The bishop's throne is on the south side next to the dean's stall, placed at an angle formed by the junction of the sanctuary with the south transept. The throne is of classical design; the canopy has a moulded architectural broken pediment.

The site of the cathedral, walled and set on the summit of a hill, gives it a loftiness from the outside which is not matched by the interior dimensions. But Clogher is an attractive example of a classical cathedral and its tidy and well-cared-for interior has a prosperous feel. It was last redecorated in 1978.

Clogher Palace, formerly the residence of the bishops, is a plain ashlar Classical mansion constructed in 1819–23. It was begun by Bishop Lord John George Beresford (1819–20) and continued by his successor, the most tragic holder of the see. The Hon. Percy Jocelyn was Bishop of Clogher 1820–22 (previously Bishop of Ferns 1809–20). After revelations of his homosexuality he was charged with an offence committed on 19 July 1822. Summoned to appear at Armagh before a court consisting of the Bishops of Derry, Dromore, Kilmore and Raphoe, he was deprived of the bishopric and ended his life as a domestic servant in Edinburgh in 1843; his companion was executed.

raise sufficient funds to re-establish Clogher as an independent diocese. Archbishop Marcus Gervais Beresford of Armagh (1862–86) strongly disapproved of the movement, but after his death, the General Synod of the Church of Ireland authorised the separation.

Clogher: the interior of the cathedral looking east, showing the shallow north transept

The awkwardness of the site of the palace, built into a hillside, has left a three-storey entrance front and a four-storey garden front. The entrance front is of seven bays with a three-bay pediment and single-storey Gothic porch with fluted Ionic columns. The garden front, overlooking a large demesne, is of six bays in the centre block, which has a high arcaded terrace across the ground floor flanked by recessed two-storey wings with canted bay windows. The accompanying deer park was sold in 1851, as was the Palace itself in 1853 after the union of the diocese of Clogher with the diocese of Armagh in 1850. It was renamed Clogher Park and became the seat of the Ellison-Macartney family until 1922. After a period as a convent for the Sisters of St Louis it was converted into a home for the elderly in 1989.

The diocese of Clogher, never very populous, was united to the diocese of Armagh in 1850 by act of parliament. From about 1870 a movement developed to separate the two and

References

1 J. G. F. Day and H. E. Patton, *The cathedrals of the Church of Ireland* (London, 1932), p. 29.
2 Jack Johnston, *St Macartan's Cathedral, Clogher* (Clogher, 1989), p. 26.
3 Ibid., p.27.
4 Ibid., p.28.
5 Ibid., p.30.
6 Ibid.
7 Ibid., p.31.
8 Joan Story, *St Macartan's Cathedral, Clogher* (Clogher, 1970), p. 27.

CLONARD

The Cathedral Church of St John

CLONARD (*Cluain Ioraird* – Erard's meadow) is about 16km west of Dublin. A monastery was founded here by St Finian *c.*520, who with St Enda of Aran is recognised as the father of Irish monasticism. Finian was born at Myshall in Co. Carlow and for many years was a monk in Wales. On his return to Ireland he founded a large number of monasteries, churches and schools. Before his death *c.*549 Finian (feast-day 12 December) had established the reputation of Clonard as one of the most important monastic schools in Ireland. Clonard numbered St Kieran of Clonmacnoise and St Columba of Iona among its students, and Finian acquired the sobriquet 'Teacher of Irish Saints'. Among the alumni of Clonard were those saints who became known as the 'Twelve Apostles of Ireland'.[1] There are no remaining traces of Clonard's famous school. 'The ancient glory of the place faded away until now it is merely a name known only to scholars, without even a broken arch or ruined wall to speak with saddening eloquence of its glorious past.'[2]

During the 12th-century reform Clonard was a natural choice for the centre of a diocese. At the Synod of Ráith Bressail in 1111 it was designated the see for West Meath, Duleek being the see for East Meath. This arrangement was altered later in the same year at a local synod of the clergy of Meath which designated Clonmacnoise as the see for West Meath and Clonard for East Meath; the alteration was confirmed at the Synod of Kells–Mellifont in 1152. The style 'Bishop of Meath' appears to have been used at the end of the 11th century but for the following century the style 'Bishop of Clonard' was generally preferred.

Clonard was the home of a number of religious houses. Apart from whatever remained of the ancient foundation of Finian, St Mary's Abbey for Arroasian canonesses and St Peter's Abbey for Canons Regular were founded in 1144, and an Augustinian priory of St John, which seems to have been used as the cathedral church, was founded between 1183 and 1186 by Hugh de Lacy. The see remained at Clonard until 1202, when Simon Rochfort, the first Anglo-Norman bishop (1192–1224), transferred it to the more secure Anglo-Norman centre at Newtown Trim. In 1200 Clonard was burnt and plundered by Ó Ciardha in revenge for the killing of his son and 'to injure the foreigners that were in it'.[3] By the beginning of the 13th century it was clearly no longer safe for an Anglo-Norman bishop to reside at Clonard.

With the burning of Clonard in 1200 and the transfer of the see to Trim in 1202, Clonard soon lost its importance. St Mary's Abbey ranked as the head house in Ireland of the Arroasian canonesses until after 1195, when it gradually declined in importance. A major transfer from Clonard to Odder took place in 1380–84. Clonard thereafter became a small dependent house and may have been abandoned by the nuns before 1535.

St Peter's Abbey and St John's Priory suffered a similar decline after the transfer to Trim. They were united at some date after 1202, but the monastery fell into financial difficulties and was described as a poor little house in 1260; in 1459 it was again in a state of dire poverty. At the time of the dissolution in 1540 the site of the abbey covered 1½ acres and contained a church, cemetery, belfry and hall, all in a state of decay.

Clonard: the mediaeval font

Parts of the monastic buildings were still standing in the late 18th century, and the following description of 1779 is all that survives: 'The entrance into this abbey, on the west side, was through a small building, with a lodge over it, which led into a small court; to the right of this court stands a small kitchen and cellar, and over them the dormitory, ranging with the river and overlooking the garden which sloped from thence to the water's edge; opposite the entrance was another small apartment, and adjoining it the refectory, which was carried for some length beyond the square, and joined the choir, a large and elegant building, most part of which still remains, and the windows are finished in a light Gothic style. On the south side of the altar, fixed in a wall, is a small double arch, in the old Saxon manner, and divided by a pillar through which iron bars were fixed; this is supposed to have been the Founder's tomb. There are many remains of walls adjoining other parts of the abbey, but in so ruinous a state that little information can be gleaned from them.'[4]

Nothing now remains of these buildings; they appear to have followed the fate of the monastic ruins at Kells in 1779, demolished to make way for the new parish church in 1821. When James Brewer visited Clonard in 1825, he noted that 'with indifference almost amounting to barbarous apathy they have lately been entirely destroyed'.[5] By 1844 Clonard was 'a poor, pitiful, tiny hamlet, indebted for very nearly all its existing importance to its post office'.[6] In 1890, John Healy noted: "The hand of the spoiler has devastated Clonard perhaps more completely than any other of our ancient churches.'[7]

The 1821 church, dedicated to St Finian, was built with a loan of £400 from the Board of First-Fruits. It was said to have replaced an old church in bad repair, probably a part of the abbey church. The price of its construction seems suspiciously small, and within twenty-two years of its completion it was described as 'a wretched-looking edifice, and in wretched repair, surmounted by a tasteless steeple about 50 feet [15.2m] high.'[8] Healy described it as 'a plainer and uglier building than even such edifices usually are in Ireland.'[9] St Finian's Church is a typical hall-and-tower church of the type erected wholesale in the early 19th century; the walls are rendered, and the square tower has battlements and pinnacles.

The interior is very plain and measures about 15.2m by 7.3m. Three pointed arch windows on the south side have wooden casements and tracery The only distinguishing features of the church are a simple pulpit of grained pine on the north side; the inscription '**YE DO SHEW THE LORD'S DEATH TILL HE COME**' painted above the east window, and a 15th-century font at the west end.

The unusual octagonal panelled grey limestone font was the sole feature of historic interest in the church and the only remnant of Clonard's great past. It is ornamented with figures in high relief slightly reminiscent of Chaucer. 'The upper panels are ornamented as follows: – One exhibits in relief a representation of the Virgin and Child, upon the ass, flying into Egypt. The next is divided *per pale* into two compartments, the first of which exhibits Joseph leading the ass, whose halter is brought over from the former panel; the second compartment of this panel exhibits a grotesque figure, holding a book, and having its lower extremity terminating in a true lover's knot. A third panel has St John baptising our Saviour, who is standing in a river, while the Baptist pours water over his head out of a vessel with his right hand; with the left he holds the arm of Christ, who has his arms placed across his breast in an attitude of devotion. A fourth panel is divided *per pale*, having in each compartment a grotesque human figure with wings, and holding a shield with both hands. The fifth panel is like the last described; and the sixth differs from them merely in the second figure's holding an open book instead of a shield. The seventh panel is also divided *per pale*, on the first compartment is the figure of a saint with wings, and holding in his right hand a loose belt which encircles his waist. This is probably for St Augus-

tine, as the hermits of the Augustinian order wore a leathern belt. The corresponding compartment contains St Peter with the key. The eighth panel is divided into two like those already described. On the first part is a bishop with a crosier, probably St Finian; and on the other is a figure with long robes and a book, in the clothing of a Canon Regular of St Augustine. In four of the lower panels consecutively, are represented angels holding shields; and in the other four are trees or shrubs. The base, which consists also of eight sides, is ornamented with leaves and flowers.'[10]

At the recommendation of the Commission on Church Buildings, St Finian's Church was closed for worship in February 1990, though it has not yet been deconsecrated at the time of writing. The Bishop of Meath and Kildare gladly supported the wish of the community that the font be placed in the local Roman Catholic church. The church bell is now one of the many eclectic features of Glenstal Abbey in Co. Limerick.

A few hundred metres to the north-west is the site of an old rath with a conical sepulchral mound crowned by a flourishing ash tree. Further to the north west is another mound marking the site of a large square fort.

References

1 The 'Twelve Apostles of Ireland':
  St Kieran of Saighir
  St Kieran of Clonmacnoise (see CLONMACNOISE)
  St Columbkill of Iona (see KELLS)
  St Brendan of Clonfert (see CLONFERT)
  St Brendan of Birr
  St Columba of Terry Glass
  St Molaisse of Devenish
  St Canice of Agnavoe (see KILKENNY)
  St Ruadan of Lorrha
  St Mobhi of Glasnevin
  St Sinell of Cleenish
  St Ninni of Inishmacsaint.
2 John Healy, *Insula sanctorum et doctorum, or Ireland's ancient schools and scholars* (Dublin & London, 1890), p. 208.
3 Aubrey Gwynn and R. N. Hadcock, *Medieval religious houses: Ireland* (Dublin, 1970), p. 64.
4 Mervyn Archdall, *Monasticon Hibernicum* (London, 1786), p. 519.
5 J. N. Brewer, *The beauties of Ireland* (London, 1825–6), ii, 182.
6 *The Parliamentary Gazetteer of Ireland* (Dublin, 1844–6), i, 425.
7 Healy, *Insula sanctorum*, p. 204.
8 *Parliamentary Gazetteer*, i, 425.
9 Healy, *Insula sanctorum*, p. 205.
10 *Parliamentary Gazetteer*, i, 425.

CLONFERT

The Cathedral Church of St Brendan

Diocese of Clonfert (Church of Ireland)

CLONFERT (*Cluain fhearta* – meadow of the grave) is a quiet little hamlet in Co. Galway consisting of a few houses, the cathedral and the ruins of Clonfert Palace. Well hidden along a series of leafy lanes it is about 8km north-east of Eyrecourt and 19.2km south-east of Ballinasloe. 'Its site is a swell or very gentle rising ground on the edge of a great expanse of dreary bog . . . it stands a little way aside from the public road, and may very easily escape the notice of the uninformed passing traveller.'[1] One 19th-century observer dismissed it as 'a small dingy unimposing structure'.[2] It is true that Clonfert is small, even by the standards of Irish cathedrals, but it has great charm and is the proud possessor of the most elaborately carved Romanesque doorway in Ireland.

A monastery was founded here by St Brendan the Navigator (486–577 or 583, feast-day 16 May) in the middle of the 6th century. Brendan has passed into history as a great voyager in the cause of spreading the Gospel and is said to have visited Iceland, Scotland and the Faroe Islands. Some centuries after his death an unknown scholar collected the oral legends about the saint into a book known as the *Navigatio Brendani* (the Voyage of Brendan) and catapulted the saint into international fame. The book was widely read by medieval scholars, translated into the main European languages, and became a textbook in the schools of Europe.

Legends about individuals in distant centuries are always subject to embroidery, and the life of St Brendan is no exception. A tradition developed that his major voyage was a search for the continent of America, and gradually the rumour circulated that he had actually found it. It is said that Christopher Columbus derived his own plans from the story of Brendan, and some historians have stated that Columbus visited Clonfert and took several Irishmen with him on his voyage.

Under the provisions of the territorial diocesan system established at the Synod of Ráith Bressail in 1111, Clonfert became the see of a diocese coextensive with the territory of Uí Maine, and the first stone cathedral was built on the site *c.*1167 by Bishop Petrus Ua Mórda (*c.*1150–1171) with the help of the King of Uí Maine. The remote site of Clonfert has probably saved the cathedral from destruction and rebuilding, and with minor alterations it is Ua Mórda's cathedral that the visitor sees today.

The little cathedral seats only about a hundred people and is partly ruined. At its greatest extent it consisted of a nave with a western tower rising from the roof, a chancel, transepts

branching nearly at the centre of the nave, and a barrel-vaulted sacristy containing a fireplace at the north side of the chancel. The oldest parts of the cathedral are the west, north and south walls of the nave, including the famous doorway, which date from *c.*1167. The chancel was added in the early 13th century and the chancel arch, tower and transepts (the north now gone) in the 15th century.

Clonfert Cathedral from the south-west

The great glory of Clonfert Cathedral is the amazing west doorway. No matter how remote the cathedral, no matter how difficult the task of finding it, and no matter how late in the day a visit has to be made, it will always be worth the effort to see this masterpiece of Irish Romanesque carving.

It consists of eight orders of jambs, all inclined inwards, surmounted first by seven orders of arches and then by a triangular pediment bordered by carvings similar to rolled ropes or cables. The rest is an extraordinary medieval picture gallery. Above the apex of the pediment two human heads protrude from the wall. In the pediment itself ten more human heads, some bearded some young and unshaven, appear between triangles, with richly carved ornamentation. Below this stage more heads are contained in the arches of a blind arcade immediately above the outermost order of the arch. The orders of the arches exhibit a variety of ornament, among them interlacing, enormous bobbles, deeply cut formalised flowers, beasts' heads and elegant rounded and engraved cusps. The capitals are a zoo of animal heads, cats, horses, donkeys and dragons, and the jamb shafts on which they stand are an anthology of mingled Celtic and Romanesque decoration. The innermost order of the door is a 15th-century blue-grey limestone replacement; it contains carvings of an abbot and a bishop and a scroll of vine leaves with an angel clutching the tendrils at the apex.

'This portal is a scheme of Christ in creation with the Trinitarian theme of the pediment repeated in the triangles separating the human faces of the redeemed that project above the animal heads, the vegetable forms, the zoomorphic interlacings and the contortions of the mineral world in the arches, capitals and shafts below them. It is a diagram of the redemption of matter – a theme worthy only of a supreme artist with the power to bring the complexity of his imaginings to order. Here at Clonfert theme and artist meet.'[3]

The west tower above the doorway was added in the 15th century and is typical of the towers erected by Franciscan friaries of that period; the parapet is a 19th-century conjectural restoration.

The nave measures 20.3m by 8.4m and has a number of 17th- and 18th-century tomb slabs set its walls at the west end. There is also a 13th-century font. North and south transepts were added to the nave in the 15th century. The north transept has long since disappeared, but the ruined south transept, measuring 6.7m square, is still standing. It is difficult to guess when the transepts were walled off from the nave, possibly in the restoration of c.1837, but the south blocking wall contains a stained glass window of 1863. The matching stonework of the north blocking wall suggests that both transepts were sealed off together. The south transept has a single lancet in its north wall and a doorway in its east wall. Its south and east walls are covered with ivy which has damaged the mortar and stonework to such an extent that the walls are unlikely to remain standing for many more years.

The chancel arch has an interesting and unusual scattering of random carvings, including a delightful mermaid with comb and mirror, no doubt intended to be an allusion to the voyages of Brendan. The chancel itself measures 8.3m by 6.7m and has a fine twin-light east window with very wide splays which incorporate blind arcading. The glass was given by Thomas O'Connor in 1897 to commemorate Queen Victoria's Diamond Jubilee. The other windows of the chancel also contain Victorian memorial glass. The chancel floor is covered with decorative high glaze and unglazed faience tiling of c.1870–80.

The throne on the south side of the chancel dates from 1850, and the altar, stalls and pulpit are probably of the same date; all are beautifully carved from local fumed oak. The sixteen stalls do not bear prebendal names or titles of dignitaries. The pulpit had four statues of the Evangelists set in its front, but the statue of St Matthew was stolen c.1985.

The cathedral was restored in 1793 and again in 1813 with the help of grants of 500 from the Board of First-Fruits. It had a small congregation which worshipped in the chancel until c.1837, when the nave was restored with a grant from the Ecclesiastical Commissioners. Further repairs were undertaken in 1856 when the cathedral was closed for several months; it reopened on 1 June in that year. Whatever the nature of the work, it was not sufficient to persuade one mid-19th-century visitor that Clonfert Cathedral was anything more than 'a small, dingy common-looking old church'.[4]

Clonfert: the west doorway

Some work was undertaken in the 1880s by Robert McLarney, rector of Clonfert at the time, although he admitted that there was 'as in the great majority of country churches in the west of Ireland, only a comparatively small congregation.' In 1884 the walls were 'thoroughly cleansed, and the pews newly painted. A new communion table and a new communion cloth were procured. A choir was formed, and a few young people were trained to sing the church music. The organ is a comparatively new one.' McLarney also reported that the sacristy was 'roofed with Danish wattles, and is quite unfit for use.'[5]

In 1890 John Healy, the Roman Catholic Coadjutor Bishop of Clonfert, predicted that it would soon be abandoned by the Church of Ireland, 'for the few persons who attend divine worship in the old Cathedral of St Brendan can hardly be called a congregation'.[6] As the Roman Catholic Diocese of Clonfert was then without a cathedral (Bishop Healy inaugurated its construction at Loughrea in 1897) there may have been some hope of acquiring it for Roman Catholic use.

Further work took place about 1899, when the interior walls were entirely stripped of the plaster with which they had been covered. The supervising architect decided not to replace it, since it was a late addition and the stone dressings of the windows were flush with the masonry walls. It was suggested at the time that the innermost order of the west door should be removed and used to provide an arched entrance to the baptistery, but this was rejected.

A new roof was put on in 1986 at a cost of £37,000 and the cathedral is generally in very good condition. But because of its remote position, it has proved impossible to maintain a regular congregation and, at the time of writing, services are held only once a month during the summer.

The diocese of Kilmacduagh was united to Clonfert in 1602, and both sees were united to Killaloe and Kilfenora in 1834. Further unions have made it part of the united dioceses of Limerick, Ardfert, Aghadoe, Killaloe, Kilfenora, Clonfert, Kilmacduagh and Emly, but the bishop is known simply as the Bishop of Limerick and Killaloe. The last bishop to reside at Clonfert was Christopher Butson (1804–36)

Among the 16th-century Bishops of Clonfert, Roland de Burgo must rank with his contemporary, Archbishop Miler Magrath of Cashel, in the adroit way that he held on to his diocese through the Reformation years. He was appointed by the Pope in 1534, but accepted the royal supremacy in 1541, having managed to expel Richard Nangle, the nominee of Henry VIII. He was pardoned by Queen Mary I in 1553, but again accepted the royal supremacy under Queen Elizabeth I. He died in 1580 after forty-six years as Bishop of Clonfert.

A gate in the churchyard wall leads to the ruin of Clonfert Palace, the former residence of the Bishops of Clonfert. It was built about 1640 by Bishop Robert Dawson (1627–43) on the site of the former palace, but was partly rebuilt in the 18th century. It is a long, low and narrow house of two storeys with an attic of dormer gables, set in an overgrown formal park. After the death of Bishop Butson the palace was no longer required by the church and was bought by J. E. Trench; it remained the home of the Trench family until the middle of the 20th century. In 1952 it became the home of Sir Oswald Mosley, but in 1954 it was badly damaged by fire which began accidentally in the kitchen; it is now derelict. The eastern end of the palace has largely been taken over by

trees. Of the driveway entrance gate on the main road, only one pier now remains; the other was recently demolished to make way for a modern house.

References

1 T. M. Fallow, *The cathedral churches of Ireland* (London, 1894), p. 80.
2 *The Parliamentary Gazetteer of Ireland* (Dublin, 1844–6), i, 442.
3 William Anderson and Clive Hicks, *Cathedrals in Britain and Ireland* (London, 1978), p. 151.
4 James Godkin, *Ireland and her churches* (London, 1867), p. 351.
5 Fallow, *Cathedral churches of Ireland* (London, 1894), p. 80.
6 John Healy, *Insulorum sanctorum et doctorum, or Ireland's ancient schools and scholars* (Dublin & London, 1890), p. 243.

CLONMACNOISE

The Cathedral Church of St Kieran

CLONMACNOISE (*Cluain moccu Nóis* – meadow of the sons of Nós) in Co. Offaly lies almost in the centre of Ireland on the Shannon plain, with hills to the south and the river the north. The nearest towns are Moate, which is 22.4km to the south-west, and Athlone, 20.8km to the north. Clonmacnoise is one of the most rewarding and fascinating monastic sites in Ireland, containing the cathedral, eight other churches, two Round Towers, and a number of High Crosses.

The founder, St Kieran the Younger, was trained for the monastic life by St Finian of Clonard and is one of the so-called Twelve Apostles of Ireland (see CLONARD). He died at the age of thirty-three in 544, 547, 548, or perhaps 556, not long after founding Clonmacnoise, and his feast-day is on 9 September. He was a friend of St Kevin of Glendalough and St Columba of Iona, and his memory is surrounded by the usual hagiographical stories that he had a charming nature and was friendly to animals. The monastery that he founded here on the bank of the Shannon owes its origin to a dream he had while studying in the Aran Islands. The dream showed him a great tree in the centre of Ireland with fruit-bearing branches sheltering the centre plain. Flocks of birds flew to it to eat its fruit and to carry the fruit to distant lands. Kieran's friend, St Enda of Aran, drew the interpretation that Kieran was the tree, that his name would become famous throughout Ireland, and that foreigners would be fed by his prayers and fasting; he should go and found his church in the centre of Ireland by the banks of the Shannon as the dream had indicated.

Land was given to Kieran by Diarmait Ua Cerbaill (O'Carroll) at a meeting-point of three kingdoms – Munster, Meath and Connacht – and the dream lasted for a thousand years. The fame of Clonmacnoise spread far beyond Ireland and came

The accession of Simon Rochfort as the first Anglo-Norman Bishop of Clonard in 1192 marked the beginning of a period in which the extension of Anglo-Norman control of that part of Ireland was accompanied by the expansion of the Diocese

Clonmacnoise Cathedral from the north-west

to the attention of the Emperor Charlemagne in the 8th century, who sent it a present *via* Alcuin of York, who went to study there. The monastery is held by many to have been the greatest centre of learning in Irish Christianity and when Pope John Paul II visited Ireland in 1979 he went to Clonmacnoise.

The monastery, as with so many other sites, came to the attention of the Vikings and was plundered or burnt on more than thirty occasions between the 9th and 11th centuries. On one particular raid a Viking leader placed his wife on the altar, where she carried out pagan rites.

The claims of the monastery to diocesan status were ignored at Ráith Bressail in 1111, which assigned West Meath to Clonard and East Meath to Duleek. Not content with this situation, Abbot Gilla Críst Ua Máel Eoin (d.1127) convened a local synod at Uisnech later in the same year which decreed the suppression of Duleek, the transfer of Clonard's jurisdiction to East Meath, and designated Clonmacnoise as the see for West Meath. The first bishop under the new territorial system was Domnall mac Flannacáin Ua Dubthaig (1111–36).

of Clonard (later styled Meath) at the expense of Clonmacnoise. By the mid-13th century the diocese of Clonmacnoise was confined to a small territory east of the Shannon where the family of Ó Máelsaechlainn (O'Melaghlin), formerly Kings of Meath, were able to maintain their authority.

Clonmacnoise remained a small and poor diocese, and the final blow came in 1552 when the buildings were sacked by the English garrison from Athlone, who removed anything of value, including the glass from the windows. 'The large bells were taken from the round tower. There was not left, moreover, a bell, small or large, an image, or an altar, or a book, or a gem, or even a glass in a window which was not carried off. Lamentable was this deed, the plundering of the city of Kieran the holy patron.'[1] It is doubtful if any of the 16th-century bishops ever were resident, and on the death of Bishop Peter Wall (1556–68) the diocese was finally absorbed into the diocese of Meath. Clonmacnoise enjoyed a brief period of revival during the period of the Confederate war, when the cathedral was restored in 1647 by Charles Coghlan, the vicar general of the diocese. But the forces of Cromwell soon ended the attempt, and since that time the cathedral and most of its satellite churches have been abandoned and ruined.

The first stone cathedral was built *c.*909 by King Flann during the abbacy of Colmán mac Ailella; it was burnt in 985 and again in 1020. It was replaced late in the 11th century by the present structure, which is the work of Cormac, grandson of Conn na mBocht, and completed at the beginning of the 12th century by Abbot Flaithbertach Ua Loingsig (1100–09). It was rebuilt in 1336 by Tomaltach MacDermot, King of Moylurg, from whom comes its later name of Teampall Mhic Diarmada.

1. *The Cathedral*

The cathedral is a single-chamber structure, 18.8m long and 8.5m wide, with a 6m-square sacristy lit by two small windows. To the left of the sacristy doorway is a piscina and a plain sedilia, part of which was removed when the chancel was added to the church at a later date. Three rows of columns divided the cathedral into parallel aisles, but little remains. The sandstone capitals of the Romanesque west doorway are probably from the 10th-century cathedral. The chancel vault and the elaborately ornamented Gothic north doorway surmounted by a figure of St Patrick, between those of St Francis and St Dominic, were built about 1460 by Dean Odo. In 1198 Rory O'Connor, the last High King of Ireland, was buried in the predecessor of the present 17th-century sacristy. A storm blew down the 'two western wings of the cathedral'[2] and it never recovered from the pillage of 1552.

2. *Teampall Doulin (or Dowling)*

This church, which lies to the south of the cathedral, dates from the 9th century. It measures 9.4m by 4.8m and has a round-headed east window. The west end was restored by Edward Dowling, who inserted a new door. A stone panel above the doorway has an ornate coat of arms and records Dowling's work.

3. *Teampall Hurpain*

This is a 17th-century structure, added on to the east end of Teampall Doulin, measuring 6.7m by 3.6m. Although it was the last church to be built at Clonmacnoise, nothing is known of its origin beyond the fact that part of it was reconstructed in 1698 and used as a place of worship by Protestants; forty years later it was in ruins.

4. *Teampall Rí*

To the east of Teampall Hurpain, Teampall Rí, also known as Teampall Máelseachlainn is 12.4m long by 5.2m wide, a church of uncertain date, possibly late 12th or early 13th century. It has two round-headed lancets at the east, splayed inwards and richly adorned with mouldings. There appears

to have been a loft or gallery at the west end, and the holes for supporting joists can still be seen. The south door is a later insertion, possibly 16th century.

Clonmacnoise: Dean Odo's doorway in the north wall of the cathedral

5. *Teampall Cheallaigh*

Only the foundations remain of this church of 1167 which occupies the site of St Kieran's Hospital. It measures 9.7m by 6.7m and was built by the head of the O'Kelly family.

6. *Teampall Chiaráin*

This diminutive oratory with mutilated antae and a good two light east window lies to the north east of the cathedral. It is the smallest church at Clonmacnoise and St Kieran is said to be buried in the north-east corner. The church of Kieran's day would have been a wooden structure and the present stone structure dates from the 10th century. There seems no reason to doubt the story that Kieran died on this site if not in this building after receiving the last rites of the church from St Kevin of Glendalough. Two crosiers, discovered here during excavations, lend weight to the story.

7. Teampall Chonchobhair

This church which stands to the north of the cathedral was founded *c.*1000 by Cathal Ua Chonchobhair (O'Connor). The O'Connors, Kings of Connacht, asked for burial rights within the monastic enclosure and granted lands to the monastery in return for permission to construct this mortuary chapel; the first interment took place in 1036. Turlough O'Connor and his son Rory, the last High King of Ireland, were interred in the cathedral. The west doorway and south window are original. It was converted into a parish church *c.*1780, restored in 1911, and is now used for the worship of the Church of Ireland monthly during the summer. It has a small courtyard formed by the old west wall of the church and the remains of the oratories constructed by the Malone family.

8. Teampall Fhinghin

Further to the north-west, at the edge of the cemetery, is this nave and chancel church with a 17m Round Tower attached. It is supposed to have been erected by Fineen MacCarthy Mór *c.*1124. The nave has virtually disappeared but there are traces of a Romanesque south doorway and a good chancel arch. The nave was 8.8m long and 4.2m wide, and the chancel is 2.5m square; there is a piscina in the south wall. There is an insoluble controversy as to whether the tower precedes the church or is contemporary. It is named MacCarthy's Tower after the family who were Kings of Munster and had burial rights at Clonmacnoise. The conical cap is intact.

9. Altar

To the east of Teampall Fhinghín is a Roman Catholic altar built in 1969. Pope John Paul II prayed here on 30 September 1979.

10. The Church of the Nunnery

An 11th-century stone lined causeway leads eastwards from the cathedral through a gate in the cemetery to the Nuns' Church, 91m distant. It was founded by Devorguilla O'Melaghlin, wife of O'Rourke, Prince of Breifne in the 12th century. There has been a church on this site since the 9th century, but the present church was completed in 1167. There is a good Romanesque doorway of four orders, the capitals adorned with a number of beasts. The chancel arch is of three orders and is heavily decorated with heads. The nave measures 10.9m by 6m, and the chancel 4.2m by 3.9m. The church was restored in 1865 by the Royal Society of Antiquaries of Ireland.

11. The Round Tower

This massive roofless Round Tower stands 18.9m high and has a basic circumference of 17.66m. It is said to have been built by Fergal O'Rourke, King of Connacht, who died in 966, and is known as O'Rourke's Tower. It was restored after lightning destroyed the conical top in 1134 and was later given a new parapeted top with eight openings to serve as a lookout. Its arched doorway is similar to that of Ardmore Tower.

12. The Castle

To the south-west of the enclosure is a ruined castle built 1214–20 by John de Grey on the site of the abbot's house burnt in 1135. The castle is said to have been destroyed by the Cromwellians in the 17th century, but there is no definite information. The remains consist of a gateway, a courtyard, and a tower which collapsed as the result of an explosion. It appears today much as it did when sketched in 1738.

13. The Cross of the Scriptures

To the west of the cathedral is the great Cross of the Scriptures, consisting of a single stone more than 3m high. It was erected by Abbot Colmán in memory of King Flann, who died in 914. The west face is covered with biblical scenes surrounding a Crucifixion. One panel shows St Kieran building his first wooden church here.

14. The South Cross

The 8th-century South Cross is 2.4m high and stands to the south-east of Teampall Hurpain. It consists of three pieces of stone decorated with rich interlacings.

15. The North Cross

Only a portion of the shaft of the 9th-century North Cross remains. It is badly worn and decorated on three sides only.

Though the monastery and diocese of Clonmacnoise are now only a memory, the name was retained for the dean of the Church of Ireland diocese of Meath, which was itself without a cathedral from the Reformation until 1955. In that year the parish church of St Patrick in Trim was designated the cathedral church of the diocese and the incumbent now holds the title 'Dean of Clonmacnoise'.

References

1 John Healy, *History of the diocese of Meath* (Dublin, 1908), i, 157.
2 Ibid.

CLOYNE

The Cathedral Church of St Colman

Diocese of Cloyne (Church of Ireland)

CLOYNE (*Cluain uamha* – meadow of the cave) is a village of about 600 inhabitants, hidden away down a series of winding lanes 25km south-west of Youghal and 12km east of Cóbh in Co. Cork. A monastery was founded here by St Colman (Colmán mac Lénéni) (522–*c.*606) in the 6th century. Colman, who was born at Muskerry, was a poet and a royal bard at the court of Cashel. Tradition states that he became a Christian after rescuing the stolen shrine of St Ailbhe (of Emly) from a lake, and that he was baptised by St Brendan of Clonfert. After preaching at Limerick and Cork, he was given land at Cloyne by Coirpre Cromm, King of Cashel. Colman's feast-day is 24 November.

The monastic annals tell very little about the history of Cloyne. There is a reference to an Abbot of Cloyne attending the Synod of Birr in 697. Cloyne, being so near the sea, suffered badly from Viking attacks during the 9th century. In 885 the abbot, the prior and several members of the community were murdered in one such raid, and there is no further reference to Cloyne until 1060.

The situation during the reformation of the 12th century is uncertain. Cloyne was not chosen to be the see of a territorial diocese at the Synod of Ráith Bressail in 1111, but there are references to the work of a Bishop Nehemias of Cloyne who died in 1149. No Bishop of Cloyne was present at the Synod of Kells–Mellifont in 1152, but the diocese was included in the list drawn up by Cardinal Paparo, the papal legate, in the same year. A Bishop of Cloyne did fealty to King Henry II in 1172, and thereafter a regular succession was maintained.

The diocese of Cloyne was formed from the territory of the large diocese of Cork. The first Anglo-Norman bishop was Nicholas of Effingham (1284–1321), but he was succeeded by Mauricius Ó Solcháin (1321–33), who was Irish, and during his episcopate, on 31 July 1327, Pope John XXII at the petition of Edward II issued a bull providing for the union of Cork and Cloyne on the death of either incumbent. There was no ecclesiatical reason for reducing the number of Irish dioceses. The proposal for union was part of an extensive and ambitious scheme to extend royal authority further into Ireland; the device of amalgamation united the more remote dioceses in the wilder parts of Ireland with those within easier reach of royal administration.

The union was not effected immediately because of local rivalries and, no doubt, determination to resist royal machinations. An unsuccessful attempt at union was made by Richard Wye on 10 September 1376 when he became Bishop of Cloyne. Bishop Adam Payne of Cloyne (1413–29) obtained further confirmation of the union from Pope Martin V on 21 September 1418, but was opposed by Bishop Milo Fitzjohn of Cork (1409–15 and for some months in 1418). The union eventually took place on the resignation of Bishop Payne in 1429 and the provision of Bishop Jordan Purcell (1429–69) to both sees.

In the Church of Ireland arrangement, Cloyne remained united to Cork (and Ross after 1583) until 1638, when it was again independent under Bishop George Synge (1638–52). After another brief period of union with Cork and Ross 1661–78, Cloyne resumed its independence until 1835, when it was again united to Cork and Ross under the provision of the Church Temporalities (Ireland) Act of 1833.

Cloyne Cathedral is a large cruciform building 51.8m long with an aisled nave and a Chapter House attached to the north-east of the chancel. The cathedral was built in the mid-13th century but partly altered in the 18th century. As the building stands today, the west wall of the nave, the nave arcades, the transepts, the chancel and the Chapter House remain from the 13th century. The east and west walls have been rendered.

In 1705 the battlements topping the nave walls were removed, and the nave roof brought down to project over the aisle roofs, giving it its present curved appearance. The rafters, some of which rest on the inside and some on the outside of the nave aisle walls, probably date from this rebuilding. The west wall was altered in 1723 to include the insertion of the present incongruous window.

Substantial alterations were made to the crossing and chancel in 1774. The aim appears to have been the restoration or redecoration of the chancel and the provision of extra seating, the nave being disused. The work was effected in the Classical style which was typical of the age but ludicrous in this Gothic cathedral.

The chancel was lengthened westwards to incorporate the crossing. Most of the chancel arch was walled up and the rest was blocked by a Classical-style wooden screen to divide the chancel from the nave. The arches leading from the crossing into the north and south transepts were similarly blocked to allow the erection of galleries on the west, north and south walls of the chancel. The west gallery contained the organ, and the north and south galleries extended one-third of the way along the walls. The ceiling was plastered and given a cornice. New stalls and a bishop's throne, 'of a painfully prim and spiritless character'[1] were inserted. 'The whole structure, in fact, has been so often and bunglingly patched, daubed, and played with by empiricism and stupidity, that a stranger might almost suppose it, on a cursory glance, to be a rude piece of masonry tastelessly constructed out of the quarried ruins of a group of fallen and variously-dated Gothic piles. The remains of ancient carved stone-work, mouldings, shafts, mullions, capitals, &c., are everywhere plastered and encrusted over with whitewash; ancient windows are filled in with masonry; while modern ones have been opened up out of all harmony with the character of the building.'[2]

This late 18th-century work mostly disappeared in further alterations in 1894, at a cost of over £1,300. The galleries were removed; the organ, which had been in the west gallery, was replaced by a new two manual organ placed in the south transept arch; the transept arches themselves, which had been walled up in 1774, were reopened. The lath-and-plaster ceiling was replaced by a pitchpine roof — and not a moment too soon: 'The old ceiling was found to be in a dangerous state, and, on the removal of a portion of it, some of the remainder fell in large mass.'[3] New choir stalls of Italian oak were installed; the sanctuary floor, formerly of wood, was inlaid with mosaic, and a new altar was presented by the canons of the cathedral. The pews were fitted with spiral brass pillars to hold oil lamps.

The 18th-century Classical wooden screen was removed and now provides an inner porch for the west door. It was replaced by a dull wood and glass screen, which at least opens up a view of the entire length of the cathedral and gives additional light to both nave and chancel; the remains of the chancel arch can still be seen. Two other screens fill the openings from the nave aisles to the north and south transepts. These functional Victorian screens do nothing to enhance the beauty of Cloyne Cathedral, and bear no comparison with the craftsmanship of the contemporary screen at Killaloe Cathedral.

Congregations at Cloyne Cathedral have not been of sufficient size, at least since the 18th century, to maintain the use of the nave. Apart from the remains of a primitive font and an 18th-century pulpit of inlaid mahogany, both in the northwest corner, the nave is now empty and unused. But this very emptiness serves well by emphasising the striking and unusual arcades, which spring from massive rectangular chamfered stone piers, without capitals or bases. Although the piers and arches are of a lower height and a different style from those at St Mary's Cathedral, Limerick, both convey tremendous strength by the common principle of size and simplicity.

The north transept, historically called 'the Fitzgerald Aisle', contains a recumbent alabaster effigy of Bishop George Berkeley who is reckoned to be the most notable bishop (1734–53) of this quiet and secluded see. Berkeley was a philosopher celebrated for his metaphysical doctrine. His most important works were *A New Theory of Vision* (1709), *Principles of Human Knowledge* (1710) and *Dialogues between Hylas and Philonous* (1713). The memorial is the work of A. Bruce Joy and was placed here in 1888. Nearby in the floor is the letter 'B', marking the burial place of two of his children: Sarah, who died in 1739, and William in 1751.

The south transept, once known as 'the Poore Aisle' or 'Poore's Aisle' after the Le Poher family, was furnished and decorated as a chapel in 1953 in memory of Patricia Ponsonby. The large south window previously had five trefoil-headed lights. It was filled in at an early date, certainly before 1730; the internal moulding is still visible, and traces of the mullions can be seen on the external wall. The transept is now badly affected by damp and is no longer used. It is difficult to predict its future without major restoration work.

Cloyne: the Round Tower, the south nave aisle and part of the south transept

The chancel is 21.3m long. The stone mullions of the east window are of unusual design and are ornamented with ogee tracery; the window dates from the 15th century but was restored in 1856; the glass is a 19th century memorial. The chapter stalls are against the north and south walls towards the west end, and the Bishop's throne is on the south wall outside the altar rails. There is a window on the north side of the chancel with stained glass by Meyer & Co. of Munich, commemorating Dean James Howie (d. 1884). A window on the south side by Patrick Pye commemorates Hugh F. Berry Dean of Cloyne (1934–52). The chancel has two lecterns, one of brass dated 1899, and an unusual iron one.

There is no sign that the cathedral ever had a tower, although Walcott, among others, refers to the collapse of a central tower.[4] The cathedral bell has always been hung in the Round Tower which stands across the street 45.7m to the north-west of the cathedral. Built of purplish sandstone, it stands 30.5m high, including the battlemented parapet which was added after the tower had been struck by lightning during a severe storm on 10 January 1749. Bishop Berkeley noted the event: 'Our round tower stands where it did but the little stone arched vault on the top was cracked. The bell also was thrown down and broke its way through three boarded stories but remains entire. The door was shivered into very many small pieces and dispersed and there was a stone forced out of the wall. The thunder clap was the largest I ever heard in Ireland.'[5] The Tower contains a Dublin-made bell of 1857 bearing the inscription 'SHERIDAN MAKER DUBLIN'.

The foundations of a small and very early building known as the 'Fire House' can be seen to the north-east of the cathedral among the gravestones in the churchyard. Measuring 9.1m by 5.7m[6] it may have been a place where a flame was kept burning perpetually, like that at Kildare, or it may have been an oratory of St Colman. One tradition says that relics of St Colman were preserved there until the early 18th century, when Bishop Charles Crow (1702–26) had them removed and the building raised to the ground.[7] This story can be treated with some degree of scepticism, since the survival of such a place after the Reformation would have been unusual and surprising.

Cloyne Cathedral has a forlorn and beleaguered appearance today. It looks like an elderly giant of quiet and ancient dignity, gently resisting the slow encroachment of weather and nature on its aged fabric.

The Bishops of Cloyne formerly lived in a small 14th-century castle in the centre of the town; this remained the episcopal residence, with breaks, until the beginning of the 18th century. In 1700 Bishop John Pooley (1697–1702) rebuilt or repaired a house adjoining the cathedral grounds, originally built by the Fitzgeralds, and made his residence there. Bishop Crow added a north wing, which was destroyed by fire in 1887. At the end of the 18th century the house had a garden of four acres and an attached farm of 400 acres. The grounds contained winding walks lined with myrtles which Bishop Berkeley had planted. The house, afterwards known as Cloyne House, was sold on the union of Cloyne with Cork and Ross on the death of Bishop Brinkley in 1835. The old castle became ruinous and unsafe and was dismantled by order of the bishop in 1797. A visitor in that year noticed 'the remains of a castle built by the Fitzgerald family, but very inconsiderable'.[8] The former palace still exists to the north of the cathedral but a road now divides it from the cathedral graveyard.

John Brinkley, the last separate Bishop of Cloyne (1826–35), was a distinguished astronomer who had held the chair of astronomy at Trinity College, Dublin, and was President of the Royal Irish Academy in 1822. A memorial to him in the cathedral shows a veiled urn in the centre, with a crozier and open book to one side, a telescope and globe on the other, and a mitre above.

The former Deanery stands about 1.5km to the north of the cathedral. It is a 18th-century house of three bays and two storeys, with a later attached wing and outhouses. It was sold c.1978–9. Abandoned by its owner some years ago, it is now falling into decay.

References

1 T. M. Fallow, *The cathedral churches of Ireland* (London, 1894), p. 43.
2 *The Parliamentary Gazetteer of Ireland* (Dublin, 1844–6), i, 470.
3 *Irish Builder*, xxxv, no. 802 (1893), p. 122.
4 Mackenzie Walcott, *The cathedrals of the United Kingdom* (London, 1860), p. 298.
5 G. L. Barrow, *Round Towers*, (Dublin, 1979), p. 68.
6 W. M. Brady, *Clerical and parochial records of Cork, Cloyne and Ross* (London, 1864), ii, 164.
7 J. C., 'St Colman of Cloyne' in *Journal of the Cork Historical and Archaeological Society*, xvi (1910), p. 142.
8 George Holmes, *Sketches of some of the southern counties of Ireland, collected during a tour in the autumn of 1797, in a series of letters* (London, 1801), pp 173–174.

COBH

The Cathedral Church of St Colman

Diocese of Cloyne (Roman Catholic)

*C*ÓBH (pronounced Cove), with a population of about 6,000 lies 22.4km south-east of Cork and has the most extensive harbour on the south coast of Ireland. Originally called The Cove of Cork, it was renamed Queenstown in 1849 to commemorate a visit by Queen Victoria. The present name was adopted in 1922.

The provision of a cathedral for the diocese of Cloyne was due to the efforts of Bishop William Keane (1857–74). His predecessors had resided at Cóbh, the most prosperous and rapidly expanding town in the diocese, since 1769. A small parish church on the site of the present cathedral had been long known as the Pro-Cathedral. On the death of Bishop Timothy Murphy in 1856, the dioceses of Cloyne and Ross were separated and Bishop Keane decided that Cloyne should have a purpose-built cathedral.

The new cathedral was ten years in the planning and was designed by Edward Welby Pugin (1834–75) and his brother-in-law, George Coppinger Ashlin (1837–1921). George Goldie (who designed the Catholic cathedral at Sligo) and J. J. McCarthy (who designed the Catholic cathedrals at Armagh, Derry, Monaghan and Thurles) were invited to submit designs, but both spoiled their chances by suggesting amendments to the conditions of the competition.

Pugin was the son of Augustus Welby Northmore Pugin (designer of the Catholic cathedrals at Enniscorthy and Killarney) by his second wife, and George Ashlin had a flourishing architectural practice at Cork. Because of their major commitments in England and Ireland, the two men later agreed to divide their work, Pugin working in England and Ashlin in Ireland. The cathedral at Cóbh then became Ashlin's sole responsibility for a while until he took Thomas A. Coleman in partnership.

After the construction of a temporary church above Bishop Street, north of the town, the old parish church was demolished in February 1868, and excavation of the site began on 25 April. Because of the difficulties of the steeply sloping site, a massive bed of sandstone quarried locally at Carrigmore and Castle Oliver had to be laid. Bishop Keane was able to lay the foundation stone, a huge block of limestone quarried at Shanballa, near Aghada, which forms the quoin at the south-west corner of the tower and is laid at a depth of 14ft under yard level. The first stone of the superstructure, the inscribed angle stone at the south-west corner of the tower, was laid on 30 September.

The original estimated cost was £33,000, but when the walls had reached an average height of 3.5m Bishop Keane decided on a more elaborate plan at a substantially increased cost, and the final price for building the cathedral rose to £235,000. The bishop died in 1874 and left his successors to cope with the problem of raising the extra funds needed to complete what was now going to be a very splendid and very expensive cathedral. Both Bishop John MacCarthy (1874–93) and Bishop Robert Browne (1894–1935) faithfully continued with the revised plans, and enough of the building had been completed to enable Bishop MacCarthy to celebrate mass in the cathedral for the first time on 15 June 1879. No work was done in the years 1883–9 because of lack of funds.

The last phase of building work began in 1911 with the construction of the octagonal limestone spire. Three years later, on 24 September 1914, a 3.3m high bronze cross, blessed by Bishop Browne, was raised to the pinnacle of the 90m spire and the cathedral was complete. The last scaffolding around the tower was removed in March 1915, and the bells were installed in May 1916. Amazingly, the tower houses 47 bells (42 hung in 1916 and a further five in 1958) hung in a rigid steel framework and shows no sign of structural damage after more than seventy years of heavy vibration caused by the pealing of 17 tons of bells. On 12 August 1919, more than half a century after the foundation stone had been laid, the completed cathedral was solemnly consecrated.

Cóbh Cathedral is constructed in a very elaborate French Gothic style using a rich variety of building materials. It consists of an aisled nave of seven bays with triforium and clerestory, transepts with eastern chapels, an apsidal chancel, and a tower and spire at the south-west corner of the nave. The cathedral measures 64m long and 36.5m wide at the transepts. Great rose windows set within high pointed arches and flanked by octagonal turrets adorn the west front

Cobh: the west front

and the transepts. The basic building material is blue Dalkey granite with cut stone dressings of Mallow limestone. Newry granite is used in the tower, with red Aberdeen granite in the pillars on the west front and the piers at the entrance to the nave. The roof is of blue Belgian slate.

Bath stone and Portland stone are used to line the inner walls. Red Midleton marble is used in the shrines and in the first confessionals of both aisles; the remaining confessionals are of red Aberdeen granite. The nave is separated from the aisles by piers of red Fermoy marble resting on bases of white Italian marble and plinths of Liscarroll limestone. The piers have richly sculpted capitals of foliage and human heads and support the tall slender clustered columns of the triforium executed in red Aberdeen granite; they in turn support the springing of the arches over the clerestory windows and the vaulted roof of Californian pitchpine. The Stations of the Cross are of Caen stone. The clustered respond columns at the end of the north aisle are of black Kilkenny marble.

The baptistery, at the entrance to the north aisle, is enclosed by a low rail of white Italian marble. The octagonal font is of white marble, and the cupola-shaped cover is of burnished brass. The windows depict the baptism of Christ in the Jordan by St John, and the baptism of the daughters of the King of Ireland by St Patrick. The Mortuary Chapel in the base of the tower has an altar of black Kilkenny marble and displays representations of the instruments of the Passion. The stained glass is by Early & Powell of Dublin.

The very high chancel arch is supported by clustered respond columns; the chancel floor is paved with mosaic, and the sanctuary piers are of green Connemara marble. Italian white marble is also used in the communion rail, which rests on red marble colonettes, and in the altar tables. The screens, throne, stalls and pulpit are of Austrian oak.

The chancel is flanked by twin chapels on both the north and south. Immediately to the north of the high altar is the Lady Chapel with an altar by Early & Powell and a mosaic floor containing the titles of the Blessed Virgin Mary in Latin. Beyond the Lady Chapel is the Blessed Thaddeus Chapel which commemorates Thaddeus MacCarthy, Bishop Cork and Cloyne 1490–92, who was beatified by Pope Leo XIII in 1895.

To the south of the high altar is the Sacred Heart Chapel. The altar is of Sicilian marble; the antependium is of Carrara marble with a background of red marble. The mosaic floor depicts the power of the Sacred Heart, with the encircling inscription '**Super Apsidem et Basiliscum ambulabis et conculabis Leonem et Draconem**' (Thou shalt walk on the Asp and the Basilisk and thou shalt trample under foot the Lion and the Dragon). This chapel is now used for baptisms; the font is the work of craftsmen from the Verolme Cork Dockyard.

Adjacent to the Sacred Heart Chapel is the Chapel of the Pietà, a memorial to Bishop Keane, which is used as a requiem chapel. The altar is of Sicilian marble and the antependium of Carrara stone. The columns are of black Kilkenny marble. The theme is in the window above the altar, which depicts the Raising of Lazarus, and the side windows, which show the Sorrowful Mysteries.

Cóbh Cathedral probably enjoys the most advantageous position of any Irish cathedral. Because of its superb hillside site, it dominates the quay in a most imposing way, standing proudly clear of all neighbouring buildings, though without any feeling of arrogance or pomposity. The exterior detail is intricate, elegant and well proportioned in a way typical of French sophistication. It south front faces out to sea, and, viewed from the quayside, it bristles with flying buttresses, gargoyles, spirelets and pinnacles, giving the impression of a royal galleon sailing in state along the horizon. This is a beautifully conceived edifice and an enduring credit to the combination of minds and hands that brought it into being.

CONNOR

The Cathedral Church of St Saviour

ONNOR (*Connere* – oak wood of the hounds) is a village in Co. Antrim 8km south-east of Ballymena. A monastery was founded here early in the 6th century, of which St Óengus mac Nissi is the first known abbot and bishop; he is said to have died in 513 or 514, and his feast-day is 3 September. The names of a few abbots and bishops are known before the Synod of Ráith Bressail established Connor as the see of a diocese for the territory of Dalriada. The first diocesan bishop was Flann Ua Sculu, who died in 1117. His successor was the famous St Malachy, who became Archbishop of Armagh in 1132 and did much to restore ecclesiastical discipline in the Irish Church.

Connor seems to have been an important place until the middle of the 14th century. In 1315 it was the scene of a military engagement in which Edward Bruce, claimant to the kingship of Ireland, defeated the Anglo-Norman forces under the command of Richard de Burgh, Earl of Ulster. The town was plundered and burned by the Scottish soldiers and never recovered its importance.

Pope Eugenius IV issued a bull on 24 July 1439 providing for the union of Connor with Down on the death or resignation of either incumbent, and this should have taken effect on the deprivation of Bishop John Sely of Down in 1442, but Archbishop John Prene of Armagh (1439–43) opposed the move, and the union was not implemented until 1453. It remained in force until Connor was re-established as a separate diocese in the Church of Ireland in 1944.

Almost nothing is known of the appearance or history of the medieval cathedral at Connor. It was restored during the reign of James I, but badly damaged during the rising of 1641. A Cromwellian report of 1657 described it as 'not in repayre'. Connor was an isolated country village with few resident members of the Church of Ireland, and there was little incentive, let alone money, to rebuild the cathedral.

Further disincentives were provided by the fact that the dioceses of Down and Connor had been held together under a single bishop since 1453, and that the cathedral at Downpatrick had since 1538 also been in ruins. In the light of these factors, it would seem likely that the rebuilding of Connor Cathedral was not seriously considered at the Restoration. Jeremy Taylor became Bishop of Down and Connor and administrator of Dromore in 1661 and devoted his attentions to the rebuilding of his beloved Dromore Cathedral. Connor was a remote village far to the north of Dromore, and a new cathedral, at the centre of a large Church of Ireland population, was an obvious course to pursue.

lin, preached at Connor and read the service of his appointment as Prebendary of Kilroot.

A plan and sketches of the old cathedral made in 1800 show a ruined, partly roofed T-shaped building with steeply pitched gables; nothing remains. The present church at Connor, built in 1811 and consecrated in 1813, stands on the site of the cathedral. The south wall of the present building runs inside the lines of the cathedral; the north wall and eastern gable are built on the foundations of the cathedral walls. Nothing of the old cathedral above ground was used at all in building the new church. Wherever the walls of the cathe-

Connor: the 19th century Church of Ireland parish church

King Charles II, by letters patent dated 17 October 1662, constituted the parish church of Lisburn, then the most important town in either diocese as the cathedral church for the dioceses of Connor and Down. Lisburn was midway between Connor to the north and Downpatrick to the southeast, and only about 10km north of Dromore.

One of the transepts of the old cathedral at Connor, was thatched with straw and continued in use as the Church of Ireland parish church. It seems to have been used, at least for a while, as though it had cathedral status. On 28 April 1695 Jonathan Swift, later Dean of St Patrick's Cathedral in Dub-

dral did not align with the those of the new church, they were blown up with gunpowder, and their remains probably lie under the present church.

To quote T. M. Fallow, the early 19th-century Church of St Saviour 'has nothing whatever of interest about it, except the fact that it is the modern representative of the ancient cathedral church . . . and occupies the ancient site'.[1] To counterbalance Fallow's dismissal, it should be said that St Saviour's Church is a good deal more attractive than the many hundreds of its contemporaries that were mass-produced in the first twenty years of the 19th century by the Board of First-Fruits.

St Saviour's Church is a plain single-chamber building with a square battlemented and pinnacled tower of three storeys with banding at floor levels attached to the west end. There is a north transept and a vestry at the north-east corner which interlocks with the transept. The only relic of antiquity is the shaft of a Celtic cross. The vestry was added in 1826–8, the transept c.1870–71. The church has never enjoyed cathedral status, and Christ Church, Lisburn is still the cathedral church of the diocese of Connor. But echoes of Connor survive in the name of the collegiate body: 'The Dean and Chapter of St Saviour Connor in the Cathedral of Christ Church, Lisburn'.

In 1844 Connor was described as 'little more than a rural hamlet . . . exhibiting the farce of a nominal city character amidst poverty, depopulation, and the utter absence of every appliance of either a great town or the seat of a bishopric'.[2] Today the village of Connor, with Kells its adjoining twin, have a more prosperous feel. St Saviour's Church sits neatly and squarely in its graveyard, with stonework mottled and weathered to just the right degree; trim, well-kept and unremarkable, but a pretty and simple country church with an ageless air.

References

1 T. M. Fallow, *The cathedral churches of Ireland* (London, 1894), pp 9–10.
2 *The Parliamentary Gazetteer of Ireland* (Dublin, 1844–6), i, 493.

CORK

The Cathedral Church of St Fin Barre

Diocese of Cork (Church of Ireland)

CORK (*Corcaigh* – marsh) is the third largest city in Ireland and the second in the Republic and stands on the banks of the River Lee close to the south coast of Ireland. It has a busy trade in agricultural produce and its industries include distilling, brewing and bacon-curing, and one of three colleges of the National University of Ireland is located here.

A monastic settlement was founded on the south bank of the main channel of the Lee at the beginning of the 7th century by St Fin Barre, a native of Connacht. He died *c.* 623, and his feast-day is 25 September. His foundation continued to be listed as one of the five principal monastic schools of Ireland until the 10th century, and it had sufficient wealth to attract the covetous eyes of marauding Vikings who, after several expeditions for plunder, settled here and carried on a flour-ishing trade. Because of the river and the proximity of the sea, it was a natural sight for permanent occupation. During one of their periodic raids the silver shrine containing the relics of St Fin Barre was removed.

Cork was close to the Dalcassian kingdom of Brian Boru and the appointment of a Dalcassian abbot is recorded in 1085 at the behest of Turlough O'Brien, the king's grandson. The Dalcassian influence may explain the large territory given to the diocese of Cork at the Synod of Ráith Bressail in 1111, since Brian's great-grandson, Muirchertach O'Brien, presided at the synod. The size of the diocese was reduced after his death in 1119 by the emergence of the dioceses of Cloyne and Ross.

Nothing is known for certain of the medieval cathedral at Cork. A cathedral was demolished in 1735, but its date of construction is impossible to fix. A crude drawing on a map of 1650 shows a building with a steeply pitched roof, a short central tower with spire, a building attached to the centre of the north wall that may have been either a transept or a chapter house, two lofty but shallow chambers on the north wall either side of the chapter house, and crosses surmounting both the east gable and the spire. Since the view shows only one side of the cathedral, it is impossible to be certain that it was cruciform. There was a chapel dedicated to St Clement, measuring 4.8m east to west and 3.5m north to south. The pulpit was on the north side near the entrance to a chapter house; the throne was on the south side and had curtains of silk damask; there was an organ loft or gallery, and burials were frequent in the nave and aisles. A visitor to the cathedral in the early 17th century noted: 'There is also a Cathedral, but in decay.'[1] It was probably in this building that the poet Edmund Spenser was married on 11 June 1594. Some medieval carved heads remain in the Chapter House of the present cathedral.

During the 17th century the cathedral was constantly repaired and patched, and it may have suffered in the rebellion and Confederate war of the 1640s. Between 1671 and 1676 a tower was added to the cathedral at a cost of £560. The first sign that a tower was being contemplated appeared in 1670 when the sum of 5 was given for that purpose by one John Folliot. This gift was followed in 1671 by the adoption of a very aggressive policy by the Dean and Chapter: 'No indenture, or setting to farm, shall be confirmed by this Chapter for any man who shall refuse to contribute to the building of the Tower of St Finbarries.'[2] On 5 April 1677 'the Chapter decreed that the sum of 20 should be given as a gratuity to William Armsteade and Thomas Smythe, in consideration of their laudable care in building the Tower of the Cathedral'.[3]

The tower had a slight batter, string courses and a triplet ogee window on the west side adorned with three carved heads. It was garrisoned by English troops in 1689–90 and the forces of King James II who held the Elizabeth Fort opposite bombarded it with cannon shot. A spire was added to the tower in 1719 by order of the chapter.[4] When the tower was demolished in 1865, a 20kg cannon-ball was discovered deep within the masonry; it now hangs from a chain in the ambulatory of the present cathedral.

A square stone font (now in the present cathedral), some carved heads (preserved in the Chapter House), a piscina (built into a wall in the grounds to the east of the cathedral), a carved doorway (now inserted in the south boundary wall), a silver gilt chalice of 1536 and a silver chalice and paten of 1638 are the only relics of this cathedral. There was a Round Tower which collapsed in 1738; its site is now occupied by the present cathedral.

At a meeting on 8 November 1733 the Dean and Chapter noted that the cathedral was 'in very bad repair and in great danger of falling', and they decided to seek the advice of the bishop on demolition and construction of a new cathedral. At a further meeting on 15 May 1734 the chapter resolved 'to go on immediately with the repairing of the cathedral, and find workmen and materials sufficient for the same'.[5] But it was only a temporary measure and on 5 September 1734 the cathedral, with the exception of the tower and spire, was condemned to demolition. On 9 April 1735, demolition presumably complete, the chapter decided to authorise construction of a comletely new building. The funds were raised by a tax on coal, levied under an act of parliament, by the Corporation of Cork. The vote in favour of levying the tax for five years was carried 13–4.

Even with the coal tax, funding the building of the new cathedral was a problem. On 9 March 1737 the Dean and Chapter decided to see the bishop 'to represent the state of the Cathedral, that all their money has now been expended, and to seek his Lordship's advice'.[6] The cathedral was not finished until early in 1738.

Whatever the crumbling condition of the medieval cathedral, and no matter how well liked its successor may have been when first erected, the Classical-style cathedral built in 1735 had sunk low in the estimation of everyone by the time of its demolition in 1865. It was an oblong building constructed of white limestone, 36.5m long, with high collegiate-style box pews, return stalls at the west end for the Dean and Chapter, and a shallow chancel decorated with stucco work at the east. On the north side was a niche occupied by a marble figure of Eloquence by the sculptor John Bacon (1740–99). It was erected in 1781 in memory of the last Lord Tracton and was moved to St Nicholas's Church on the demolition of the cathedral in 1865. The bishop's throne was in the centre of the south wall of the nave facing the pulpit on the north wall. The 17th-century tower and spire stood at the west end with a vestry and chapter room attached to its north and south sides respectively. Entrance to the cathedral was through the base of the tower. The spire of

St Fin Barre's Cathedral, Cork: the Angel of Resurrection at the apex of the chancel roof

1691 was replaced by a larger, curiously shaped spire in 1751–2, and a new peal of eight bells was hung. The cathedral was provided with a new roof in 1816, 'the old one being decayed'.[7]

Nobody liked the 18th-century cathedral. 'Architectural beauty was not aimed at, and certainly not achieved. It was unworthy to be the mother church of the capital city of the Province of Munster.'[8] Another critic described it as 'an unsightly edifice and there is nothing within its walls to compensate for the deformity of its exterior'.[9] As demolition was being contemplated in 1861 Caulfield called it a cathedral 'which the smallest hamlet in England would contemptuously reject'.[10] After its demolition in 1865, the *Dublin Builder* called it 'a shabby apology for a cathedral which has long disgraced Cork'.[11]

The Parliamentary Gazetteer of Ireland issued a withering condemnation in 1844: "It is a plain, massive, dull, tasteless, oblong pile, totally destitute of what is usually regarded as cathedral character, and possessing hardly a claim to any sort of architectural consideration. The old tower rises from the west end, and is surmounted by an octagonal spire of most unsymmetrical proportions; the body of the church affects the Doric Order, but has windows with wooden sash frames, and presents hardly a feature of attraction to either the superficial observer or the artist, and the interior is distinguished from that of an ordinary parochial place of

St Fin Barre's Cathedral, Cork: from the east

worship only by the bishop's throne and the stalls of the dignitaries. A pointed doorway (in the tower) is the only one of even the remnants of the ancient structure which draws the attention; it is recessed and richly moulded; it consists of two distinct arches, ornamented in low relief – the outer by cluster columns and a cinquefoil head, and the inner by bold and well-relieved mouldings.'[12] This red sandstone doorway can be seen set in the south boundary wall; the inner arch is of freestone and the outer arch is of limestone.

A rare favourable comment was made in 1797 by John Harden who thought 'the Cathedral Church of St Finbarrys very neat & the service & Organ delightfull'.[13] But this was an exceptional view, and in 1861 the chapter decided to demolish this despised building and replace it with a cathedral more worthy of the designation. The only relics are the 18th-century entrance gates and some of the carved choir stalls in Irish oak now in the Masonic Hall in Tuckey Street. One contemporary observer reported that its demolition 'has excited but little regret.'[14] But the chancellor of the cathedral lamented its passing, suggesting that it could have been kept and used as a parish church, a new cathedral presumably being built elsewhere.[15]

After an open competition which attracted sixty-eight entries from the United Kingdom and Europe, the plans of William Burges of London were chosen; the runner-up was Sir Thomas Deane, who was to build Tuam Cathedral. Burges was only thirty-five years old and wrote excitedly in his diary: 'Got Cork.' His design and methods proved to be controversial. One of the conditions was that competitors must submit designs costing no more than £15,000. Burges's design was estimated to cost £25,000–£30,000, and many of the competitors angrily protested that they could have submitted more beautiful designs if they had ignored the rule on cost. Another complaint was that his design allowed only 466 pew sittings, whereas the competition rule had called for a cathedral to seat 700. Burges replied, with an innocence that sounds less than genuine, that he had not thought for a moment that the figure of £15,000 was meant to cover the cost of the whole cathedral, only to build something essential for divine worship; no cathedral, complete with towers and spires, could be built for £15,000, nor could it be built in one generation. Future generations would build the towers and spires. To the second charge he pointed out that with use of the transepts, a congregation of 738 could be seated.

On 20 October 1864, when the restoration of St Patrick's Cathedral in Dublin was complete, a faculty was issued for building a new cathedral at Cork, and services were held in the 18th-century cathedral for the last time on Sunday 23 October 1864. Perhaps not realising the glory that was to arise from the ashes, the cathedral organist adopted a very gloomy note by playing the 'Dead March' from *Saul*

at the conclusion of the evening service. "During its performance many of the old congregation loitered about the Cathedral, and took one longing, lingering look at the building they were about to bid farewell to for ever.'[16] The foundation stone of the new cathedral was laid on 12 January 1865, and four days later the demolition of the old cathedral began.

The new cathedral was consecrated on 30 November 1870, although the three towers and spires were not completed until 1879. After the consecration Bishop John Gregg (1862–78) announced that he had raised the £30,000 necessary to complete the towers. His announcement, during the course of a sermon, was followed by a rendering of Handel's 'Hallelujah Chorus'! The bishop, who had been enthroned in the old cathedral and laid the foundation of the new, survived to lay the top stones on the western spires in April 1878, one month before his death. In the following year his son and successor, Bishop Robert Gregg (1878–93), completed the cathedral when he laid the top stone of the great central tower. The total cost was £40,000. Not everyone liked the design; Richard Rolt Brash, a contemporary historian of Irish medieval architecture, described it as 'the perfect abortion of a cathedral'.[17] But no one doubts that St Fin Barre's Cathedral is one of the most remarkable sights in Ireland.

The plan is cruciform, consisting of an aisled nave, transepts and an apsidal chancel with ambulatory. Its total length is 49.7m; the width is 17.4m in the nave and 24,7m at the crossing, and the central tower is 73m high. The style is early French Gothic, a transitional mixture of the massive masonry of Romanesque with the pointed arches and geometric traceried windows of Gothic. The exterior is of white Cork limestone, and the main entrance is through three deeply recessed doorways on the west front. The nave piers are of Bath stone, the crossing piers are of grey-brown Stourton stone, and the apse piers are of red Cork marble. The walls of the nave, transepts and ambulatory are lined with red and dove-coloured Cork marble.

The font is of red Cork marble, supported on a central column of the same and surrounded by six others of green marble resting on a white marble base. The lectern is of solid brass, 3m in height, with profiles of Moses and David, and is studded with Italian rock crystals. It was designed by Burges for the Cathedral of Our Lady of the Vineyards at Lille in France. Burges had won the competition, but was never invited to execute the design. The pulpit is circular and made of stone with a rim of red Cork marble, standing on a central column surrounded by four piers, all of the same local marble and with stone caps, standing on a plinth of grey marble. It was painted in 1933 by Eileen Dann. When it was first installed a contemporary observer remarked: 'On the whole its resemblance to some large vat was, to my mind, very practical.'[18]

The nave is separated from the chancel by a low white-veined marble wall. The capping of the wall is inset with alternate slabs of red and green porphyry between intermediate squares of lapis lazuli and bezants of gold mosaics.

The painted chancel roof shows Christ in Glory surrounded by adoring angels and was executed in 1935 by Professor E. W. Tristram in accordance with Burges's designs. The bishop's throne, an incredible 14m in height, dominates the chancel and was made by Walden of London. It rests on a large plinth of red Cork marble. On its wooden panels are carved the heads of more than twenty of the more prominent Bishops of Cork; a carved wooden figure of St Fin Barre is set high up on the roof of the throne.

The chancel is separated from the sanctuary by a low brass screen. The altar is of oak and rests on a plinth of black marble. The reredos is of Painswick stone, alabaster, marble and mosaic. The floor of the sanctuary has a mosaic pavement worked by Italian artists, executed in Paris and using marbles from the Pyrenees. It depicts Matthew 13:47 in which the Kingdom of Heaven is likened to 'a net which was thrown into the sea and gathered fish of every kind.' The coloured pavement continues down into the choir, where the pattern becomes geometric.

St Fin Barre's Cathedral is a magnificent and startling creation in the French Gothic style. Approached from the southwest, this astonishing building suddenly rears up with all the marvellous strength of its elaborate and complex architecture, causing eye and mind to boggle at the sight. Another has described its weight, power and majesty thus: 'It crouches, heavily muscled, like some tumescent beast, waiting to spring.'[19] Despite the fact that its height greatly exceeds it length, the proportions somehow work. The soaring towers and spires and the lofty majesty of the exterior deceive the observer and the small size of the cathedral is not appreciated until the interior reveals the fact. 'Such richness and beauty have not elsewhere been condensed into so small an area.'[20] The building is unique in Ireland, but that was of no concern to Burges; he was a dreamer who lived long before his time: 'I was brought up in the 13th-century belief, and in that belief I intend to die.'[21] The architecture of the city that surrounded his cathedral was not his concern, and in ignoring it, he has given Cork, and Ireland, an architectural wonder of which to be proud. Without doubt it is the most richly decorated and, of its kind, the most beautiful cathedral of the Church of Ireland.

The Bishop's Palace to the west of the cathedral is a compact three-storey block with a fanlight doorway, built by Bishop Isaac Mann (1772–88) on the site of an earlier palace, a rambling building said to have dated from the 16th century.

References

1 C. A. Webster, *The diocese of Cork* (Cork, 1920), p. 276.
2 Richard Caulfield, *Annals of St Fin Barre's Cathedral, Cork* (Cork, 1871), p. 37.
3 Ibid., p. 40.
4 Ibid., p. 58.
5 T. M. Fallow, *The cathedral churches of Ireland* (London, 1894), p. 48.
6 Caulfield, *Annals of St Fin Barre's Cathedral, Cork*, p. 66.
7 Ibid., p. 92.
8 J. G. F. Day and H. E. Patton, *The cathedrals of the Church of Ireland* (London, 1932), p. 143.
9 Maurice Carey, *Saint Fin Barre's Cathedral* (Cork, 1984), p. 4.
10 Richard Caulfield, *A lecture on the history of the Bishops of Cork, and the Cathedral of St Fin Barre* (Cork, 1864), p. 36.
11 *Dublin Builder*, 1 Jan. 1865, p. 9.
12 Fallow, *Cathedral churches of Ireland*, pp 48–49.
13 Michael Quane, "Tour in Ireland by John Harden in 1797" in *Journal of the Cork Historical and Archaeological Society*, lx, no. 192 (1955), p. 80.
14 James Godkin, *Ireland and her churches* (London, 1867), p. 338
15 Caulfield, *Annals of St Fin Barre's Cathedral, Cork*, p. 102.
16 Ibid.
17 Charles Handley-Read, "St Fin Barre's Cathedral" in *Architectural Review*, cxi, no. 844 (June 1967), pp 423
18 *Irish Builder*, xx, no. 443 (1878), p. 163.
19 J. M. Crook, *William Burges and the High Victorian dream* (Chicago, 1981), p. 199.
20 Day and Patton, *The cathedrals of the Church of Ireland*, p. 145.
21 Carey, *St Fin Barre's Cathedral*, Cork, p. 9.

CORK

The Cathedral Church of St Mary and St Anne

Diocese of Cork (Roman Catholic)

CORK's Roman Catholic Cathedral was among the earliest of the post-Reformation Catholic cathedrals. It stands at the junction of Gerald Griffin Street and Roman Street and replaced an earlier church, built in 1730 by Bishop Thaddeus MacCarthy (1727–47) and known as the North Chapel or the Bishop's Chapel. Nothing is known of its appearance beyond a contemporary reference which described it as built 'in a Large and Sumptuous Manner.' (1)

Construction of the present cathedral began in 1799 during the episcopate of Bishop Francis Moylan (1787–1815), and the cathedral was dedicated on 22 August 1808 in the presence of the Archbishops of Dublin and Cashel. Moylan was typical of many Roman Catholic bishops in 18th century Ireland, taking a strong a line against any rebellion by Catholics against the civil authority. During and after the insurrection of 1798 and the French invasion of Ireland he issued pastoral instructions to his Diocese warning Catholics against 'those Atheistic principles of French Fraternity, which have deluged Christendom with blood and carnage'.[2] 'I felt it my duty to admonish warn you against the direful evils that riot and insubordination must inevitably entail for yourselves and your poor families.'[3] It may be coincidental that construction of the cathedral was beginning as the bishop issued his pastoral guidelines.

Little is known about the earliest stage of the building. An old tub-shaped Holy Water Font bearing the date 1799, now standing in the main porch of the south transept of the cathedral, provides the only evidence that construction began in that year. The new 'Chapel of the Blessed Virgin Mary', as it was called, was designed in the shape of a tau cross, consisting of a nave, galleried side aisles, transepts and an apse. The building was 33.2m long, 18.8m wide at the nave and aisles, and 27.4m wide at the transepts. The general style was Gothic 'the windows of the upper story being highly pointed, and those of the lower story, together with the doors, consisting of flat arches in trefoil form; and it is supported by cluster columns painted to represent jasper and porphyry with gilt bands.' The apse was 'highly ornamented with rich capitals, flutings, mouldings and the figure of the Mystical Dove', which were 'gilt, silvered or painted' to represent lapis lazuli or other precious marbles.[4]

The high altar was 4.5m long and surmounted by a tabernacle 3.3m high. Embossed on its door was the Lamb of the Apocalypse resting on the Book of Seven Seals. Above, in high relief was a representation of a Pelican feeding its young. On either side were monumental piers, upon each of which stood an angel supporting a four-lamped chandelier. Two kneeling angels graced the columns on either side of the tabernacle door. Each supported in one hand a chandelier similar to those flanking the pelican, and in the other hand each carried a palm branch intertwined with ears of corn, vine leaves and grapes. The palm branches united to form a canopy for Exposition of the Blessed Sacrament. This impressive tabernacle, described as 'unquestionably the first of its kind in Ireland' was of carved and gilt woodwork, and made in Lisbon by Italian craftsmen at a cost of £600.[5]

The identity of the architect of the Chapel is unknown. Francis Johnston of Dublin, an early exponent of the Gothic Revival, is one possibility; he designed a number of Gothic-style churches and chapels at the beginning of the 19th century. Sir Richard Morrison of Midleton, Co. Cork (1767–1849), first President of the Royal Institute of Architects of Ireland from 1839 has been suggested, as has Fr Matt Hogan, architect and priest, who designed churches in the environs of Cork. There is no consensus of the opinion. But the matter is now of academic interest since the cathedral has been subjected to so much alteration and addition that little remains of the original building.

The building was substantially damaged by an arson attack on 3 June 1820. The attack is said to have been sectarian in origin, and motivated by a controversial sermon on the Blessed Sacrament, preached on the Feast of Corpus Christi. With Emancipation becoming a distinct possibility, fears and animosities were running at a high level, and only with difficulty could the priests of the cathedral restrain members of their congregation from burning down the neighbouring Church of Ireland parish church of St Anne, Shandon.

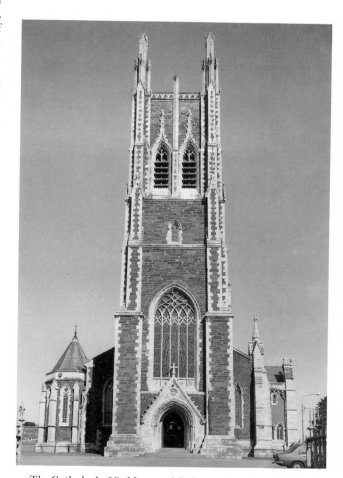

The Cathedral of St Mary and St Anne, Cork: the west front

The cathedral remained little more than a shell before rebuilding work began in 1828. The chosen architect was George Richard Pain (c.1779–1838) George and his brother John were pupils of Nash and came to Ireland c.1818. James went to Limerick but George remained in Cork. George Pain followed the *tau*-shape of the earlier building, but his interior design was described as 'one of the richest specimens of florid Gothic in Ireland.'[6] Pain's cathedral was 44.1m in length and 12.8m high. The north and south galleries were not rebuilt, but a large gallery was provided at the west end.

The chapter stalls were on the north and south sides of the chancel, and the bishop's throne was on the north side. The high altar was backed by a very high reredos reaching almost to the roof and adorned with twenty-seven wooden statues of the angels and apostles, each more than 1m high, carved in 1822 by the sculptor John Hogan (1800–58). The tabernacle was surmounted by a baldachino nearly as high as the reredos. The altar was flanked by curtained doorways which led to the sacristies. Above the doorways were two high pointed windows on either side of the reredos.

The alterations of 1963–4 have left only the seven bay aisled nave to indicate the style of Pain's work. The nave is divided from its aisles by clustered columns of marblised wood, probably with an iron or brick centre. The nave has elaborate stuccoed lierne vaulting which gives a somewhat dark and heavy feeling to the nave in contrast to the lofty and bright sanctuary; it has the feeling of the iron vaulting of a 19th century railway terminus. A vast gallery of sculptured nameless saints can be seen in the niches at clerestory level. The windows have trompe l'oeil decoration. The Stations of the Cross are small carved wooden panels dating from 1963–4. There is an organ gallery at the west end, above which can be seen a good west window, also dating from the reconstruction of 1963–4, depicting the Holy Spirit; the organ is of German make and was purchased in 1924. The heptagonal shaped former baptistery at the north west, added in the 1860s, now houses a shrine to the Blessed Virgin Mary. Mahogany confessional boxes are sited in the north and south nave aisles.

Pain's work was continued with the construction in 1862–1867 of the very florid west tower. The construction of the tower was due to phenomenal efforts of Canon Daniel Foley (d. 1875). Canon Foley had decided that the cathedral should have a tower, but because of the shortage of funds, he himself acted as clerk of works, director of operations, mason and labourer. It is not clear whether the Canon was actually the architect of the tower, or whether that function was filled by Sir John Benson, the City Architect of Cork. The tower is the most interesting feature of the exterior. It is built of irregular blocks of dark-red sandstone with limestone dressings, and has elaborate but oddly truncated pinnacles. Despite the addition of the tower, the cathedral was described in 1869 as 'an edifice worthy only – in external appearance at least – of a country parish.' The tower itself was called 'a memorial of the great zeal and perseverance of an humble priest who sought in some degree to rescue the Cathedral from obscurity.'[7]

Perhaps conscious of these criticisms by the *Cork Examiner*, and also of the rising glory of Burges' Cathedral of St Fin Barre (1865–79) on the other side of the Lee, Bishop William Delaney (1847–86) convened a meeting of Cork citizens in 1868, to discuss the further improvements to the cathedral. The tower tended 'to make the meanness of the church building more conspicuous'[8], and Benson was asked to produce designs for a total reconstruction of the cathedral. He proposed to enlarge the cathedral by extending its length from 44.1m to 71.9m, its width from 18.8m at the nave and 27.4m at the transepts, to 19.05m and 35.5m respectively, and the tower from 46.3m to 85.3m by the addition of a spire. He produced an impressive vision of a cruciform cathedral, transepts with rose windows, a fleche at the crossing, and an apsidal chancel lit by very tall Decorated windows. Had his designs been effected, Cork would now possess two French Gothic cathedrals on either side of its river.

Benson's design progressed very little beyond the visionary stage. He strengthened the buttresses of the tower, and added the parapets and pinnacles, and the 14th century style west door, but no further work was done after July 1869, and the rest of his plan was abandoned, probably on the grounds of cost.

Following the liturgical decrees of the Second Vatican Council (1962–5), Bishop Cornelius Lucey (1952–80) decided to reorder the cathedral. The result was a savage destruction of the entire east end of the cathedral, and the removal of many memorials, including that to Bishop John Murphy (1815–47) by John Hogan can be seen in the mortuary chapel. It shows two boy angels on either side of a bust of the bishop, supporting mitre, staff and crozier. The memorial to Bishop Francis Moylan by Turnerelli can be seen in the small-group liturgy chapel. The 1730 foundation stone of the early cathedral, sited high on the wall in a prominent place near the Twelfth Station, was quite unnecessarily covered by plaster.

George Pain's transepts and apse were demolished and the present shallow three bay transepts and a three bay aisled chancel were built in 1963–4 to designs by J.R. Boyd Barrett. The new design extended the cathedral eastwards by a further 21.3m, and provided a new sacristy, conference room, mortuary chapel, and a complex of basement rooms. The new sanctuary has facings of limestone, pre-cast concrete and bes-stone, which harmonises with the limestone/sandstone construction of the 19th-century tower and spire, without reproducing its style.

The new sanctuary has a quadripartite vaulted ceiling, a parquet floor of oak and mahogany, and a communion rail of mahogany. The stained glass windows – the centre one representing the Crucified Christ – are set in abstract designs of blue, green and yellow. The east window has trompe l'oeil moulding. All other side windows in the cathedral are geometrical in character and have neutral colouring relieved only by purple uprights; a crucifix-motif is built into each of these windows. The cathedra is in the north chancel aisle, flanked by three chapter stalls on each side; six further stalls are in the south chancel aisle; throne and stalls are made of oak. The former high altar, of white marble with panels of mosaic and onyx colonettes, has been retained, though superseded by a new oak altar. The 19th-century oak pulpit, wine glass in shape and hexagonal in plan, has been retained at the south west of the new sanctuary. The panels portray scenes depicting the Annunciation, the Nativity, the Flight into Egypt, the Crucifixion, and the Assumption of the Blessed Virgin Mary. Presumably there were at one time flanking side altars in the north and south chancel aisles, which now have a feeling of emptiness.

The north transept has been screened off from the body of the cathedral by a partition of wood and glass to provide a small chapel separate from the cathedral; it appears to be unused at present. The south transept contains a late 19th-century Pieta of white marble.

The tower, although massive and heavy, is easily the most attractive part of the cathedral; the combination of the rich, dark-red sandstone and the off-white limestone is very striking. Sandstone and limestone were used to construct the nave and chancel but the shades are paler; tower and chancel are so different in this respect that there is almost a degree of mutual embarrassment. But the contrast between the two stones is strong and gives the building some style.

The Cathedral Church of St Mary and St Anne is a composite architectural entity from several periods; an 1828 nave, an 1862–7 tower and a 1963–4 chancel and transepts; the work of successive architects who have, with due regard for their predecessors in the task, attempted to complete the cathedral, while leaving their own mark. Moving from the low dark nave to the lofty bright sanctuary is much like moving from one building to another. Looking from the west end of the nave to the new sanctuary is not unlike seeing light at the end of the tunnel.

The cathedral is an odd and interesting mixture; a tantalising architectural curiosity, with the incomplete tower standing as a symbol of Benson's unfulfilled vision. The type of Gothic that he envisaged would not find favour in these days of liturgical and architectural simplicity. But if his plans had been implemented, Cork's Roman Catholic cathedral would have been a fitting companion to its Church of Ireland counterpart across the river.

References

1 M. A. Bolster, *Cathedral of St Mary and St Anne* (Cork, n.d.), p. 4.
2 Francis Moylan, *Pastoral instruction to the Roman Catholics of the diocese of Cork* (Dublin, 1798), p. 14.
3 Francis Moylan, *Doctor Francis Moylan to the lower order of the Roman catholic inhabitants of the diocese of Cork* (Cork, 1799).
4 Bolster, *Cathedral of St Mary and St Anne*, p. 6.
5 Ibid., pp 6–7.
6 Ibid., p. 9.
7 Ibid., p. 13.
8 Ibid.

DERRY

The Cathedral Church of St Columb

Diocese of Derry (Church of Ireland)

LONDONDERRY, with a population of 63,000, is the second city of Northern Ireland and a prominent commercial centre. It stands on an oval hill above the River Foyle in Co. Londonderry still surrounded by 17th-century walls. The official name 'Londonderry' has been in use since the royal charter of 1613, but it was known as 'Derry' (Doire – oakwood) for nearly a thousand years before that date, and it is usually known as such today. Both the Roman Catholic and Church of Ireland bishops have always been styled Bishops of Derry.

A monastery was founded here by the great St Columba (feast-day 9 June) on this wooded hill to the west of the Foyle *c.* 545 or 546. The site of his monastery may possibly be that now occupied by St Columb's Cathedral, but there is no firm evidence. Columba was born in Co. Donegal in 521, into a minor ruling family. he left Derry in 563 to found a monastery on Iona off the Scottish coast and died there in 597. He is also known as Columcille, meaning Columba of the churches, an allusion to the many churches that he founded.

The Synod of Ráith Bressail in 1111 created a diocese for Tír Conaill, and after hesitating between Derry and Raphoe, the synod selected the latter. Ardstraw was chosen as the see for a diocese comprising the western part of the territory of Cehel Tír Eogain (Tyrone), excluding the Inis Eogain (Inishowen) peninsula, which was assigned to Derry–Raphoe, as well as the east of Co. Londonderry, which was assigned to Connor. It is not clear how far Ardstraw functioned as diocesan see. No names of bishops have been recorded, and it was replaced at the Synod of Kells–Mellifont by the obscure site of Ráith Lúraig (better known as Maghera). The choice was motivated partly by the wish to affirm Tír Eoghain control over the eastern part of what is now Co. Londonderry, and secondly by a desire for an episcopal see which not be overshadowed by the great Columban church at Derry, whose abbot was given mitred status in 1158. But Derry was too important for this situation to last, and *c.* 1247 Bishop Gilla in Choimded Ó Cerballáin (*c.* 1230–79) transferred the see from Maghera to Derry; the transfer was confirmed by Pope Innocent IV on 4 November 1254.

St Columb's Cathedral, Derry: the chancel

A church, later known as Dubh-Regles (Black Abbey), was the earliest known church on the site; its ruins were still visible in 1520, but nothing now remains. Derry and its churches were burned in 1135 and 1148, and Dubh-Regles was superseded in 1164 by a new large church, constructed a short distance away by Abbot Flaithbertach Ua Brolcháin which was to become the cathedral of the diocese. Known as Templemore (great church) it was 73m long and is said to have been one of the most splendid ecclesiastical buildings in Ireland before the arrival of the Anglo-Normans. Dubh-Regles and Templemore stood in the district now known as Long Tower, immediately outside the city walls to the south-west of the present cathedral.

During the course of the rebellion of Shane O'Neill (1566–7) the English garrison used the cathedral as an arsenal. An accidental explosion in 1568 left Templemore and much of the city in ruins. The garrison withdrew, and Derry was left to its own devices until government forces under the command of Sir Henry Docwra reoccupied the city in 1600. Docwra demolished the medieval ruins, with the exception of the tower, and used the stonework for fortifications. It is thought to have been a 10th-century Round Tower and was still standing in 1689; only the stump, used as an ice-house, remained in 1802, and this has now gone. the Roman Catholic Church of St Columba (known as the Long Tower Church) stands on the site.

After the suppression of another insurrection by Sir Cahir O'Doherty in 1608 James I invited the city of London to colonise 'the late ruinated city of Derry'. The City Corporation founded The Honourable the Irish Society in 1610. In 1613 the society received a royal charter of incorporation, one of its provisions being that the city was to be renamed Londonderry. the earthwork fortifications of Sir Henry Docwra, which had been overrun in 1608, were replaced by the present stone walls between 1614 and 1618.

The cathedral having been demolished, its congregation had to make do with a repaired medieval fragment of St

Augustine's Abbey. A visitation of 1622 reported that 'The Cathedral Church of St Colum of Derry hath not so much as any ruins left. Neither is there any other Cathedral or Parish Church built insteade thereof, within ye City of Londonderry. The small Church called S. Augustines which yet remayneth and is not yet capable of half ye auditory, belongeth to a disused Monastery.' The small 19th-century Gothic Revival St Augustine's Church on the West Wall, fronting Grand Parade, stands on the site of the abbey.

In 1628 the foundations of the new cathedral were laid on a new site at the summit of the hill within the city walls. It was built by William Parrott and completed in 1633 at a cost of £4,000 and dedicated to St Columb. A stone inside the porch includes the famous inscription indicating the generosity of the City of London's Irish Society:

> IF STONES COULD SPEAKE
>
> THEN LONDONS PRAYSE
>
> SHOULD SOUNDE WHO
>
> BUILT THIS CHURCH AND
>
> CITTIE FROM THE GROUNDE

The cathedral had an aisled nave, a short chancel accommodated within the body of the nave, a south porch and a short west tower; galleries were added to the aisles in the Georgian period. the parapets of the aisles and clerestory were crenellated. Although parts of the cathedral have been rebuilt, the masonry throughout is rubble schist with sandstone. A spire of wood covered with lead originally surmounted the tower. The lead was taken down and stored while repairs were undertaken, and it provided a useful supply for bullets during the siege of 1689, when the cathedral suffered considerable damage. The spire was converted to provide a platform for artillery fire and was subsequently dismantled.

A new spire was constructed in 1776–8 on the orders of the eccentric and colourful Frederick Hervey, subsequently 4th Earl of Bristol, who became Bishop of Derry at the age of thirty-eight in 1768. The Earl-Bishop provided £1,000 to raise the height of the tower by 6.4m and add an octagonal pyramidal spire of ashlar with a gilt copper ball crowned by a copper weather-vane at the summit. The new spire raised the total height of the structure to 69.4m. Inevitably the spire was found to be too heavy for the tower, and the Earl-Bishop lived to see both taken down in 1802, one year before his death. A new tower was erected in the same year with the help of the Irish Society, and the cathedral was reopened in 1805.

The 17th-century roof was removed and replaced in 1820–23, the cathedral remaining roofless for a year. A new ashlar spire was added to the tower, possibly to designs by John

Bowden, bringing the height to 58.2m. The massive western four-storey tower has thin clasping buttresses, regular string courses and octagonal pinnacles. Both tower and spire blend well with the 17th-century cathedral.

In a restoration of 1861–2 Joseph Welland removed the north and south Georgian galleries from the aisles, leaving the west gallery in position; the entrance porch in the tower was refitted with Minton encaustic tiles; and the box pews were removed from the body of the nave and replaced with the present pews. The bishop's throne, now on the south side of the nave between the fifth and sixth piers, was placed there by Welland in 1861. The 18th-century Chinese Chippendale mahogany chair is set within an impressively carved and pinnacled 19th-century throne. The brass eagle lectern was a gift in 1868.

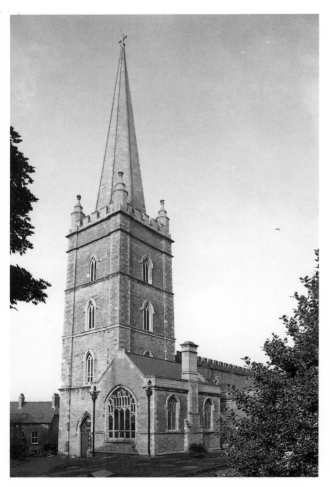

Derry: the west end of St Columb's Cathedral

Further alterations were made in 1885, when John Guy Ferguson extended the nave by an extra bay to the east and added a two-bay aisled chancel which contains the chapter stalls. The eastward extent of the 17th-century cathedral is marked by the external semi-cylindrical turrets on the north and south walls. Ferguson added the crocketed dome finials. The chancel is 10.6m long and was added in accordance with the intentions of the original builders. The foundations had been laid in 1633 and were discovered during building operations. The chancel is divided from the nave by a stone screen with quatrefoil piercings set within round frames.

The east window had been provided with its unusual tracery, part perpendicular, part foliated, by Welland. Ferguson kept it and inserted it in the new chancel. The smaller Decorated windows of the side chapels are Ferguson's own design. A small and ill-designed chapel was created in the south chancel aisle in memory of Mary Irvine, who died on 4 July 1972; the altar, cross and candlesticks are uncomfortably small. The north chancel aisle houses the organ. The seven-bay aisled nave is now 34.7m long and has a clerestory which rests on arcades springing from octagonal piers. Ferguson also removed the plaster vaults from the nave and aisle roofs and replaced them with the present Perpendicular timber trusses. Carved representations of the heads of the Bishops of Derry act as corbel stops for the main trusses.

In 1889 further improvements were made by Thomas Drew, who removed the nave pulpit and replaced it with the present octagonal pulpit of Caen stone with brown marble shafts, on the north side of the crossing. Drew also added the ornate and fussy reredos of Caen stone which makes the usual mistake of rising above the window-sill and obscuring part of the east window; it contains mosaic cartouches of the four Evangelists together with St Patrick and St Columba. The central part was given by the clergy ordained in the cathedral. Drew also added the Chapter House and vestry at the south-west in 1910.

All the stained glass is post-1860; the east window of *c.*1865 depicts the Ascension and Christ's charge to the Apostles. The recent troubles in Northern Ireland claimed most of the glass in the north nave aisle, which was shattered by a bomb blast in 1989. Detailed photographs have enabled it to be replaced. The aisle windows are in groups of low cusped lancets, three in the south aisle and four in the north, set within a flat, shallow, segmental arch with a segmental hood mould above.

The cathedral possess a peal of thirteen bells, the two oldest of which were presented by the Irish Society in 1614 and 1620. In 1638 Charles I presented five larger bells, and a further bell was added, in 1671. It was these bells which 'rung most chearfully' when the news of a relieving force was received by the citizens of the town after a siege lasting 105 days in 1689. They were recast in 1928, and further five bells were added.

The former Bishop's Palace adjoining the cathedral in Bishop Street stands on the site of an Augustinian convent. The palace was built *c.* 1761 in the episcopate of Bishop William

Barnard (1747–68). It is a square Georgian five-bay block of three storeys; the central three bays are recessed. it was largely rebuilt in the late 18th century for the Earl-Bishop and repaired for Bishop William Knox (1803–31) at the beginning of his episcopate after temporary use a a barracks. The palace has been used as a Masonic Hall since 1945. The spacious Georgian Deanery, adjacent to the cathedral, is still in use, although its has been damaged many times by bomb attacks on the adjacent courthouse.

St Columb's Cathedral is an interesting example of 17th-century Ulster Gothic, known as Planter's Gothic or Gothic Survival. As a product of the reformed church, it was de-signed as a rectangular auditorium, which it remains, even with the addition of Ferguson's chancel. The high site of the cathedral sheltering behind the old city walls, its but-tresses, lancet windows, domed turrets and crenellated para-pets, give it a somewhat fortified and defensive appearance. Given the history of the city and its successive cathedrals, this is not surprising. Derry has been the focus of much trouble in the current period of strife, and the cathedral has been subjected to a number of serious bomb attacks, causing many of its congregation to leave the area.It is to the credit of successive clergy, organists and members of the choir and congregation that St Columb's Cathedral con-tinues to function, maintaining a full choral cathedral serv-ice, refusing to bow to the intimidation of periodic acts of violence. On a positive and encouraging note, defiant marches of reconciliation have taken place in recent years between St Columb's and St Eugene's, its sister cathedral in Derry.

DERRY

The Cathedral Church of St Eugene

Diocese of Derry (Roman Catholic)

*T*HE decision to build a cathedral for the Roman Catholic Diocese of Derry was taken at a public meeting in the Long Tower Girls' School in February 1838. But the early years were occupied with fund-raising and the foundation stone was not laid until 26 July 1851. The guid-ing force behind the construction was Bishop Francis Kelly, who was Coadjutor Bishop of Derry from 1849 until 1864, when he succeeded the elderly Bishop John MacLaughlin as Diocesan Bishop; he remained Bishop of Derry until his death on 1 September 1889 at the age of seventy-seven. Bishop Kelly is buried in the vault below the cathedral sanc-tuary, and the east window, showing the Crucifixion with seven Irish saints below, was given in his memory in Decem-ber 1891.

St Eugene's Cathedral is built on a triangular hillside sight bordered by Great James Street, Infirmary Road, Francis Street and Creggan Street. The basic building material is green schist with Mourne granite dressings and sandstone tracery in the windows; the west front is of granite. It is a plain Gothic Revival building 'conceived in the hard, spare, Gothic introduced into Ireland in the early 1840s by Pugin'.[1] The first architect, whose name is unknown, was reported to have 'made grave errors in building the foundations'[2] and was swiftly replaced by J. J. McCarthy (1817–82), who was assisted by Charles Whelan. McCarthy was the Irish Pugin of his day and influenced the development of Gothic Revival architecture in Ireland during the second half of the nine-teenth century. The builder was Robert Maxwell, and the total cost, excluding later additions, was £40,000. Former Derry residents who had emigrated to the U.S.A. contrib-uted £4,000; the remainder was raised in the city and the diocese.

The construction of the main body of the cathedral took twenty-two years, and the building was dedicated on 4 May 1873. The Bishop's Palace in the cathedral precincts, also by McCarthy, was completed in the same year. Because the building of Catholic schools was perceived to be a priority at the time, construction of the spire was delayed until April 1899. Work began in August 1900 and was completed in June 1903. The 14th-century-style 78m spire with crocketed pinna-cles was designed by E. J. Toye. Toye added cusped and crocketed canopies for six statues in 1904, and the gate lodge was constructed in the same year. The cathedral was sol-emnly consecrated in April 1936.

St Eugene's Cathedral is a nine-bay rectangle internally di-vided into a six-bay aisled nave and a three-bay aisled chan-cel, both with clerestory. The total internal measurements are 66.1m long by 22.8m wide; the height of the roof to the outer ridge is 29.2m. the nave is 47.8m long and 10.6m wide. The two eastern bays constitute a rather short chancel, and the nave aisles extent to form flanking chapels to the chan-cel. The arcades are supported by piers of Scottish freestone with Corinthian capitals. The nave has a hipped, panelled ceiling with the shafts of the roof trusses resting on twenty-six corbel heads. When seen from the exterior, a slightly lower roof indicates the chancel, but there is no appreciable differ-ence on the interior. The east gable has buttresses and paired octagonal finials. There is an entrance porch on the second bay of the south chancel aisle.

The bishop's throne, by Meyer & Co. of Munich, was in-stalled in April 1898. Meyer also provided much of the stained glass for the cathedral between 1880 and 1896. The original pulpit, font and reredos, by Early & Powell, were of Caen stone with red Middleton marble and green Clifden marble and were installed in 1878. The pulpit had a spire and canopy of Austrian oak by Ferdinand Stufflesser & Co. and was designed by E. J. Toye in 1906. The altar rail was of Caen

Interior of St Eugene's Cathedral

stone supported by marble pillars with iron tracery forming arches in between. An elaborate carved stone organ gallery at the west end is supported by columns of dark-grey polished granite.

A temporary wooden altar was inserted in May 1967 in accordance with the liturgical requirements of the Second Vatican Council (1962–5), and this was replaced by a more extensive but still temporary reordering in December 1975, when a dais and altar designed by Liam McCormick & partners were installed. Although temporary, they remained in position until 1989, when a professional and permanent reordering took place.

A thorough and complete restoration of St Eugene's Cathedral took place in the period 1985–9 at a cost of nearly £1.2 million. An inspection of the exterior in 1985 revealed that the stonework of the tower and spire and the tracery of the windows was in need of urgent restoration, and the entire slate roof had to be replaced. The fine hillside site had exposed the cathedral to the ravages of the weather, and the industrial pollution of an urban atmosphere had contributed to the staining and deterioration of the exterior. As well as the requirements of Vatican II, the smoke produced by the burning of votive candles for more than a decade had made a redecoration of the interior a necessity.

The first phase of the work took place between June 1985 and March 1986 and involved the re-slating of the roof, the replacement of some badly damaged stonework, and the complete repointing and cleaning of the exterior.

The cathedral had always suffered from inadequate sacristy space, and a second phase of work, completed in March 1988, involved the construction of a new sacristy adjacent to the old sacristy, which was converted into two reconciliation (confessional) rooms. The new sacristy has a conference room above and a new boiler room and store in the basement. This new block has a steeply pitched slated roof and a facing of Donegal granite. In a recess above the doorway between the cathedral and the sacristy can be seen eight wooden figures which used to adorn the canopy of the old pulpit.

The third phase of work took place between June and December 1989. The cathedral was closed for six months to allow a complete cleaning and restoration of the interior and a permanent reordering of the sanctuary to replace the 'temporary' work of 1975. The walls and ceilings were cleaned and repainted; the sandstone windows, columns and arcades were cleaned; the Caen stone reredoses and Stations of the Cross were also cleaned, and the cathedral was generally provided with a new floor covering and new oak pews. The cathedral was also made more accessible for the disabled. Fourteen new standard brass electroliers were installed in the nave. The ceiling is now a dusky pink colour with some stencil decoration.

The reordered sanctuary includes a new floor of Sardinian granite, and a new altar, ambo, font, celebrant's chair and tabernacle baldachino of Carrara and Macedonian marbles.

Derry: St Eugene's Cathedral from the south

The tabernacle itself is of silver-plated bronze and was made and decorated by Peter Donovan of Kilkenny. Some panels from the pre-1967 high altar and pulpit have been incorporated into the lower part of the original reredos, which has been retained. The shrine to Our Lady remains in the south chancel aisle, and a new altar has been created in the north chancel aisle for visiting priests to say private masses. The bishop's throne is on the south side of the new sanctuary. The circular font on the north side bears the inscription 'SPRINGS OF THE LORD GIVE HIM GLORY AND PRAISE FOR EVER'.

The entire restoration work of 1985–9 was under the supervision of Joseph Tracey, and the result is a credit to Bishop Edward Daly and the priests and people of the diocese who laboured to raise the large sum required to produce this clean and bright cathedral.

The newly restored cathedral was rededicated on Sunday 17

December 1989. 'We can say "Rejoice" because we now have this beautiful Gothic cathedral restored and maintained to serve this diocese and city...in coming centuries. by carrying out this work, we have been responding to the Lord's command, "not to lose faith" in Him. We have been handed on that faith by those who built this cathedral more than 100 years ago and we are now in our turn, handing on that same faith to those who are to come in future generations.'[3]

References

1 Alistair Rowan, *North-west Ulster* (London, 1979), p. 383.
2 Ibid.
3 From the sermon by Bishop Edward Daly at the rededication of St Eugene's Cathedral on Sunday 17 December 1989.

DOWNPATRICK

The Cathedral Church of the Holy and Undivided Trinity

Diocese of Down (Church of Ireland)

DOWNPATRICK, 33km south of Belfast and 51.2km north-east of Newry, is the ancient county town of Down, overlooking the marshy vale of the River Quoile. The town was a place of importance long before the arrival of St Patrick in the 5th century and was anciently called Dún Da Léith-Glas (fort of the two broken fetters), or simply An Dun (the fort). Patrick converted local chieftains and founded a monastery on land given to him by the ruler of Ulidia. Traces of the ditch and bank of a large hill-fort, Ráth Celtchair, the site of Patrick's monastery, can be seen to the south-west of the cathedral.

St Patrick died at Saul, 3.2km to the north-east, about the year 461. But the place of his burial caused some contention between Armagh and Down, both desiring to have the honour. Eventually, neither side being willing to give way, the body was placed on a cart to which two untamed oxen were yoked. They were then released without guidance. 'They went forth and stopped on the site of the present Cathedral of Downpatrick where, since the year 700, when MacCumacthenius wrote, the body has been believed to lie, for that ancient writer tells us that when they were building a church at Downpatrick, the workmen coming on the relics of St Patrick were compelled to desist by the flames which issued from the tomb.'[1]

The reputed grave of the saint lies in the churchyard to the south-west of the cathedral. The site is marked by a piece of fanciful Victorian romanticism, a great unhewn slab of granite inscribed with a Celtic cross and the name PATRAIC in Gaelic characters. The slab was placed on this site in 1901 by Francis Joseph Bigger of the Belfast Naturalist Field Club. The reasons for the choice of this site are unclear; there is no proof that this is the site of the saint's grave. But there is no serious dispute that he is buried at Downpatrick, 'for it is an unbroken tradition of such antiquity that he who denies it may safely question the evidence for the Saint's existence at all'.[2]

The town was designated as the see of a diocese for the territory of Ulidia at the Synod of Ráith Bressail in 1111, and the first diocesan bishop was Mael Muire who died in 1117. In 1124 Máel Maedoc Ó Morgair (St Malachy) became Bishop of Down and set to work to repair, enlarge and beautify the cathedral; but because of later destruction, it is unlikely that any of his work remains.

Among the Anglo-Norman newcomers to Ireland was an adventurous knight, John de Courcy, who in 1177 put into practice an audacious plan to convert the kingdom of Ulster (then comprising the area of the present counties of Antrim and Down) into an independent principality of his own. De Courcy marched north to Downpatrick, which he took after a hard-fought campaign, thereafter using it as his seat. Some six years later the 'relics' of St Patrick, St Brigid and St Columba were 'discovered' at Down, and de Courcy took the opportunity to rename the town Downpatrick (*Dún Pádraig* – fort of Patrick). He expelled the secular canons from the cathedral in 1183 and replaced them with Benedictine monks from Chester, reconstituting the ancient monastery as a Benedictine priory. Down was the only Irish cathedral chapter in the care of the Benedictine Order. To appease the native Irish he ordered that the dedication of the cathedral be changed from 'the Holy and Undivided Trinity' to 'St Patrick of Down'; the ancient dedication was restored in 1609.

The cathedral suffered on several occasions during various squabbles for control of Ulster. In 1204 de Courcy's lands were granted to the rival de Lacy family by King John who had become suspicious of his increasing power. While at prayer in the cathedral de Courcy was seized by the de Lacys, but not before he had killed fourteen of his assailants. He escaped and ravaged Down in alliance with the King of Man but never regained control of his Ulster territories. The rest of his life is obscure. He was reconciled to King John in 1210 and died *c.* 1219.

The fighting for control of Ulster seems to have affected the cathedral, since as early as 1220 the Bishop of Down sent some of his monks to England with a shrine containing relics of St Patrick and others 'begging some little place of refuge until his church should be rebuilt'.[3] The cathedral and town were damaged by an earthquake in 1245 and plundered by the Scots in 1315, when the cathedral was burnt. The continuous strife between the Irish and the English settlers prevented much in the way of restoration from being done. By the beginning of the 16th century, the cathedral was described as 'gone to ruin in walls and roof'.[4] It was rebuilt in 1512, but wrecked in 1538 and used for the stabling of horses by Lord Grey, the Lord Deputy of Ireland, as part of the suppression of the monasteries. Grey's destruction of the cathedral formed one of the charges on which he was executed in 1541. The cathedral then remained in ruins until it was restored late in the 18th century.

Previous writers about Downpatrick Cathedral have long believed the present cathedral to be only the chancel of the medieval cathedral. It was a widely held assumption that the nave and transepts were destroyed in one of the many catastrophes that befell the town. This theory is now generally discredited. The nave and transepts, if they were ever built, would have made the cathedral a building of considerable extent, as what remains measures 32.6m long and 17.4m wide. More substantial evidence has been provided by excavations which have failed to reveal any trace of foundations of the conjectured nave and chancel. There is no proof that they were ever built, and the history of the several destructions of the cathedral suggests that they may not have been.

Though it was roofless and desolate, the Dean and Chapter still thought of the old building as the cathedral church of the diocese, and restoration plans were considered from time to time. In 1637 Bishop Henry Leslie wrote to Archbishop Laud of Canterbury telling him of his plan to restore the cathedral and seeking his aid in procuring a government grant. No money was forthcoming, and the Confederate war of the 1640s, followed by the Cromwellian regime, ended the proposal.

Downpatrick Cathedral remained in ruins for 250 years, and in 1662, a royal charter of Charles II, raised the parish church of Lisburn to the status of a cathedral church to serve both the diocese of Down and the diocese of Connor, whose cathedral was also in ruins. Despite this, the Dean and Chapter still regarded the ruined building as the cathedral church and during the first half of the 18th century three bishops were enthroned and five deans were installed in the old cathedral.

Downpatrick Cathedral from the north-west

Even in its ruined state the cathedral was an impressive site. John Wesley, the founder of Methodism, visited Downpatrick in 1778 and was moved by what he saw: 'It is a noble ruin, the largest building I have ever seen in the Kingdom. Adjoining it is one of the most beautiful groves covering the side of the sloping hill.' Another eye witness in 1744 said: 'It stands within 200 paces of the Town on the Ascent of the Hill, and is yet venerable in its Ruins.'[5] Small items connected with the cathedral were occasionally unearthed, such as lead, stained glass, carved stones and occasionally human bones. In c.1728 an Agnus Dei (a figure of a lamb representing Christ) was found 'which being.....Freestone, an ignorant Servant maid brayed it to Powder for domestick uses'.[6]

In 1790, owing to the energy of Dean William Annesley (1787–1817) and the 1st Marquess of Downshire, an act of parliament was sponsored to permit the restoration of the cathedral, and a grant of £1,000 was made by the crown. The restoration may have envisaged the construction of nave and transepts, since difficulty in raising funds compelled the planners to curtail their plans and restore the chancel alone.

Most of the restoration work was finished by 1818, but the construction of the octagonal vestibule and perpendicular tower was delayed for several years because of lack of funds. When Richard Mant became Bishop of Down and Connor in

Downpatrick: the south side of the nave shows the bishop's throne

The ruins of the cathedral were described by Archdall in 1786: 'The roof was supported by five handsome arches which composed a central aisle of twenty-six feet in breadth, two lateral ones of thirteen feet each, and the whole structure is one hundred feet long. The heads of the pillars and arches, the tops of the windows, the tops of the windows, and many niches in the walls, were adorned with a variety of sculptures, some parts of which yet remain. At the east end is a very lofty and magnificent window, and over it are three handsome niches, in which niches the pedestals, whereon stood the Saints Patrick, Colomb, and Brigid still remain. Adjoining the east end of the church are two square columns in one of which was a winding staircase leading to the roof.'[7]

1823, the work still remained to be done. 'The building at a distance looks well, and would be a fine feature in the county, if the tower were completed; but from deficiency of funds, that has not been carried above the level of the roof, and whether it will be ever raised higher depends, I suppose, upon the liberality of the gentlemen of the county.'[8] Liberality was forthcoming, and the tower was completed in 1826. Dean Annesley did not live to see the completion of the work for which he had laboured hard, giving 300 p.a. from his own income; he died in 1817.

The appointed architect was Charles Lilly, who was less concerned with preservation and restoration of surviving detail than with desiring to produce an overall medieval effect; as a result, much surviving medieval work was probably obscured. It is not clear how much of the medieval cathedral remains and to what period it dates. It is unlikely that anything now standing predates the burning by Edward Bruce in 1315, but there may be substantial stonework dating from the restoration of 1512. The east window and the three small niches above were retained by Lilly, and many of the capitals of the piers are original 14th- or 15th-century work. But the present appearance of the cathedral is mainly an 18th-century architect's conjectural restoration of how the medieval cathedral should have looked — even if it actually did not.

Downpatrick Cathedral is essentially a rectangle, 33.5m long by 19.8m wide, with a pinnacled three-storey tower at the west end. At either side of the eastern gable is a square turret, and above the east window are three small arched niches, described by Archdall in 1786, containing mutilated effigies of St Patrick, St Brigid and St Columba. Previous authors have described it as 'a stately embattled building',[9] a view deriving in part from bristling obelisks which rise from the aisle parapets like silent sentries.

The interior is arranged in a manner not unusual in Ireland; the entire building is treated as a cathedral 'choir'. This arrangement was designed to suit a building that was of both parish church and cathedral church status. The officiant is separated from the cathedral chapter by the congregation, and the throne of the bishop is set in the midst of the people. More or less similar arrangements can be seen at Achonry, Cashel, Cloyne, Killala, Leighlin and Rosscarbery Cathedrals.

Five pointed arches of cut freestone supported by massive piers of rubble masonry divide the building to produce side aisles. The ceiling, springing from corbels between the arches, is groined in plaster and ornamented with bosses of foliage. The westernmost bay is divided from the others by a wooden screen, on the eastern side of which are canopied returned stalls for the Dean and Chapter. The organ above the screen was built by the English organ-builder Samuel Green for George III in the late 18th century. It is alleged to have spent its early life in one of the royal chapels, though there is no evidence for this, before the king presented it to the cathedral in 1802. It was rebuilt in 1914 and 1966, but Green's original pipework remains intact.

The congregation are accommodated in bow-fronted collegiate-style pews facing in towards the central aisle. The bishop's throne is placed at the centre of the north side. The centre area between the pews is now filled with movable chairs which replaced Victorian pews that were not part of Lilly's restoration and added later only to provide additional seating. The nave and sanctuary are lit partly by standard electroliers. The sanctuary floor is paved with mosaic, and the altar is raised on three steps of grey marble. A wooden

reredos overshadows and dominates the wooden altar, leaving it almost invisible; it would benefit by the addition of a frontal and candles. The high east window above contains stained glass by Ballantyne of Edinburgh.

The south aisle houses an 11th-century granite 'font', discovered in a yard in English Street in 1927 and placed in the cathedral in 1931. It had served as a watering trough for many years and may originally have been the base of a cross.

Nothing remains of the monastic buildings which stood on the north side of the cathedral; whatever remained was removed in the 18th-century restoration. A number of ancient tombstones were certainly destroyed at the time of the restoration. But the worst loss was the Round Tower which had stood next to the cathedral since before 1015. It was 20.1m high, with an inside diameter of 2.4m and was removed allegedly because it was unsafe but more likely because its presence spoiled the appearance of the proposed restoration; its stones were used in the construction of the present tower. The Round Tower stood on the west side of "St Patrick's Grave" on raised ground which may conceal its foundations.[10] To the east of the cathedral is a reconstructed 9th- or 10th-century High Cross which formerly stood in the centre of the town. The fragments were re-erected in the cathedral grounds in 1987.

Downpatrick is one of a handful of Irish cathedrals without a parish, and this caused severe problems at the time of Disestablishment in 1871. The cathedral was left totally disendowed and was even closed for a brief period as a place of worship. For a time its future was in doubt, and there was a strong possibility that it would have to be abandoned. Since Down, Dromore and Connor were united dioceses under a single bishop, and unlikely to be separated, was there any point in maintaining a cathedral at Downpatrick when those at Dromore and Lisburn would be sufficient for all requirements? The debate was settled on 8 March 1872 when the Bishop of Down, Dromore and Connor presided at a meeting of the gentry and nobility of Co. Down to discuss the future of the cathedral. The meeting agreed 'that the cathedral of Down should be kept up as a diocesan cathedral'[11], and that subscriptions should be raised for its support; it was estimated that £400 p.a. would be required.

Downpatrick Cathedral survived the catharsis of Disestablishment, and continues to survive, with a dedicated congregation, who have undertaken two major restorations in recent years. In 1952–3, the windows were reframed and reglazed; three of the pinnacles were restored; the stonework around the tower windows was replaced; and the roof slates and timbers were replaced, repaired or treated; all at a total cost of £53,000. A second major restoration, at a cost of £600,000 took place in the years 1985–7, during which time the cathedral was closed. The exterior was sandblasted, and the interior walls were replastered and painted. The central Victorian pews were removed, and the black and white tiled pavement on which they had stood was replaced by flagstones. The cathedral was rehallowed on 29 October 1987.

Although the site has a long history, there is very little genuine medieval detail to be seen at Downpatrick Cathedral. The building is really an 18th-century architect's vision of how he would have liked a medieval cathedral to have looked. It can be seen as the first of the 19th-century 'thorough' restorations of dilapidated or ruined cathedrals, to be followed by Armagh, Kildare, and St Patrick's and Christ Church in Dublin. But for all that it represents Charles Lilly's highly subjective vision of Gothic architecture in the Middle Ages, Downpatrick Cathedral should not be derided as the product of an unlearned and immature attempt to reconstruct a medieval building. It would be fairer and kinder to say that, in the chronicle of Ireland's cathedrals, Downpatrick represents the early flowering of a fascination for romanticised images of the Middle Ages; it is a product of the infancy of the Gothic Revival, when that movement was still governed by exuberant imagination. Within thirty years of the completion of Downpatrick, exuberance and imagination had been suffocated by scholarship.

The passing of time has aged and mellowed Downpatrick Cathedral, allowing it to acquire a greater air of antiquity than perhaps it deserves.

References

1 J. G. F. Day and H. E. Patton, *The cathedrals of the Church of Ireland* (London, 1932), p. 42.
2 Ibid.
3 Down Cathedral Restoration Committee, *Cathedral of the Holy Trinity of Down, restoration 1952* (Downpatrick, 1952), p. 8.
4 Day and Patton, *Cathedrals of the Church of Ireland*, p. 45.
5 Charles Smith, *The antient and present state of the county of Down* (Dublin, 1744), p. 27.
6 Ibid., p.29.
7 Mervyn Archdall, *Monasticn Hibernicum* (London, 1786), p. 116.
8 W. B. Mant, *Memoirs of the Rt. Rev. Richard Mant, Lord Bishop of Down and Connor, and of Dromore* (Dublin, 1857), p. 161.
9 Day and Patton, *Cathedrals of the Church of Ireland*, p. 45.
10 Smith, *Antient and present state of the county of Down*, p. 220.

DROMORE

The Cathedral Church of Christ the Redeemer

Diocese of Dromore (Church of Ireland)

DROMORE (*Druim mór* – great ridge), a town of about 3,000 inhabitants on the River Lagan, lies about 25km west of Downpatrick and 107km north of Dublin. The story goes that St Patrick was celebrating mass in the church of one of his disciples when he saw through the east window a host of angels hovering over a neighbouring valley. Afterwards Patrick declared that a monastery would be founded on that spot. The monastery was founded in the early 6th century by St Mo-Cholmóg (better known as Colman), who, according to different traditions, was a native either of Argyll or of Ulster. He was a friend of St Óengus mac Nissi of Connor and is said to have been the teacher of St Finian of Clonard. He is the titular saint of at least one church in Scotland, Inis Mo-Cholmaig, and of Llangolman in Wales. His feast-day is 7 June. Successive cathedrals at Dromore bore the dedication 'St Colman' until 1603. The style 'Christ the Redeemer' was ordered for the rebuilt cathedral by letters patent of James I.

By the 10th century the monastery had become rich and powerful and had acquired extensive possessions; but like so many Irish monastic foundations, it was a tempting target for the Vikings, and Dromore was frequently raided. By the time of the 12th-century reformation of the Irish Church Dromore was insignificant enough to be ignored at the Synods of Raith Bressail and Kells-Mellifont, and no Bishop of Dromore did fealty to King Henry II in 1172.

Dromore was a late arrival in the diocesan system. The first mention of the diocese occurs in 1197, and it is likely that it was created by a local synod held at Dublin in 1192 by Matthew Ua hÉnna, Archbishop of Cashel and papal legate. The reason for the creation of this new diocese in the province of Armagh at such a late date is uncertain, but very little is known about Dromore in the 13th and 14th centuries. It was one of the smallest and poorest of the Irish dioceses; indeed, by 1487 it was so small and so poor that the Archbishop of Armagh wrote to Henry VII telling him that the revenues of the see amounted to only 40 p.a., 'so that none would remain upon the bishopric'.[1]

In the 15th century Dromore was treated virtually as a titular see, with little regard for the needs of the diocese. Between 1420 and 1501 a succession of bishops of Dromore lived in England, acting as suffragans of English dioceses: John Chourles (1420–33), Marcus (?1410–29), Nicholas Wartre (1419–45), Thomas Rackelf (1429–53), William (?–1431), David Chirbury (1431–51), Thomas Scrope (?1434–40), Thomas Radcliff (1450–54/5), Richard Messing (1457–63), William Egremond (1463–1501). At one time four absentee bishops, all monks or friars, claimed the title simultaneously. The list is hopelessly confused.

Some degree of order seems to have prevailed towards the end of the 15th century with the appointment of a Frenchman, Yvo Guillen (1480–83) and then by a Greek, Georgius Braua (1483–99). Both bishops appear to have been normally resident at Dromore ignoring the claims of the absentee Bishop Egremond (suffragan in York 1463–1501). But it is clear that in the 15th century, Dromore was of little importance.

gest a completely new cathedral. Buckworth also began work on the construction of a new palace, but the outbreak of the rebellion of 1641 ended his brave effort to make amends for the neglect of centuries, and the cathedral, the unfinished palace, and the town of Dromore were wrecked in the fighting. The ruins could still be seen in 1657 when the cathedral was described as having 'parts of the walls sufficient, part ruined, without covering, doors or windows.'[3]

The revival of the fortunes of the diocese came with the arrival in 1661 of Jeremy Taylor as Bishop of Down and

Dromore: the interior looking from the nave to the north aisle

Given the poverty of the see and the succession of first titular and then foreign bishops, it comes as no surprise to learn that the medieval cathedral was in ruins by the time of the Reformation and remained so until the early 17th century; there is no record of its style or appearance. Its date of construction is unknown but there is a reference to the creation of a cathedral chapter in 1240.

In 1609 James I endeavoured to restore the decayed and impoverished see by endowing it with extensive properties in the neighbourhood. Theophilus Buckworth was appointed bishop in 1613 and began the process of rebuilding the ruined cathedral. How much of it survived is unclear. In 1622 he described it as 'almost new builded, covered, glassed, and in part furnished with seats'[2] which would tend to sug-

Connor and administrator of Dromore. His fame rests on his two great works, *Holy Living* (1650) and *Holy Dying* (1651). Stressing temperance and moderation in all things, they became classics of Anglican spirituality. The beauty of his prose and the power of his preaching made him a celebrated figure. George Rust, who succeeded him as Bishop of Dromore, preached Taylor's funeral sermon and paid great tribute to his predecessor. 'He had the good humour of a gentleman, the eloquence of an orator, the fancy of a poet, the acuteness of a schoolman, the profoundness of a philosopher, the wisdom of a chancellor, the sagacity of a prophet, the reason of an angel and the piety of a saint.' Taylor was not quite the saint some have depicted; he was harsh in his treatment of Presbyterians and Catholics. But he cared assiduously for the little diocese of Dromore. Of the three ruined cathedrals in his dioceses, it was Dromore that he chose to rebuild, and for it he always retained affection. When he died at Lisburn in 1667, his last wish was to be buried at Dromore, and he lies there in a vault beneath the chancel.

Jeremy Taylor's cathedral was a single-chamber building, measuring approximately 30.4m by 6m, with a tower, but much of it has been obliterated by later alterations. The only remaining 17th-century parts are the south and west walls of the nave, built of split-stone rubble with squared granite quoins. The work of alteration appears to have begun in the third quarter of the 18th century. When Bishop Thomas Percy (1782–1811) arrived at Dromore, he wrote that the cathedral 'had gone to such decay, that it required to be repaired and almost rebuilt a few years before I came here, and the old Pavement &c. had been entirely removed.'[4]

Bishop Percy, poet, antiquarian and author of *Reliques of Ancient English Poetry*, began the process of extending the cathedral in 1808. He constructed a transept on the north side of the nave which became known as the 'Percy Aisle'; the transept had a recess on the north wall in which it was intended to erect a memorial to Taylor. Since 1871 this arched recess has been occupied by the organ, by Connacher of Huddersfield. The tower was demolished and replaced by the present plain battlemented western tower; and the oak-shingled roof was replaced by slate.

The work continued in 1870, when the cathedral was extended eastwards. Two bays were added to the east side of Bishop Percy's transept; the north bay is now an entrance porch, and the south bay is the baptistery. At the same time an apse was added to the chancel. The apse was criticised for being a 'French' addition, and its lancet windows for departing from the style of the 17th-century windows with their simple tracery. Dromore Cathedral achieved its present appearance only in 1899, when five bays, including a galleried porch, were added to the west side of the Percy Aisle and a baptistery was constructed at the west end. The font is a late Victorian memorial and replaces the 17th-century font, which now stands in the tower porch. This late 19th-century work has turned the cathedral into the unusual double rectangle that can be seen today.

The nave and its adjoining twin, the Percy Aisle, are both seven bays long and divided by an arcade of seven low-pointed arches which rest on piers, alternately cylindrical and octagonal, with short shafts and large capitals and bases. The pews of the Percy Aisle face east for the first three bays from the west end, and then south towards the nave for the remainder. The chancel and sanctuary constitute the seventh bay of the nave.

The chancel steps are marble, and both chancel and sanctuary have a polychromatic tiled floor. The sanctuary panel-

ling, altar and choir stalls, all made from oak, are memorials inserted during a general redecoration and refurnishing in 1952–53. The altar, without the benefit of a frontal, is virtually invisible. The bishop's throne on the north side of the chancel, and a memorial brass, were added in memory of Jeremy Taylor in 1894. Oak-canopied chapter stalls on the north and south sides of the chancel were installed at the same time. A niche on the south side of the chancel contains an ancient stone with a floriated cross which, for some no doubt highly implausible reason, is known as 'St Colman's Pillow'. Also on the south wall is the King's Standard of the Royal Horse Guards (Blue), which was borne behind Edward VII at his coronation in 1902; it was presented to the cathedral by the Earl of Clanwilliam.

The pulpit occupies a prominent but odd position at the centre of the south wall. Made of Caen stone with marble colonettes, and standing on a mosaic floor, it commemorates James Saurin, the last separate Bishop of Dromore before the diocese was united to Down and Connor in 1842.

Dromore Cathedral is basically a pleasant and comfortable 19th-century church of unusual shape and interior arrangement, grafted on to two 17th-century walls, and most of the interior furnishings are late 19th or 20th century. The repeated enlargements of the 19th century, no doubt necessary to accommodate worshippers, have created an interesting building in which there is no single area of focus to which the worshippers can direct attention. The 'double church' arrangement of nave and north aisle, with an expanse of pews and dispersed focal points, leaves the visitor feeling uncertain of where to sit or which way to look; this is not helped by the distinct separation and distance between the pulpit and the altar, which tend to compete for attention.

There are a few fragments of antiquarian interest but none of them is structural. St Colman's Pillow, a Celtic High Cross in the churchyard, restored and erected there in 1887, and a Bible used in the cathedral destroyed in 1641, are the only evidence of other ages which have otherwise been entirely obliterated.

The Bishop's Palace was built c.1781 by Bishop William Beresford (1780–82). When Bishop Percy was appointed to succeed him in 1782, he discovered that the palace was still unfinished and he remained in Carlisle until the summer of 1783. The palace was sold in 1842 after the death of Bishop Saurin. It was used as a school in the late 19th century; then it was empty and fell into ruin and was demolished after the Second World War. The diocese of Connor was detached in 1944, but Down and Dromore remain united. In the Roman Catholic arrangement, the diocese of Dromore remains independent and its cathedral is at Newry.

References

1 J. G. F. Day and H. E. Patton, *The cathedrals of the Church of Ireland* (London, 1932), p. 53.
2 Ibid. p.54.
3 E. D. Atkinson, *Dromore: an Ulster diocese* (Dundalk, 1925), p. 89.
4 Arthur Tillotson (ed.), *The correspondence of Thomas Percy and Edmund Malone* (Lousiana, 1944), p. 204.

DUBLIN

The Cathedral Church of the Holy Trinity
(commonly called Christ Church)

Diocese of Dublin (Church of Ireland)

THE name of the capital city of Ireland was given to it by the Vikings when the established a permanent settlement there *c.*841, beaching their galleys at the *Dubh Linn* (dark pool) below the ford at the head of the navigable tideway. To the native Irish it was *Baile Átha Cliath* (town of the hurdle ford) where a wicker bridge crossed the River Liffey. The Viking name has stuck and Dublin, with a population of some 526,000 is now the largest city in Ireland and the capital of the Republic. The city is bisected, west to east, by the Liffey, which is embanked throughout its course through the city. With the exception of the two heavily restored Church of Ireland cathedrals, few buildings in the city pre-date the middle of the 18th century. But Dublin is still comparatively unspoilt, though derelict and run down in places, and its large tracts of fine Georgian squares and terraces have allowed it to retain an 18th-century appearance.

There are traditions of an early bishopric of Dublin with dates in the 7th and 8th centuries. But the tradition is no earlier than the 17th century and is now dismissed as unhistorical. Any Christianity in the area of the Dubh Linn would have been temporarily extinguished Christianity by the arrival of the Vikings *c.*841. The town was probably always overshadowed by the fame of St Kevin's foundation at Glendalough in the Wicklow Mountains to the south.

Intermarriage between the Vikings and the Irish eventually brought conversion to Christianity. In 1028 Sitric Silkbeard, Viking King of Dublin from 989 until his deposition in 1042, went on pilgrimage to Rome. At some date soon after his return he gave to a bishop named Donatus (*c.*1028–1074) 'a place whereon to build a church to the Holy Trinity'.[1] Sitric gave money and some rich farmland in Co. Dublin, the first of many grants of revenue which financed the cathedral for some 800 years until the disestablishment and disendowment of the Church of Ireland in 1871. King Sitric's cathedral,

which stood on the site of the present Christ Church Cathedral, is known to have had a nave and 'wings' (transepts), but nothing survives.

This Viking diocese of Dublin recognised the jurisdiction of the Archbishop of Canterbury for most of the 11th century, but shortly after 1096 Bishop Samuel refused to accept the jurisdiction of Archbishop Anselm. Since Dublin was not included in the list of dioceses at the Synod of Ráith Bressail in 1111, it must have occupied a very irregular position during the lifetime of Bishop Samuel Ua hAingliu, who died in 1121. Dublin was gradually incorporated into the Irish Church in the mid 12th-century and elevated to metropolitan rank at the Synod of Kells-Mellifont in 1152.

The Anglo-Norman invasion under the command of Richard, Earl of Pembroke (better known as Strongbow) seized Dublin in 1171. Shortly afterwards Strongbow joined with Archbishop Laurence O'Toole and the Prior of Christ Church in a scheme to rebuild the cathedral. O'Toole, who had been Abbot of Glendalough before his appointment to Dublin, converted the cathedral administration from a secular chapter to a foundation of Augustinian Canons Regular shortly after his appointment in 1162. The cathedral remained an Augustinian priory until 11 May 1541 when, with the dissolution of the monasteries, Robert Castle, the last prior, became the first dean.

The chancel and transepts were rebuilt in the period after 1172, and some of the building work done at that time, although restored, can still be seen, particularly in the south transept, where the round arches and chevron moulding of Romanesque predominate. The rebuilding of the nave was completed in the first half of the 13th century in the Early English style. The perfectly preserved crypt is contemporary with the 12th- and 13th-century rebuilding. Strongbow saw little of the work completed, dying in 1176 at the age of about forty-six. He was buried in the south aisle.

Because of destruction and rebuilding, all that remains of the 13th-century nave is the north wall. It was built by masons from Somerset, and its rich carving is reminiscent of Wells Cathedral. The stone was brought from the quarries at Dundry to Bristol and then shipped to Dublin. Transportation was not difficult, and the use of English stone gave the masons the advantage of working with a familiar material. It was as easy to bring the stone from England as to chance the hazards of quarrying it in the wilder parts of Ireland and transporting it overland.

The cathedral has suffered damage necessitating rebuilding at various stages in its history. In 1283 the spire, chapter house, dormitory and cloister were destroyed by fire. In 1316 the rebuilt spire was blown down in a storm which may also have damaged the east end of the cathedral; it was rebuilt again in 1325–31. The large east window was destroyed in a storm in 1461. Parts of the cathedral, probably including the tower, were rebuilt in 1608.

In 1358 the 12th-century chancel was demolished and replaced by a 31m-long chancel which stretched 12m further to the east of its predecessor. The reason for the construction of this chancel is unknown but may have been motivated by a desire to replace permanently structures erected temporarily after the storm damage of 1316. The work was carried out during the archbishopric of John de St Paul (1349–62) and the new chancel was afterwards known as the 'Choir of John de St Paul'. It had a noticeable incline towards the north caused by the builders using the south wall of the old Lady Chapel (formerly the Chapel of St Nicholas) erected independently of the cathedral. The Lady Chapel was built outside the cathedral 'and therefore its divergence from the axis of the nave was of no consequence; but when its outer wall was made use of to save the cost of building a new north wall to the Choir, this divergence became of the utmost importance, and involved a blemish and an unsightliness which no architectural skill could have entirely surmounted . . . There never was any great exhibition of such skill, and the new Choir, with its awkward bend, its absence of groining, and its want of architectural features, must have formed a sad

contrast from the first, to the exquisite art displayed in the western half of the cathedral.'[2]

The Victorian restoration deemed the Choir to have neither beauty nor architectural merit, and it was demolished in the 19th-century rebuilding; the stump of its eastern wall can be seen in the grounds outside the Chapter House. Fortunately the two westernmost arches of Strongbow's chancel were not disturbed during the building of the 14th-century chancel, nor a third arch built into the north side of the chancel wall, and these still remain.

The worst damage was done on 3 April 1562 when the nave vaulting collapsed, bringing down the roof and the south wall, which had been built on a peat bog. The wonder is that the north wall remained standing since it has an outward inclination of 30.5cm as a result of subsidence; it only remains standing owing to the external flying buttresses. The ruin was repaired in the most functional way, the beautiful south arcade being replaced by a 'hideous blank wall' and the vaulting with 'mean and naked rafters'.[3] The south aisle was completely shut off from the nave and later used as a chapter room and library. The medieval tiled floor, covered

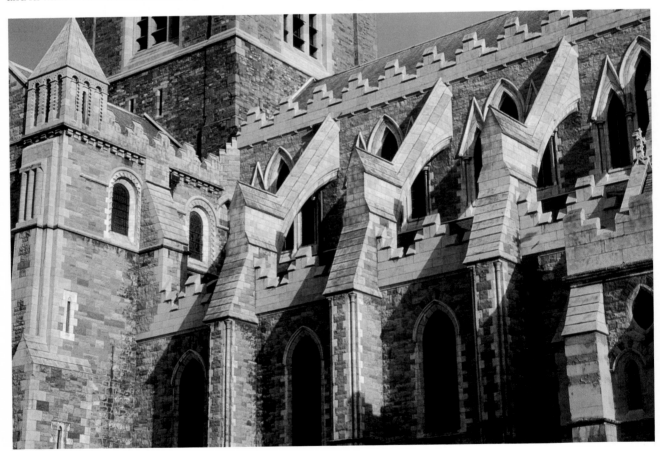

Christ Church Cathedral, Dublin: the south side

by the debris of the falling roof, was covered by a wooden floor. Ugly though the work was, it was probably all that could be done in the troubles of the early Reformation years.

The period from the mid-16th century to the mid-19th century appear to have been one of grim decay for both the Dublin cathedrals. The crypt of Christ Church was used by shopkeepers whose shops had doors opening into St John's Lane and the churchyard, but a 17th century description of the crypt reveals a sorry picture: 'the vaults from one end of the minster to the other, are made into tippling rooms for beer, wine and tobacco, demised all to popish recusants, and by them and others so much frequented in time of divine service, that though there is no danger of blowing up the assembly above their heads, yet there is of poisoning them with fumes. The table used for the administration of the blessed sacrament in the midst of the choir [is] made an ordinary seat for maids and apprentices.'[4]

A significant factor in the decline of Christ Church was that from 1681 until 1887 no occupant of the office of dean could give the cathedral his undivided attention. Because of the desolation caused in the mid-17th century by rebellion and war and the subsequent activity of Cromwell, many historic properties and endowments had been wrecked or lost. The diocese of Kildare was very poor and had no provision for the maintenance of its bishop. Since the Dean of Christ Church was paid the princely sum of £600 p.a., compared with only £50 for most of the clergy, the solution was to appoint Dean William Moreton as Bishop of Kildare in 1682, and allow him to retain his office as Dean of Christ Church. For the following 145 years a succession of nine dean-bishops had a dual allegiance – to the cathedral and to the diocese – a arrangement that probably brought no benefit to either. The situation was ended by the Church Temporalities (Ireland) Act of 1833. Under its provisions, the diocese of Dublin and the diocese of Kildare were to be united at the next vacancy. Accordingly, when Dean-Bishop Charles Lindsay died in 1846, the posts of Dean of Christ Church and Bishop of Kildare were separated. Since the 1833 Act had transferred the dean's income to the Commissioners of Church Temporalities, there was now no provision for a dean, so the same act decreed that the Dean of St Patrick's should also be Dean of Christ Church. From 1846 to 1872 Deans Henry Pakenham and John West successively cared for both cathedrals. By 1872 it had become clear that the arrangement was satisfactory. Although Dean Pakenham endeavoured to give equal time to both cathedrals, Dean West was only interested in St Patrick's, and both deans spent most of their time and energy on the restoration of St Patrick's, neglecting Christ Church. From 1872 to 1887 the Archbishops of Dublin were deans of their own cathedral, until these posts were separated with the appointment of William Greene as dean.

By the mid-19th century Christ Church was an architectural mess in very poor condition. 'The central tower was sup-

ported on arches rudely wrought in limestone and covered with whitewash; the tower itself was solidly built, but mean and bad in all its details . . . The north wall was in a dangerous state; the piers, built of small pieces of freestone with an interior of limestone rubble, were cracked and bulging in all directions. The triforium and clerestory were much out of perpendicular. The groining of the north aisle had fallen, and the north aisle wall, being out of perpendicular, had been propped up by an enormous mass of masonry like a vast

Christ Church Cathedral, Dublin, c. 1833

continuous buttress, thus closing (and preserving) all the windows . . . The chancel was shut off from the church by a solid screen . . . The walls were covered with wretched plaster panelling, cornices and pinnacles. The floor was badly paved, and the choir aisles had galleries. Throughout the church not one ancient window remained open.'[5]

The status of Christ Church had also been affected by the construction of the Chapel Royal in Dublin Castle in 1814. Whereas the Lord Lieutenant and members of the viceregal court and household had worshipped each Sunday in the collegiate-style box pews of the Choir of John de St Paul, the new Chapel Royal was now much more convenient, and more elegant.

St Patrick's Cathedral had been thoroughly restored in 1860–64. Similar work was needed at Christ Church to avoid a future that seemed to point towards further decay and eventual ruin. In 1871 Richard Chenevix Trench, Archbishop of Dublin, received an unexpected letter from Henry Roe, a wealthy Dublin whisky distiller. In an act of extraordinary generosity he offered to underwrite the total cost of restoring the cathedral and to build a Synod House beside it. 'In offering this as my donation to the disestablishment of the Church of Ireland, I wish especially to make it a thank offering to the Great Head of the Church for mercies granted me ... It is my earnest desire that this Cathedral (when restored) may prove useful to the Church of Ireland at large by being connected, as in past ages, with her synodical government; and I further hope that its ancient distinction as a Cathedral may be maintained, and its fine choral services continued in all their past efficiency.'[6] Roe's interest and generosity may have been kindled by reading a report describing the state of the cathedral and calling for its restoration. The report was published in 1869 and was written by Edward Seymour, a prebendary of Christ Church and a cousin of Roe.

The architect George Edmund Street was invited to submit proposals. Street delivered an astonishingly radical plan which called for the demolition of two-thirds of the cathedral, based on a guiding principal of reconstructing the cathedral built by Strongbow and Archbishop O'Toole. It was radical if only because it envisaged the destruction of so much medieval and Tudor fabric. The ease with which it was accepted in official quarters can be partly explained by the unsightly appearance and unstable condition of the cathedral, and partly by the fact that the entire cost was immediately available.

Shortly before the work of demolition and restoration began, a certain William Butler made copious measurements of the old cathedral for the purposes of record. During his examination of the building he recorded the following encounter with a crowd of children who were curious about his work: 'Judging by the positive neglect which was shown to this cathedral, some members of other denominations were impressed with the belief that we really did not require it at all; and it was widely circulated among a certain class, at the time I was making my measurements, that the heads of the Roman Catholic Church in Dublin were contemplating the purchase of what they called their old rights. I may mention that one day, when taking some dimensions about the western door, I was surrounded by a pack of ragged urchins, a class pretty numerous about that classical locality, and was asked the following question: "Misther, is this goin' to be a chapel?"[7] "Certainly not," said I. Immediately there was a general yell of disapprobation, and I could gather the follow-

ing remarks from the young zealots: "Yes, it is; we'll have it yet, as we had it before: d'ye think we'll let the auld swaddlers[8] have it: ye needn't be measuring it; it'll be pulled down." This was followed by a shower of stones and mud which naturally compelled me to take refuge inside the cathedral.'[9]

Christ Church Cathedral, Dublin: the central tower and the south transcept

At the same time as he was involved with the rebuilding of Christ Church, Street was also working on the rebuilding of Kildare Cathedral, where a greater proportion of the medieval fabric survived. Christ Church was rebuilt in seven years, but the work at Kildare took twenty-five years, since it had no Henry Roe to underwrite the cost.

The work at Christ Church began in 1871, and the cathedral was reopened on 1 May 1878. The total internal length is 58.8m, the width of the nave is 17.6m, and the width at the transepts is 27.1m. The height of the nave is 20.7m.

The long 14th-century chancel was removed and replaced with a conjectural reconstruction of Strongbow's 12th-century apsidal chancel on its original foundation. The plain south wall was also removed and replaced with an arcade, triforium and clerestory to match the 13th-century north arcade. The aisles were rebuilt and the entire cathedral vaulted in stone. Battlements were added to the eaves and to the parapet of the tower, and a five-light window inserted into the west gable wall. All the windows were filled with stained glass. There was some hope that the wall might contain remnants of the piers and arches of the old south arcade, but when the plaster was removed only the shattered eastern arch remained.

The arrangement of the triforium, which is united to the clerestory stage, is unique in Ireland. Marble shafts rise from each opening of the triforium straight up to the clerestory level, and the trefoil-headed arch of the centre opening in the triforium is repeated in the clerestory. The arrangement owes much to Pershore Abbey in Worcestershire, and is reminiscent of that of Wells Cathedral. English west-coast influences are marked throughout the building.

In the collapse of 1562 the debris of the roof which had collapsed on to the floor of the nave was simply levelled and paved over. When this was removed during the restoration, the remains of the 13th-century tiled floor was revealed; sixty-three different patterns of tile were recovered and some were relaid in the floor of the Chapel of St Laurence O'Toole off the south transept. The design of the 19th-century encaustic tiling which covers the entire floor of the nave was carefully copied from the surviving 13th-century tiling.

The delightful baptistery opens off the north nave aisle and stands on the foundations of the north-west porch. It is the one exception to Street's rule of reproducing as far as possible the 13th-century cathedral. Street felt that the cathedral should have a chamber rather than a font somewhere within the cathedral, and he turned the ancient porch into a baptistery. The font is constructed of a variety of Irish marbles.

Almost opposite the entrance to the baptistery, on the south side of the nave, are two recumbent effigies; one crossed-legged in chain armour, and the other a small half-length figure. The first was for long alleged to be a representation of Strongbow on the site of his tomb, but this is no longer seriously believed. One account says that the effigy was brought from a church in Drogheda by Sir Henry Sidney in the mid-16th century to replace a memorial damaged in the fall of 1562. The effigy displays the arms of the FitzOsbert family of Drogheda, which lends credence to the story. The other figure is probably part of the original Strongbow monument and not(as tradition has it) a representation of his son whom he allegedly cut in half for showing cowardice in battle.

Until 1871 Christ Church, as the cathedral of the Established Church in the capital city, was used for many state functions. Successive Justiciars, Lords Lieutenant, Lords Deputy, Lords Justices and other representatives of the crown swore their oaths of office in the cathedral. On 24 May 1487 the pretender Lambert Simnel was crowned 'King Edward VI' in Christ Church with a golden circlet taken from an statue of the Blessed Virgin Mary at the Church of St Mary del Dam. The old Civic Pew, designated for the Lord Mayor of Dublin or his representative, can be seen in the easternmost bay of the north nave aisle; it has a carving of the arms of Dublin and a stand for the city mace; the State Pew, formerly used by the Lord Lieutenant and now reserved for the President of Ireland, is in the corresponding bay of the south nave aisle.

The inclusion of a chancel screen in 1872 as part of the restoration aroused criticism on the ground that it obstructed the view. But, to be fair to Street, his guiding principle was the reconstruction of the cathedral as it had existed in the early 13th century, and there would certainly have been a screen at that time. The Choir of John de St Paul was separated from the nave by a solid screen. Constructed of yellow Mansfield stone on a base of red Cork marble, the 19th-century screen is surmounted by a cross copied from the ancient Cross of Cong. The lower part of the screen which is now open was originally filled up to a height of 1.2m with solid alabaster diapered panelling, but this was later removed. It could be criticised on the ground that it is Victorian Gothic rather than an attempt to produce an accurate copy of a medieval Gothic screen; but even so the screen is beautiful piece of work. The adjacent stone pulpit has columns of green Connemara marble. The hand-wrought brass lectern on the south side is medieval. The screen is set at the entrance to the crossing, creating a choir beyond with carved oak stalls for the Dean and Chapter, and the throne of the archbishop.

Beyond the choir is the sanctuary, which is surrounded by an ambulatory. Directly behind the main altar is the Lady Chapel, which was built on ancient foundations in 1871. To the north is the Chapel of St Edmund the King, and to the south is the Chapel of St Laud (Bishop of Countances in the 6th century), which was destroyed c.1315 and rebuilt on its ancient foundations in 1871; it contains the heart of St Laurence O'Toole. To the north east, beyond the Chapel of St Edmund, are the Library and Chapter House and other official buildings connected with the cathedral, all designed by Street. The first bay on the south side of the ambulatory contains a very unusual find in Dublin: an urn containing the ashes of Major Marko Zekou Popovich, Hereditary Royal Standard-Bearer of Montenegro, who died in London on 26 October 1934.

The north transept contains the fine organ by Kenneth Jones of Bray. Installed in 1982, it replaced an 1857 organ by Telford of Dublin and includes some of its pipework. The cathedral Choir School was forced to close in 1972 because of lack of space and facilities. But the replacement of the boy choristers by sopranos and altos has enabled the performance of a wider repertoire of music to enrich the liturgy of the cathedral.

The most substantial remaining portions of the medieval cathedral are the south transept and the crypt. The south transept has an interesting mixture of Romanesque, and Gothic architecture. The entrance arch to the Chapel of St Laurence is Romanesque, composed of stones found on the site, although the chapel itself is the work of Street. There is also a fine external Romanesque doorway in the south wall of the transept. Against the west wall is a massive memorial to the 19th Earl of Kildare (1675–1744) by Sir Henry Cheere (1703–81), whose work can also be seen in Westminster Abbey. The 12th-century crypt consists of an aisled nave and apse and three square-ended eastern chapels. The nave is divided from the aisles by low arcades resting on short thick square piers.

The grounds contain the remains of the conventual buildings which were occupied by the Augustinian canons who served the cathedral from the 12th to the 16th centuries. The medieval Chapter House (c.1230), which stood beside the south transept, has been excavated, revealing moulded 13th-century work. The present Chapter House, which is attached to the north-east of the cathedral, is part of Street's work and stands on the site of the old Chapel of St Nicholas, which was used as the cathedral Lady Chapel from the 14th to the 18th centuries. It was 21.1m long and removed by Street. The only remaining evidence is the arch leading to the choir ambulatory, which is 13th-century work. It was used for many years by a Hugenot congregation.

The 19th-century Synod Hall is connected to the cathedral by a covered bridge, a Victorian 'Bridge of Sighs', which crosses the main street down to the Liffey. The tower is a substantial rebuilding of the tower of the Church of St Michael and All Angels. This diminutive church was founded in the 11th century. As with the cathedral and many other Dublin churches, it was for many years in a ruinous condition. It was rebuilt in 1676 and again, on a smaller scale, in 1815, when it measured 18.2m by 7.6m. It was built for a congregation of 200, but there were only 76 parishioners at the time. St Michael's was still in use in 1868, but was demolished during the restoration of Christ Church to make way for the Synod Hall. The tower, mainly 17th century but standing on medieval foundations, was carefully incorporated into the Synod Hall. The hall ceased to be used as the meeting place of the General Synod of the Church of Ireland in the 1980s, the victim of an almost total lack of parking space and other modern amenities. The building is for sale at the time of writing.

In 1731 houses were built for the dean, the cantor and the chancellor, in Fishamble Street adjacent to the cathedral. These were abandoned after a few years, and no residence has since been provided for any member of the chapter in the neighbourhood of the cathedral.

The restoration of Christ Church at a total cost of £250,000 was an impressive act of generosity on the part of Henry Roe. It may be justifiably questioned for its cavalier approach to much medieval fabric, especially the demolition of the 14th-century chancel, but nonetheless the restoration has left an interior that is warm, welcoming, intimate and dignified. The joins between the work of the 12th/13th and the 19th centuries are quite apparent, but no matter. Christ Church is a fine building and not to be dismissed as a mere Victorian pastiche. Street's careful preservation of the beautiful north nave arcade, using it as the yardstick in the creation of a very sympathetic cathedral around it, deserves praise. It could be argued that the loss of medieval fabric in the quest for authentic reconstruction was unnecessarily destructive. But the descriptions of Christ Church in the years before 1871 indicate that something drastic needed to be done, and also perhaps that nothing of great beauty was sacrificed. Christ Church may not have the mixed and muddled appearance of its pre-restoration days, but it has symmetry and harmony; another century and it will have antiquity.

Standing on its island site, around which traffic swirls at an alarming speed, Christ Church presents an attractive composition. With its lofty central tower containing a peal of thirteen bells, boldly projecting transepts, flying buttresses and battlemented walls, the cathedral is an imposing sight from the north bank of the Liffey. The view is spoiled to an extent by the construction of two office blocks on Wood Quay in recent years; they are to be deplored for marring the view of the cathedral and breaking the rhythm of the south bank.

References

1 Edward Seymour, *Christ Church Cathedral, Dublin* (Dublin, 1869), p. 27.

2 Ibid.

3 Ibid.

4 W. H. Grindle, *Irish cathedral music* (Belfast, 1989), p. 20.

5 Ward & Lock, *Illustrated historical handbook to the Irish cathedrals* (London, 1889), p. 274

6 E. H. Lewis-Crosby, *A short history of Christ Church Cathedral, Dublin* (Dublin, 1949), p. 30.

7 Roman Catholic churches were referred to as 'chapels' at the time.

8 An early nickname for Wesleyans, and applied later by Roman Catholics to Protestants and Dissenters generally. It is supposed to come from an early Methodist preacher who preached on the text 'Ye shall find the babe wrapped in swaddling clothes.' A Roman Catholic who was present and to whom the language of scripture was something of a novelty thought that this was ridiculous and called the preacher a 'swaddler' in derision.

9 William Butler, *Christ Church Cathedral, Dublin* (Dublin, 1874), p. 8.

DUBLIN

The National Cathedral and Collegiate Church of St Patrick

(The National Cathedral of the Church of Ireland)

ALTHOUGH St Patrick's Cathedral is one of the best known cathedrals in Ireland, it is, in the correct definition of the word, no more a cathedral than Westminster Abbey is an abbey. St Patrick's is a cathedral in name and by courtesy only, since it is no longer the seat of a diocesan bishop. Despite the widespread belief that a cathedral is no more than a large church, it is only the bishop's "cathedra" or throne which confers cathedral dignity upon any church. The vast size of many cathedral churches is due partly to contemporary prevailing perceptions of the status of the episcopate, partly to the status and influence of the church, and partly to the funds available at the time of construction. The size of the building does not constitute the *sine qua non* of a cathedral.

Until the disestablishment of the Church of Ireland in 1871 St Patrick's was a co-cathedral (with Christ Church) of the Archbishop of Dublin; since then it has been "The National Cathedral of the Church of Ireland". The title and the implied function were devised at the time of Disestablishment to end the centuries-old anomaly of a diocese with two cathedrals, to maintain St Patrick's as a Church of Ireland place of worship, and to recognise that, because of its history, reduction to the status of a parish church was not an appropriate option.

St Patrick's was given a unique constitution and status not unlike that of Westminster Abbey in England. It has the appearance of a cathedral constitution, being governed by a chapter consisting of the four traditional dignitaries – dean, precentor, chancellor and treasurer – and a college of twenty two prebendaries. But St Patrick's is not subject to the jurisdiction of any bishop. Although stalls are allotted to them in the chancel, neither the Archbishop of Armagh nor the Archbishop of Dublin have any authority in St Patrick's, and neither may carry their croziers there. The dean is styled "Dean and Ordinary" and possesses all the power and authority of a bishop within the cathedral and its precincts, saving only the administration of such sacraments as are the preserve of the episcopate. The cathedral has a common relationship to all the dioceses of the Church of Ireland, and each diocese is represented in the chapter. Twelve of the prebendaries are appointed individually by the twelve diocesan bishops, nine are appointed by the Dean and chapter, and the prebendal stall of Cualaun is annexed to the Archbishopric of Dublin.

The origin of St Patrick's Cathedral dates to the time of the saint, who is said to have baptised converts in a well close to the site of the present cathedral. During the course of excavations in 1901 a site, conjectured to be that of the well, was uncovered. The well appears to have flourished until the 16th century. A small wooden church was built at the site and was probably later replaced by a church of stone, but nothing definite is known of the site until Archbishop John Comyn brought it into prominence at the end of the 12th century.

The Anglo-Norman invasion of Ireland seized Dublin in 1171. In 1180 the death of Archbishop Laurence O'Toole provided Henry II with the opportunity to appoint one of his trusted followers to the see and extend royal influence in the Irish Church. John Comyn was a Benedictine monk from Evesham in Worcestershire with a reputation for being an able judge, diplomat and administrator. He was consecrated Archbishop of Dublin in 1182 and arrived in Ireland in 1184.

The Archbishop's Palace stood next to the Danish cathedral at Christ Church, whose precincts lay within the jurisdiction

St Patrick's Cathedral, Dublin: from the south east

of the civil authorities. Comyn's relations with the authorities and with the troublesome Augustinian Canons Regular of Christ Church were far from cordial. This seems to have prompted him to build a palace and a church on his own land outside the city walls, thereby exercising unfettered jurisdiction. Because of its historic associations, Comyn moved a short distance to the south to live adjacent to the old Church of St Patrick, and this church, being served by a

St Patrick's Cathedral, Dublin: the south side of the chancel

college of secular canons, was easier to control than the Augustinian Regulars. He rebuilt it "in hewn stone in the form of a cross, rightly goodly to be seen with fair embowed works, fine pavements and an arched roof overhead with stonework".[1] The church was dedicated on St Patrick's Day 1192 to "God, Our Blessed Lady Mary and St Patrick". The new episcopal residence, known as the Palace of St Sepulchre, remained the residence of the Archbishop of Dublin, although much rebuilt, until 1806, when it was sold to the state and became a police barracks.

Comyn's successor, Henry de Loundres (1213–28), issued two charters establishing the offices of dean, chancellor, treasurer and precentor about 1220–21. The charters were confirmed by Pope Honorius III on 6 March 1221, and the establishment of St Patrick's as a cathedral church was complete. De Loundres, like Comyn, is thought to have distrusted monastic chapters and wanted a cathedral chapter that would submit easily to his jurisdiction.

Continued quarrels and lawsuits inevitably characterised relations between the rival chapters of the secular canons at St Patrick's and the Augustinian canons at Christ Church, especially at the time of elections to fill the vacant see; the lengthiest dispute caused an eight-year vacancy in 1271–9. A compromise agreed in 1300 known as the Pacis Compositio provided that Christ Church should be recognised as the older and "mother" church of the archdiocese; archbishops were to be consecrated there, and the cross, ring and mitre were to be kept there; burials of archbishops were to take place in the two cathedrals alternately unless they wished to make other arrangements;[2] synods were to be held alternately, but provincial councils were to be opened and closed in Christ Church.

The new status of St Patrick's inevitably gave rise to the feeling that even with Comyn's rebuilding it had insufficient dignity to be the cathedral church of an archbishop, and an appeal was launched in 1225 to rebuild it on a more impressive scale.

The present cathedral, although heavily restored, and with some additions, represents the outline and appearance of the mid-13th-century cathedral dedicated in 1254, a year before the death of Henry de Loundres's successor, Archbishop Luke (1230–55). The Lady Chapel behind the main Altar was added in 1270 by Archbishop Fulke de Sandford (1257–71), who is buried in the north chancel aisle. There was a tower and spire at the north west of the cathedral, but the spire was blown down in a storm in 1316, and both the tower and the north-west corner of the nave was damaged by a serious fire in 1362. The tower was rebuilt by Archbishop

Thomas Minot in 1370 and has since been known as Minot's Tower. About 1544 the nave vaulting collapsed at the west end, destroying many monuments, and the whole cathedral was in a semi-ruinous condition from the 17th to the 19th centuries.

St Patrick's has none of the sense of elevation enjoyed by Christ Church. It stands on marshy lowland, making the provision of a crypt an impossibility; the moist clay caused endless floodings to the cathedral. As early as 1437 a commission was appointed to inquire into the obstruction of the water coming near to the cathedral. Damage was done in 1493 by the overflow of the River Poddle (which now runs underground), and, on the petition of the Dean and Chapter, parliament enacted that the inhabitants of the precincts were to be responsible for keeping their drains clear. In 1687 the whole city was inundated and the water level rose "above the desks" in the cathedral. In 1744 the Dean and Chapter were obliged to ask the Chapter of Christ Church for permission to hold their Lenten services there as St Patrick's was "dangerous to assemble in from the late floods". In 1762 "the excessive rains, which fell in October this year occasioned such floods that there was five feet depth of water in the choir."[3] Further floodings were recorded in 1778, 1783, 1791 and 1795. Five great inundations occurred in the second half of the 18th century, "all of which took place on a Saturday". Similar floodings took place from time to time in the 19th century, and although the water level is only 2.2m below the floor of the nave, an effective system of drainage now prevents the recurring flooding of previous centuries.[4]

There are other references to the dilapidated state of the cathedral. In 1633 the Lady Chapel behind the main altar was in ruins and a lath-and-plaster wall filled the arch, blocking the view of the chapel. During the Cromwellian period the cathedral was used for courts martial and for the stabling of horses, but this is a familiar story about cathedrals during Cromwell's regime. An appeal to the citizens of Dublin at the Restoration in 1660 spoke of "the decayed and ruinous state of the ancient and once most famous and beautiful church of St Patrick, occasioned by the sacrilege and impiety of these later times".[5] By the end of the 18th century the cathedral was in a terrible state. In 1787 the "stone arch over the choir" was in a state of decay. In 1792 the south wall was leaning 60cm out of the perpendicular, and the nave roof was propped up with wooden scaffolding for a quarter of a century afterwards. The north transept, screened off and used as the parish church of St Nicholas Without from the mid-14th to the early 19th centuries, was ruined by 1784, and the south transept, used as the chapter house, was in a dangerous state.[6] The cathedral architect reported to the Lord Lieutenant in 1805 that £16,318 15s 9d would be needed for restoration but suggested that it would be economical to rebuild at a total cost of £81,600. Fortunately the plan never came to fruition. Piecemeal restoration took place during the first half of the 19th century: the nave was re-roofed in

1812–14; the north transept was rebuilt in 1821–6; the west door and west Perpendicular window were rebuilt in 1832–4; and the Lady Chapel was restored by Dean Henry Pakenham in 1845–52. But when Thackeray visited St Patrick's in the early 1840s, he spoke of the greater part of the building being "suffered to remain in gaunt decay".[7]

The major work of restoration was undertaken at the expense of Sir Benjamin Lee Guinness in the years 1860–65 at a total cost of £160,000. Five bays of the south nave aisle were rebuilt; the south wall was rebuilt of Irish granite; the triforium bays of the nave had long since disappeared and were rebuilt; the clerestory was refaced, except on the north side of the chancel and at the east end; the west clerestory of the south transept was rebuilt; a new roof was provided for the nave; the north transept was reconstructed, replacing the unsympathetic rebuilding of 1821–26; the south front of the south transept was renewed; two flying buttresses were added to the north side of the nave; and a porch was added to the south-west corner of the nave; the Perpendicular window in the west wall of the nave was replaced by the three-light Early English window which echoes the triple lancets in the east wall of the Lady Chapel. Two of Sir Benjamin's sons, Lord Iveagh and Lord Ardilaun, underwrote the cost of further work at the end of the 19th century, and in 1899–1904 Lord Iveagh paid for the restoration of the choir, including the replacement of the lath-and-plaster ceiling by the present stone vaulting.

Because of these several restorations, little remains of the original 13th-century fabric, and there is no stained glass earlier than the mid-19th century. Although the building probably looks much as it did in the 13th and 14th centuries, most of the stonework has been replaced. The most authentic remaining portions are the three eastern bays of the north side of the nave, the vaulting of the south transept with its eastern wall and aisle, and the north and east walls of the chancel. Archbishop Minot's limestone tower is much as it was when completed in 1370, although the granite spire was added in 1749; it was extensively cleaned and repointed in 1974. The tower is 44.8m high, and the spire adds a further 30.7m, making a total height of 75.5m.

The cathedral is bordered on the north by a pleasant garden known as St Patrick's Park which was laid out in 1903 by the generosity of Lord Iveagh. The land was at one time occupied by residences for cathedral officials, but for several generations it had deteriorated into tenements, reckoned to be the worst in Dublin, so that the cathedral stood "in the midst of a dense mass of narrow, filthy, putrid thoroughfares".[8] A visitor in the days before the park was laid out confirmed the dreadful location of St Patrick's: "It stands in a locality which is one of the lowest in the city, surrounded by a dense, impoverished population, occupying decayed and half-ruinous houses, where nearly all sanitary arrangements are neglected . . . the spectator looks upon a mass of filthy lanes and alleys, squalid dwellings, pestilential slaughter-houses, and the lowest kind of shops for the sale of old furniture and refuse of all souls which surround the cathedral, and cover all the space between it and Christ Church, about a quarter of a mile distant."[9]

St Patrick's Cathedral is 91.4m long by external measurement and 87.1m by internal. The nave is 40.3m long, and the chancel 17.2m; both are 9.1m wide (excluding the aisles). The Lady Chapel behind the main altar is 16.7m long. Both nave and chancel are 17.1m in height. The nave is eight bays long, the chancel has four bays, and the transepts have three bays each.

The nave piers and arches are built of Somerset stone with a core of Irish limestone; the casing of Caen stone was added during the Pakenham and Guinness restorations. Two piers on the north side were found to be unstable and were rebuilt in Portland stone in 1903. The three piers on the north side nearest the west end were rebuilt by Archbishop Minot in the 14th century after the fire, and the arcades are of Cheshire stone. The encaustic floor tiles were added in 1882 at a cost of £1,600; their design was based on medieval tiles found under the floor of the south transept. The nave roof is a lath-and-plaster restoration of 1863, but the groining of part of the south nave aisle is medieval.

The great monument against the south wall, at the west end is "the very famous, sumptuous, glorious tombe" of black marble and alabaster, erected by the 1st Earl of Cork in 1631 in memory of his second wife. Lord Cork subsequently spent much of his time and money rebuilding Lismore Cathedral. Formerly standing in the chancel, the tomb was placed in its present position in 1863. On the south aisle adjacent to a door leading to the robing room is bust of Jonathan Swift, author of *Gulliver's Travels*, who was Dean of St Patrick's 1713–45. The bust is of Carrara marble and was given to the cathedral in 1775 by a nephew of the dean's Dublin publisher, over whose shop door it had once stood. Swift is buried in the nave, the exact spot being marked by a brass plate. A memorial to his life-long companion Stella is on the other side of the robing room door.

The baptistery at the south-west of the nave is the oldest part of the cathedral and contains vaulting of an earlier date than the rest of the building and it may have been the entry to Comyn's church. The floor is paved with medieval tiles removed from the altar floor of St Paul's Chapel in the south transept. Nothing remains of the ancient font which formerly stood against one of the piers on the north side of the nave. The floor tiling and the font were placed here in 1863 during the Guinness restoration.

The pulpit on the north side of the crossing is of richly carved Caen stone resting on a large central pier surrounded by slender colonettes of red marble. It was given by Sir

Benjamin Lee Guinness as a tribute to Dean Henry Pakenham, who died on Christmas Day 1863 as the restoration was nearing completion. The pulpit tester, not part of the original design, was added a short while afterwards. The brass lectern on the south side of the crossing was presented in memory of Dean Henry Jellett, who died in 1902.

The south transept was used as the Chapter House at least from the 15th century until the mid-19th century. The old Chapter House door is still preserved. It has a hole which was created in 1492 to enable Lord Ormond and Lord Kildare, two quarrelling noblemen, to shake hands from opposite sides. Kildare "pursuing Ormond to the chapter-house doore undertooke on his honor that he should receive no villainie, whereupon the recluse craving his lordship's hand to assure him his life, there was a clift in the chapiter-house doore, pearsed at a trise, to the end both the earles should have shaken hands and be reconciled; but Ormond surmising that this drift was intended for some further treacherie, that if he would stretch out his hand, it had been percase chopt off, refused that proffer; until Kildare stretcht in his hand to him, and so the doore was opened, they both imbraced, the storme appeased, and all their quarrels for that present rather discontinued than ended".[10]

The north transept is a rebuilding of 1863 on the model of the south transept, except for the western aisle, which is medieval. The beautiful columned spiral staircase to the organ loft only dates from 1901. It was designed by Sir Thomas Drew, who based it on a similar staircase in Mayence Cathedral. The stained glass in the triple window was inserted in the 1930s as a memorial to Lord Iveagh, who died in 1927. The medieval transept was used as the parish church of St Nicholas Without from the middle of the 14th century to the early part of the 19th century. It was reincorporated into the cathedral as part of the Guinness restoration and now houses colours of disbanded Irish regiments which have been laid up in the cathedral.

The chancel is essentially the result of the 1901–4 restoration. The groined roof of the chancel is part of the restoration, but follows the lines of the ancient wall ribs. The triforium arcades rest on shafts of Irish limestone. The mosaic floor of the sanctuary, the steps of black Kilkenny marble and the carved oak sedilia are also part of the Iveagh restoration. The five windows above the eastern arch depict St Patrick, St Columba and St Brigid, with allegorical figures on each side. The stalls of the four dignitaries, the dean, the chancellor, the treasurer and the precentor, are at the four corners of the choir, the dean's stall being at the south-west. Thrones for the two archbishops are on the north (Armagh) and south (Dublin) sides of the choir to the east of the chapter stalls.

The pre-restoration ceiling was pale blue with gold stars and may have been so decorated for the installation of the Prince of Wales as a Knight of St Patrick in 1868. One of the attractive features of the chancel is the mass of colour provided by the banners of the Knights Companions of the Most Illustrious Order of St Patrick. This Order was founded by George III in 1783 as an honour for Irish peers to mirror the Order of the Garter in England and the Order of the Thistle in Scotland. Because of the national reputation, of the cathedral it was chosen to be chapel of the order, and it remained such until the disestablishment of the Church of Ireland in 1871. New knights of the Order were solemnly installed in the cathedral, and their banners and plates of arms, together with the mock helmets and swords, were placed above their stalls. By wish of Queen Victoria, the banners of the knights of the order at the time of Disestablishment remain in position. Some of the banners on the south side were restored after a fire on Good Friday 1940 which destroyed several of the stalls. The Order is now in a state of desuetude, since the changed circumstances of Irish politics after 1922 have made further conferments unlikely for the time being. The banners add great dignity to the chancel, though Thackeray dismissed them as "tawdry old gimcracks of the most illustrious order of Saint Patrick (whose pasteboard helmets, and calico banners, and lathe swords, well characterise the humbug of chivalry which they are made to represent)".[11] A statue of the Marquess of Buckingham, first Grand Master of the order, stands in the north nave aisle; the marquess is wearing the robes of the order.

The aisled Lady Chapel to the rear of the main altar is part of the 13th-century cathedral. In 1663 it was given by the Dean and Chapter for the use of a congregation of French Protestant refugees who had arrived in Dublin. They used the chapel continuously until 1816, by which time they had, by a process of gradual assimilation with Irish culture, ceased to exist as a separate identifiably French group. They added galleries to the chapel and used the Chapel of St Stephen on the south side as their vestry room. For the first quarter of the 19th century, when the north transept was in ruins, the Lady Chapel was also used the parishioners of St Nicholas Without. It then became the Chapter House until the Pakenham restoration of 1845–52. The dean planned to restore it as a chapel for the Order of St Patrick, but although nothing came of the idea, the chapel was rebuilt from the floor, reproducing the original design. The roof is supported by slender piers of four detached Purbeck marble shafts clustered around a core of Caen stone. The attractive Gothic arcading, which forms a dado, was added in the 1930s. The east windows were inserted in 1864 as a memorial to Dean Pakenham. The Lady Chapel is flanked by the south chancel aisle, which terminates in the Chapel of St Stephen, and the north chancel aisle, which terminates in the Chapel of St Peter; the groining of both aisles is medieval.

St Patrick's Cathedral is unique among Irish collegiate and cathedral foundations in that the Morning and Evening Offices are sung every day. There is a Choir School in the precincts, and a foundation of lay vicars choral augmented by supernumeraries.

Since 1871, when St Patrick's became the National Cathedral of the Church of Ireland, it has been used extensively for national occasions, and Dean Victor Griffin (1969–91) did much to encourage the recognition and use of the cathedral as a national building. In 1974 the cathedral was the setting for the funeral of Erskine Childers (President of Ireland 1973–4).

References

1 J. H. Bernard, *A history of St Patrick's Cathedral, Dublin* (Dublin, 1903; ed., Dublin, 1940), p.5.
2 Since 1191 fifteen archbishops have been buried in Saint Patrick's and a further nine in Christ Church.
3 W. M. Mason, *The history and antiquities of the Collegiate and Cathedral Church of St Patrick, near Dublin* (Dublin, 1820), p. 447.
4 Bernard, *History of St Patrick's Cathedral, Dublin*, p. 7.
5 Ibid., p. 12.
6 Ibid., p. 13.
7 W. M. Thackeray, *The Irish sketch-book* (London, 1843), ii, p. 312.
8 *The Parliamentary Gazetteer of Ireland* (Dublin, 1844–6), ii, p. 115.
9 James Godkin, *Ireland and her churches* (London, 1867), p. 164.
10 Bernard, *History of St Patrick's Cathedral, Dublin*, pp 57–8.
11 Thackeray, *Irish sketch-book, ii, 312.*

DUBLIN

The Pro-Cathedral of the Immaculate Conception of the Blessed Virgin Mary
(commonly called St Mary's)

Diocese of Dublin (Roman Catholic)

THE origin of a post-Reformation Roman Catholic cathedral in Dublin lies in the pre-Reformation Cistercian Abbey of St Mary. Its lands extended eastwards along the north side of the Liffey from the present Four Courts, north to Constitution Hill, and eastwards to the sea. The abbey was dissolved in 1539, and by the beginning of the 17th century its ruins were being used to stable horses; the remaining traces can be seen in Meeting House Lane. The name was kept alive by the creation of two parishes dedicated to St Mary: a Church of Ireland parish in 1697, and a Roman Catholic parish in 1707. The Church of Ireland parish erected its church in 1697 in Mary Street. In 1986 the church was given to the Greek Orthodox community, who used it as their cathedral. By the end of the same year, however they were asked to leave, since the building was considered a dangerous structure.

Twenty-two years after the creation of the Roman Catholic parish of St Mary, sufficient funds had been raised to allow the construction of a chapel in Liffey Street. A contemporary document described it as small but neat, with the 'altar railed in, steps ascending to it of oak, fore part of the altar covered with gilt leather, and name of Jesus in glory in the midst. On the altar is a gilt tabernacle with large gilt candlesticks.' It had two galleries, 'several pews for better sort, and two sprinkling pots of black marble in the chapel yard', presented in 1760.[1]

In 1786 John Thomas Troy arrived in Ireland as the new Roman Catholic Archbishop of Dublin. The new archbishop, who had returned to Ireland in 1777 after twenty years amid the architectural triumphal grandeurs of Rome, was shocked by the state of the chapels and mass-houses that he found. The metropolitan church of the archbishops had been St Nicholas's, Francis Street (the church was rebuilt in 1829), but in 1797 Archbishop Troy petitioned the pope to use the small church of St Mary's, Liffey Street instead. The request was granted, and the archbishop began raising funds for the building of a 'new dignified and spacious church'.

Ten years later Drogheda Street (later forming part of O'Connell Street) was widened towards the west to align it with Sackville Street and become Dublin's main thoroughfare. A site in the new development was offered for the erection of a new Catholic church, but there were fears about Protestant reaction to a Catholic church in such a prominent position, and the hardening of attitudes after the 1798 rebellion, persuaded those closely involved that a less conspicuous site might be more prudent. The O'Connell Street site is now occupied by the General Post Office.

By 1803 sufficient funds had been raised to purchase the Dublin mansion of Lord Annesley which stood on the corner of Marlborough Street and what was then known as Elephant Lane, later Tyrone Place, and now Cathedral Street. It was purchased for £5,100, but funds were far below what was needed to begin work immediately. In the meantime the building was leased to the Barracks Board. When their lease expired in 1814, the board was given notice to quit, demolition began, and the foundation stone of the new church was laid on Easter Tuesday 1815.

The identity of the architect is a mystery. The winning design was sent from Paris and was marked with the letter 'P', and there is still doubt today about the identity of 'P'. Some believe that it was John Sweetman, a Dubliner living in exile in Paris since the 1798 rebellion; others that it was Louis Hippolyte le Bas, architect to the Emperor Napoleon I. Those who support the candidature of Sweetman point to the interior of the pro-cathedral being copied from the fine Classical church of St Philippe de Reule in the Rue St Honore which had only recently been completed. Those who support le Bas state that St Mary's closely resembles his Parisian church of

Notre Dame de Lorette. They also point to the secrecy of the architect's identity, which would have been necessary because of the fact that England was at war with France in 1814.

One argument against le Bas is the fact that early records speak of the plans being drawn up by an amateur.

In August 1821 a flag was flown from the top of the dome to show that the shell was complete. Archbishop Troy died in May 1823 at the age of eighty-five. His remains were temporarily laid to rest elsewhere, since the vaults of the new church were leased to the Commissioners of Inland Revenue for the storage of spirits. The arrangement ceased in 1824, and the vaults became the burial place of over 900 benefactors of the church. The appointment of Troy's successor, Archbishop Daniel Murray (1823–52), gave new impetus to the building work, and the cathedral was finally dedicated on 14 November 1825 in the presence of most of the Irish bishops. The internal decoration of the building was continued after the dedication, and the total cost of the building was £45,000.

The pro-cathedral is a Classical Revival building, one of the last to be built before the Classical style was swept aside by the craze for Gothic. The building is 45.7m long and 34.4m wide at its greatest width. The centre of the dome is 21.3m above floor level. A view of the exterior presents the pro-cathedral as a low and massive structure, but the interior is relatively small.

St Mary's was intended at the time of planning to be the most impressive Catholic church in Ireland and a structure that would rival the finest Church of Ireland churches. It would be fair to say that it now fails in both respects. Both the Roman Catholic Church and the Church of Ireland possess some very fine and handsome cathedrals which far outshine St Mary's. The cramped site does the cathedral no service by making it impossible to view or photograph it from any distance.

The entrance portico is a copy of the Temple of Theseus at Athens. Six fluted Doric columns of Portland stone, 9.1m high and 1.5m in diameter, rest on granite plinths and support a plain triangular pediment. The interior is in the style of a Roman basilica ending in an apse. Twenty-two fluted Doric columns without bases or plinths rise from the floor to support a barrel vault; further similar columns support the aisle roofs. The nave is separated from its aisles by oak railings with carvings of lotus flowers along the bases. The coffered dome was an afterthought and not well liked. It

St Mary's Pro-Cathedral, Dublin: the west front

sits lightly on four round arches including the semi-circular apse dome, which contains a white and blue frieze of the Ascension by John Smythe and two large flanking semi-circular windows added in 1908. One visitor thought that the dome was a mistake: 'It is no help to the preacher and constitutes a serious and unhappy departure from the graceful lines and principles of Grecian art.' Another critic thought a dome would have looked well when supported and balanced on the converging arms of a cruciform edifice, 'otherwise, it is but a beautiful deformity'.[2]

and ventilation of the building. There are two marble sculptures by Thomas Farrell in the south and north aisles, commemorating Archbishops Daniel Murray (1823–52) and Paul Cullen (1852–78). Archbishop Cullen became Ireland's first-ever resident Cardinal when he received the red hat in 1866. The north aisle contains the Altar of St Laurence O'Toole and a major reliquary of the saint. It was erected here by Archbishop John McQuaid (1940–72) as a memorial to his predecessor, Archbishop Edward Byrne (1921–40).

Interior of St Mary's Pro-Cathedral, Dublin (1900 photograph)

The interior of the pro-cathedral was ornately decorated in 1886 at beginning of the episcopate of Archbishop William Walsh (1885–1921) with Biblical scenes, saints' heads and Latin inscriptions, all of which were covered over in a later refurbishment. The stained glass window in the apse (concealed at the time of writing), depicting Our Lady of the Immaculate Conception flanked by St Laurence O'Toole and St Kevin, belongs to the same period. The rounded organ gallery at the west end was constructed in 1893. The organ itself was rebuilt in 1971 by J.W. Walker & Sons, but is housed in the original case of 1908. The marble and mosaic side altars of Our Lady and the Sacred Heart were added in 1908, together with the semi-circular north and south windows below the dome, which improved the light

During preparations in 1928 for the celebration of the centenary of Catholic Emancipation the portico on the Cathedral Street side was walled up between the Doric columns, and St Kevin's Chapel in the northern flank became an open space within the church. The justification was the need to create as much additional floor space as possible to accommodate the large numbers expected for the great occasion. Another building, used as St Kevin's Chapel, was built to the north of the pro-cathedral at the rear of the Parochial Houses, fronting on to Thomas Lane. The chapel is rectangular and lit by seven high level diocletian windows. Above the white marble altar is a painting representing St Kevin, framed by a Corinthian segmental arch. The Stations of the Cross are mid-19th-century Flemish paintings.

The liturgical requirements of the Second Vatican Council caught up with St Mary's as they did with every other Catholic church. The sanctuary area was redesigned by Cathal O'Neill, Professor of Architecture at University College, Dublin. The floor was raised, enlarged and paved with Portland stone. A new altar replaced the original high altar carved by Peter Turnerelli (1774–1839), a prominent Irish sculptor who was for several years Sculptor in Ordinary to the royal family. Thankfully the architect decided to retain the front panel of the Turnerelli altar, depicting two kneeling angels, and incorporate it into the new altar, which was dedicated on 31 January 1982. One victim of the work was the original carved oak pulpit, which is stained to give it the appearance of mahogany. The pulpit was modelled on the choragic monument of Lysicrates at Athens and represents a section of the monument. It is still in the cathedral, but now stands disused in a corner of the south aisle.

The official title of 'pro-cathedral' was first used in the 1880s, and its used was confirmed by Archbishop Walsh. It emerged from a long-held nationalist feeling that one of the two medieval cathedrals should be 'returned' to the Roman Catholic church. Christ Church had been constituted the cathedral church of the Archbishop of Dublin by papal authority, and no Roman Catholic archbishop has ever petitioned for the decision to be revoked. The title became fixed in the early years of the 20th century, when plans were floated to build a new cathedral. After the Easter Rising of 1916 and consequent destruction of parts of the city centre, a plan for a new Dublin was drawn up, including provision for a new Roman Catholic cathedral on the north side of the city. Nothing materialised, and in a revised plan of 1946 the proposed site was moved to the quays. However, the diocesan authorities preferred building on the south side of the city, and the park in Merrion Square facing the Parliament Buildings was bought in the 1920s. During the episcopate of Archbishop John McQuaid (1940–72) the scheme remained under active consideration, but after his death in 1973, a more realistic approach led Archbishop Dermot Ryan (1972–85) to give the park to the city in 1974.

Although the Roman Catholic diocese of Dublin still lacks a proper cathedral church, the time for such buildings is probably now past. Given the strenuous efforts of fund-raising during the eighty-three years it took to build St Anne's Cathedral in Belfast, it seems a great pity that the same should not be done in Dublin to provide this capital city with a greater cathedral for its large Catholic population. But for the time being at least St Mary's continues to function as the mother church of the diocese without the full title of 'cathedral church'.

The present age has been conditioned by the 19th-century Gothic Revival not to think well of the 18th-century Classical Revival. St Mary's was unfortunate enough to be built at the very end of the Classical Revival. Had plans been drawn up five to ten years after its completion in 1825, a very different

building might have emerged. But even examined on its merits, the pro-cathedral is of little architectural interest; this plain, severe Greek temple lacks the degree of ornamentation of the later Classical Revival, as exemplified by the cathedrals of Cavan and Longford. The inherently cumbersome and dull design is not helped by its location in the cramped side streets of central Dublin. Were it to stand on some promontory in the sun-drenched whiteness of the Mediterranean, there might be room for a kinder assessment.

The interior is in need of redecoration, and the wall of the apse, badly affected by dry rot, is now shielded by blue-painted boarding, concealing in the process the two altars of Our Lady and the Sacred Heart. But the pro-cathedral is a well-used, living, working church. 'St Mary's is neither ancient nor awesome. Its site was a compromise, and it does not have an impressive façade of statuary, an exquisite rose window or a magnificent spire to be seen from afar. However, neither is it a museum; it is a living church, and it continues to be as Archbishop Troy wanted it to be, a heart for the city and an active house of God.'[3]

References

1 Mary Purcell, *Dublin's Pro-Cathedral* (Dublin, 1975), p. 5.
2 Ibid., p. 13.
3 Dermod McCarthy, *St Mary's Pro-Cathedral, Dublin* (Dublin, 1988), p. 25.

DULEEK

Duleek Cathedral

DULEEK (*Daimh liag* – stone house) is a village in Co. Meath 36.8km north-west of Dublin and 6.4km south-west of Drogheda. The first stone church in Ireland is said to have been built here by St Patrick, who gave charge of it to St Cianán. With Patrick, Cianán is supposed to have been a disciple of St Martin of Tours. He died *c.*500, and his feast-day is 24 November.

The diocese of Duleek was established at the Synod of Ráith Bressail in 1111 to provide a diocese for East Meath. A local synod which was convened at Uisneach later in the same year overruled this choice and substituted Clonmacnoise. However, Duleek was recognised as a diocesan see at Kells–Mellifont in 1152 and three possible bishops are known: Gilla Mo Chua mac Camchuarta, who died in 1117; Congalach, described as 'Coarb of Cianán', who died in 1127; and Áed, not specifically styled a bishop, who died in 1160. No Bishop of Duleek took the oath of fealty to King Henry II in 1171–2, and whatever shadowy existence the diocese may have had seems to have been ended by submission to the rights of Clonard.

The Celtic foundation was succeeded by an Augustinian priory founded by Hugh de Lacy in 1182 and dedicated to St Mary. Part of the ruined priory church still stands in a graveyard adjacent to the now disused Church of Ireland parish church. After the dissolution of the priory in 1537 the church continued to be used as a parish church, but it was in poor condition by the 17th century. James I gave away the charity lands that supported the church, and later reports indicate that it suffered during the Confederate war of the 1640s. A visitation in 1693 found a sorry state: 'There are still standing

except the architectural shadow. Two 10th-century High Crosses lie to the north and south of the parish church.

The parish church, dedicated to St Keenan (Cianán), was built in 1819 at a cost of £1,579, most of which was provided in the form of a loan from the Board of First-Fruits. The architect was John A. Trotter (1790–1842), and, at the time of writing, a statue of his grandfather, Judge Thomas A. Trotter, who represented Old Leighlin in the Irish parliament, stands in an alcove on the ground floor of the tower.

Duleek: the south aisle of the priory church looking east

the walls of a large fair church and chancell, with two aisles adjoining to it, but all out of repair these fifty years, except the porch, where the parishioners assemble to divine service . . It had been a large fair church and had organs and bells before the wars.'[1] In 1786 Duleek was described as 'this almost desolated village . . . From the ruins which are everywhere, we must suppose it was a town of note.'[2]

All that remains is the south aisle with its 14th-century south wall and 13th-century north arcade. The east window was reconstructed in the 16th century. The aisle contains the head of a 15th-century High Cross, the 15th-century Preston-Plunkett altar tomb and the tombs of the Bellew family. There is a square tower, also of the 15th century, and the concave curve in its north west corner shows that it was built around an older Round Tower of which nothing remains

There are two remaining 19th-century memorials, but the church, which was closed and deconsecrated in 1967 as part of a reorganisation of parishes, is now gutted and the interior is an eerie sight. The west gallery is in an advanced state of decay, and it cannot be much longer before it collapses; no doubt the roof will follow in due course.

The site of the abbey and the parish church is now depressingly derelict and forlorn, and it is to be hoped that funds may be found to improve its appearance.

References

1 John Healy, *History of the diocese of Meath* (Dublin, 1908), ii, 14.
2 Mervyn Archdall, *Monasticon Hibernicum* (London, 1786), p. 533.

ELPHIN

The Cathedral Church of St Mary the Virgin

ELPHIN (*Ail Fionn* – rock of the clear spring) is a market village in Co. Roscommon with a population of about 500, situated on the road from Roscommon to Boyle. Roscommon is 28.8km to the south, and Boyle is 25.6km to the north-west. It stands on the summit of a ridge running east–west, 'well and pleasantly situated on high ground in the midst of a fertile country.'[1]

Tradition says that Ono, son of Oengus, offered his house to St Patrick *c*.450, who renamed it Ail Fionn and placed his disciple St Assicus in charge. Assicus, who died *c*. 490 (feast-day 27 April) is said to have been 'an admirable worker in precious metals; and in his capacity as a goldsmith, greatly adorned his cathedral church with articles of his handicraft'.[2] He is said to have been succeeded by his nephew Bite (Batheus), but there are no further records of the monastery until the 12th century, when Elphin was established as a diocese for east Connacht. No trace remains of an edifice that could be linked to Assicus, and the last cathedral to stand on the site was a plain and insubstantial building. The surviving remains present a sad and pathetic picture.

A cathedral was built *c*. 1240 to replace one destroyed by fire in 1235. This building was itself partly destroyed during the rebellion of 1641 and was rebuilt by Bishop John Parker (1661–7). In 1685 Bishop John Hodson (1667–86) transferred an estate to certain trustees, half of which was to be used for 'the maintenance of a Grammar School in the town of Elphin' and the other half for 'the supporting, repairing, amending, beautifying and adorning the cathedral church

of Elphin, as the bishop and Dean and chapter should direct'. The Bishop Hodson Grammar School still exists, and although the entire governing body, headed by the Bishop of Kilmore, Elphin and Ardagh, are members of the Church of Ireland, there are no longer any Church of Ireland families in the neighbourhood and all the pupils are Roman Catholic.

By 1757 either the income from the remainder of the bishop's estate had dwindled in size, or it was no longer being used for the purpose intended, because the cathedral was in a ruinous condition. Most of the roof had fallen in, and the walls were in a dangerous state. A thorough rebuilding in 1757–8, with the help of a grant of 300 from the Board of First-Fruits, included the demolition of the 17th-century cathedral and any surviving medieval remains. Among the 18th-century Bishops of Elphin was Charles Dodgson (1775–95), grandfather of Charles Lutwidge Dodgson, better known as Lewis Carroll and author of *Alice in Wonderland*.

The cathedral was described in 1810 as 'neither large nor splendid'[3]; whether because of inadequate size, poverty of architecture or structural problems, the nave was rebuilt in 1823 under Bishop John Leslie (1819–54). Leslie was the last separate Bishop of Elphin: the dioceses of Kilmore and Ardagh were added to his care in 1841. A more flattering but slightly inaccurate reference of 1837 described the cathedral as 'a plain modernised building...with an ancient square tower . . . The interior is very neat.'[4] In 1844 it looked 'not unlike an English barn jostled up against an ancient steeple; yet it has quite a neat interior, – though a singularly plain one for a cathedral; and its old tower is square, narrow, tall, and considerably dilapidated, its summit ragged, and its sides disfigured by broken plaster'.[5] 'But being situated on the brow of a hill and in the centre of only miserable cabins it can be seen miles distant rising over the trees.'[6] The final addition to Elphin Cathedral was a short apse of Caen stone constructed in 1872.

The cathedral was an oblong building about 24.3m long excluding the apse, and 8.5m wide, 'a plain good-sized room, fitted up as well as circumstances will permit, for divine service.'[7] The bishop's throne and chapter stalls were at the east end of the nave, the dean's stall being on the north side. The pulpit was also on the north side, and the reading desk was on the south. The lectern and the font occupied unusual positions, being in the centre of the nave in between the pulpit and desk, the lectern being closer to the altar. There were four round-headed windows in the north wall. The ceiling was plastered and had a plain curved cornice.

A high square tower was attached to the west end of the cathedral. When William Warburton became Dean of Elphin in 1853, he was told that the tower had been some 6m higher but was partly demolished by high winds and not rebuilt to its former height.[8] This seems an unlikely story, considering that surviving pictures of the cathedral show a very tall tower out of proportion to the small cathedral. It had a curious crenellation not unlike the rim of a crown. It is not clear exactly how much of the medieval cathedral survived the destruction of 1641, but the descriptions in 1837 and 1844, quoted above, speak of an 'ancient' tower or steeple, which might be an indication of some medieval and 17th-century stonework. The tower was constructed partly of small stones and partly of brick and by the end of the 19th century had been coated with Portland cement and paint; it contained a clock which struck on a bell of 11 cwt.

The life of Elphin Cathedral was ended by a fierce storm on 4 February 1957 which wrecked the building. The roof was almost completely stripped of slates, and the roof timbers and ceiling were seriously damaged. The diocesan synod, meeting at Longford on 11 July, decided to abandon the cathedral and move the see of the dioceses of Elphin and Ardagh to Sligo. The decision was ratified by a meeting of the General Synod of the Church of Ireland in the following year, and Elphin Cathedral was formally deconsecrated on 17 November 1958. The stalls of the canons and dignitaries were transferred to St Patrick's Cathedral at Trim.

On 25 October 1961 the Church of St John the Baptist in Sligo was raised to the status of cathedral church for the dioceses of Elphin and Ardagh. In deference to Elphin, its dedication was changed to 'St Mary the Virgin and St John the Baptist'.

The ruined cathedral was mostly demolished in 1964 and the stones used in the construction of an interdenominational school. What little remained was partly rebuilt and restored in 1982. Custody was transferred from the Church of Ireland to Roscommon County Council in 1985. The neglected remains stand in an equally neglected graveyard at the east end of the town. Nothing survives to a height of more than 3m, and what does survive is in a deplorable state.

The structure is entered by a round-arched doorway on the north side of the nave at the west end. There is a small vestry or chapter room at the south west. The east and west walls are 1.5m high and the south wall about 2.5m high. It has a plaque to the memory of Oliver Goldsmith (1728–74), the poet, playwright and novelist, who was educated at the diocesan school before moving to Athlone. Edward Goldsmith, cousin of the poet's grandfather, was Dean of Elphin 1700–22. The plaque, erected in 1935 by the Goldsmith Society, contains the line 'Where genius dwelt and grew in classic halls' — an irony considering the state of the cathedral today.

The remains of Elphin Cathedral from the north-west

The north and south walls of the nave are approximately 1m high and have a number of memorials, including one to William Warburton, Dean of Elphin 1853–1900. Immediately outside the apse, against the south wall, is a crude stone construction resembling a chair, standing on red and black square tiling, which is alleged by a sign above to be 'The Throne'. This 'throne' is a ridiculously clumsy and ugly composite invention and probably no older than the restoration of 1982. It may indicate the site of the bishop's throne but, as a relic of Elphin Cathedral in its functioning days, it is a worthless fake.

Three steps lead up to the apse, which contains five round-arched windows and is brick-lined from the floor to the window sills. Part of the floor tiling remains and shows red, green, white and brown geometric patterns. Fallow wrote that the apse was constructed 'in a semi-medieval style, and scarcely harmonises with the domestic architecture of the rest of the inside of the cathedral'.[9] An embarrassingly crude representation of an altar consisting of a stone slab on four pillars, stands at the centre of the apse. This 'altar' has nothing whatever to do with the history and architecture of the cathedral; its crude workmanship links it with the 'throne' as an artificial construction from post-demolition days, presumably intended only as an indication of the position of the former altar.

Elphin Cathedral is a pathetic-looking ruin today. A tower of indeterminate date, a nave of 1823 and an apse of 1872 constituted the cathedral as last in use, but the 'rebuilding' of 1982 makes one suspect that perhaps even parts of the surviving low walls date from the late 20th century. The 'throne', the 'altar' and the 'chancel steps' are blatantly bogus and are designed, presumably, to give the modest 19th-century cathedral a much greater sense of antiquity than it actually possessed.

The Bishop's Palace was situated on the road to Boyle, about 400m from the cathedral. It was 'a spacious, comfortable old-fashioned country house behind a small lawn and shrubbery'.[10]

References

1 T. M. Fallow, *The cathedral churches of Ireland* (London, 1894), p. 84.
2 Ibid.
3 Nicholas Carlisle, *A topographical dictionary of Ireland* (London, 1810), p. 157.
4 Samuel Lewis, *A topographical dictionary of Ireland* (Dublin, 1837; repr., Washington, 1970), i, 598.
5 *The Parliamentary Gazetteer of Ireland* (Dublin, 1844–6), ii, 174.
6 Mackenzie Walcott, *The cathedrals of the United Kingdom* (London, 1860), p. 307.
7 Fallow, *The cathedral churches of Ireland*, p. 85.
8 Ibid., pp 84–85.
9 Ibid., p. 86.
10 *The Parliamentary Gazetteer of Ireland*, ii, 174.

EMLY

The Cathedral Church of St Alibeus

ALIBEUS, Elibeus, Ailbhe or Ailbe, who lived in the early 5th century, was one of four bishops that St Patrick found already in Ireland on his arrival. There are a number of conflicting and untrustworthy stories of his life. One account says that he was abandoned when a baby and left under a stone where a she-wolf suckled him. Other stories say that he had constant dialogue with the angels and was guided by them. It would be safer merely to record that he was a shadowy contemporary of Patrick; his feast-day is 12 September.

Emly (*Imleach iubhair* – borderland of the yew trees) is a village of about 1,000 people, 13.6km to the west of Tipperary. Because of the story of Alibeus being in Ireland before Patrick, the see of Emly is officially listed by the Vatican as being founded in the 4th century. This would make it many years older than Armagh and gives it the distinction of being the oldest continuous see in Ireland. It was certainly important enough to be the metropolitan see for the province of Munster until 1152, when it was supplanted by Cashel at the Synod of Kells–Mellifont. Emly suffered badly from violence and neglect throughout its history. The cathedral and the Round Tower were either burnt or pillaged by the Danes in 845, 847, 851, 866 and 968, and by other hands in 1058, 1089, 1116, 1152, 1154, 1162 and 1192.

Very little is known of the medieval cathedral. Records of the repeated pillagings and burnings of the 12th century are followed by a report that the cathedral was in a bad state of repair in 1363. The diocese was neglected in the 15th century, two of its bishops being absentees earning their living as suffragans in English dioceses. It probably suffered badly during the upheavals of the 16th century. On the death of Bishop Raymund Burke in 1562, Queen Elizabeth I nominated no successor, and Emly was amalgamated with Cashel in 1569, when both dioceses had become too poor to maintain bishops of their own. An act of the Irish parliament united the dioceses indicating by its wording that Emly was to be completely absorbed by Cashel: 'Henceforth for ever the said bisshoprickes and dioceses of Cashell & Imolye shalbe adjudged made and reputed & taken as one hole & intire diocese of Cashell & by that name shalbe knowen & used and not as several dioceses.'[1] In spite of this explicit suppression of Emly, the two dioceses, although united under one bishop remained separate and distinct, with clearly defined boundaries, each retaining its own cathedral church and chapter.

After the union with Cashel 'thus disrobed of its consequence, Emly fell a sacrifice to time, and because, though yet a village, a scene of desolation. Originally its situation was much more beautiful than at present, being immediately seated on a considerable lake, consisting of two hundred acres, which on account of its value, was nearly drained by the neighbouring proprietors in the year 1718.'[2] The lake extended westward by the line of the Dromcomogue river to Knocklong and eastward to an area westward of Ballymire and north of Duntryleague.

The cathedral was still in ruins in 1607, but was ordered to be rebuilt at the charge of the clergy and laity in 1611. Not much work had been done by 1615, when it was reported that 'the Church is down, the Chancell is in good state, yet standing'.[3] A Roman document of 1620 states that 'the cathedral has a choir, sacristy, belfry and cemetery, but the nave is in ruins', and also that 'the building was profaned and for some time derelict but was roofed by the Catholics for the use of the heretics'.[4]

Apart from a simplistic representation on the chapter seal, the only illustration of the the medieval cathedral is a sketch made by Thomas Dinely in 1680. His drawing shows a partly roofed small and rectangular Gothic-style building with a Decorated six-light east window and a stepped buttress at the north-east angle. Crosses surmount the gables. A passage leads from the north side to what looks like the stump of a Round Tower. Part of the Round Tower was still standing in the 18th century, but there is now no surviving trace. Dinely's drawing shows to the south an adjacent gabled ruin which looks as if it might have belonged to the 15th-century; it has a broken window not unlike that of the cathedral. It is possible that the cathedral was wrecked during the rising of 1641, though there is no mention of the town in the events of that year. It was described as being in a bad state of repair in 1693.

The simple church shown on the seal of the diocese was said, by those who remembered it, to have been a fair representation of the old cathedral. In the centre on the north side was a medieval tower with characteristic stepped Irish battlements and crowned by a low stunted spire. The doors and windows of the building appear to be of 17th-century design, which leads to the conclusion that the body of the cathedral had been repaired if not rebuilt at that time.

In 1715 an order was made for the construction of a pulpit, four stalls and a throne for the archbishop, and the cathedral appears to have been in satisfactory condition for most of the 18th century. New windows were inserted in 1780. A Glebe House was built close to the cathedral in 1782–4, the

building being superintended by the vicar, who lived in a tent during construction. In 1783 the floors of the cathedral were described as well flagged, with the exception of the south side, which had an earth floor and no pews, but the west end had been damaged by constant ball-playing.[5] By 1787 the north wall was so damp that its plaster was falling off, the south wall was soaking water, and rain was coming in through the roof in several places. The pews were also in a state of decay, no doubt through the damp. Repairs were undertaken in 1790–91, and in 1792 the cathedral was declared to be in 'elegant order'. But the structural problems of Emly Cathedral seem to have been insoluble, and in 1811 the roof and ceiling were so decayed that there was no possibility of repair. Instead of making every effort at preservation, the Dean and Chapter decided that the limits of patching and mending this dilapidated cathedral had been reached and that a new cathedral was the only possible solution.

The old cathedral was not immediately demolished, since its ruins were apparently still standing in 1844,[6] but it was abandoned and dismantled in 1821, and services were being held in the rectory in 1822. Rebuilding was deferred because of economic depression – another way of saying that insufficient funds had been raised. Architects were appointed in 1824, and the new cathedral was completed in March 1827. It was designed by the Pain brothers, George Richard (c.1793–1838) and James (c.1779–1877). Both were pupils of John Nash, who was instrumental in establishing them as architects and builders in Ireland. They had an extensive practice as designers of churches and castellated houses in the province of Cashel.

There was nothing of any great note about the new cathedral. It was a small and simple Gothic Revival building, 'a handsome structure of hewn stone, in the later English style, with a lofty spire'.[7] It was constructed with a loan from the Board of First-Fruits, and the total cost was £2,521 11s 9d. The exterior gave the impression of a cruciform shape, but, as at Ennis, the traditional area for the chancel was walled off to provide a vestry. This was typical of the Pains, who usually emloyed a *tau*-cross (T-shape) in the design of their churches, with a western tower and tall spire. The altar was set against this wall, and a three-decker pulpit was placed in the centre of the crossing in front of the altar. There were shallow transepts and a tower and spire at the west end. The building was repaired after damage by a storm in The 'Big Wind' of 1839 and repaired again in 1853.

By the middle of the 19th century it was clear that Emly Cathedral was an anachronism. 'The appearance of Emly, even aided with the decent form of its present parish-church [*sic*] and the ruin of its quondam cathedral, is prelatic dignity, first humbled and beggared, and next held up to utter derision.'[8] The presence of the structure, dignitaries and prebendaries of a cathedral church in such a small and remote place, was increasingly difficult to maintain and to justify in an area whose population was overwhelmingly Roman Catholic. The congregation was never very large, and the population of Emly was fast declining. Standing at 4,500 in 1841, it had fallen to 2,551 in 1868 of whom only 31 were members of the Church of Ireland. The population continued to fall steadily until 1971, when it stood at little more than 1,000. These statistics sealed the fate of Emly Cathedral. Disestablishment of the Church of Ireland in 1871 was the beginning of the end, and the cathedral was closed soon afterwards. Emly was united to the neighbouring parish of Cullen.

After the dissolution of the chapter the archdeacon was assigned a stall in Cashel Cathedral, and the union of the two dioceses first envisaged in 1568 at last took effect.

A new Roman Catholic church dedicated to St Ailbe was built close to and parallel with the site of the cathedral. It was designed by George Ashlin, the architect of Cóbh Cathedral, and constructed of limestone from quarries at Hospital and Knockcarron. The total cost was £14,500. The foundation stone was laid on 30 May 1880, and the church was completed and dedicated to St Ailbe on 6 January 1883. It is a fine building with a clerestoried nave, aisles and chancel,

Emly: St Ailbhe's Cross and the 19th century Roman Catholic Church

Canon Maurice Power, the Roman Catholic parish priest of Emly, offered to buy the building for £2,000. His offer was refused partly on legal grounds, but mainly owing to the objections of Maurice Day (Bishop of Cashel and Emly, Waterford and Lismore 1872–99). The bishop's grounds for objection are not on record, but there was some bitterness between the two churches in the years after Disestablishment. The cathedral was dismantled in 1877, and part of the stonework used to build a new church at Monard. The cathedral bell was moved to Mealiffe church, and the cathedral chalice and paten are now in the GPA–Bolton Library at Cashel; the paten bears the inscription 'For the Cathedrall of Emly'.

and a tower on the north side. In the Roman Catholic arrangement of dioceses, Emly is united to Cashel, and the church is of parish and not cathedral status, but it can be taken as the modern representative of the old cathedral church.

Very little remains to be seen at Emly today. The old graveyard, marking the site of the two cathedrals, is still there; the cathedral of 1827 stood on rising ground in the centre, its medieval predecessor a short distance to the east. Built into the wall by the left-hand pier of the gateway is a stone with the following inscription in raised Roman characters: '**LO-**

CUS IN QUEM INTRAS TERRA SANCTA EST. R. JONES P'CENT' (The place wherein you enter is holy ground. R. Jones Precentor). Robert Jones was ordained deacon and priest in 1622 and became Precentor of Emly in 1628. In the rising of 1641 the precentor was robbed of 'books and other property . . . worth 100, and he was also dispossessed of a farm in Ballyholohan, and as well lost his Precentorship, which was worth 140 per annum'.[9]

There are two items of antiquity in the graveyard. St Ailbe's Well is 24.6m north of the present church. It is about 7m deep and surrounded by a circular cut stone wall which was erected by the order of the cathedral chapter in 1827. Unfortunately the well is now completely encased by a concrete cover with the exception of a small manhole.

In the south-west of the graveyard is an ancient Celtic sandstone cross known as St Ailbe's Cross, said to mark the burial place of the saint. Its present height is 1.5m, though a further 1.5m, are thought to be buried below ground. In 1694 two local magistrates obtained permission from William Palliser (Church of Ireland Archbishop of Cashel 1694–1727) to demolish the cross and close the well since they encouraged 'eye-dolatry'. Fortunately, for whatever reason, their intentions were not put into effect.

For many years Precentor Jones's tablet was the only visible reminder of Emly's cathedrals. However, in 1960 the wheel came full circle with the demolition of Monard church. Canon Laurence Meaney (Roman Catholic parish priest of Emly 1939–70) managed to acquire fragments of the medieval cathedral and returned them to Emly. A stone tablet bearing the coat of arms of Sir Maurice Hurley, which had been erected in the medieval cathedral in 1632 as a memorial to his two wives, and transferred to the 1827 cathedral, was moved again in 1877 to Monard, where it was built into the north gable. A second part of the memorial with a Latin inscription of nineteen lines was set in the boundary wall of the new schools at Emly. Both these tablets have now been returned to the graveyard at Emly and are set in the boundary wall opposite the sacristy of the Roman Catholic church.

The centenary history of St Ailbe's Church, published in 1982, mentioned that 'up to recently', certain pieces of ancient stonework, presumably retrieved from Monard church, could be seen piled up by the side of the church. These comprised: a large circular stone basin with two ears, said to have been the font; an oblong stone which seems to have been a chute from the gutters; a small square pillar with a cross and the letters IHS carved upon it, which is said to have supported the altar; and various portions of tracery and mullions. Most of them have now disappeared. Three capitals can still be seen, two bearing human faces and foliage designs, and the third bearing the mitred head of a bishop. These can be seen on the perimeter wall of the right-hand side of the church grounds. There are also a few ancient

stones bearing curved designs set in the walls of the Sacristan's House, which stands on the left-hand side of the graveyard.[10]

These are the few surviving fragmentary remains of Emly's cathedrals.

References

1 St J. D. Seymour, *The diocese of Emly* (Dublin, 1913), p. 92.
2 Mervyn Archdall, *Monasticon Hibernicum* (London, 1786), p. 654.
3 St J. D. Seymour, *The succession of parochial clergy in the united dioceses of Cashel and Emly* (Dublin, 1844), p. 96.
4 Thomas Duhig, *St Ailbe's Church, Emly, 1882–1982* (Emly, 1982), p. 13.
5 Ibid.
6 *The Parliamentary Gazetter of Ireland* (Dublin, 1844–6), ii, p. 176.
7 Samuel Lewis, *A topographical dictionary of Ireland* (Dublin, 1837; repr., Washington, 1970), i, p. 3.
8 *The Parliamentary Gazetteer of Ireland*, ii, p. 176.
9 Duhig, *St Ailbe's Church, Emly, 1882–1982*, p. 34.
10 Ibid., pp 34–35.

ENNIS

The Pro-Cathedral of St Peter and St Paul

Diocese of Killaloe (Roman Catholic)

ENNIS (*Inis* — river-meadow) is the busy county town of Co. Clare and is of little architectural interest. It lies 35km to the north-west of Limerick and 67.2km south of Galway. Clare has been at the forefront of Irish politics in the 19th and 20th centuries. At the centre of Ennis is is a column commemorating Daniel O'Connell (1775–1847), the Irish nationalist who was elected M.P. for Clare in 1828. In the grounds outside the county courthouse is a monument to Eamon de Valera (1882–1975) who represented Clare in the Dail from 1917 to 1959 and was President of Ireland 1959–73. The only significant remnant of antiquity is the ruin of a 13th/15th century Franciscan friary, by the bridge over the River Fergus, founded *c.*1250 by one of the O'Briens of Thomond. The nave and chancel are the oldest parts of the friary; the other structures, including the tower, transept and sacristy, date mainly from the late 15th century.

A Roman Catholic chapel was built in what is now Chapel Lane in 1735, and it remained the principal place of Catholic worship until 1842. The building still stands and is now used as a community centre.

On 21 October 1821 a parochial meeting was held to consider the future, since the chapel was now too small to hold the increasing number of worshippers and 'it is useless to attempt any enlargement of it, the approaches being narrow, offensive and inconvenient'. The meeting resolved to build a new chapel 'in such a situation as to combine the accommodation of the Inhabitants, with the improvement of the town'.[1] Despite this resolute beginning the building of Ennis Cathedral was dogged by lack of funds, by disputes and by other problems until the day that the last stone was put in place in 1874.

Nothing happened for seven years, owing to a minor famine in 1822. Then followed an acrimonious dispute between Dean Terence O'Shaughnessy, the parish priest of Ennis, and his curate Fr Patrick MacDonogh, concerning the Ennis jail chaplaincy. In addition, worsening relations between Catholics and Protestants ensured that the project did not get the support from Protestants that had been hoped.

In January 1828 Francis Gore, a Protestant, donated a site for a nominal rent. Six weeks later the dean issued guidelines to the competing architects: the church was to be T-shaped, 36.5m long, 15.2m wide in the nave and 30.4m wide at the crossing. The T-shape plan was common in early Catholic churches and was copied from the Presbyterian pattern which developed in the 17th century. A public meeting of clergy and laity was held in the old chapel on 23 April 1828 to inspect the plans. The dean pointed out that the new church would one day be the cathedral church of the diocese of Killaloe, since it was likely that Ennis would be the future residence of the bishops, and in the light of this he suggested that it might be appropriate to set up a committee which would both consider plans and be responsible for raising funds. The meeting agreed and a committee of thirty members chaired by a Protestant and including two others was formed.

The winning design was by Dominic Madden, a well-known architect of the day. Madden had been commissioned to design the Roman Catholic cathedrals at Ballina and Tuam, construction of both of which had begun in the previous year, 1827. Madden's established reputation in the field of cathedral building, may have influenced the planning committee to choose his design, its merits apart. But cathedral building in Ireland was still in its infancy at this stage, and the architectural doctrines of the Pugin–McCarthy era were still in the future. The style of Madden's three cathedrals at Ballina, Ennis and Tuam is a very simple form of Gothic, though Ennis is notably different from Ballina and Tuam.

Work was in progress on the foundations in June 1828 but nothing more was done until 1831 because of a dispute between Dean O'Shaughnessy and the Franciscans, who had opened their own chapel in Ennis in December 1830. Their right to do so was contested by the dean, who saw Franciscans drawing on limited financial resources which were needed for the cathedral building fund. After an appeal to Rome amicable relations were restored in 1832. Hardly had one dispute been settled than the pugnacious dean was in conflict with another group of religious for exactly the same financial reasons. The Christian Brothers, whom he had initially welcomed, arrived in Ennis in 1827. Relations deteriorated in 1833, and in November 1834 the dean was suspended from office for publicly denouncing not only the Brothers but also one of his own curates who had supported them. The Brothers eventually left Ennis in 1840, only to return in 1854 at the request of O'Shaughnessy's successor, Dean John Kenny.

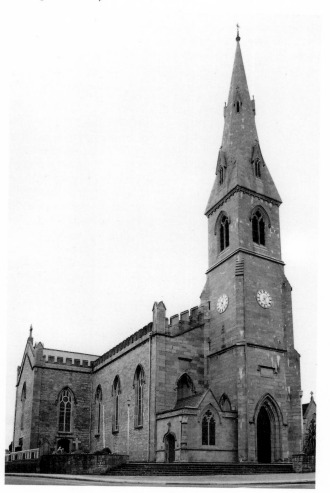

Ennis Cathedral from the north-west

Work on the cathedral, which had stopped for the duration of the dispute, began again in November 1836 after a morale-boosting visit from Patrick Kennedy, the new Bishop of Killaloe (1836–50). Work proceeded slowly, and it was not until January 1841 that the walls had reached a height to allow the construction of a roof. The first mass was said in the still unfinished cathedral on 4 September 1842, the dean delivering 'a lengthy and eloquent discourse at the joy he felt in being able to meet them in the edifice, to which he had devoted so much of his time and attention'.[2]

The cathedral was dedicated by Bishop Kennedy on 26 February 1843. Much remained to be done, principally the building of the tower and spire, but the onset of the Great Famine in 1845 brought the work to a halt, as it did at Killarney Cathedral and elsewhere in Ireland. Dean O'Shaughnessy died in 1848 and was buried in the cathedral he had done so much to build. He was aged about eighty-six or eighty-seven at the time of his death, which says much about his behaviour in the preceding twenty years. He was an old man in a hurry to see a cathedral built in his lifetime and would allow nothing to get in the way. The work was eventually stopped by a natural disaster which even he was powerless to sweep aside. He is commemorated by a brass plaque in the floor of the cathedral which possibly marks his burial place.

The cathedral was still unfinished in 1850 and in debt to the extent of £800. A priest was dispatched to England to raise funds, and sufficient money had been collected to pay for the erection of a gallery in one of the transepts at a cost of £115. On 18 June 1871 a meeting of the church committee decided to proceed with construction of the tower and spire. The work was undertaken by Maurice Fitzgerald, who, conceivably with some slight modifications, implemented Madden's design. A slow-down in fund-raising meant that the work was not completed until 23 October 1874, nearly two years after the scheduled date, and at a cost of £1,500. The three-storey diagonally buttressed tower is surmounted by a broach spire making a total height of 42.6m. The flanking porches have ogee-headed doorways.

The cathedral is built of limestone ashlar and has a crenellated parapet and tall pointed windows with tracery. The original façade has been partially obscured by the porches, but the original doorways can still be seen from the inside.

The interior of the cathedral was completed by 1861 under the supervision of J.J. McCarthy. The arcades and piers, the panelled ceiling and the organ gallery at the west end are the work of McCarthy, as were the altars and reredos. There is an aisled nave of six bays with clerestory, and transepts of two bays each. Slender Doric piers with fanciful tracery in the spandrels support a coffered ceiling of floral patterned square panels divided by white ribs, dating from a reroofing of 1957–8. The timber piers and arches are purely decorative and not load-bearing in any way. They were installed by McCarthy for the purpose of creating two side aisles which he may have considered essential to the design of a cathedral. Both transepts have galleries, and there is an organ gallery at the west end of the nave. The transept galleries have chaste Gothic panelling on their fronts – that of the organ gallery is bolder. The fluted stoups beside the transept doorways have square-headed dripstones. The former Mortuary Chapel is in the south-west corner of the nave; it is partially walled in dark marbles and has a mosaic of the Virgin and Child. The former baptistery, in the north-west corner of the nave, contained a memorial font of 1912, now gone. In its place is a shrine to Our Lady of Lourdes. The Stations of the Cross are good painted plaster casts in deep relief.

Of McCarthy's three altars, all of Caen stone, alabaster and Irish marbles, the two transept altars, dedicated to the Sacred Heart and the Blessed Virgin Mary, remain; the high altar was removed in the reordering of 1973. The reredos rests on a plinth of Caen stone and consists of an arcade of polished marble shafts with moulded bases and carved caps. The tympana contain busts of Christ, the Blessed Virgin Mary, St Celestine, St Bridget and St Mary Magdalen. The spaces below and between the shafts are filled with paintings by John Early representing St Senan, St Paul, St Peter and St Flannan. Further paintings, depicting St John and St Patrick, can be seen above side doors in the reredos which lead into the sacristy and offices behind. The altars were consecrated on 6 and 7 July 1861 by Bishop Michael Flannery. An organ was installed at the same time at a cost of £1,000.

Following his appointment as coadjutor bishop in 1889 Bishop Thomas MacRedmond (1891–1904) came to live at Ennis, and the completed church at last became the pro-cathedral of the diocese of Killaloe. Bishops Michael Flannery (1859–91), Thomas MacRedmond (1891–1904) and Michael Fogarty (1904–55) are buried within the cathedral, and Bishop Joseph Rodgers (1955–66) is buried in the grounds.

Ennis Cathedral is almost totally devoid of representational stained glass. While every other cathedral was filling its windows with memorial stained glass as quickly as possible, Ennis has only one such window, erected in the former baptistery in 1903 in memory of Fr Dan Fogarty, Administrator of Ennis 1878–88. A memorial to Dean James Barrett on the south wall has fluted Doric columns supporting a broken pediment. On the north wall is a memorial to Fr John Meagher, who died on St Patrick's Day in 1866. It consists of a white-painted bust set in an elaborate Gothic niche.

Some renovation was undertaken in 1894, but the cathedral remained substantially unchanged until Vatican II reordering of 1973. The work took six months to implement, and the cathedral was formally re-opened by Bishop Michael Harty on 21 December. The altar rails, pulpit and high altar were removed, though the reredos was allowed to remain, and a new altar, ambo, font and tabernacle pillar of Wicklow granite, designed by Andrew Devane, were installed at the crossing. The bronze tabernacle door is embellished with enamelled representations of five loaves and two fishes. The cathedral was provided with new flooring, and the entire building was repainted. The tower clock, which was installed to commemorate the Holy Year of 1950, was removed and replaced by the clock from the old cathedral at Mullingar, which had been in store since the demolition of that cathedral in 1933.

At the rear of the cathedral is the presbytery, built about 1870. It is a polychromatic structure of red brick with blue and yellow brick banding, coigns, arches and window dressings.

The Pro-Cathedral of St Peter and St Paul is a comparatively modest and simple structure, its style governed as much by geography and budget as by architectural whim. It would be inaccurate to describe it as a great work of architecture, and unfair to dismiss it as uninteresting. Allowances need to be made for the fact that it is an early Roman Catholic cathedral dating from pre-triumphalist days; that it stands in the remote west of Ireland; that money was not as plentiful as it might have been in Dublin or Belfast; and that the building as one sees it today is the work of two architects – a marriage of Madden's exterior and McCarthy's interior.

References

1 *Limerick Reporter*, 6 Sept. 1842.
2 Ibid.

ENNISCORTHY

The Cathedral Church of St Aidan

Diocese of Ferns (Roman Catholic)

ENNISCORTHY (*Inis coirthe* — island of the memorial stone) is a market town in Co. Wexford, 120km south of Dublin, 11.2km south of Ferns and 24km north of Wexford, standing on the banks of the River Slaney at the limit of its navigation. It grew up around a 13th-century castle which now houses the County Museum. There were two religious houses at Enniscorthy. An early mission house or chapel, founded here by St Senan of Scattery Island *c.*510, evolved into an Augustinian priory in the 13th century and was suppressed in 1539; it stood on the west bank of the river about 1.6km south of Enniscorthy. There was also an Observant Franciscan friary in the town founded *c.*1460, but also suppressed in 1539. The site of the friary is now occupied by other buildings.

Enniscorthy became the see town of the Roman Catholic Bishop of Ferns at the beginning of the 19th century. Bishop Patrick Ryan (coadjutor 1805–14, diocesan 1814–19) was the first to reside in the town. A pro-cathedral was built on the site of the present cathedral on Duffry Hill, in 1809, but lasted for only forty years. In 1838 Bishop James Keating (1819–48) called a public meeting to decide the future of the building, which was too small for its congregation and in need of repair. Temporary repairs were carried out in 1839 under the direction of Augustus Welby Northmore Pugin (1812–52), who was commissioned to design a new cathedral.

Pugin firmly stamped his mark on Gothic Revival architecture in the 19th century, but Enniscorthy Cathedral is one of his less well-known works. The site is cramped, and the ground falls away sharply to the river. Because of this limitation, Pugin designed a building that was narrow, but long and lofty, and, probably for the same reasons, it is aligned north—south instead of east–west.

Pugin modelled Enniscorthy Cathedral on the ruined Tintern Abbey in Wales, and the cathedral is a three-quarter-size version of Tintern with a high-walled but very long-aisled nave of six bays, an aisled chancel and transepts of the same height, and a central tower. The plan departs from Tintern in that the cathedral chancel has three bays instead of the four at Tintern, no eastern chapels in the transepts, and a tower (that at Tintern having collapsed long ago). Tintern's walls are well buttressed, whereas those at Enniscorthy are clear except for the substantial buttresses along the aisles and at the corners. The vestries, chapel and baptistery outside the chancel aisles are not present at Tintern and were later additions to Pugin's design.

Pugin thought that the only thing of beauty at Tintern was the west window, and this (or the south transept window) provided the unusual motifs for the large windows in the nave, chancel and transepts: a row of extremely acute and barbed-looking trefoils over slender lights with trefoiled heads and under roundels filled with trefoils, quatrefoils, cinquefoils and hexafoils.

Pugin's plan called for the new cathedral to be built around its old cathedral, which could then remain in use until the new cathedral was ready. The foundation of Pugin's cathedral was laid in 1843 and in 1846 the first mass was said in the completed chancel and transepts. The nave was completed in 1849, and the old cathedral was demolished.

The state of the almost complete cathedral was not entirely to the satisfaction of Pugin, who complained about the behaviour of Bishop Keating's successor, Bishop Myles Murphy (1850–56): 'The cathedral I built, at Enniscorthy, has been completely ruined. The new bishop has blocked up the choir, stuck the altars under the tower!! and the whole building is in the most painful state of filth: the sacrarium is full of rubbish, and it could hardly have been worse if it had fallen into the hands of Hottentots.'[1] There was, conceivably, some degree of friction between architect and bishop. It is possible that Bishop Murphy cared little for the internal decoration of a building which had consumed so much of the time and attention of his predecessor. Bishop Murphy died in 1856, and his successor, Bishop Thomas Furlong, commissioned J. J. McCarthy, who later acquired the name and reputation of 'the Irish Pugin', to complete the interior in accordance with Pugin's designs. The work was probably finished by 1860, when the cathedral was dedicated.

Pugin designed a tower with two stages, the lower with four lancets and the upper with two traceried openings in each face. The tower was constructed in 1850, and a spire was added in 1871–2. But the weight of the spire was too heavy, and the tower began to sag. Both tower and spire were taken down and rebuilt in 1872–3, the tower losing its lower stage with small lancet openings. A mortuary chapel and baptistery were added in 1915. An extensive scheme of restoration took place in the years 1936–45; the cathedral was reroofed because of problems with damp, new pews of Austrian oak were added, the west window was filled with stained glass, and new Stations of the Cross (to replace those provided in 1885) were erected. With the completion of the work and the clearing of all debts, the cathedral was solemnly consecrated in 1945.

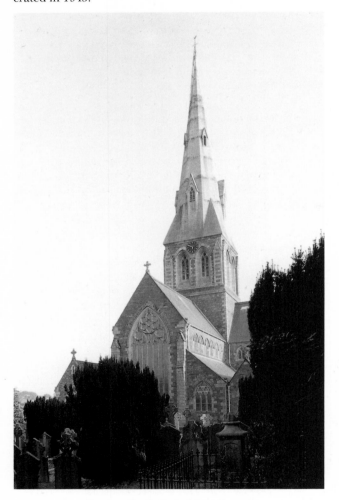

Enniscorthy Cathedral from the east

The cathedral is built of granite blocks ranging from grey-blue to deep green in colour and incorporates stones from the old Franciscan friary. The friary tower collapsed at about the time that work on the cathedral began, and Bishop Keating obtained permission from the landlord, the 3rd Earl of Portsmouth, to remove the stones for use in the construction of the cathedral.

The cathedral has an aisled nave with clerestory and a limestone tower and spire with lucarnes, at the crossing. The nave and aisles are only 15m wide, but the total length is 53m, and the spire is 69m high.

The steeply pitched timber ceiling has unusual webbing with trusses resting on stone corbels. The five-bay nave is divided from its narrow aisles by arcades resting on cylindrical granite piers laid in drums, with simple carved capitals and bases. The shallow transepts are only a little wider than the nave aisles and have lofty five-light stained-glass windows. The chancel has aisles separated from it by arcades of delicate Gothic arches, with pierced quatrefoil openings, resting on slender marble colonnettes. The altars on the (liturgical) north and south sides of the chancel, are dedicated to St Aidan and the Blessed Virgin Mary respectively. The seven-light east window has Decorated tracery. The marble high altar and reredos, by Pearse & Sharpe, are still in position, but pointedly ignored by seating which faces towards the crossing.

The new granite altar and lectern, on a dais at the crossing, were installed in 1970 in conformity with the requirements of the Second Vatican Council. A tau-rood, by Enda King, is suspended from the tester above the new altar, and the general arrangement is quite successful. A list of names of the Bishops of Ferns in painted scrolls adorns the four piers of the crossing.

The grounds of the cathedral were given free by the 4th Earl of Portsmouth in 1897. The wrought-iron entrance gates and granite piers and the boundary railings were given in 1920.

Enniscorthy Cathedral is not the most memorable of Pugin's designs, but it is worth seeing because of the good use he has made of a difficult site. There is nothing especially distinctive about the exterior, with the exception of the coloured granite blocks, but the black-and-white decoration of the interior is striking. 'Altogether the aspect and arrangements of this church show that comfort and economy were the objects of its founders rather than ostentatious display or architectural pretensions.'[2]

References

1 Benjamin Ferrey, *Recollections of A. N. Welby Pugin and his father, Augustus Pugin* (London, 1861), p. 125.

2 James Godkin, *Ireland and her churches* (London, 1867), p. 300.

ENNISKILLEN

The Cathedral Church of St Macartin

Diocese of Clogher (Church of Ireland)

ENNISKILLEN (*Inis Ceithleann* — Ceithleann's island), situated on the River Erne, is a town of about 10,500 inhabitants, and the county town of Fermanagh. The island that lies at the heart of the town was always of strategic importance for control of the valley, and during the Middle Ages it was a key stronghold of the Maguire family. In 1611 James I granted the island, together with considerable estates, to Captain (later Sir) William Cole. A royal charter in 1613 constituted the island as the borough of Enniskillen. Thereafter Enniskillen became an important stronghold of Protestant settlers; the town became a rallying-point in 1641 during the Confederate war, and again in 1689–90, when the inhabitants repelled an attack by the forces of James II.

The first rector was appointed in 1622, and a parish church, dedicated to St Anne, was built on one of the two hills in the centre of the island probably *c.*1627. The 19th-century cathedral which today stands on the site of this church occupies a commanding position in the centre of the city, the tip of its octagonal spire being 45.7m above ground-level.

The first church was about 15m long and roofed with shingles which were replaced by slates in 1739. It had a tower to which a spire was added in 1721 at a cost of £58 17s 2d; it was repaired and increased in height in 1734, but reduced again in 1832 because of structural instability. Only part of the tower remains from the 17th-century church; it was incorporated into the present structure during the 19th-century rebuilding. A small three-light lattice window and a stone bearing the date 1637 can be seen above the main entrance door. The tower formerly had a large 17th-century sundial on its south face which was unfortunately removed when the the three-train chiming clock was installed in 1936. There is also a stone commemorating William Pokrich who died in 1628. It was recovered from the graveyard when the church was rebuilt in 1842 and is set in the west wall of the nave near the entrance; it is inscribed with the last words of Thomas Cromwell: 'GRAUNT ME MER[CIFUL SAVIOUR T]HAT NOW DEATH HATH S[HUT UP THE EYES OF MY] BODY YET THE EYES OF MY SOULE MAY STILL BEHOLD AND LOKKE UPPON THEE AND WHEN DEATH HATH [TAKEN A]WAY THE USE OF MY TOUNG YET MY HEART MAY CRY AND SAY LORD INTO THY HANDES I COMMEND MY SOULE LORD JESUS RECEIVE MY SPIRIT.'

By the beginning of the 19th century the church could no longer accommodate the growing number of parishioners, and extensions were built in 1826. By 1832 the spire had become so unsafe that it was demolished, and the opportunity used for a complete rebuilding. The total cost of the work was £5,000, and the new building was dedicated on 7 June 1842. It was designed either by Thomas Elliott of Ballygonnell or by William Farrell, regional architect of the Ecclesiastical Commissioners with Elliott as the contractor. Its style has been described as 'an old-fashioned, naive Perp[endicular] style first introduced into Ireland by the Paine brothers thirty years before',[1] but there are many points of similarity with the Planter's Gothic to be seen in the architecture of St Columb's Cathedral at Derry. The only further major alteration was the extension of the chancel by 5.1m in 1889; the oak pulpit, standing on a plinth of grey-veined marble, was installed at the same time.

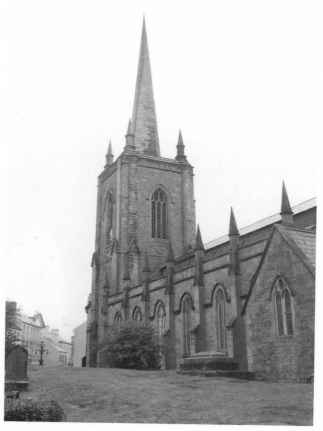

Enniskillen Cathedral from the south-west

The size of Enniskillen's population increased substantially in the early years of the 20th century, and the parish became one of the largest in the diocese of Clogher. Long before St Anne's was formally given cathedral status in 1921, the possibility was probably discussed in certain quarters, and alterations were made to the cathedral in anticipation of such a change. At the time of the extension of the chancel in 1889, during the incumbency of Canon Charles Ovenden (1886–1911), stalls were provided for the diocesan chapter 'in case of the church being converted into a cathedral'.[2]

In 1921, on the proposal of Lt-Col. John Madden (1870–1935) of Hilton Park in Co. Monaghan, the General Synod of the Church of Ireland decided that St Anne's Church should become a cathedral church for the diocese of Clogher. The decision was taken while Archdeacon James MacManaway was Rector of Enniskillen (1917–23). In 1923 he was elected Bishop of Clogher, and was succeeded at Enniskillen by his brother Hugh MacManaway (1923–50), who was given the honorific title of Dean of Clogher in 1932.

The circumstances and reasoning behind the General Synod's decision are somewhat obscure. The claim was made that Clogher itself was a small and remote village, with a comparatively small cathedral, and difficult to reach from most parts of the diocese. The same could be said of many Church of Ireland dioceses, but it was deemed necessary in Clogher to resolve this apparent difficulty by adding a second cathedral. The General Synod provided that St Anne's Church would become the second cathedral church of the Diocese, rather than that it would supplant Clogher Cathedral. The two cathedrals were to have equal rights, and each new Bishop of Clogher is usually enthroned in both cathedrals, and new prebendaries can be installed in either cathedral. One scents, perhaps, an underlying degree of triumphalism behind statements made at the time: 'It is not unlikely that the final residence of the Bishop will be placed in Enniskillen the most important town with the largest church congregation in the diocese, and the most convenient town of access to the greater number of the parochial clergy.'[3]

Dedicated to St Anne, mother of the Blessed Virgin Mary, for more than two hundred years, the elevation of the church to cathedral status brought an abrupt, confusing and quite unnecessary change of dedication. The dedication to St Anne was dropped and the 'new' cathedral took on the dedication of the ancient cathedral -St Macartin – although, for unknown reasons, the spelling is slightly different from that at the 'old' cathedral at Clogher which is dedicated to St Macartan.

In 1923 the east end of the cathedral was reordered under the supervision of the architect R. Caulfield Orpen. The west gallery organ was abandoned and replaced by a new instrument in the north-east corner of the nave; the corresponding south-east corner was formed into a vestry; the floor space between was raised two steps and formed into a choir containing the bishop's throne and the chapter and choir stalls, all made of carved oak; and the sanctuary was panelled with coloured marbles. The throne was presented in 1923 by Lt-Col. Madden and his wife.

The cathedral plan is an aisled nave and clerestory of six bays and a shallow chancel and sanctuary. The nave has galleries on three sides, marked off by a painted wooden balustrade, and supported by clustered cast-iron columns. The west gallery contains the old organ by John Smith of Bristol which

was in use from 1830 to 1923; only the case remains. The Renaissance font at the west end of the nave below the gallery is of sandstone carved with an interlaced border around the rim set like a sundial on a turned baluster. It was presented in 1666 by William Vincent, rector at the time. The pews are of pine, and the aisles are tiled.

The cathedral contains the colours and several monuments of the two regiments connected with the town, the Royal Inniskilling Dragoons and the Royal Inniskilling Fusiliers. The Inniskillings ceased to exist in 1968, being amalgamated in that year with the Royal Irish Rangers. The Regimental Association suggested that a chapel be provided for them in the cathedral, and in 1970 the north aisle was converted into a small Regimental Chapel. The design, by John Storie, provided a coffered ceiling of cedar and the separation of the aisle from the nave by a wrought-iron screen. The ill-proportioned and impractical altar is made from teak in a design typical of its date. The chapel is used for an annual service by the Regimental Association.

The choir contains a number of memorials to the descendants of Sir William Cole, who rose through the ranks of the peerage in the 18th century: Barons Mount Florence in 1760, Viscounts Enniskillen in 1776, and Earls of Enniskillen in 1789. On the south side of the chancel is a statue of the 2nd Earl of Enniskillen (1768–1840) in the robes of a Knight of St Patrick. On the north side is a statue of his brother, General Sir Galbraith Lowry Cole (1772–1842), who fought in the Peninsular War of 1808–14. A small stained-glass window near this statue commemorates the 3rd Earl of Enniskillen (1807–86). The east window contains stained glass by William Warrington of London, inserted in 1856 in memory of Jane, wife of the 3rd Earl, who died in May 1855. The crypt contains the remains of many members of the Cole family, whose seat was at Florence Court, 13.6km southwest of Enniskillen. The property was made over to the National Trust in 1954, and the 6th Earl and his wife left the house in 1973. The 7th and present Earl lives in Kenya.

On a strict interpretation of the words 'cathedral church', it can be argued that the position of Enniskillen Cathedral is anomalous and confusing, and its elevation to such a status can be regarded as the reflection of an imperfect understanding of episcopacy and ecclesiology. There can only be one cathedral church and one 'cathedra' in a diocese, and the provision of two such buildings for the diocese of Clogher, unique in the Church of Ireland, is a state of affairs for which geography and population are unsatisfactory explanations.

The interior of Enniskillen Cathedral looking east

A practical and more realistic view is to accept that this co-cathedral has the twin advantages of its position (at the heart of the most populous town in the diocese of Clogher) and its size (with a seating capacity of 800–1,000). On these grounds it is an obvious setting for large diocesan services and other events.

References

1 Alistair Rowan, *North-West Ulster* (London, 1979), p. 277.

2 W. C. Trimble, *The history of Enniskillen* (Enniskillen, 1919–21), iii, 899.

3 Ibid.

FERNS

The Cathedral Church of St Edan

Diocese of Ferns (Church of Ireland)

FERNS (*Fearna* – place of alders), once the capital of the King of Leinster, is a pleasant village of 800 inhabitants in Co. Wexford, 18km south-east of Gorey and 11.2km north of Enniscorthy. The history of the town is closely linked with St Edan of Clonmore, also known as Máedóc-Edan or Áed or Aidan, but more commonly as Mogue. Mogue is a contraction of Mo-Áed-Óg. The prefix Mo signifies endearment and the suffix Óg is the diminutive of affection. Mogue was a Welshman trained at St David's Abbey at Menevia. Tradition says that St David died in his arms and that Mogue succeeded him as abbot. On the strength of that tradition, a claim was later made from Wales to establish Welsh jurisdiction over Ferns since it had been founded by a Welsh abbot. By tradition Mogue became a bishop *c.*598 and died in 625; his feast-day is 31 January.

Mogue was given land at Ferns by the King of Leinster in thanksgiving after victory at the battle of Dunboyke in 598. The semi-circular wall around the graveyard marks the rampart he erected to protect his church and monastery. His piety and learning attracted many visitors to Ferns in search of education and for a while it ranked with Clonmacnoise and Glendalough as one of the more important Celtic schools.

There is a reference to 'the stone church of Ferns' in 787, a time when stone buildings were still rare. The Abbot of Ferns seems to have exercised some pre-eminence over the heads of the other religious communities of Leinster, and St Mogue and his successor St Moling (d. 697, feast-day 17 June) are sometimes, though erroneously, described as Archbishops of Ferns.

The town and monastery were plundered several times by the Vikings in the 9th and 10th centuries, and a gap of more than a century in the list of abbots, indicates disturbance and disintegration. Ferns was burned in 1154 by Dermot MacMurrough, King of Leinster. The king later repented of his action and refounded the monastery in 1169 as a priory for the Canons Regular of St Augustine. He died in 1171 and was buried at his own request, 'near the shrines of St Moedhoc and St Moling'.[1] A cross-shaft covered with a key pattern is said to mark his grave. The ruins of the priory lie to the south of the cathedral and can be recognised by a tower which is square at the base and round for the upper part. The north wall of the church is still standing, and the chancel once had barrel vaulting. To the north of the chancel is the sacristy, from where a staircase leads to a room where the sacristan lived and another room over the chancel. The foundations of the cloister are to the south of the church.

A new cathedral was built in the 13th century by Bishop John of St John (1223–53), the first English Bishop of Ferns. It was intended to be on the same scale as that completed later at Kilkenny and the plan was very similar. It had an aisled nave, transepts and a central tower, and a long chancel with aisles for nearly half its length.

In 1570 the Lord Deputy, Sir Henry Sidney, suggested that the collegial residence might be moved from Ferns, then declining in importance, to St Mary's Church at New Ross, a growing river port town. But the Dean and Chapter refused to move and addressed a petition to the Lord Deputy: 'We, whose names are hereunto subscrybed, will sticke whyle wee live [to the Cathedral Church of Ferns], and wee have agreed for buildinge and repairinge the same, to our great charges, and meane to bring the same to suche plighte, to the uttermoste of our powers and liabilitie, whereby wee may be there residente, according to our firste institucion and creacion, for the behofe, commoditie and great comforte of all our countery and diocese.'[2]

Several writers have stated that the town and cathedral were burnt in 1575 by the O'Byrnes of Wicklow under Fiach MacHugh O'Byrne but, surprisingly, the exact date of the disaster is unknown. The chapter letter of 1570, protesting at the proposed move of the see to Ross, was long thought to refer to the attitude of the Dean and Chapter after the burning, but it is dated 7 April 1570. This raises the possibility that the burning of the cathedral took place in the late months of 1569 or the early months of 1570, but there is no reference to such a disaster in official contemporary papers and correspondence. If the date 1575 is accepted, then the letter of 1570 may have been quoted to Queen Elizabeth I as evidence of the tenacity of the chapter. By Order-in-Council the queen commanded the O'Byrnes to rebuild the cathedral.

The rebuilding in 1577 was 'parsimonious and destructive'.[3] The spaces between the arches of the nave were walled up, the tower was retained at the crossing, and the aisles, transepts and chancel remained in ruins. The eastern portion of the chancel was dismantled and rebuilt on to the east end of the nave, so that the 13th-century lancet windows have been preserved. But it seems that despite this rebuilding, Ferns Cathedral never really recovered from its traumatic destruction in 1575, and it entered a long period of neglect and decay. In 1589 the cathedral 'was sometime a church well-adorned and maintained, but now in great ruins and decaie, the bishop and chapter not remaining there at all.'[4]

Ferns Cathedral from the south-east

By 1599 the see of Ferns was valued at only £30 per annum and the diocese was amalgamated with Leighlin in the following year. In 1611 the Irish parliament considered the position of the cathedral 'now ruined' and declared that it should be re-edified at the charge, of both the clergy and the laity of the diocese.[5] Nothing is known of work done in the 17th and 18th centuries apart from a reroofing in 1672 and a rebuilding of the tower in 1759–61. A drawing of the cathedral made in 1786 shows a single-chamber church with a short tower capped by a squat pyramidal roof, a ruined south transept, and the ruins to the east of the cathedral. In

1810 Ferns Cathedral was described as 'small, and quite plain'.[6]

Substantial alterations were made in 1816–17 with a grant of £500 from the Board of First-Fruits. The cathedral was extended westwards by incorporating the north and south walls of the tower; a new, narrower and higher tower was built on to the west wall of the nave, and a Chapter House was added to the west side of the new tower.

A speculative reconstruction of the original outline of the cathedral is complicated by the remains of an early 13th-century building standing 23m to the east of the present cathedral. The east and west walls have gone but the north and south walls each have a range of seven lancets. Several suggestions about its original purpose have been put forward. It may have been a medieval parish church, though the parish altar is more likely to have been in the nave of the cathedral. It may have been a choir for the monks of the Augustinian priory to the south (the church of which may have been thought insufficiently important in c.1240), since the substantial lighting from high-set windows was favoured by the Augustinian Canons; but the building is axial with the cathedral and well away from the priory. A third possibility is that it was a chapel enclosing the tomb of St Mogue, the original founder of the see, but this Irish practice is unlikely to have been adopted in an area where English rule dominated.

The fourth and obvious possibility is that these walls are the remains of the chancel of the cathedral destroyed in 1575, and this is a widespread and long-held belief. The perfect alignment with the present cathedral and the complete absence of east and west walls support this theory; the problem is the contrast in floor levels, that of the cathedral being more than 1m above that of the ruin. But very little is known about the destruction and rebuilding by the O'Byrnes in 1575–77 and the rebuilding of 1816–17. Details of the architectural history of Ferns Cathedral are so scanty that this theory cannot be easily dismissed and archaeological excavation may in due course find a link between the two buildings.

The following description gives a good picture of the state of Ferns in the middle of the 19th century: the cathedral 'is a small barn-like structure . . . with the usual heavy square tower. The bishop's "throne" is an elevated pew, now used as a reading desk. The "stalls" of the dean and chapter are small seats in two dark corner pews at the bottom of the church, under the gallery, and over each, in faded letters on the mouldy walls, is the title of the dignitary to whom it belongs. The dignitaries were screened from vulgar eyes by curtains, which became a useless piece of furniture when their glory had departed, and so the Rector has very properly turned them to account as window-blinds to keep the glare of the sun off the pulpit during divine service. The congregation on this great holiday [Good Friday] was a mere handful, perhaps twenty persons.'[7]

After many years of neglect, an extensive Gothicising restoration began in 1901, under the inspiration and aegis of Thomas Brownell Gibson, Rector of Ferns 1896–1925, and Dean of Ferns 1908–26. The work can be summarised as follows. A new chancel arch was built, from which hangs a plain cross; and the flat plaster ceiling of 1816–17 was replaced by a panelled pitch-pine roof; four of the pillars of the nave arcade, which the O'Byrnes had walled up, were opened out; the west gallery was reduced in size and given the former Georgian sanctuary rails as a balustrade; the box pews were removed and replaced with the present pine pews; the return Georgian chapter stalls, at the west end of nave, were removed to the Chapter House and replaced by the present pine stalls, formerly in St Canice's Cathedral, Kilkenny; the bishop's throne was also removed to the Chapter House in 1907 and replaced by the present throne in memory of Bishop William Pakenham Walsh (1878–97); the altar was given in 1902, and the present simple oak sanctuary rail in 1903.

The chancel has a polychromatic tiled floor and is brightly lit by a central window of five stepped lancets within a moulded frame, single lancets on either side, and two vesicae above. The chancel steps and altar plinth are of black marble. A double piscina can be seen on the south wall of the sanctuary. The carved stone and white marble reredos depicting the Last Supper was erected in 1918.

A window on the south side of the nave contains a fine stained-glass representation of St Patrick by Kathleen O'Brien of An Túr Gloin (see LOUGHREA); it was inserted in 1931 to commemorate Dean Thomas Brownell Gibson, A recumbent effigy of a bishop in the south-west corner of the nave was for some time thought to represent St Mogue and may once have marked the place of his burial. But the vested and mitred figure is 13th century and the common belief is that it is a representation of Bishop John of St John. The organ gallery is supported by two pillars of limestone encased in stop-fluted wooden columns with Doric capitals.

Instead of being the large aisled cruciform church that it was, Ferns Cathedral is now aisleless, only a little more than half the 55m length of the original building; a neat and tidy little cathedral set on high ground, with nothing much left of its great past. It has a square battlemented western tower with pinnacles, with a small Chapter House on its west side. Dating the cathedral is difficult because of rebuildings and restorations, but the eastern part, with the exposed piers in the north and south walls, is the remaining remnant of Bishop John of St John's 13th-century work, saving only that the ruined walls to the east of the cathedral may also be remains of his cathedral. The north and south walls themselves are at least partly 16th century, and the western part, together with the tower and Chapter House, is early 19th century.

By the roadside which skirts the churchyard is St Mogue's Well, said to have been sunk by St Moling. The well-house was constructed in 1847.

On the hill to the north-east of the cathedral are the remains of the 17th-century Church of St Peter, a nave-and-chancel church which incorporates a Romanesque window in the south wall of the chancel and two Gothic lancets in the east gable, possibly taken from other churches.

There is a 13th-century castle on high ground at the north-west end of the town which was the site of a stronghold of the Kings of Leinster. Built by William Marshal, Earl of Pembroke, it was for long the residence of the Bishops of Ferns; it has been ruined since 1649.

Ferns Palace was the residence of the Bishop of Ferns and Leighlin until 1836. A large square stone house, it was begun in 1785 by Bishop Walter Cope (1782–7) and completed by Bishop William Preston (1787–9); it was plundered and severely damaged in the rebellion of 1798. It ceased to be used after the death of Bishop Thomas Elrington (1822–35), when Ferns and Leighlin were united to Ossory. The palace was burnt down in 1960. Only a small part of its porch remains, standing in a large field (formerly parkland) on the Gorey side of Ferns. However the courtyard and arched entrance are in good condition, having been made into a dwelling-house and egg farm, called The Palace.

The former Georgian Deanery was sold c.1969, when the present Deanery was built close by.

References

1   J. F. G. Day and H. E. Patton, *The cathedrals of the Church of Ireland* (London, 1932), p. 114.
2   Ibid., p.115.
3   Ibid.
4   T. H. C. McFall, *An account of the history of Ferns Cathedral Church* (Dublin, 1954), p. 10.
5   Ibid., p. 9.
6   Nicholas Carlisle, *A topographical dictionary of Ireland* (London, 1810), p. 157.
7   James Godkin, *Ireland and her churches* (London, 1867), p.273.

GALWAY

The Cathedral Church of Our Lady Assumed into Heaven, and St Nicholas

*Dioceses of Galway, Kilmacduagh and Kilfenora
(Roman Catholic)*

GALWAY (*Gaillimh*) with a population of 38,000 is the largest town of the ancient province of Connacht. It lies at the mouth of the River Galway, 211.2km west of Dublin and 102.4km north-west of Limerick. It is a thriving city, an important market and industrial centre, and houses one of the three consituent colleges of the National University of Ireland. The city originated with the seizure of the territory by Richard de Burgo in 1232–43 and the construction of a castle. The grant of letters patent in 1396 establishing Galway as a royal borough effectively removed it from the influence of the de Burgo family, and it became a firm bulwark of the crown in the west of Ireland. At the same time its isolation from Dublin, combined with increasing prosperity derived from trade with France, Flanders, the Baltic and Spain, fostered a spirit of independence, and Galway developed into a city-state ruled by a merchant oligarchy. In 1484 the chief officer of the town was granted the title of mayor.

Galway lay within the territory of the diocese of Annaghdown, which was suppressed by papal decree in 1327 and amalgamated with Tuam. A church dedicated to St Nicholas was founded by the Lynch family about 1320, and in 1484, with the appointment of the first mayor, the Archbishop of Tuam promoted it to collegiate status. Papal confirmation was granted on 8 February 1485. Collegiate churches were governed by a chapter in much the same way as cathedral churches, and Galway's chapter consisted of a 'warden' and eight other priests. The warden had some episcopal jurisdiction, though without the full authority of a bishop, over the town of Galway and neighbouring parishes. Collegiate churches were comparatively rare in Ireland — Galway and Scattery Island being the two most prominent examples. The right of appointing the warden and priests was given to the mayor, bailiffs and freemen of Galway.

The warden and chapter were expelled by Queen Elizabeth I in 1568 and St Nicholas's Church passed into the hands of the reformers; it remains in the possession of the Church of Ireland to this day. The church, standing in Market Street, is a plain building with a central tower of *c.*1500 crowned by a curious pyramidal steeple of 1683. It has been altered many times since the 14th century, but the original outline remains. The church passed back into Roman Catholic hands for brief periods in 1643–52 and 1689–91, but otherwise mass was celebrated in private houses.

An unofficial Catholic warden and college continued to exist, appointed by an unofficial Catholic mayor and bailiffs who were secretly elected by the Catholic 'Freemen' of the parish. But by 1792 resentment was beginning to surface against this limited franchise, and protests and complaints were sent to Rome. The difficulty was resolved in 1831 when the wardenship was abolished and Galway became the centre of a new diocese.

A small chapel, dedicated to St Nicholas, was built in Middle Street in 1750 and enlarged in 1816, and from 1831 it became the pro-cathedral of the diocese of Galway and remained such for 130 years. No thought was given to building a full cathedral at that time and such funds as were available were used to build parish churches and schools in the new diocese. A cathedral building fund was launched in 1876 with a bequest of £500 by a Mr Murray of Kinavara, but the project was not pursued seriously until many years later.

The interior of Galway Cathedral looking east

Impetus was given with the enlargement of the diocese in 1883. The two small neighbouring dioceses of Kilmacduagh and Kilfenora to the south had been held together since 1750. In 1883 they were both added to the care of the Bishop of Galway. Because Kilfenora is in a different ecclesiastical province, the Bishop of Galway and Kilmacduagh is technically only the the Apostolic Administrator of Kilfenora.

The need for a suitable cathedral church to serve all three dioceses was recognised, and towards the end of his episcopate Bishop Francis MacCormack (1887–1908) acquired the site of an old military barracks at O'Brien's Bridge further south of the present cathedral and bequeathed £3,000 to the cathedral fund on his death in 1909. The task was continued by his successors, and by 1936 the fund had reached £108,000.

The plan for building a cathedral began seriously with the arrival of Bishop Michael Browne, whose long episcopate (1937–76) saw the work finished. The Bishop abandoned the

planning the foundation stone was laid on 27 October 1957 by the Archbishop of Armagh, and seven years later, on 15 August 1965, the building was dedicated to Our Lady Assumed into Heaven and St Nicholas by Cardinal Cushing, the Pontifical Legate, in the presence of President Eamon de Valera. Robinson died before the completion of the cathedral, but his son-in-law and partner, Frederick Browne, with his wife, was present at the dedication ceremonies.

The cathedral is constructed of rough-hewn greenish-grey Galway limestone. It measures 91m long, 48m wide at the

Galway Cathedral

site at O'Brien's Bridge in 1937 because it was too small and because (with remarkable prescience) it was felt to have insufficient parking space. A suitable alternative presented itself in 1939 when the Irish government found that it no longer had any need for the early 19th-century gaol. The building was handed over to the County Council in 1941, who in turn handed it over to the bishop. The gaol had been demolished by the end of the year, but there was no question of building work during the course of the Second World War, and it was not until 1949 that John J. Robinson of Dublin was charged with designing a new cathedral. After several years of meticulous

transepts, 44m high to the top of the cross on the copper dome, and seats 2,000 with standing room for a further 1,000. The total cost, excluding the internal equipment, decoration and furnishing, was £600,000. The main entrance faces north and consists of a portal with a tall Romanesque arch which projects beyond two towers. The towers have Italianate cupolas which are unfortunate fussy additions to the Celtic simplicity of the rest of building. The entrance front and transepts have unusual rose windows which are for once genuinely rose-shaped and not simply round.

A narthex leads into a wide nave of six bays with clerestory divided from narrow side aisles by Romanesque arches resting on plain concave chamfered piers. The high altar and throne are sited at the crossing, and the retrochoir beyond has flanking chapels. The baptistery on the ground floor of the western tower contains a font carved from a single piece of black marble.

The floor of the wide central aisle is of sepia Connemara marble with panels in red and white marble. The pews are made from Utile mahogany from West Africa, and the floor below is of red tile. The Stations of the Cross in Portland stone were designed by Gabrielle Hayes. The coffered and barrel-vaulted wooden ceiling is of red cedar from the Pacific coast of America. It sits a little uneasily on the clerestory and might be more appropriate in a palazzo. A stone vault would have been better. Above the narthex is the organ gallery, with a stone balustrade stretching the whole width of the nave. The organ was constructed by the Liverpool firm of Rushworth & Dreaper.

Immediately before the crossing, the nave is flanked by the Mortuary Chapel to the left and the Chapel of St Fachanan (of Kilfenora) to the right. The Mortuary Chapel has a mosaic showing Christ rising from the dead, with two small circular mosaics showing the heads of Patrick Pearse (leader of the Easter Rising of 1916) and President John F. Kennedy. The Chapel of St Fachanan commemorates the small diocese of Kilfenora and contains a fresco of the saint with crozier standing before one of the High Crosses.

The crossing itself has four high and wide Romanesque arches with mosaics of archangels occupying the pendentives. The circular band above is inscribed in mosaic with the words 'GLORIA IN EXCELSIS DEO ET IN TERRA PAX HOMINIBUS BONAE VOLUNTATIS' (Glory to God in the highest and in earth peace, good will towards men). The octagonal dome above has two levels of windows grouped into three on each facet. The lower windows are blind; the upper windows have yellow glass which imparts a warm glow to the dome. The four piers of the crossing are linked by the white marble communion rail. The floor is of beige Portuguese marble, and the altar is a single large slab of white Carrara marble. The throne and stalls are of Utile mahogany.

The retrochoir of three bays has a great mosaic of the Crucifixion designed by Patrick Pollen on the south wall. The timing of the planning and construction accounts for the oddity of the retrochoir. The cathedral was planned before the Second Vatican Council; it was constructed during the Council; and its interior arrangement reflects post-Council liturgies. The sanctuary splendidly positioned beneath the great dome at the crossing really makes the retrochoir unnecessary, and one has a slight feeling of sitting in the storeroom at the back. It was presumably designed to be the chancel and became redundant when the Second Vatican Council made cruciform churches unfashionable.

The retrochoir is flanked by the Chapels of St Nicholas and St Colman. St Nicholas's Chapel has a 17th-century limestone triptych set in the wall above the altar depicting the Coronation of the Blessed Virgin Mary as Queen of Heaven. The crypt below the chapel contains the remains of four former Bishops of Galway. St Colman's Chapel commemorates the diocese of Kilmacduagh and has a fresco depicting St Colman vested as a bishop in the act of blessing a family. The Round Tower of Kilmacduagh is depicted in the background.

Galway Cathedral has a slightly Iberian feel, no doubt intended to recall the town's medieval trading links with Spain, but its architectural style generally defies classification. Its round arches and unplastered stonework evoke an early Romanesque architecture, but the Renaissance cupolas on the towers are pointless additions, as are the towers themselves. But the cedar roof and marble flooring of the interior are most un-Celtic. The general sense of elevation is not helped by the lack of a plinth and the surrounding prairie of tarmac; trees and grass would have created a more authentically Celtic environment. The flat, exposed site remorselessly displays every feature of the building to instant gaze. A parapet atop the walls would have given the building a more 'finished' appearance and perhaps helped to bridge the rather stark gap between the plain and simple style of the body of the cathedral and its incongruous Renaissance dome and cupolas.

Endless minor criticisms could be made of Galway Cathedral because it mixes styles and defies architectural categorisation. But to what end? Why dismiss a building as an architectural disaster when it does catch the eye, and when its interior has an unmistakably warm and welcoming atmosphere. That is sufficient redemption for any architectural deficiency. As Bishop Michael Browne himself put it in 1966, 'We did not set out to build a new masterpiece or to initiate an architectural revolution. We had no higher ambition than to build a church which would be solid, dignified and worthy of Galway.'[1]

References

1   B. Donohoe, 'Galway's new cathedral' in *Capuchin Annual* (1966), p. 406.

GLENDALOUGH

The Cathedral Church of St Peter and St Paul

GLENDALOUGH (*Gleann dá locha* – glen of the two lakes), 46km directly south of Dublin, is probably the most atmospheric and best preserved of the monastic sites in Ireland. Set by two lakes at the junction of two wooded valleys high in the Wicklow Mountains and reached by a narrow winding road bordered with gold-flowering gorse, Glendalough still evokes the atmosphere of prayer and meditation that governed its days and nights for a thousand years until the 16th century. There is a great stillness and silence about this place, which not even the presence of the large numbers of tourists can entirely obliterate. This remote and lonely valley, shielded by its high wooded mountains, has an impressive natural beauty, but it is not 'pretty'. It has a brooding atmosphere and 'on a dull day this sacred precinct can evoke the most profound melancholy'.

The foundation of Glendalough is ascribed to St Kevin (*Cóemgen* – the fair born), a member of a ruling tribe in Leinster. He was educated by St Petroc of Cornwall, who was in Ireland at the time, but the official biographies of his life contain largely romantic and untrustworthy legends. Kevin built a church on the south bank of the Upper Lake some time in the 6th century, moving later to the opening of the valley, where he died in 618. His feast-day is 3 June. Devotion to his memory continued long after his death, and pilgrimages still go to the ruins of the abbey that he founded. The monastery was centred around the Upper Lake, but as it grew, it spread down the valley beyond the Lower Lake to the junction of the two rivers. The main river is the Gleanealo, which enters the valley by a waterfall at the western end, connects the Upper and Lower Lakes, and then leaves the Lower Lake to join the Glendasan river and empties into the sea at Arklow. The main group of buildings, including the cathedral, which constitute the remains of the monastic foundation, were built here at the junction of these two rivers.

The diocese of Glendalough, established at Ráith Bressail, bordered Dublin to the south and west, and included territories in south Kildare that were soon to be settled by the Anglo-Norman invaders. As the see remained in Irish territory, there was strong royal pressure to unite it with the diocese of Dublin which was under royal control. The union of Dublin and Glendalough was confirmed by Pope Innocent III on 25 February 1216 and Pope Honorius III on 6 October 1216.

Although some historians have detected political machinations by the Anglo-Normans in the affair, equal attention should be paid to the testimony of the Irish about the fate of diocese of Glendalough, which was not decided without due consideration. Cardinal John Paparo, papal legate to Ireland in the early 13th century, visited the site and recommended

suppression of the diocese. He was was supported by the Archbishop of Tuam in a submission to Innocent III. 'Although that holy church in the mountains was from early times held in great reverence on account of St Kevin who lived there as a hermit, it is now so deserted and desolate and has been so for forty years, that from being a church it has become a den of thieves and pit of robbers, and because of the deserted and desolate wilderness there are more murders committed in that valley than in any other part of Ireland.'[1] The only problem with this convenient corroboration is that Felix Ó Ruanada, the archbishop in question, was

Glendalough: the Round Tower

a prominent advocate of the submission of the Irish church to the Normans.

The last substantive Bishop of Glendalough was William Piro (1192–1212). The diocese still has a nominal existence, in that the Archbishop of Dublin is still styled Bishop of Glendalough, but the two sees have been held together for centuries. There is still an Archdeacon of Glendalough whose stall is in Christ Church Cathedral, Dublin.

The union of the two dioceses inevitably depended on the extent of royal control of the area. Glendalough was evidently troublesome enough for the monastery to be sacked and burnt by the English in 1398. The diocese of Glendalough was temporarily revived in the 15th century when the English had lost control of the territory in and around the Wicklow Mountains. A Dominican friar named Denis White secured provision as Bishop of Glendalough in 1481 and held out for some sixteen years. 'The archbishops of Dublin could not obtain quiet possession till 1497, in which year, on 30th of May, a surrender was made in the cathedral of St Patrick, Dublin, by Friar Dennis White, who had long usurped that see in opposition to regal authority; from this aera, Glendalough has continued a desert.'[2] Altogether there were some eight bishops recorded after the suppression of 1216, but it seems that Denis White was the only one who got possession. In 1494, for example, Pope Alexander VI appointd Ivo Ruffi, an Italian Friar Minor 'on the death of John'.

After the union with Dublin, Glendalough sank into relative obscurity, though it seems to have remained active until the 16th century. The last abbot was Christopher St Lawrence, whose rule came to an end with the suppression of the monasteries. From that date the buildings began to fall into ruin. The Priory of St Saviour was an overgrown heap of debris by 1770.

The monastic site is entered by a round-arched gateway dating anywhere from 900 to 1200; it formerly had a second storey. Inside on the right is a large stone with an inscribed cross set into the wall.

There are a number of ruins scattered over a distance of 2.4km along the valley. Moving from the top (west) of the valley to the bottom (east), these are:

1. *Teampall na Sceillig (Church of the Rock)*

Standing 6m above the south shore of the Upper Lake are the slight remains, mainly a reconstruction on old foundations, of a small rectangular church roughly 7.6m by 4.2m internally, with a twin-light east window. The earliest church in the glen, it probably stands on the site of Kevin's original church. The church possibly dates from the 7th century and the east window from the 10th. To the west is a walled enclosure with a paved causeway in which the wattle-and-daub huts of the first monastery may have stood. The site is only approachable by boat.

2. *St Kevin's Bed*

In a cliff on the south bank of the Upper Lake is St Kevin's Bed, a small man-made cave 2.1m by 1.2m, 9.1m above the

water. It can be approached with difficulty by land, but more easily and usually by boat. It certainly predates St Kevin, and may be a Bronze Age (1800–1500 B.C.) rock tomb of the type to be seen in Sicily and Normandy. Legend relates that the hermit chose this inaccessible place as a refuge from the attentions of pursuing females. One of them, named Kathleen, with 'eyes of most unholy blue', was undaunted and succeeded in finding the saint's hideout. Awaking one morning to find her standing beside him, the enraged Kevin pushed her into the lake!

A section of the chancel arch of Glendalough Cathedral

3. *St Kevin's Cell*

The foundations of a roughly circular stone hut traditionally said to be have been St Kevin's house. It measures 3.4m east to west and 3.2m north to south. It lies to the west of Reefert Church and high above it on a spur.

4. *Reefert Church*

Overlooking the Upper Lake are the remains of Reefert Church. Built of granite, probably about 1100, it belongs to the transitional period between Early Christian and Roman-esque architecture. The nave is 8.8m long and 5.3m wide. The chancel is 4.2m long and 2.6m wide. The doorway is of the old flat-headed type, but the windows are round-headed, and there is a plain rounded chancel arch which, with the upper parts of the walls, was rebuilt in the 1870s. Projecting corbel stones held wooden rafters. The name derives possi-bly from Ríogh-feart, meaning royal cemetery. The church stands on a site always regarded as the burial place of the local chieftains, the O'Tooles. In the surrounding graveyard are a number of Early Christian gravestones as well as a cross with interlacing decoration. The modern enclosing wall and terracing date from 1875.

5. *Unidentified Church*

The foundations of a church can be seen on a platform north of the Poulanass brook opposite Reefert Church. It measures about 10.6m east to west, though the east wall has been destroyed, and 6m north to south. The west wall is almost 1m high.

6. *Stone Fort*

A circular stone fort with thick stone walls built of dry stone masonry. The outside diameter is 20.4m. The fort is near the eastern shore of the Upper Lake, not far from Reefert Church.

7. *St Mary's (or Our Lady's) Church*

In the fields west of the graveyard is the Church of St Mary, believed to have been the first building in the lower valley, and marking the site of St Kevin's grave. It may date from the 10th or 11th century or earlier; some have dated it to the late 6th or early 7th centuries. The chancel is 12th-century Ro-manesque. Internally the nave measures 6m in width and 9.7m in length. The chancel is 6m in length and 5.3m in width.

8. *The Round Tower*

The Round Tower is 30.48m high, the doorway is about 3m above ground. Its conical cap is a reconstruction of 1876,

Glendalough: St Saviour's Priory

partly with stones found lying inside the tower. The tower is constructed mainly of the mica-schist of the valley interspersed with blocks of light-grey granite.

9. *The Priest's House*

A tiny rectangular building of uncertain function, probably 12th century, with the remains of a Romanesque arch on the exterior of the east wall. It may have been a mortuary chapel, or a shrine to house the relics of St Kevin. Apart from the lower sections of the walls, the Priest's House is mainly a reconstruction of 1875–80, based on a drawing made in 1779, when the building was almost complete. Above the south door is a fragmentary lintel with representation of an ecclesiastic or monarch flanked by two abbots. The name of the building is modern and derives from two or more Catholic priests having been buried there during the 18th century.

10. *The Cathedral*

The cathedral, a simple nave-and-chancel structure with a sacristy, probably dates from the 10th century, though the chancel is a late 12th-century addition. The total length is about 29.2m, the nave being 14.7m in length and 9.1m in width. Built of mica-schist and granite, it has projecting antae which probably supported a timber roof, a square-headed west doorway and two round-headed windows high in the south wall. The chancel is 7.6m long and 10.6m wide. It has two windows in the north wall and one in the south, besides a tall, narrow and round-headed east window with a wide inward splay. Under the south window is a recess which contained the aumbry and piscina. The late 12th-century chancel arch has been partly rebuilt, but only the springing on the north and south sides remains. The arch was of three orders with chevron carving. Under the south window in the chancel can be seen an aumbry and piscina in a single recess.

The cathedral is the largest church in the valley and still the most imposing structure in the group despite being choked by gravestones on all sides. This graveyard is an unfortunate addition to Glendalough and has no antiquity about it whatever; most of the stones date only from the last three centuries.

11. *St Kevin's Church*

Perhaps the most distinctive building in the valley is the church which has unfortunately acquired the ridiculous name of 'St Kevin's Kitchen'. The 'Kitchen' is in fact a two-storeyed oratory given its name by the chimney-like round bell-turret growing out of the roof at the west end. The church is of the same period and type as those of St Columba at Kells, St Flannan at Killaloe, and St Mochta at Louth. It consists of a 12th-century barrel-vaulted lower chamber with a loft above. A sacristy and chancel were later additions to the east end. The sacristy still stands, but the chancel, still standing in 1772, collapsed at a later date. The present entrance is the chancel arch, the original square-headed west entrance having been blocked up. The surviving portion measures 6.9m long by 4.4m wide, and the walls are 1.1m thick. The church contains a collection of minor fragments placed there in 1911–12.

As the only roofed building in Glendalough, St Kevin's Church was used as a Catholic church from 1810 to 1850. A rough altar of stones and turf was observed by a visitor in 1810. The church would have served the mining village beyond the Upper Lake, where up to a hundred men lived and worked mining lead and copper between 1800 and 1880.

12. *St Kevin's Cross*

To the south is St Kevin's Cross (*c*.1150), a granite monolith, 3.3m high. It was once said to mark the burial place of the saint, but is probably no more than a boundary mark.

13. *Bullaun*

Crossing the steam to the south of St Kevin's Church and following a path to the left, there is a granite bullaun – an artificially hollowed stone – into which, according to legend, St Kevin used to milk a mysterious white doe, to provide food for a child he found abandoned at his hermitage.

14. *St Kieran's Church*

A small nave-and-chancel church lying 10.9m to the southeast of St Kevin's Church. It was only discovered during the repairs of the 1870s. Nothing remains apart from the foundations and the walls to the height of a little more than 1m. The base of a stone altar was found, and a south door to the chancel which possibly led to a sacristy of which nothing remains. The structure is assumed to be the church erected for St Kieran close to the church of St Kevin, but is probably not contemporary with the 6th-century saint. The nave measures 5.7m by 4.4m, and the chancel 2.8m by 2.6m; the walls are 0.8m thick.

15. *Trinity Church*

On the north side of the Lower Lake is Trinity Church, belonging to the same transitional period as Reefert Church, perhaps 11th or 12th century, with a round-headed east window and a plain but perfect semi-circular chancel arch, but with a flat-headed west doorway. A round tower stood on an annexe at the west end. It was covered with ivy and collapsed during a storm in 1818. Only the north wall of the annexe was standing in 1839; the south and west walls were level with the ground, but were rebuilt during the repairs of the 1870s. There are corbel stones on the exterior for holding wooden rafters. The nave is 8.9m long by 5.3m wide, and the chancel 4.1m long by 2.7m wide. Trinity Church is built of undressed mica slate with some granite blocks in the walls. The finely-jointed voussoirs of the chancel arch are of granite.

Trinity Church was founded by St Mo Chuaróg, a disciple of St Kevin, in the 7th century, but the present building is 9th/10th century and probably stands on the site of the original foundation.

Although roofless, it is a very well preserved, neat and sturdy little church with an appealing solid simplicity. It is surrounded by a dry stone wall which, for some inexplicable reason, is surmounted in part by ugly barbed wire fencing.

16. *St Saviour's Priory*

The 12th-century Church of St Saviour preserves the best Irish Romanesque decoration in the valley. The nave is 12.5m long and 6.1m wide. The chancel is 4.2m long and 3.5m wide. The decorated chancel arch survives, but some stones were incorrectly replaced when the building was restored in 1877. The jambs are carved with dragons, and a gruesome raven eating a human head; one of the capitals of the piers is carved with a wolf whose tail is intertwined in the hair of a human head. The church is said to have been founded by St Laurence O'Toole, but it may be earlier than his time. The nave was reconstructed when a new building was added in the later medieval period. A staircase led to a second floor, of which nothing remains, above the chancel.

The building is best approached by an unmade road on the south side of the lake, and the visitor first catches a glimpse of the simple round-headed doorway in the south-east wall of the nave along an avenue of trees. The reward for persevering along this difficult access is to discover the most delightful place in Glendalough – tucked away in a grove of trees by the river at the lower end of the valley. The site of the priory was once an open field sloping down to the river, but now a plantation of conifers shrouds the buildings from view.

The priory is surrounded by a dry-stone and earth wall which at one time sprouted several Scots fir pines; they were still standing in 1971, but have since been cut down. A secluded place, perhaps unvisited by most travellers to Glendalough, St Saviour's has a secret and slightly magical atmosphere that would delight a child. This is a pleasant place and a welcome relief from the general level of chatter found in the centre of the monastic city around the cathedral.

The site of Glendalough has always exercised a fascination for those who have seen it, if only for its haunting scenery. Thomas Carlyle went to Glendalough in 1849 and found himself surrounded by 'hideous crowds of beggars'[3] offering to act as guides; he remembered the valley as 'the grimmest spot on my memory'.[4] But others have felt something of the atmosphere that drew Kevin to this place 1,400 years ago: 'Here the mountains cast a melancholy shadow on the inferiour (lower) valley, contracting every prospect; and so awful, sovenerable is the scene, that, even to a momentary beholder, it appears as if formed for a study of the eremitic life.'[5]

References

1 John Watt, *The church in medieval Ireland* (Dublin, 1972), p. 121.
2 Mervyn Archdall, *Monasticon Hibernicum* (London, 1786), p.765.
3 Thomas Carlyle, *Reminiscences of my Irish journey in 1849*, (London, 1882), p. 77.
4 Ibid., p. 78.
5 Archdall, *Monasticon Hibernicum*, p. 765.

KELLS

KELLS (*Ceanannas* – head abode) is a small market town of about 2,600 inhabitants situated near the wooded banks of the River Blackwater in Co. Meath, 17.6km north-west of Navan and 68km north-west of Dublin. It was once a royal capital and subsequently a famous monastic centre of learning, but very little remains.

A late and untrustworthy tradition states that St Columba received a grant of land from a local chieftain and founded a monastery here *c*.550. There is no definite reference to a monastery at Kells before 804, when the monastic annals record that 'Cennanus was given to Colmcille the musical without battle.' This may be a quotation from an early poem, the date being a later addition. Since Iona had been burnt by the Vikings in 802 and sixty-eight monks of the community were slain in 806, it would be reasonable to infer that Kells was founded *c*.804 as a place of refuge for the monks of Iona. In 807, Iona having been raided three times by the Vikings, the headquarters of the league of Columban monasteries was transferred to Kells. But Kells was itself raided in the same year and the church destroyed. A new church was finished in 814. Four further Viking raids took place between

920 and 1019. The town was burnt in 1170 and again by Edward Bruce in 1315, and the monastery was dissolved in 1551.

The great reforming synod of 1152 which bears its name not surprisingly designated Kells as the see for the kingdom of Breifne. After the Anglo-Norman settlement of north Co. Meath, this part of the Diocese of Kells was absorbed into the Diocese of Meath. An unnamed Cistercian was chosen as Bishop of Kells c.1185 but ejected by the Bishop of Meath. The last Bishop of Kells M. Ua Dobailén died in 1211, and the small diocese which had maintained its independence with difficulty for about sixty years was absorbed into Meath by Bishop Simon Rochfort.

The monastery is remembered for the richly illuminated and decorated Book of Kells, a late 8th- or early 9th- century Gospel book of 680 pages written in Latin, now in the library of Trinity College, Dublin. It is often described as the most beautiful book in the world. Some scholars hold that it was written at Iona and carried for safety to Kells. It was stolen from the western sacristy of the great church at Kells in 1007 but later recovered. During the Cromwellian wars it was sent to Dublin for safe-keeping, and presented to Trinity College by the Bishop of Meath in 1661. A crozier made in the abbey is now in the British Museum.

Considering the reflected glory given to Kells by the synod and the book which bear its name, the present-day town is a disappointment, and there are only a few remnants of its great past; certainly very little to detain the traveller.

There is an oratory known as St Columba's (or Colmcille's) House, a traditional 12th-century oratory of the type to be seen at Glendalough, Killaloe and Louth. It has a steeply pitched roof and stands on the highest point of the hill on which the town is built. It was part of the monastery and was used as a residence as well as an oratory. It measures about 7.3m by 6.4m externally, with a height of 11.5m, and the walls are 1.2m thick.

There is also a 27m-high Round Tower dating from before 1076, when, according to ancient records, an Irish chieftain was murdered inside it. It has a 9th-century doorway which may be a later insertion. The tower is built of limestone, though the doorway and its surrounds are of three different types of sandstone – reddish-purple, light-brown and grey. Unusually, it has five windows near the top, possibly to watch the five roads entering the town. It stands by the south gate of the graveyard of the Church of Ireland parish church, which itself occupies the site of the ancient monastery enclosure.

Apart from these two fragments, nothing survives of the monastic buildings, or of the abbey church that would have served briefly as the cathedral church of this ephemeral

diocese. The monastic church was cruciform with a large chancel. It was restored in 1578 after being 'i utter ruyn and decaie',[1] but the large bell-tower is the only remaining portion of this church, and much of it probably dates from the Elizabethan restoration. The chancel was still in use as the parish church in the late 17th century and was demolished to make way for the present parish church, a large plain building of 1778. Perhaps to celebrate this act of vandalism, a spire was added to the tower in 1783 by Lord Bective.

Kells: the Round Tower and Cross

There are a number of High Crosses at Kells:

1. *The Market Cross*

This is so-called because it stands in Market Square at the centre of the town. It possibly dates from the 8th or 9th centuries, and its shaft is 2.5m high. The main scene shows the Crucifixion, depicting Christ without a halo. The base has a frieze of horse and foot soldiers. The top of the shaft and part of the wheel is broken. It was used as a gallows in 1798 and lay prone for a century afterwards.

2. *The South Cross*

This cross, which is 3.4m high and stands close to the Round Tower, is the most complete and elaborate Cross at Kells. It is decorated on all four sides and may be older than the Market Cross.

3. *The West Cross*

This incomplete cross, of which only the shaft remains, stands in front of the church door; the base and shaft are more than 3.5m in height. There are two inscriptions on the west panel requesting prayers for Muireadach and Artgal.

4. *The East Cross*

This cross was never finished; on the east face are a Crucifixion and a panel of four figures.

5. *The North Cross*

A well-decorated small conical and socketed base near the bell-tower was intended to hold the shaft of a cross which no longer exists.

References

1 John Healy, *Historical Guide to Kells (Ceanannus Mór), County Meath* (Dublin, 1930), p. 22.

KILDARE

The Cathedral Church of St Brigid

Diocese of Kildare (Church of Ireland)

KILDARE (*Cill Dara* – Dara's church) is a market town of 4,000 inhabitants in Co. Kildare, about 52km south-west of Dublin on the road to Portlaoise. It is one of the most famous sites in Ireland, being intimately bound up with the life of St Brigid.

Brigid (Bridget and Bride are alternatives to be found in church dedications) ranks with St Patrick and St Columba as one of the principal figures in the earliest years of Irish Christianity. Accurate details about her life are scarce, and most of the stories that surround her memory have their basis in much later legends. She was born about 453, the daughter of Dubhthach, a pagan chieftain of Offaly, and Broicseach, his Christian bondmaid.

The story goes that, while she was pregnant, Broicseach was sold to a druid at Faughart, 6.4km north of Dundalk in Co.

Louth. Faughart has long been a centre of pilgrimage; the present shrine dates from 1933 and contains a relic of Brigid. The druid was converted to Christianity, and Broicseach and Brigid were then reunited with Dubhthach who arranged that his daughter should marry an Ulster chieftain. The prospective husband was sensitive to the fact that Brigid inclined to the cloistered life and helped her to found a monastery in Kildare towards the end of the 5th century; 480 is the generally favoured date. When she was grudgingly granted as much land at Kildare as her handkerchief would cover, it miraculously expanded to cover the land she needed for her monastery! She died early in the 6th century on 1 February in a year placed anywhere from 521 to 528 inclusive. She was buried initially at Kildare, but her remains were removed to Downpatrick to protect them from repeated Danish attacks on Kildare. When the relics were destroyed at the Reformation, her head was saved and taken to Neustadt in Austria, and from there to the Jesuit church at Lisbon in 1587.

Brigid is widely venerated in Ireland, and there are places in every part of the country called Kilbride or Kilbreedy which received their names from churches founded by her or in honour of her; there is even a church in the city of London (St Bride's, Fleet Street). Her memory is surrounded by the usual hagiographical stories of generosity to the poor and love for animals whom she protected from local hunters. The reality is that the true facts of her life have long been obscured by clouds of pious devotion; too much time has passed and too many romantic legends have developed to construct an accurate record of her life.

What does emerge from the opaque mists of the 5th and 6th centuries is the memory of a woman of remarkable fame and influence, whose stature was such that for more than a thousand years after her death her successors as Abbesses of Kildare were given precedence over the bishops of Ireland. One interesting theory suggests that because of her pre-eminent fame and the lasting status of her successors, Brigid may have been the high priestess of a powerful pagan cult who led her entire community into Christianity. There was also a pagan goddess called Brigit whose festival was kept on 1 February. The fire-house on the north side of the cathedral may have originated with a pagan sacred fire subsequently adopted as a symbol of the light of Christ.

The foundation at Kildare began as a community of nuns but developed at some date into a double monastery for men and women, presided over by the abbess styled the *comarbae Brigde* (heir of Brigid). The community of men was headed by an abbot and there was a bishop on the staff. Brigid selected a bishop named Condleth (who died *c.*520) to assist her in the rule of the house. Kildare is therefore the first clear example of a monastery with a bishop under the rule of the head of the institution – in this case an abbess. It is not clear whether the office of abbot was identical with that of bishop before c.700 but thereafter it was separate and appears to have lapsed after 967.

A record of c.630 describes a church at Kildare, probably a wooden building. 'A lofty and spacious building, adorned with pictures, divided into three parts by timber partitions. One part comprised the east end or sanctuary. The timber wall dividing this from the rest was decorated with painted figures and linen hangings, and at its opposite extremities were two doors, through one entering the bishop and his monks and officiating priests and through the other the

until the dissolution of religious houses in 1540–41, but its importance declined after the coming of the Anglo-Normans.

Kildare became the seat of the powerful Fitzgerald family, and Bishop Ralph of Bristol (1223–32) began the construction of the present cathedral in 1223. It was enlarged and embellished in 1482, but later bishops were not so assiduous. The period of decline began with Bishop Alexander Craik (1560–64), who exchanged the manors and lands of the diocese for ready cash. 'By this exchange the very ancient See of Kildare was reduced to a most shameful poverty . . .

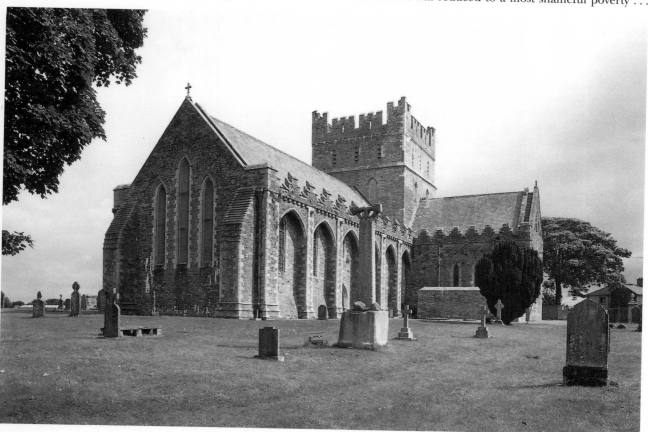

Kildare Cathedral from the south-west

abbess and her virgins and widows among the faithful, when going to partake of the banquet of the body and blood of Jesus Christ.'[1]

Kildare's importance declined from the 12th century. The unique pre-eminence of the Abbess of Kildare was hardly in a position to survive the introduction of territorial dioceses, and she was deprived of her privilege of precedence over bishops at the Synod of Kells–Mellifont in 1152. The Anglo-Norman invasion of 1170 took the process further. The men's community dwindled to a few priests serving the cathedral and is later said to have been taken over by Augustinian Canons Regular. A small women's community remained

and . . . he did more mischief to the See than his successors have ever been able to repair.'[2] Bishop William Pilsworth (1604–35) found a ruinous cathedral when he took possession of the diocese and tried to recover the lands alienated by Craik. He had no success 'and therefore determined to have a share in the spoil by leaving his bishopric poorer than he found it'. A visitation of 1615 found the cathedral 'now altogether in ruins'.[3]

Kildare suffered major damage during the rebellion of 1641. The north side of the central tower was broken down by a battery which demolished the north transept as well, and the nave, chancel and south transept were left roofless. Thomas

Price (Bishop of Kildare 1661–7) took no interest whatever in proposals to restore the cathedral and refused to spend anything despite offers of financial help.

Restoration work was not begun until the arrival of Bishop William Moreton (1682–1705). Moreton had enjoyed the princely sum of £600 p.a. as Dean of Christ Church Cathedral in Dublin. Given the poverty of the diocese of Kildare, he was allowed to retain his deanery, so beginning a link which was to last until 1846. During his episcopate the chancel alone was rebuilt for use as the cathedral church and was consecrated on 29 June 1686. The rest of the cathedral was allowed to remain a deteriorating ruin. The west wall of the nave was still standing in 1738, but had fallen by the mid-19th century and been replaced by 'a modern wall'.[4]

The new chancel, built in a style typical of the late 17th century, was a jarring and unharmonious addition to the ruins of the medieval cathedral. George Edmund Street, the 19th-century architect who re-created the medieval cathedral, thought that walls, especially the north wall, were 'old, though modernized in all their architectural features.'[5] Presumably this statement means that they incorporated medieval masonry, but photographs of the rebuilt chancel show no visible remains.

This 17th-century 'pro-cathedral' was of little architectural interest apart from 'a large Gothick window much decayed' which was replaced by a Venetian window in the early 18th century.[6] Photographs show a very plain hall with rendered walls, round arched casement windows and a pointed roof reaching to the height of the crossing arches of the central tower, with a small chimney on the south side. The interior had a flat plastered ceiling. A small low Chapter House with a quaint stepped battlement parapet was added in 1738 at the angle between the chancel and the ruined south transept. In 1856 a slender bell-tower, also having a stepped battlement parapet, was built in the corresponding angle with the north transept. The remains of that transept, already substantially destroyed, were cleared to make way for the tower.

By 1869 the fabric of the pro-cathedral was in such a state of disrepair that demolition seemed the only possible option. The walls were cracked in many places and too weak to bear the new roof which was then badly needed. Under the terms of the Irish Church Act of 1869, which disestablished the Church of Ireland, the cathedral was vested in the parishioners of Kildare, and a deputation discussed the question of restoring the 17th-century cathedral with the Dean and Chapter. They were unable to make any promise of financial help, and very little money can have been available in the neighbourhood. Carlyle visited in Kildare in 1849 and thought it 'one of the wretchedest wild villages I ever saw; and full of ragged beggars'.[7]

Although funds were not immediately available, it was suggested that if restoration were to be contemplated, it might extend to the ruined nave, tower and transepts, instead of being limited to the 17th-century chancel. The architect George Edmund Street, then engaged on rebuilding Christ Church Cathedral in Dublin, was commissioned to produce a report on the feasibility of complete restoration of a building which had been a steadily deteriorating ruin for more than 240 years.

Street's report, which appeared in October 1871, bore a marked resemblance to his plan for Christ Church Cathedral. It called for the demolition of the 17th-century chancel, the 18th-century Chapter House and the 19th-century tower, the last being only fifteen years old. In their place would be a complete reconstruction of the medieval cathedral, incorporating the ruined remains, at an estimated cost of £5,000. It was bold and visionary report, and the decision to accept its recommendations was courageous.

The interior of Kildare Cathedral looking east

The plan provoked scorn and opposition. Richard Rolt Brash, an historian of Irish medieval architecture, and a contemporary of Street, thought the use of the word 'restoration' was fraudulent. 'What is there to restore?' he wrote. 'Two dilapidated nave walls, one transept, and a portion of one side of a tower; remnants of crumbling masonry that we know to a certainty has been unroofed 140 years, and most certainly a century more. I have heard Mr Street's name mentioned in connexion with this so-called restoration, but I can scarcely imagine that an architect of his reputation would for one moment advise so preposterous an undertaking. Having myself some forty years experience in building and architecture, I unhesitatingly assert that no true restoration of Kildare Cathedral is possible; there may be a sham restoration, under the plea of which a new building may be constructed in the same style as the ruins which present to us.'[8] Brash's opinion provoked an angry rejoinder from Thomas Cooke Trench, honorary secretary of the Restoration Committee who quoted from Street's report in support of the restoration.

Preparation of plans and raising of initial finance took a further four years, and work began on 24 August 1875. The 17th-century cathedral and its appendages were demolished in 1877, and the nave, tower and transepts were complete by 1881 when work stopped. The general political and economic difficulties of the time caused serious financial difficulties to many Irish landlords, and the flow of funds ceased.

After further public appeals, sufficient funds had been raised to enable work to begin again in 1890, and within six years the chancel, sanctuary and interior furnishings were complete. Street had died in 1881, and his work was completed by J. F. Fuller, the diocesan architect. The final cost was £12,000. Archbishop Edward Benson of Canterbury preached his final sermon at the reconsecration ceremony on 22 September 1896. He died on 11 October on his journey home, and the stained glass of the west window was inserted in his memory.

Although the joins are apparent in places, Street's work blends well with the 13th-century masonry. The chancel, the north transept, the west wall and most of the great central tower are the work of Street. The north and south walls of the nave, the south transept and the south wall of the central tower, although restored and reroofed by Street, are what remain of the 13th-century cathedral. The north and south walls of the nave and chancel have buttresses joined by pointed arches and crowned by stepped battlements to form an unusual arcade of deeply recessed window bays.

The reredos and arcading in the sanctuary are by Fuller and have attracted criticism. Their pointedly late Victorian Gothic style does not sit well with Street's painstaking reconstruction of the medieval building. In natural light they clash with the surrounding cathedral and seem to be crude attempts to enhance and beautify a beauty already existing, but in artificial light they acquire a soft pink glow and the discordance seems to lessen. The east window above is a memorial to Dr

Samuel Chaplain (1826–91), County Surgeon of Kildare, who did much to initiate the work of restoration. Most of the cathedral glass is late 19th or early 20th century; a poorly designed 1960s window on the south side of the nave was inserted in memory of Dean George Graham, who died in 1962.

The chapter stalls at the crossing beneath the central tower are carved from oak and have acorn and oakleaf carving; the bishop's throne is at the south-west corner of the chancel. The chapter is of a unique constitution in that it consists of a dean and dignitaries (precentor, chancellor, treasurer and archdeacon) and one remaining prebendary (of Geashill), but also of first, second, third and fourth canons who took residence on behalf of the rest of the chapter, a curious custom made more curious by the election of one of their number to take residence on behalf of the other three. The titles are continued, though most of the positions have been vacant for many years, and no vestige of the old residence duties remains. The painted stone pulpit with red and green marble colonettes, was erected in 1887, and the brass 'eagle' lectern in 1896.

There are a few ancient monuments in the cathedral, mostly of the Fitzgerald family (Earls of Kildare and later Dukes of Leinster) in the south transept. The remains of their burial vault can be seen outside the east wall of the chancel. The south transept also contains the restored altar tomb of Bishop Walter Wellesley (1529–39), placed there in 1971, and a lead-lined stone font resting on shafts of black Kilkenny marble, presented in 1879.

The nave has a Victorian polychromatic tiled floor; the westernmost bay was screened off below window level in 1952 to form a vestry. The simple granite font at the south-west was discovered in 1890 in ground on the north side of the cathedral, and brought into use for baptisms in the 1920s. A roughly dressed crude piece of granite, about 1m high, the font was lined with lead at one stage and has no drain. Because of its appearance, claims have been made that it is the original font of St Brigid's church and it was restored and placed in the cathedral. Some authorities have suggested that it may have had other origins and merely been put to use as a font.

The Round Tower to the west is 33m high and one of the finest in Ireland, though its conical top was replaced by battlements in the 1730s. Its solid base is 16m in circumference. The lowest 3m are of blocks of well dressed and evenly coursed granite, above which the masonry changes to the rubble work of local limestone. This suggests that the granite base may be the remains of an earlier destroyed tower. The doorway, 4.6m from the ground, was of dark-red sandstone in four receding orders carved in floral and geometric patterns which date it to the 12th century. It was embellished with a triangular hood moulding set into the wall above the outer order. The windows, one in each of the four storeys, have narrow slits on the outside and wide splays on the inside, quite unlike any of the other Round Towers. The tower is one of the few that can still be climbed. As part of a general restoration programme for the whole cathedral, it is intended to give the tower a reconstructed conical cap using new stones at a cost of £30,000.

To the north of the cathedral are the remains of St Brigid's Fire-House. After her death the nuns kept a fire burning here perpetually. They would tend it themselves by rota for nineteen nights and leave it for the saint herself to tend on the twentieth night. Allegedly it never went out. Henry de Loundres, Archbishop of Dublin 1213–28, is said to have ordered it to be extinguished in 1220, thinking it a relic of heathen days, but it was rekindled by local people and allowed to burn until the suppression of the monastery. One wall was still standing in the 18th century, but only the foundations remain today.

To the south-west is a restored High Cross. The shaft was used from 1686 as an altar step in the rebuilt chancel and the head was left lying in the graveyard near the base. The cross was restored in late Victorian times. To the south-east is a disused burial chamber which has acquired the misnomer 'St Brigid's Kitchen'.

The rebuilding of Kildare Cathedral was a challenging enterprise, and the result is a strong and impressive building with a greater appearance of antiquity than is to be seen, for example, at Christ Church in Dublin. Some criticism was directed at Street for 'spoiling a beautiful ruin', but his own words more than answer this objection. 'A few years more, and what remains of this interesting church may have become a thing of the past. Each winter's rain and frost help to disintegrate the very fabric of the walls, and that which is possible now may not be possible ere long.'[9] Brash's objections to the use of the word restoration may have been justified in 1875, but Street's plan has at least preserved what remained of the medieval cathedral.

At the time of writing, Kildare Cathedral is facing a major restoration project due to last four-five years and costing £250,000. Although the 19th-century masonry has lasted well, the mortar holding it together has all but rotted away and only the weight of the stonework is holding the building together. The cathedral is now the spiritual home of only twenty-five Church of Ireland families, but affection for the building stretches beyond denominational boundaries, and in these ecumenical days support for the restoration is encouragingly widespread.

There is no Bishop's Palace for the diocese of Kildare as the bishopric had been held jointly with the deanery of Christ Church, Dublin throughout the 18th century. Dublin and Kildare were united in 1846 on the death of the Hon. Charles Darymple Lindsay (Bishop of Kildare 1804–46). The two

dioceses were separated in 1976 and Kildare was united to the diocese of Meath. This union required the removal of Meath from the province of Armagh to the province of Dublin. Since the Bishop of Kildare together with the Bishop of Meath has the style of 'Most Reverend', normally reserved for archbishops in the Church of Ireland, and takes precedence over all other Irish bishops, it is appropriate that they should be held together.

References

1 J. G. F. Day and H. E. Patton, *The cathedrals of the Church of Ireland* (London, 1932), p. 98.
2 J. T. F. Paterson, *Kildare: the cathedral church of Saint Brigid* (Kildare, 1982), p. 31.
3 T. M. Fallow, *The cathedral churches of Ireland* (London, 1894), p. 28.
4 Paterson, *Kildare: the cathedral church of Saint Brigid*, p.31.
5 Fallow, *The cathedral churches of Ireland*, p. 26.
6 Ibid., p. 27.
7 Thomas Carlyle, *Reminisicences of my Irish journey in 1849* (London, 1882), p. 70.
8 *Irish Builder*, xvii, no. 379 (1875), p. 277.
9 Fallow, *Cathedral churches of Ireland*, p. 28.

KILFENORA

The Cathedral Church of St Fachan

Diocese of Kilfenora (Church of Ireland)

KILFENORA is a little market village (population 125) in a remote part of western Co. Clare, about 28km from Ennis and 5km from Ennistymon. It is set in a hollow of hills in the centre of The Burren, an eerie carboniferous limestone landscape formed as a result of glaciation thousands of years ago. The etymology of the name Kilfenora is uncertain; some authorities give *Cill fionnabhrach* (church of the white brow or meadow), while others give *Cill Fhionnurach* (Fionnuir's church).

The earliest history of the site before the establishment of the diocese in 1152 is extremely obscure. A monastery is said to have been founded here in the 6th century by St Fachan (who may be identified with St Fachtna who founded Rosscarbery), but the earliest historical reference is in the year 1055, when it was burnt by Murtough O'Brien; renovations were carried out in 1056 and 1058. It was plundered in 1079 and accidentally burnt in 1100.

Kilfenora was ignored by the Synod of Ráith Bressail in 1111. But it was sufficiently prominent to achieve diocesan status at the Synod of Kells–Mellifont in 1152, to represent the sub-kingdom of Corco Mruiad. Kilfenora was one of three dioceses carved out of diocese of Killaloe. Roscrea and Scattery Island lost their diocesan status within a few years, and Kilfenora was the only one to survive any length of time.

Records of the succession of Bishops of Kilfenora provide very limited information. An unnamed Bishop of Kilfenora took the oath of loyalty to King Henry II in 1172; his two successors are known only from their initials. The first named bishop, Johannes, was appointed in 1224, and many of his successors in the 13th and 14th centuries are also known only by their Christian names.

tion is somewhat confused. There are references to a Bishop John O'Neylan between 1541 and 1572, but it is not clear whether his allegiance was to the crown or to the pope. Murtough O'Brien was nominated in 1573, and a bishop-elect named Daniel in 1585; whether or not they ever took possession of the diocese is uncertain.

A picture of this small and remote cathedral early in the 17th century is given by Bernard Adams (Bishop of Limerick 1604–26 and Bishop of Kilfenora 1606–1617). In 1615 the bishop reported to the royal commissioners that there were ten canon's portions belonging to the cathedral, each valued at fourteen shillings. The dean, treasurer, chancellor and

Kilfenora Cathedral from the south-east showing the ruined chancel and sacristy

The certainty about the diocese of Kilfenora is its position as almost the smallest of the Irish dioceses. The diocese is roughly 29km long and 14.4km wide at its greatest extent, and covers an area of 54,977 hectares (135,746 acres); only the diocese of Waterford (27,074 hectares or 66,851 acres) is smaller. Kilfenora is slightly smaller than its neighbouring diocese of Kilmacduagh (56,562 hectares or 139,660 acres) and both are about half the size of the diocese of Ross (102,949 hectares or 254,197 acres).

A measure of the insignificance of the diocese is found in the fact that the list of Bishops of Kilfenora after the Reforma-

precentor each held one of the canon's portions; one was 'sequestered this yeere onely for the reparacion of the cathedrall church'; the five remaining portions were held by 'Willm Neland deacon, Murtoghe o Daveryn minister, Andreas McGillisaught A Protestant's sonn and a student at the Colledge att Dublin', Derby Nestor A Protestant', and 'Mathew Powell A minister's sonn'. By 1694 the dean was holding eight canon's portions. The bishop also reported that 'The Dean Donnellon is revolted to popery,' and that 'The Ilandes of Aron auncientlye belonginge to the Bishopricke of Kilfenoraghe which are five markes rent. Where also there are twoo Prebendes belonginge to the

Cathedralle Churche the one named Disart Brecken the other Killurly. But I could never get anything out of the said Ilandes since I had commendam of the Bishopricke which is almost Tenn years.'[1]

The Aran Islands, referred to by the bishop refers, lie 45km south-west of Galway. Formed by a ridge of carboniferous limestone, the three islands, Inisheer, Inishmaan and Inishmore are generally barren and stony, most of the soil being produced by a compost of sand and seaweed. The islanders are largely Irish-speaking. The islands were Christianised *c.*490 by St Enda who was given them by Aengus, King of Munster.

Because of the remoteness, poverty and insignificance of the diocese, it was often difficult to find a candidate willing to become Bishop of Kilfenora. In 1628 Richard Betts was nominated Bishop of Kilfenora by Charles I, but when he arrived in Ireland and saw the reality for himself, he declined and returned to England. 'I have no wish to become Bishop of the poorest See in Ireland.'[2]

The see was subsequently offered to and accepted by James Heygate in 1630; he died in 1638, and again there were problems in finding a candidate. Bishop John Bramhall of Derry (Archbishop of Armagh 1661–3) pressed Viscount Wentworth (later Earl of Strafford), Lord Deputy of Ireland 1633–41, to consider one way of increasing the revenue of the see to make it more attractive to suitable candidates. 'You have answered nothing about the Bishopricke of Kilfenora, which is so poor in itself that no man asks it of the king, and his Majesty is graciously pleased that your lordship would think of some parsonage or vicarage or donative that might for ever be annexed to it.'[3]

In his letter to Archbishop Laud of Canterbury, Wentworth followed Bramhall's advice. 'The old bishop of Kilfenora is dead, and his bishopric, one of those which when it calls goes a begging for a new husband, being not worth above four score pounds to the last man . . . The fittest and only person we have here that will accept it is Mr Robert Sibthorpe, a Bachelor of Divinity, but then he will expect to hold in commendam his Treasurership of Killaloe, the Rectory of Tradaree and some such other benefice as may chance to be conferred upon him. In truth, the gentleman is honest and able. If you like not of this, I know no other here who will accept it.'[4]

Evidently Sibthorpe's conditions were met, because he accepted the appointment and became the last separate Bishop of Kilfenora. It has long been impractical to maintain Kilfenora as a separate diocese in either the Church of Ireland or the Roman Catholic Church. No appointment was made by the crown in the period 1541–1606, and it was held with Limerick from 1606 to 1617. Since the death of Bishop Sibthorpe in 1661 Kilfenora has been united with various dioceses and is unlikely ever to be a separate diocese

again. In the Roman Catholic arrangement, Kilfenora was united to Kilmacduagh in 1750, and both were joined to Galway in 1883. Much is made of the fact that the pope is the titular Bishop of Kilfenora; but there is nothing extraordinary about this. Although geography is the natural link between Kilfenora and Galway and Kilmacduagh, Kilfenora is in the province of Cashel, while the other two are in the province of Tuam. Because of this, the diocese of Kilfenora has been left technically vacant, and nominally in the care of the See of Rome, the Bishop of Galway and Kilmacduagh being the Apostolic Administrator.

Kilfenora: effigy of a bishop on the north side of the chancel

The poverty of Kilfenora in the 17th century was continued in the 18th and 19th centuries. On his tour of Co. Clare in 1780 the schoolmaster John Lloyd visited Kilfenora and found it to be an 'old, ruinous, village . . . though, still, in the centre of a respectable, good, neighbourhood'.[5] When Richard Mant (Bishop of Killaloe and Kilfenora 1820–23) visited Kilfenora in 1820, he called it 'the worst village that I have seen in Ireland, and in the most desolate and least interesting country'.[6] In 1868 the population of the diocese of Kilfenora was

23,042, of whom 224 belonged to the Church of Ireland; of those 224, only 30 resided at Kilfenora itself. Thirteen parishes were grouped into three benefices. At the time of writing Kilfenora Cathedral is the only remaining Church of Ireland place of worship in the diocese of Kilfenora. The Roman Catholic diocese of Kilfenora contains only nineteen parishes.

Kilfenora Cathedral is small and very simple. It was built in the Transitional style of the late 12th century and may have been constructed after the foundation of the diocese. There is some evidence of alteration and extension in the 14th or 15th century, but little remains. This plain, battered, rugged and partly ruined little building, called the Cathedral Church of St Fachan, has no splendour whatever. But it conveys the feeling that its survival has been a long and constant struggle. It stands on windswept sloping ground on the edge of the village; its walls of cyclopean blocks were rough-cast at one time, but this is now crumbling away.

The cathedral has three distinct sections. The nave, which is roofed and used, and the chancel and the sacristy, which are both roofless and disused. The sacristy is attached, like a transept, to the north-east of the chancel. The nave, which measures 20.6m long and 6.3m wide, was also ruined until c.1837, when it was fitted up as a parish church with the help of a grant of 421 from the Ecclesiastical Commissioners. Local tradition, recorded over a hundred years ago, says that until shortly before 1800 'the chancel was roofed and had an oak ceiling, painted blue with gold stars'.[7] It is possible that the chancel was still roofed and used in 1810.

The west wall of the nave has a crude stepped gable which has been likened to 'a pile of emigrants' luggage, with a rabbit hutch or birdcage overhead'.[8] There is a little bell-turret at the apex topped by a small stone pyramid. The wall is buttressed at the north corner and has a two-light window. It also has a very narrow lancet through which arrows could be fired, perhaps a survivor of less tranquil days. The north wall has a two-light window at the west end and two other windows now blocked. As it faces out towards open country, this side of the cathedral presents the appearance of a fortress. A magnificent head of a bishop projects above the south wall door.

The interior of the nave need not detain the visitor for long. It is simple, functional and almost undatable, devoid of decoration or ornamentation of any kind. It has a white panelled board ceiling, plastered walls painted yellow, and a flagstone floor. The large square stone font resting on four square shafts on the south side, could well be contemporary with the cathedral. The sides of the font have primitive carving, but the central column with its hole to drain water into the ground is missing. This form of baptismal font is typical of the 13th century, and its decoration so resembles that on one of the capitals on the east window of the chancel

and those on the pinnacles of the west gable that it may have been made for the cathedral c.1200.

There are five rows of high-backed pine pews on the north and south sides. The triple-lancet east window, through which the ruined chancel can be seen, has wooden sash-frame windows. The altar below the window is flanked by what at first sight appears to be three pulpits, two on the south side and one on the north side. In 1894 T. S. Fallow wrote that the one on the north side was the pulpit, and the other two were desks for the clerk and the parson. It would be interesting to know the source of his information, since he admitted that he was unable to visit Kilfenora.[9] It is more likely that the very high 'desk' on the south side is the pulpit, with the desk for the officiant below, and the clerk's desk or lectern on the north side. All three are in a very dilapidated condition. The modern bishop's throne is on the north side.

The north and south walls have 14th- or early 15th-century arcades of four bays each, perhaps indicating that the nave at one time had aisles. The bays on the south wall contain wooden-sash frame windows set in narrow lancets with deep reveals. The easternmost arch on the south wall springs from a carved corbel depicting the head of an ecclesiastic. The third bay on the north wall contains 17th- and 18th-century memorials of the MacDonogh family. A memorial of 1752, now hidden by the side of a pew, bears the following inscription: 'Here lie the remains of Dr Patrick MacDonogh son of the above Donaldus and grandson of The Craven – He was a dignatory [sic] of the Church of France and of Romish Ireland – He was intimately acquainted with men of the first rank.'[9]

The ruined chancel is more interesting. It measures 10.8m in length and 6.3m in width, and its walls are nearly 1m thick. The east wall has a three-light east window typical of Irish Transitional architecture. The three lancets are separated by slender triangular piers with carved capitals and the whole window is rounded and framed by moulding; the north capital is carved with foliage, the south capital with five figures in a joint act of devotion. The lancets are about 6m in height, the central 39.6cm wide, and the others only 27.94cm wide. There is an elaborately screened recess in the north wall, often thought to be a sedilia. But the seats between the piers are too narrow, and it is more likely to be a wall tomb of the 15th-century. There are two effigial grave slabs on either side of the window, neither in their original position. One is of a 14th-century bishop, the other a primitively carved representation of a cleric, possibly 13th-century. Opposite the 14th-century recess is a double sedilia with a plain dividing shaft, and east of this is a square aumbry. The doorway and windows in the south wall are 15th-century insertions.

The rectangular building attached to the north-east of the chancel may have been a sacristy; it was known in the last century as the 'Lady Chapel'. It may have been the O'Brien

Chapel, mentioned by earlier historians of the cathedral. It has three windows on the east wall: two are lancets, the third has mostly gone. The west wall has a lancet and an external door. There is a low double piscina on the east wall, but the dividing shaft has gone. The south wall, which abuts the chancel, has two arched recesses; the western arch has a small doorway giving entry to the chancel.

On the north wall of the chancel is a large memorial tablet to the seven children of the fearsomely named Neptune Blood (Dean of Kilfenora in the mid-17th century, and a kinsman of the Colonel Blood who attempted to steal the crown jewels in the reign of Charles II). Their ages range from five to sixteen and their dates from 1683–1700. The dean was one of the very few clergy who were still in office in 1661 after twenty years of rebellion and protectorate; no doubt he was protected by the remoteness of Co. Clare. The cathedral possesses a fine Dublin made chalice of 1665 given by the dean. A small circle of silver was removed from the chalice at some time, and Co. Clare folklore tells that it was made into a silver bullet with which to shoot a witch. At the time of writing the chalice is kept in a bank in Ennis and is no longer in use.

The one surprising object in Kilfenora Cathedral is the new bishop's throne. It was donated in 1981 by a schoolteacher from Shannon who wanted to mark the occasion on 10 May that year when Walton Empey (Bishop of Limerick, Ardfert, Aghadoe, Killaloe, Kilfenora, Clonfert, Kilmacduagh and Emly 1981–5) was enthroned as Bishop of Kilfenora, the first enthronement in the cathedral for centuries. Bishop Empey later remembered the occasion with great fondness: '[Kilfenora] is a Cathedral, and I felt that it was only right that I should be enthroned there in order to give encouragement to that tiny community and also to witness to the Church of Ireland presence in the area . . . It was a wonderful day and almost everything ceased in the village for the occasion. They hung out bunting in the streets . . . and the reception was extremely warm. I vested in the Roman Catholic church and was led over to the Cathedral by the parish priest and I think it was the local Irish Countrywomen's Association who put on a splendid reception in the Community Hall afterwards . . . it was a memorable day and will linger long in my memory.'[10] The precedent set by Bishop Empey in 1981 was not followed by his successor, Bishop Edward Darling in 1985, who was enthroned only in the cathedrals of Limerick and Killaloe.

Kilfenora is well known for its High Crosses which surround the cathedral:

(1) Standing near the western end of the cathedral is the so-called 'Doorty Cross'. This 12th-century cross displays the figure of a robed Christ with an interlaced knot below, and below again a large figure riding a donkey which stands on a roof. The other side shows a bishop with crozier standing above two smaller crozier-carrying figures. This cross is thought to commemorate the establishment of the diocese of Kilfenora.

(2) Near the doorway to the cathedral is the shaft of a 13th- or 14th-century Cross.

(3) Near the gate into the graveyard is an unusual Cross without a ring, c.1300–1500.

(4) Near the ruined sacristy is a plain hexagonal pillar with a simple cross-head, probably post-Reformation.

(5) Standing in a field to the east of the graveyard is a 13th- or 14th-century cross with a figure of Christ standing on the end of a two-strand rope which rises from a large gable-shaped area at the bottom of the cross-shaft.

(6) Another 12th-century cross stood in the same field until 1821 when it was taken to Killaloe; it now stands in Killaloe Cathedral. (See KILLALOE for further details).

The former Deanery, a Georgian house of c.1815 with two floors and three bays, stands about 1.5km to the north-west of the cathedral. There has been no resident dean at Kilfenora since the beginning of the century, and no resident priest since 1931. At the time of writing the cathedral is cared for by the Rector of Ennis.

References

1 T. M. Fallow, *The cathedral churches of Ireland* (London, 1894), pp 55–6.

2 Averil Swinfen, *Kilfenora Cathedral* (Ennis, 1986), p. 5.

3 Philip Dwyer, *The diocese of Killaloe from the Reformation to the close of the eighteenth century* (Dublin, 1878), p. 189,

4 James Frost, *History and topography of County Clare* (Dublin, 1893), p. 106.

5 John Lloyd, *A short tour: or, An impartial and accurate description of the county of Clare, with some particular and historical observations* (Ennis, 1780), p. 11.

6 W. B. Mant, *Memoirs of the Rt Rev. Richard Mant, Lord Bishop of Down and Connor, and of Dromore* (Dublin, p. 128).

7 Swinfen, *Kilfenora Cathedral*, p. 5.

8 Ibid., p. 6.

9 Fallow, *Cathedal churches of Ireland*, p. 53.

10 Letter to the author, 24 Oct. 1989.

KILKENNY

The Cathedral Church of St Canice

Diocese of Ossory (Church of Ireland)

KILKENNY lies 116.8km south-west of Dublin and 48km north of Waterford. The history of this interesting and comparatively unspoilt Anglo-Norman town begins in the 6th century with St Canice, who is alleged to have established a cell on the hill now occupied by the cathedral which bears his name. His name also survives in the name of the town itself, Kilkenny (*Cill Chainnigh* meaning Church of Cainneach or Canice, which is the Irish form of Kenneth). Canice, a Pict by race, was born in Co. Derry *c.*525 and died *c.*599. He was trained for the monastic life by St Finian of Clonard and St Cadoc in Wales. He accompanied St Columba on his visit to meet Brude, King of the Picts, in Scotland and is said to have founded churches on the islands of Mull, Tiree, South Uist, Coll and Kintyre. He was the first to build a church at the place now known as St Andrew's. His feast-day is kept on 11 October.

Kilkenny is built around two hills, one crowned by the castle, the other by St Canice's Cathedral. Kilkenny Castle was the property of the Butler family from 1392 until 1967. Kilkenny itself virtually the creation of the Butler family (Earls and later Marquesses of Ormonde), possessors of one of the three great earldoms into which that part of Ireland controlled by Edward III was divided. Its winding passages and lanes give it the air of a medieval university town. It rivalled Dublin as a seat of government, being an occasional residence of the Lord Lieutenant, and a regular meeting place of the Irish parliament. Having flourished from the 14th to the 17th century, it was besieged, captured and sacked by Cromwell in 1650 and thereafter began to decline. The decline accelerated in the 19th century, and the population of Kilkenny dropped by two-thirds.

St Canice's Cathedral is one of the finest of the Irish medieval cathedrals and the second largest of its date in Ireland. Built of local limestone rubble masonry, it measures 64.62m long and 35.66m wide across the transepts; only St Patrick's Cathedral in Dublin is larger. In the reign of Elizabeth I it was described as 'a worthy foundation as well for gorgeous buildings as for notable liuyings'.[1] At the Restoration in 1661 Bishop Griffith Williams (1641–72) called it 'the great and famous, most beautiful cathedral church of St Keney',[2]

The name of one 10th-century abbot/bishop is known, and a wooden church on the site was destroyed by fire in 1087. But history effectively begins with the establishment of the territorial diocese of Kilkenny at the Synod of Ráith Bressail 1111. A few years later it was renamed the diocese of Ossory (Osraige) after the district, and remains so.

A further burning took place in 1114, and a new cathedral was constructed in the mid-12th century. The massive foundations of this building, which was of some size and importance, lie on either side of the present chancel. Its font, made from Kilkenny marble, is to be seen in the present cathedral.

St Canice's cathedral is cruciform, with an aisled, clerestoried nave of five bays, a south porch, transepts, and a partly aisled chancel. There is a squat tower at the crossing, scarcely higher than the apex of the chancel, nave and transept roofs that surround it. Hugh de Rous, the first Anglo-Norman Bishop of Ossory (1202–18), began construction soon after his appointment to the see, and the chancel may date from his episcopate. The transepts and the chancel aisles are the work of his successor Bishop Hugh de Mapilton (1251–60). The whole cathedral was completed during the episcopate of Bishop Geoffrey St Leger (1260–87). The different dates are represented by the different stones used; the dressings and ornamental features of the chancel and transepts are sandstone, and those of the nave are limestone. The nave arcades rest on quatrefoil columns which echo the theme of the quatrefoil clerestory windows above.

On 22 May 1332 the original tower, 9–12m higher than the present structure, collapsed, falling on the side chapels and involving the western portion of the chancel in its fall, 'a most terrible and pitiful sight to behold'.[3] Restoration was begun by Bishop Richard (Ledred) Leatherhead (1317–61) in 1354. The tower was not raised to its original height, probably because of a belief that the piers were not strong enough to support it and a desire to avoid a repetition of the catastophe. It would seem that the repair was not entirely satisfactory, since about a century later Bishop David Hacket (1460–78) ordered the erection of the lierne vaulting to support the tower. The north-west pier of the crossing may be 13th-century, but the other three date from the 14th-century reconstruction. The north transept contains a 13th-century stone chair with arms ornamented with foliated bosses, known as St Kieran's Chair. The Bishops of Ossory have been enthroned in this chair for centuries.

Bishop Ledred was buried on the north side of the high altar. A niche on the north wall of the sanctuary contains the effigy of a bishop fully vested, with mitre and crozier, but on his feet are the sandals of a Franciscan friar. Ledred was the only Franciscan to occupy the see, so this effigy can probably be identified as his monument.

Ledred filled the cathedral windows with stained glass, and the three great lancets of the east wall were especially admired. In 1645 the papal nuncio, Archbishop Rinuccini, was so impressed by the glass that he offered to buy it for £700.

St Canice's Cathedral, Kilkenny, looking east

The cathedral chapter refused to sell, and unfortunately the glass was smashed in 1650 by Cromwell's soldiers, who were said to have stabled their horses in the cathedral. As a town of considerable importance, and the headquarters of the Catholic Confederation, Kilkenny probably suffered more at the hands of Cromwell than most other towns in Ireland. It was a devastation from which the town never really recovered. Bishop Griffith Williams (1641–72) sadly recorded the damage done to the cathedral. 'They have utterly defaced, and ruined, thrown down all the Roof of it, taken away five great and goodly Bells, broken down all the windows, and carried away every bit of the Glass, that they say was worth a very great deal; and all the doors of it that Hogs might come, and root, and Dogs gnaw the Bones of the dead.'[4] Bishop Williams returned from exile in 1660 and did what he could to restore the cathedral devoting his first year's income to the purpose. But having done all that he was able to do, he wrote that 'yet a thousand pounds more will not sufficiently repair that church'.[5]

Whatever kind of building Bishop Williams may have found on his return, it had certainly been repaired by 1673, when the Chapter Book records that the cathedral was whitewashed and new flagstones were laid. Neither were likely to have been done in a building that was still derelict and roofless.

Despite the efforts of successive bishops, the cathedral fabric deteriorated, and when Bishop Richard Pococke (1756–65) was enthroned, the cathedral was in 'a most ruinous condition.'[6] This claim is contradicted by the chapter accounts and by the fact that Pococke's work was concerned largely with beautifying the church rather than with structural repair. The bishop collected a fund of £1,191 15s and contributed 100 guineas himself. He concentrated his efforts on providing the chancel with new fittings and furnishings, but with little understanding of the principles of Gothic architecture. Elaborate stalls, a bishop's throne, galleries and pews were inserted in the chancel, 'being of fine grained oak, the whole well executed, but in the Ionic style, which, it need hardly be said, was most unsuitable'.[7] The altar was given a new cover of purple velvet embroidered with gold lace, above which was a painting of a 'glory' which the bishop had brought back from Italy. The medieval screen was raised in height to block and separate the chancel from the nave. Some work was possibly done to the walls of the chancel which were described in 1860 as 'Italianesque'.[8]

Pococke's Classical work was similar to the contemporary alterations at Cloyne Cathedral but equally out of sympathy with Gothic. It was the product of an age that admired the Classical style and regarded Gothic architecture as barbarous, and it was done with the best of intentions. 'That a man just returned from foreign travel, at the period when he lived, should prefer the Grecian architecture, of the Ionic style, to the Gothic, is, however, nothing wonderful, and,

perhaps, we should be grateful that his active and liberal disposition did not lead that prelate to remodel the entire building in the former style.'[9]

Pococke was succeeded by Bishop Charles Dodgson (1765–75), grandfather of Lewis Carroll, author of *Alice in Wonderland*. No further major work was undertaken on the cathedral until 1850, when the squat spire-shaped roof of the tower was removed. This was followed in December 1853 by the removal of the wall between the chancel and nave. The lower 4.8m was a blank wall constituting the medieval rood-screen. Access to the chancel was gained by a simple Early English central doorway with jambs and voussoirs made of a soft yellow sandstone. Loose rubble-work masonry filled the gap between the top of the screen and the arch above.

St Canice's Cathedral, Kilkenny from the south-west

A thorough and more sympathetic restoration took place in the years 1864–70 as a result of the efforts of Dean Charles Vignoles. The chosen architect was Thomas Newneham Deane, thirty-six years old at the time of his appointment in 1863, who had begun work on the construction of the nave, transepts and choir of Tuam Cathedral in 1861. Whereas he had a free rein at Tuam to construct a cathedral from the ground, Kilkenny was not in a serious state of decay, no part of it had collapsed, and the uniform style of the basic structure had been untouched since the 14th century. He liked Gothic architecture and his restoration was broadly sympathetic and conservative. The Georgian woodwork was completely removed; windows and arches, blocked up for centuries were reopened. Deane provided the nave and transepts with massive hammer-beam roofs which, while unknown in Irish medieval Gothic architecture, are splendid additions to St Canice's.

Deane had estimated the cost of restoration at £10,000, which proved inadequate and caused some bitterness with the chapter. Nevertheless, the restoration continued, and the bulk of it was completed by the time of Deane's resignation in May 1870.

Still further bitterness might have been caused had Deane still been the architect ten years later. The ceiling that he erected consisted of timber slatting laid and nailed on to rafters without being rabbeted or tongued and grooved. Consequently, about twelve years later, there were complaints that 'all the joints of the boarding have opened to a greater or lesser extent, allowing free excess to the outer air, which rushes in with greater or less force according to the direction of the wind ... creating great draughts and making the church most uncomfortable'.[10]

The east window was filled with stained glass in 1875 to replace the glass smashed by the Cromwellians. The 19th-century glass faithfully imitates its medieval predecessor and depicts the life, passion, resurrection and ascension of Christ. George Edmund Street was consulted in 1876, but seems to have done little; only the screen in the south chancel aisle can be attributed to him.

Work continued into the 1890s under Richard Langrishe, a local architect, who was responsible for the interior of the south porch and the fittings in the Lady Chapel. Stalls for the chapter and choir, carved at Bruges from Danubian oak to a design by Richard Langrishe, were added in 1904; their pine predecessors were given to Ferns Cathedral.

The sanctuary was provided with a pavement of Irish marbles, grey from Tyrone, green from Connemara, red from Kerry, and black from Kilkenny. The dull reredos of Kilkenny marble framing three panels of white marble was added in 1921 as a memorial to the 3rd Marquess of Ormonde.

St Canice's Cathedral is impressive in its spacious simplicity. It is one of the best cathedrals in Ireland from the aspects of position, preservation, architectural detail and furnishings. The view of the chancel from the west end is a beautiful sight; lit by a profusion of stained-glass windows, it has a soft silvery-grey luminescent quality. 'As one stands at the west end of the nave, the eye is carried forward, through the great arches of the crossing, to the three lofty lancets of the east window, surmounted by a rose ... There is no nobler vista in any church in Ireland.'[11]

There is a Round Tower close to the gable wall of the south transept. It stands 30m high and has battlements instead of the traditional conical roof. It is built of mountain limestone and local dolomite and gritstone and could date from anywhere between 700 and 1000.

The Bishop's Palace, to the north of the cathedral, is a Georgian house built 1736–45 on the foundations of the medieval palace. At the eastern end of the palace is a 14th-century keep with a groined ground-floor ceiling. Excavations in 1962–3 revealed a stone staircase in the east wall of the first floor and a slit window in the north wall. This is probably part of the bishop's residence built by Bishop Ledred. In 1760 a Doric colonnade, incorporating a robing room, joined the palace to the north transept of the cathedral. The colonnade was subsequently demolished, and a road now passes between the cathedral and the palace garden, but the robing room still remains a feature. The palace was restored in 1963.

To the south-west of the cathedral is the attractive 17th-century Deanery and the Library and Registry, which is also the residence of the Bishop's Vicar, a title unique in cathedral establishments. The Library contains a rare and valuable collection of about 3,000 16th- and 17th-century books.

The dioceses of Ferns and Leighlin were united to Ossory in 1835, and in 1976 the three dioceses were joined to the united dioceses of Cashel, Waterford and Lismore.

References

1 Adrian Empey (ed.), *A worthy foundation: the Cathedral Church of St Canice, Kilkenny* (Portlaoise, 1985), p. 9.
2 Ibid., p. 45.
3 H. E. Day and J. G. F. Patton, *The cathedrals of the Church of Ireland* (London, 1932), p. 106.
4 Ibid., p. 107.
5 Ibid., pp 107–108.
6 Ibid., p. 108.
7 Richard Langrishe, *Handbook to the Cathedral Church of St Canice, Kilkenny* (Kilkenny, 1879), p. 9.
8 Mackenzie Walcott, *The cathedrals of the United Kingdom* (London, 1860), p. 314.
9 James Graves and J. G. A. Prim, *The history, architecture and antiquities of the Cathedral Church of St Canice, Kilkenny* (Dublin, 1857), p. 91.
10 *Irish Builder*, xxi, no. 463 (1879), p. 99.
11 Day and Patton, *Cathedrals of the Church of Ireland*, p. 112.

KILKENNY

The Cathedral Church of the Assumption of the Blessed Virgin Mary

Diocese of Ossory (Roman Catholic)

St Mary's Cathedral (as it is usually known) stands in Blackmill Street on the highest point in the city and was built on the site of an old mansion called Burrell's Hall. The cathedral was built to replace a chapel, also dedicated to St Mary, which stood outside St James's Gate at the end of what used to be the bishop's town house; it was built in 1771 and replaced a chapel of 1700. After the completion of the cathedral, the old chapel remained in use, and part of it still remains.

The foundation stone of the cathedral was laid on 18 August 1843 during the episcopate of Bishop William Kinsella (1829–45). It was designed by William Butler in a rather hard and angular Gothic Revival style which contains elements of Early English and Decorated. It is allegedly based on the plan of Gloucester Cathedral and has a conspicuous tower at the crossing. The main building material is grey Kilkenny lime-stone from the Black Quarry. A contemporary observer described the new cathedral as 'very beautiful indeed; the magnificent tower is too large and lofty in proportion to the length of the nave, but it has a grand effect when seen from a distance'.[1] The disproportionate size of the tower may be partly explained by the fact that the planned length of the nave was shortened by one bay; but the high ground on which the cathedral is built does much to accentuate the loftiness of the tower.

Bishop Kinsella died in 1845 when the walls of his cathedral were still only about 2m high. The work was continued through the famine years by his successor, Bishop Edward Walsh (1846–72), who consecrated the cathedral on Rosary Sunday, 4 October 1857 at a ceremony that lasted nearly three hours. Relics of SS Cosmas and Damian were placed under the high altar, and of St Clement under the Lady Altar. The total cost amounted to £25,000.

For the practical purposes of worship, the cathedral was completed in 1857, but work on the interior and on surrounding associated buildings continued until the end of the century. Railings were erected around the cathedral in 1862, and a new organ and organ gallery were installed in 1866 at a cost of £1,000. The cathedral presbytery was built in

St Mary's Cathedral, Kilkenny, looking east

the same year. A new sacristy, to replace the use of the crypt below the high altar, was constructed to a design by William Hague in 1887 and connected to the cathedral by a cloister. In the years 1887–93 a heating system was installed; two inner porches were constructed at the west end of the nave aisles and the centre porch was remodelled. The marble altar rail was extended to the side walls by James Pearse of Dublin who also constructed the altar of the Sacred Heart. Pearse was one of the best-known monumental sculptors then working in Ireland; his other claim to fame is that he was the father of Patrick Pearse, the leader of the Easter Rising in 1916.

Between 1893 and 1899 the roof was overhauled, the sanctuary furnished, the baptistery constructed, the altar of St Joseph erected, new seating provided for the aisles, the entire cathedral cleaned and painted, and the cathedral grounds laid out. There was also installed a new font of white marble supported by a large pillar of Galway granite in the centre surrounded by four pillars of green Connemara marble. All the additional work was carried out under Hague's supervision. The total cost was £20,000, and the cathedral was solemnly reopened on 9 April 1899.

Within thirty years further restoration was needed. In 1928 £28,000 had to be spent on repairs to the leaking roof and restoration of the external turrets, which had to be taken down and rebuilt; the organ was renovated at a cost of £2,500; the floors of the sanctuary and side chapels were covered with mosaic; pitch-pine seats were placed in the aisles and transepts, and new stalls of Austrian oak were provided for the choir. No further major work was done until the reordering of the mid-1970s.

St Mary's greatest asset is its hilltop site and conspicuous tower. The 56.8m-high tower has a pierced battlemented balustrade with pierced and spired corner turrets. Larger versions of these turrets do sentinel duty on the west front, the transepts and the apse. The cathedral is 49.3m long; the side aisles are each 4.5m wide, and the nave is 9.1m wide, making a total width of 18.2m; the total width at the crossing is 18.2m. The statue outside the west door, representing St Patrick, was erected in 1909 to commemorate the silver jubilee of Bishop Abraham Brownrigg of Ossory (1884–1928).

St Mary's Cathedral is cruciform in plan, very lofty yet relatively small; its height and comparatively small internal space echo St Fin Barre's Cathedral in Cork. The five-bay nave is separated from its aisles by arcades resting on clustered columns; there is a triforium in the eaves of the aisles. The nave is lit by twin-light windows in each bay with small trefoil windows above. The clerestory has triple-light windows, and the theme is continued and echoed at the same level by double-arched recesses in the transepts. A large Decorated window at the west end is now partly obscured by the organ case. The trusses of the timber-vaulted roof are supported by semi-cylindrical pilasters which descend through the

clerestory and triforium stages to meet the springing of the nave arcades and rest on the capitals of the clustered columns. The tower rests on four symmetrical arches at the crossing. The Stations of the Cross are large 19th-century oil paintings in Gothic frames.

The apsidal chancel has nine stained-glass windows, six tall windows, with glass by Early & Powell, above three smaller ones. The lower apse windows are set in deeply recessed and pointed arched bays. The mosaic floor by Bourke of London depicts the emblems of the four Evangelists. The ceiling is richly painted, and the murals are by Westlake of London. The Italian marble high altar by J. L. Robinson is still in position, though disused since the reordering of the chancel and sanctuary in the mid-1970s; the reredos was built by Messrs Ryan of Great Denmark Street, Dublin. The apse has flanking and disused side chapels of the Blessed Virgin Mary and St Joseph. There is a marble statue of the Blessed Virgin Mary by Benzoni.

St Mary's Cathedral, Kilkenny from the north-west

Reordering in line with the decrees of the Second Vatican Council took place in the mid-1970s. Complete new lighting and heating systems were installed. A dais was erected between the four piers of the crossing and covered with a dark-red carpet. The new altar, with bronze figures depicting scenes from the life of Christ, the president's chair and the lectern are of black Kilkenny marble, and are in accord with the surrounding dark stonework of the cathedral. The tabernacle, also of Kilkenny marble, is set between vertical panels of marble behind the president's chair. The new altar was blessed and consecrated on 4 October 1977. Although the designs are contemporary, the new furnishings somehow blend well with the surrounding cathedral. The very blackness of Kilkenny marble, no doubt chosen for being a local material, complements the dark-grey limestone and substantially reduces the visibility, and therefore the obtrusiveness, of the new arrangements. The same designs, repeated in a light-coloured marble or stone, would be unwelcome detractions from the sense of the numinous in this cathedral. Feelings of reverence and devotion are often heightened by the atmosphere of mystery that accompanies darkness.

References

1   James Godkin, *Ireland and her churches* (London, 1867), p. 311.

KILLALA

The Cathedral Church of St Patrick

Diocese of Killala (Church of Ireland)

KILLALA is a fishing village, with a population of about 600, 10.4km north-west of Ballina and 9.6km east of Ballycastle in Co. Mayo. The derivation of the Irish form of its name *Cill Alaidh* is obscure; *aladh* means 'variegated' or 'piebald' which would give the odd translation 'the variecoloured church', perhaps an allusion to some external decoration. Some have simply and mistakenly assumed that Killala means 'the church of St Ala'; but there is no evidence for the existence of a saint of that name.

The see is one of the many alleged to have been founded by St Patrick who consecrated St Muredach (*alias* Murtagh or or Murdoch) as the first bishop and built the first church on land given by a local chieftain. The site is certainly an old one. An elaborate but inaccessible 9th-century souterrain can be found in the grounds of the cathedral. It lies to the south-east of the cathedral and was discovered at the end of the 19th-century by workman digging a grave. The souterrain suggests that the site may well have been an old rath. Muredach is an obscure figure from the mists of the early 6th century who ended his life as a hermit on the island of

Inishmurray. His feast-day is 13 August. Nothing is known of his successors beyond a list of names.

The diocese of Killala was established at the Synd of Ráith Bressail in 1111 to correspond with the territory of the Uí Fiachrach, a sept claiming descent from Fiachrach, son of King Dathi. Until the early 13th century several Bishops of Killala were styled 'Bishops of the Uí Fiachrach'. The Uí Dubhda (O'Dowds) came to be the most prominent family in the area. When Norman-Welsh settlers arrived after 1235, the power of the O'Dowds began to wane. They held on to some territory as late as the early 17th century, but the arrival of Cromwell ended their power. Only the diocese of Killala remains as an indication of the geographical extent of their authority.

Killala Cathedral from the south-west

The first recorded diocesan bishop was Ua Máel Fogmair I, who died in 1137. Very little is known about the successive cathedral churches of the see. There is no record of the appearance of the medieval cathedral, although Bishop Thomas Orwell (1390–98) obtained a grant of indulgences for those who visited the cathedral and gave alms for its repair. Probably wrecked in the troubles of the 16th century, it was certainly in ruins in 1611, and proposals for its re-edification were laid before the Irish parliament that year.[1]

Since the notorious Miler Magrath (see CASHEL) was Bishop of Killala 1613–22, it is most unlikely that any repair work was undertaken during his tenure of the see, and the cathedral was still in ruins in 1645. The Roman Catholic Bishop of Killala, Francis Kirwan (1645–61) managed to gain possession of the cathedral in 1645 during the rebellion of the Confederate war. He found the cathedral church and the whole Diocese of Killala to be in a 'deplorable state', the cathedral church itself being 'tumbled to the ground'.[2] He built a wall around the bishop's house and began to rebuild the walls of the Lady Chapel 'which was attached to the old walls of the cathedral'.[3] Further restoration was halted by the arrival of Cromwell's army in 1652.

After the troubles of the 16th and 17th centuries, Killala settled down into the quiet and sleepy village that it remains. The only event which disturbed its peace was the French invasion at the end of the 18th century. On 22 August 1798 two French frigates sailed into Killala Bay carrying 2,000 troops under the command of General Humbert. His intention was to raise a rebellion and attack England through what he saw as the backdoor of Ireland. He occupied Killala and established his headquarters in the Bishop's Palace. He and his troops were forced to surrender on 8 September to Lord Cornwallis at Ballinamuck, Co. Longford. Bishop Joseph Stock (1798–1810) was holding a visitation of the diocese at the time, and, together with his family, the dean and some of the clergy, he was held prisoner. The bishop later wrote an account of his experiences acknowledging the kindness of his captors.

Killala Cathedral today is essentially a late 17th-century building, constructed during the episcopate of Thomas Otway (Bishop of Killala and Achonry 1671–1680). A blocked 13th-century Gothic doorway in the south wall, known as the Dean's Door, is the only substantial survivor of the medieval cathedral, although there are traces of medieval stonework in the walls. The only subsequent alteration to the cathedral was the addition of a stone spire in the first half of the 18th century.

The cathedral stands on high ground which sharply falls away to the bay. It is a plain rectangle with a square tower and spire at the west end, and a vestry attached like a transept to the north side of the chancel. The battery below the east window is the only unusual feature. The cathedral is in every respect typical of the auditory building which was deemed sufficient for a 17th-century reformed church. Its style can be seen as the forerunner of the churches that were erected wholesale across Ireland in 1810–21 by the Board of First-Fruits. The roof is of ornamental exposed timber trusses. There are four round-arched windows in the south wall and three on the north, all with elementary wooden tracery. The east wall has a small rose window above a pointed arch window. This latter window has some panes of coloured glass which do nothing to improve its appearance; plain glass

throughout would have been better. The sanctuary is panelled in painted wood to a height of 2m.

The internal furnishings of the cathedral follow the arrangement of many Irish cathedrals, the whole building being constituted a 'choir', and the congregation being placed between the chapter stalls and the altar. Although the building is, ecclesiologically, a cathedral, for all practical purposes, it is no more than a parish church. In many Church of Ireland cathedrals, members of the chapter are usually non-resident, their full-time work being elsewhere than at the cathedral. The provision of chapter stalls in the traditional 'choir' area, between the congregation and the altar, for a chapter whose members would rarely be seen at cathedral services, would be pointless. Killala Cathedral in 1845 adopted the sensible arrangement of siting the eight chapter stalls in return position, below the large detached gallery at the west end.

Killala: the Dean's Door

The bishop's throne stands in the sanctuary against the north wall. The font is under the west gallery on the north side. The lectern is next to the officiant's desk on the south wall outside the altar rails; the pulpit is on the corresponding north side. The north and south walls are lined with a well-preserved and magnificently archaic set of box pews which have been badly grained. Their doors, high partitions and cushioned benches prevent any meaningful liturgical revision at Killala in the foreseeable future.

Walcott speaks of the cathedral being 'modernised in 1817 into a commonplace parish church'.[4] He gives no record of what was actually done, though it was perhaps at this time that the external walls were rendered. James Collins (Dean 1844–71) made strenuous efforts to improve the fabric of the cathedral, and also the standard of its services, which had lost their 'characteristics of cathedral service'[5] after the union of Killala with Tuam in 1834. He also re-erected the chapter stalls which had apparently been removed after 1834. But the death of Dean Collins in 1871, and the disestablishment and disendowment of the Church of Ireland in the same year, left the cathedral dependent on voluntary contributions and effectively ended his efforts. By the early 1920s a former worshipper at the cathedral described it as follows: 'This very old sanctuary, which was in my early boyhood filled with a great and grand congregation under the light and eloquence of Dean Collins. Now a mournful silence pervades the long aisle at the usual Sunday and Holy-day services.'[6] 'The decay began from the time the Moy was diverted from its natural course by Ballysokeery and Moyne Abbey to its present flow out through Bartra Banks. That was about the year 1845. Captain Wright, for long years Harbour Master at Ballina Quay, sailed his schooner up by Killala and Moyne . . . Crowds of men could be got for 6d per day...The change took all the old shipping, life and traffic from Killala, and so its decay set in.'[7]

A further restoration took place at the end of the 19th century in response to an appeal for funds to supplement the voluntary contributions of the congregation 'which have proved quite inadequate to meet the common needs of keeping it wind and weather proof, the parish being a very poor one, and having of late years lost many of its resident parishioners, through death or migration. Hence it is we are constrained to make this public appeal to all friends of the Chuch, so that this ancient and venerable building may not be allowed to fall into complete decay; and it is our hope to obtain at least sufficient to refit the chancel, etc., and to put the whole fabric externally and internally in thorough repair.'[8]

The building was last restored in 1962, and further major restoration is presently under way. The exterior walls were rendered in cement plaster, probably in 1817, which gave the cathedral a hard and plain appearance. The rendering was removed in 1991, revealing the very attractive stonework beneath, including traces of 13th-century work. The interior is in need of redecoration, and this will take place as soon as funds are available.

There is little to interest the visitor to Killala Cathedral beyond its historic associations, and the curious sight of the box pews. Mrs Delany, wife of Dr Patrick Delany, Dean of Down in the mid-18th century, was a regular visitor to Killala, and her comment still holds good: 'The church is neat but you would not dream it was a cathedral.'[9] At the time of writing it ministers to thirty seven families.

A 25.5m-high 12th-century Round Tower, built of oolitic limestone, stands 73m to the north-west of the cathedral on a bluff overlooking the harbour. Its plinth is 0.9m high, and the doorway 3.3m above ground level. The tower was struck by lightning in 1800 and was repaired by Bishop Verschoyle c.1840. A lightning conductor has been attached to prevent further disaster.

The former Bishop's Palace was known as Killala Castle. In 1810 it was described as 'a very small and ruinous house, ill situated and ill contrived, at the edge of a very fine demense. But the present Bishop is making such additions and improvements as will render it a very comfortable residence.'[10] In its last manifestation, the castle was a tall plain three-storey L-shaped building with a gable-ended tower block at the end of one of its arms. On the death of Bishop James Verschoyle (1810–34), the united dioceses of Killala and Achonry were united to Tuam, and the castle was sold. It was a family residence for some years, then it became a warehouse, and was demolished in the 1950s to make way for a housing estate. It stood to the south of the cathedral. The former Deanery, across the street on the north side of cathedral, has also now been sold.

References

1 John Lynch, *The portrait of a pious bishop; or The life and death of the Most Rev. Francis Kirwan, Bishop of Killala* (Dublin, 1864), pp 170–71.
2 Thomas McDonnell, *The diocese of Killala from its inception to the close of the penal times* (Monaghan, 1976), p. 119.
3 Ibid., p. 120.
4 Mackenzie Walcott, *The cathedrals of the United Kingdom* (London, 1860), p. 316.
5 T. M. Fallow, *The cathedral churches of Ireland* (London, 1894), p. 88.
6 James Greer, *The windings of the Moy* (Dublin, 1924), p. 17.
7 Ibid.
8 T. M. Fallow, *Cathedral churches of Ireland*, pp 88–9.
9 W. H. Grindle, *Irish cathedral music* (Belfast, 1989), p. 54.
10 Nicholas Carlisle, *A topographical dictionary of Ireland* (London, 1810), p. 217.

KILLALOE

The Cathedral Church of St Flannan

Diocese of Killaloe (Church of Ireland)

KILLALOE is a town on the border between Co. Clare and Co. Tipperary. It lies in a valley on the west bank of the Shannon at the point at which it leaves Lough Derg on its way to Limerick, 20.8km distant, and the sea. The valley is formed by the Slieve Bernagh Mountains of Clare and the Arra Hills of Tipperary. The border between Clare and Tipperary runs along the middle of the Shannon at this point, and Killaloe in Clare is linked to its twin town of Ballina in Tipperary by a splendid bridge of thirteen arches.

Killaloe was close to the birthplace of Brian Boru, the great High King who succeeded in uniting Ireland in 1002–14. Towards the end of the 10th century Brian, approaching the height of his power, made Killaloe the capital of his Dalcassian kingdom in Clare; there is no mention of Killaloe in the Irish annals before that date. In the light of this royal patronage Killaloe was a natural choice for a territorial diocesan see at Ráith Bressail, superseding the greater prestige and antiquity of the two island churches of Iniscattery (Scattery Island) in the Shannon estuary, and Inishcaltra in Lough Derg.

St Flannan, whose name survives in the dedication of the cathedral, is a shadowy figure of whom nothing reliable is known. He sprang into prominence solely because of the fame of the king. His date is uncertain, and the 12th-century biography of him is historically worthless. He has been confused with the 7th-century saint of the same name who worked in the Hebrides for several years and gave his name to the Flannan Islands; this identification is certainly incorrect, but he may perhaps be identified with Flannan of Cill Ard in West Clare who died in 778. St Flannan's feast-day is on 18 December.

The name Killaloe derives from *Cill Da Lua*, meaning 'the church of St Dalua (or Molua)', and there are grounds for believing that a saint of that name at one time had a small church at Killaloe; but the tradition is late and open to question. His sanctuary on Friar's Island in Co. Tipperary was a place of pilgrimage until 1929. Plans for the Shannon Hydro-Electric Scheme envisaged raising the level of the river and therefore the submergence of the island. Because of the importance of the place, it was decided to dismantle St Lua's Oratory and re-erect it in the grounds of the Roman Catholic Church at Killaloe; the work was completed by July 1930. The Oratory is a small nave-and-chancel church of the 9th- or 10th-centuries, built of yellow sandstone.

Killaloe was established as a diocese at the Synod of Ráith Bressail in 1111, and Máel Muire Ua Dúnáin was the first diocesan bishop. Although prominent at the synod, he held the diocese for only a short time and died as a monk at Clonard in 1117.

There would certainly have been a church at Killaloe in the time of Brian Boru, but it was probably demolished to make way for the cathedral built by Domhnall Mór O'Brien (King of Munster 1168–94) *c.* 1180. His cathedral had a brief existence being destroyed soon afterwards by Cathal Carrach of Connacht, in retaliation for raids made by the king into west Connacht. The only relic of the O'Brien cathedral is a Romanesque doorway incorporated into the extreme southwest corner of the present nave. The present cathedral belongs to the Transitional period between Romanesque and Gothic. Construction began *c.*1182, and the nave was completed *c.* 1225.

Very little is known of the building until the 17th century. The cathedral was possibly damaged during the troubles of the 16th century; partial restoration was under way in 1622, when Bishop John Rider (1613–32) reported to the royal commissioners: 'Concerning ye cathedrale church of Killaloe called Ecclesia Sti fflanani Laonensis: the quire of it is in very good repair, and adorned wth a new pulpit and with many new faire and conveniente seats: and ye roofe well timbred and slatted, and ye church well glassed . . . But for ye body of ye said church, it belongs to ye parishioners to build, who have brought all theyr materialls in place, erected theyr scaffolds, and I hope this summer it will be finished.'[1] The walls of the nave are original 13th-century work, and the bishop's comments may refer only to a re-roofing.

Cathedral records record further work in 1676, the rebuilding of the screen at the crossing in 1707, and the repairing of the south transept and nave in 1708. The extent of the work in 1708–11 appears to have involved considerable restoration since the chapter accounts record a bill for £10 'for throwing down the wall of the south isle [*sic*] of the church, and for carrying rubbish out'.[2] On the assumption that the screen is the one that was demolished in 1885, it was a stone wall about 1m thick. In 1725 the gate and stone piers were erected, and shortly afterwards the chancel was re-roofed.

Bishop William Knox (1794–1803) undertook some internal repairs and raised the height of the tower in 1795 by 4.5m; it was raised again in 1892 by a further 1.5m to the present 24.3m, to allow the hanging of a peal of bells. Before Knox's day the cathedral tower had no parapet or battlement and was surmounted by a pyramidal roof whose base was smaller than the roof of the tower on which it sat. A similar pyramidal cap was to be seen on the tower of St Canice's Cathedral, Kilkenny, until the mid-19th-century restoration. The pyramid itself was topped by an iron pillar and weather-vane bearing the date 1682. Bishop Knox's motive in raising the height of the tower is uncertain. Some say that it was to make

Killaloe Cathedral from the east

room for bells; others ascribe it to a more frivolous motive: 'The tower, which was previously not well visible from the Bishop's palace, Clarisford House, might be so elevated as to make a pleasing and appropriate picture in the prospect.'[3]

A later observer thought the additions by Knox to be in a style that was 'tottally incorrect',[4] though whether this comment applies only to the raising of the height of the tower, or to internal work, is uncertain. It is tempting to speculate that Bishop Knox, if not one of his predecessors, subjected the cathedral to a classicising restoration of the kind that took place at Cloyne, Ferns and St Mary's, Limerick.

Killaloe Cathedral is cruciform cathedral with an aisleless nave, transepts, chancel, and central tower, built of yellow and purple sandstone. The east and west gables have square clasping buttresses. It measures 47.7 long, 9.15m wide and 11.7m high. James Godkin described it in the mid-19th century as 'a small dingy old church'.[5] Since he used exactly the same words to describe Clonfert Cathedral, his comment need not be taken too seriously.

The dark disused nave bears a strong resemblance to the nave of Leighlin Cathedral, which is also 13th century. It is 18.6m long and 9.15m wide and has an impressive resonance which has not been lost on past visitors. George Holmes found that it produced 'an uncommon lengthened and solemn echo from our footsteps'[6] and John Harden found it 'remarkable for the prolongation of sound, supporting the human voice for half a minute or near it'.[7] The nave is dimly lit, the north and south walls having only two lancet windows each. There is also a single lancet, 6.1m long and 61cm wide, set in the west wall above the entrance doorway.

The Romanesque doorway, which now frames a window at the south west corner of the nave, has a hooded moulding over four orders springing from four shafts. The first order has a design of chevron and lozenge patterns. The left-hand pillar is missing, except for the small indented stand at the base. The second order has carvings of animals in high relief, their tails wrapped around the hair of human heads. The third order has a pattern of foliage. The fourth order has an architrave deeply cut into alternate chevrons and recesses, moulded and beaded and ending in serpent heads. There are over one 130 patterns of plants and animals, no two of which are exactly alike. A precise replica of the doorway can be seen between two reception rooms in Glenstal Castle in Co. Limerick; it was executed in 1841 for Sir Joseph Barrington, for whom the castle was built.

An ancient tombstone incised with a cross, 162cm by 60cm, is set in the floor of the recess of the doorway. Tradition says that it marks the burial place of Murtough O'Brien, great-

grandson of Brian Boru. He died in 1119 and was the last of the Dalcassians to be High King of Ireland.

Close by the Romanesque doorway is one of the few Ogham stones in the country with an additional Viking Runic inscription. The runes read: 'Thorgrimr carved this cross' and the Ogham: 'A blessing on Thorgrimr'. The stone was discovered in 1916 and dates from about A.D. 1000. Thorgrimr may have been a Viking convert who carved the stone as an act of expiation for his part in the pillaging of churches and monasteries.

Killaloe, the Romanesque south doorway

Also beside the doorway, set up against the west wall, is a 12th-century High Cross. It has no connection with Killaloe, being brought here from the graveyard of Kilfenora Cathedral in 1821 by Richard Mant (Bishop of Killaloe and Kilfenora 1820–23), an amateur archaelogist, to stand outside Clarisford, the Bishop's Palace. 'On a visit to Kilfenora, in 1820, where there had been five or six stone crosses, I found two or three broken and lying on the ground, neglected and overgrown with weeds. On expressing my concern that these remnants of ecclesiastical antiquity were left in such a state, the clergyman of the parish proposed to send me one of them, which he said might be done without difficulty or danger of giving offence, as when they were brought to that state the people had no regard for them. One was accordingly sent to Clarisford, and I caused it to be erected among some trees in a picturesque spot, between the house and the canal.'[8] The cross fell and broke in 1934 and was re-erected in the cathedral for protection. The action of the bishop in transferring the cross from its original position is questionable, but its location inside the cathedral has at least preserved it from further weathering. No one seems to have thought of the obvious move of returning it to its original position at Kilfenora.

The nave is divided from chancel, transepts and crossing by an elaborate Gothic oak screen made by a carpenter from Cork and erected in 1885; it replaced a stone wall that was 1m in thickness. The screen is an impressive piece of carpentry and has a rose window. The four arches of the crossing have plainly chamfered ribs, and a quadripartite vault supports the tower. On the north side one of the corbels supporting the arches ends in a well-propotioned.little horse.

Killaloe, the High Cross from Kilfenora

The transepts are now closed off from the crossing. The north transept had been walled off from the crossing by the middle of the 19th century, and a floor was inserted to provide two rooms; the lower room is used as a vestry (formerly a schoolroom in the 19th century), and the upper room was used as the bishop's registry. The wall dividing the north transept and the crossing, may have been constructed during the alterations of Bishop Knox at the end of the 18th century. There is a staircase in the north-east corner of the tower.

The south transept is separated from the crossing by a wood and glass screen and by the organ to form an attractive chapel which has recently been restored. It contains a medieval font of yellow sandstone with the unfinished carvings of a cross and medieval foliage on one face. A flight of steps in the thickness of the east wall leads to a staircase in the south-east corner of the tower.

The chancel is 19.8m long and the same width as the nave. There are four lancet windows on each side. The corbels between the windows are richly carved, one showing six kilted figures holding hands and kissing each other. The bishop's throne and chapter stalls are outside the altar rails at the east end of the chancel, the throne being on the south side. Before the demolition of the stone wall and the erection of the present oak screen, the chancel of the cathedral was arranged in the form of a 'choir', with return chapter stalls at the crossing.

The flooring of Killaloe Cathedral becomes progressively elaborate from west to east. The floors of the nave and crossing are covered with flagstones; the chancel floor is tiled; and the sanctuary floor is covered with grey-veined marble, the altar itself standing on a plinth of black marble. The brass altar rail was given in 1894. The east wall has four aumbries, three of which were discovered and reopened in 1852.

The north and south walls of the chancel each have four deeply splayed lancets, but the three east windows are the most strikingly beautiful sight at Killaloe. Each window is 0.5m wide; the central window is 9.2m high and the other two 7.7m. The shape of the top of each window — the central window round-arched, and the flanking windows pointed — indicate that the cathedral was built in the Transitional phase between Romanesque and Gothic. The windows contain stained-glass by Warrington of London, inserted in 1865 in memory of Lord Riversdale (Bishop of Killaloe, Kilfenora, Clonfert and Kilmacduagh 1839–61) showing Christ surrounded by his twelve Apostles. The splays are decorated with a herringbone and lozenge pattern. The three windows add a striking dignity to the simple whitewashed walls. There is a magical quality about them which retains the gaze of the beholder but is difficult to analyse. Slenderness, height, closeness to each other, stained glass contrasting with the surrounding whitewash, brightness of light shining in the dark – all contribute to produce a captivating beauty which leaves the visitor desiring to know more of the glory of which they are but messengers. 'Of all the many marvellous sights . . . there are few to compare with the perfect simplicity of these pencils of light. They are like angelic presences.'[9]

Outside the cathedral, a few metres to the north, lies the early 12th-century St Flannan's Oratory, in a perfect state of preservation though minus its chancel. It measures 11m long by 7.6m wide. It has a good Romanesque doorway of three orders. The much-weathered capitals have animal and foliate carving. There is a small loft above. Its steeply pitched stone roof is similar to St Kevin's Church at Glendalough, St Columba's House at Kells and St Mochta's House at Louth.

Clarisford, the former Bishop's Palace, is a late 18th-century block of three storeys built 1774–8 by Bishop Robert Fowler (1771–9). It was sold after the amalgamation of dioceses in 1976.

Although virtually unknown, Killaloe Cathedral has found a number of admirers. Crossing the bridge into the village, 'the visitor finds himself at the little collection of houses upon which the title of city is conferred by this most antique-looking of cathedrals. In an age of energetic, not to say frantic, rebuilding and restoration, it is consolatory to find a venerable church which seems to have suffered nothing from the hand of man for many centuries past. Builders and masons, with their dire scraping tools and hideous rasping processes, have not yet invaded the solemn precinct of Killaloe.'[10] Standing at a bend in the Shannon, it seems to nestle comfortably and securely in its wall-surrounded, tree-lined churchyard, exuding an air of confident well-being, and looking much as it did when it was built.

The diocese of Killaloe is now one of a collection of united dioceses which cover most of south Connacht and north Munster. Kilfenora was added to Killaloe in 1752. Clonfert and Kilmacduagh were added in 1836. All four, together with the diocese of Emly, were added to Limerick, Ardfert and Aghadoe in 1976, to form the most cumbersomely titled bishopric in the Church of Ireland, or anywhere else for that matter – Limerick, Ardfert, Aghadoe, Killaloe, Kilfenora, Clonfert, Kilmacduagh and Emly. Wisely, the bishop of these collected dioceses is known simply as the bishop of Limerick and Killaloe. In the Roman Catholic arrangement, the diocese of Killaloe remains independent, and the pro-cathedral is at Ennis.

References

1 Philip Dwyer, *The diocese of Killaloe from the Reformation to the close of the eighteenth century* (Dublin, 1878), p. 129.
2 Ibid., p. 457.

3 Michael Quane, 'Tour in Ireland by John Harden in 1797' in *Journal of the Cork Historical and Archaeological Society*, lviii, no. 187 (1953), p. 82.
4 Dwyer, *Diocese of Killaloe*, p. 452.
5 James Godkin, *Ireland and her churches* (London, 1867), p. 309.
6 George Holmes, *Sketches of some of the southern counties of Ireland, collected during a tour in the autumn, 1797, in a series of letters* (London, 1801), p. 48.
7 Quane, 'Tour in Ireland by John Harden in 1797', p. 82.
8 W. B. Mant, *Memoirs of the Rt Rev. Richard Mant, Lord Bishop of Down and Connor, and of Dromore* (Dublin, 1857), p. 128.
9 William Anderson and Clive Hicks, *Cathedrals of Britain and Ireland* (London, 1978), p. 169.
10 T. M. Fallow, *The cathedral churches of Ireland* (London, 1894), p. 57.

KILLARNEY

The Cathedral Church of the Assumption of the Blessed Virgin Mary

Diocese of Kerry (Roman Catholic)

THE town of Killarney (*Cill áirne* – church of the sloe) lies in the valley of the Flesk on the north-east side of Lough Leane in Co. Kerry, 84.8km south-west of Cork and 32km south-east of Tralee. It has a largely undeserved reputation for being one of the great tourist centres of Ireland. In fact the town is of little interest and has become famous only because of the great natural beauty of the surrounding lakes and mountains. The one sight in the town that is worth seeing is the Early-English-style Gothic Revival cathedral by Augustus Welby Northmore Pugin (1812–52).

The Roman Catholic diocese of Kerry (co-terminous with the Church of Ireland Diocese of Ardfert) was ruled by vicars apostolic from the mid-16th century until the early 18th century, with the exception of a brief few years in the 1640s. The 18th-century Bishops of Kerry resided at Dingle, Kilcummin, Tuogh, Listowel and Tralee, from 1720 until 1775. In the latter year Bishop Francis Moylan (1775–87) established the see at Killarney.

Before the construction of the present cathedral there was a small chapel in Chapel Lane, of which the font survives in the baptistery of the present cathedral. The idea of building a cathedral was begun by Fr Joseph O'Sullivan, curate of Dingle, who roused the enthusiasm of Bishop Conelius Egan (1824–56) and the 2nd Earl of Kenmare (1788–1853), a local landowner.

A subscription list was opened in 1828, and a building committee was formed in 1836; Fr O'Sullivan was transferred to Killarney in that year and placed in charge of the committee.

Killarney Cathedral from the south-west

By 1840 the committee had collected only £900, but, undaunted, they commissioned Pugin to design a new cathedral. He presented a number of designs to the committee, one envisaging a great central tower at the crossing, and another a spire at the same point 91m high. His design drew some inspiration from the ancient ruined cathedral at Ardfert, most notably in the slender triple lancets in the east wall, which are repeated in the west wall and in each transept.

A site was acquired from the Presentation Brothers, and the foundation stone was laid in the summer of 1842. Funds were still short, only £1,232 10s 7d having been raised by subscription between 1828 and 1842, and a public appeal were made in Ireland and in the U.S.A. Work continued, under the supervision of Richard Pierce of Wexford (Pugin being unable to undertake personal supervision) until May 1848, when the full effects of the failure of the potato crops in 1846 and 1847 were felt and the Great Famine spread throughout Ireland. Work then stopped and the unfinished shell was boarded up. No work was done for five years, and during that time the two men who had done so much to produce the cathedral, both died. Fr O'Sullivan died in October 1851, and Pugin in September 1852.

Construction was resumed at the beginning of 1853, and J. J. McCarthy, a friend and colleague of Pugin, succeeded him as architect. Two years later, the total cost having risen to £20,000, the cathedral was free of debt, substantially complete, and ready for divine worship. On 22 August 1855 it was consecrated and dedicated to the Assumption of the Blessed Virgin Mary in the presence of McCarthy and Edward Pugin, the architect's eldest son, who said later that of all the sixty-odd churches designed by his father, Killarney had been his father's favourite. Bishop Egan, now elderly and frail, had been taken to the cathedral in a chair on the previous day and was moved to tears when he surveyed the building that he had helped to begin twenty-seven years earlier. A local journalist described it as 'more like a dream from the Middle Ages than a thing of modern reality'.[1]

Although the cathedral was now usable for worship, it was still unfinished. Pugin's design for a great central tower was left for a future generation to build. An organ was installed in 1869, and minor additions were made by Bishop Egan's successors, but the final effort began in 1907. Bishop John Mangan sent priests to the U.S.A. and to Australia to raise funds to complete the work begun in 1842. The firm of Ashlin & Coleman, who had designed Cóbh Cathedral, were appointed to complete the work of Pugin and McCarthy. The nave and side aisles were extended westwards by 8.2m to create two new bays; a new sacristy and mortuary were built; pinnacles were added to the flanking turrets at the west end, and a pinnacle at the east end to join one already there; the crossing piers were strengthened, and the great tower and spire, 86.8m high, were constructed above at a cost of £36,500. The work was completed and the cathedral finished in 1912.

Killarney Cathedral is set in spacious grounds on a level site reminiscent of the plain of Salisbury Cathedral. Pugin used grey, red and brown sandstone with dressings of limestone. This creamy exterior contrasts with the grey of the slate roof, spire and pinnacles and gives the cathedral a softer appearance than it might otherwise have had. The plan is cruciform, with an aisled nave of six bays, clerestory, transepts and an aisled chancel of four bays. The cathedral is 62m long and 34.7m wide at the transepts. The height, from the floor to the apex of the nave roof, is 25.9m. The former baptistery, off the north nave aisle, has a double font, mosaic work and a coffered vault with stencil designs. The former Mortuary Chapel, off the south nave aisle, lacks the original floor. The gallery at the west end of the nave contains an organ by Telford & Son, erected in 1869. During the restoration of the early 1970s it was rebuilt and divided, to reveal the lower part of the west window.

The appearance of the interior of the cathedral was changed virtually beyond recognition by a extensive programme of restoration in 1972–3. It was clear throughout the 1950s and 1960s that the cathedral was reaching the stage of requiring major renovation, but Bishop Daniel Moynihan (1953–69) gave all his attention to building schools in the diocese. It was left to his successor, Bishop Eamonn Casey (1969–76), to launch a fund-raising campaign at a public meeting in the town hall on 18 December 1970. It was felt that nothing short of a thorough restoration of the whole building would be sufficient, taking into account the requirements of the Second Vatican Council. Bishop Casey was able to tell the meeting that his predecessors had inaugurated a fund for repairing the cathedral and that this now stood at £50,000. A committee of eight lay residents and nine priests was established to supervise the work. The work lasted from April 1972 until July 1973, and the total cost was £278,500. The designer was Ray Carroll of Glencullen, Co. Dublin, and the supervising architect was Daniel J. Kennedy of Tralee.

Carroll adopted a very radical restoration design, and apart from a few small areas, nothing of the former interior interior remains to be seen. Carroll, while applauding the soaring strength of Pugin's design, was sharply critical of his devotion to the architecture of the Middle Ages, which reflected a very different understanding of liturgy from that in force since the mid-1960s. 'His philosophy of architecture, prompted as it was by excellent principles of expressing sacredness and mystery and his enduring mastery of his craft, by its very power served as a major restraint on the development of liturgy . . . His concept of a church building harshly divorced the activity of the altar from the distant people . . . Many lovers of Pugin's work the world over would have been grateful to the people of Killarney had the building been left as a museum of Victoriana. I believe, however, that to do so would not have been in the age-old tradition of the living Church. In the end it would have been a false service to Pugin. It is better that his building should have been given a new lease of life . . . a new life conforming with the development of thought in theology and liturgy.'[2]

The greatest single change of the 1972–3 restoration which has either shocked or delighted visitors to the cathedral, whether Pugin experts or not, is the removal of all the internal Victorian plasterwork, which had been badly affected by damp. The rubble stonework underneath was revealed and cleaned by sandblasting, and the result, although not what Pugin intended, is an eye-catching display of the strength and force of his arches. They look a little strange springing from the smooth cylindrical piers below, but the rough stone gives the lofty and soaring interior a light bluish-grey colour and perhaps links Killarney less with Victorian Gothic Revival and more with its ancient parent at Ardfert.

The original reredos, altar and screens were removed, the floor of the crossing was raised to the level of the former sanctuary, and a new sanctuary was created at the crossing, allowing the high supporting arches to form a canopy over

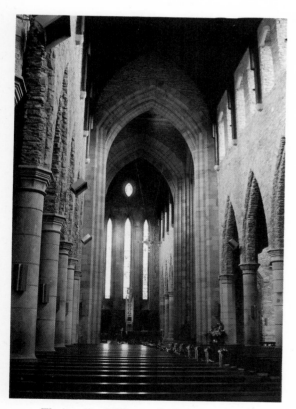

The interior of Killarney Cathedral looking east

the new altar, pulpit, throne and chairs, all made of Tasmanian oak. In conformity to the requirements of the new liturgy, that the font should be close to the sanctuary area, a new font consisting of a limestone bowl, was fitted into the angle between the south-west pier of the crossing and the first pier of the south nave arcade.

In the north transept the former St Patrick's Altar was removed, but the former Blessed Sacrament Altar, off the east side of the transept, was allowed to remain unchanged. The furnishings are by Lane & Lewis of Dublin, who worked on Pugin's other Irish cathedral, at Enniscorthy. The sculptured work in the reredos represents scenes from the Old Testament which can be linked with the Eucharist. The spiral columns supporting the mensa of the altar have rich mosaic work. The chapel is now used for the Altar of Repose on Maundy Thursday.

The north chancel aisle was formerly the Chapel of St Joseph. It was emptied during the restoration, and the only memory of its former use is the rather sad plaque on the easternmost column, recording the fact that the chapel was 'decorated and fitted for divine service' by John Morrogh Bernard and Francis Mary Blount. Bernard was the grandson and heir of Hanoria Maria Raymond, who had bequeathed the five-acre site on which the cathedral stands to the Presentation Brothers. The proposal to build the cathedral technically invalidated the bequest. Bernard stood to inherit the land in the case of such invalidation, but in a rare act of generosity, he drew up new leases, allowing the site to be used for the cathedral. As another author has noted, 'It is one of the sadder results of the renovations that this plaque is all that remains to commemorate him and his family.'[3]

The south chancel aisle, formerly housed the Chapel of St Brendan (adjacent to the chancel) and the Lady Chapel. The Chapel of St Brendan was intended under the reorganisation of 1972–3 to become the Chapel of the Blessed Sacrament; for a few years after 1973 it functioned as such, the Sacrament being reserved in a tabernacle set on a limestone pedestal. But in the late 1970s the present Blessed Sacrament Shrine (designed by Heinz Gernot of Cologne) was erected in the former chancel, and the chapel is now known as the Day Chapel.

The former Lady Chapel is now known as the Kenmare Chapel. The chapel was laid out in memory of the 2nd Earl of Kenmare, who died in 1853. The floor is tiled with representations of the Kenmare coat of arms and motto: *Loyal en tout* (loyal in everything). Below the chapel is a vault containing the remains of members of the Browne family (Viscounts Kenmare from 1689, Earls of Kenmare from 1801; the 7th and last Earl of Kenmare died in 1952). The entrance to the vault is covered by the flagstones which also carry the coat of arms of the family. It was opened, probably for the last time, to receive the remains of Mrs Beatrice Grosvenor (1915–85), niece of the last Earl of Kenmare, who died on 15 June 1985.

References

1 *Tralee Chronicle*, 24 Aug. 1855.
2 J. McKenna, T. Egan, Ray Carroll and D. J. Kennedy, *St Mary's Cathedral, Killarney* (Tralee, 1973), pp 32–33.
3 Tomás Ó'Caoimh, *Killarney Cathedral* (Dublin, 1990), p. 25

KILMACDUAGH

The Cathedral Church of St Colman

KILMACDUAGH Cathedral lies 4.8km south-west of Gort in the strange landscape of the Burren in the extreme south of Co. Galway. The Burren is an area of bare limestone hills and terraces covering about 80 square kilometres formed by glaciation many thousands of years ago and certainly one of the most weird and fascinating landscapes in Ireland. 'There is a sternness and coldness of character about Kilmacduagh, where all mountain and plain, as far as the view extends, seems one vast sheet of limestone.'[1] In this desolate lanscape set against the backdrop of the rounded curve of the Burren mountains are to be found the leaning Round Tower and the ruined cathedral with its sprinkling of attendant churches which constitute all that remains of the heart of the old diocese of Kilmacduagh.

It was here that Colman, son of Duach, founded his episcopal see c.610, giving rise to the name Kilmacduagh (*Cill meic Duach* -church of the son of Duach). The original church was built for him by his kinsman Guaire Aidni, King of Connacht. One needs to be careful of hagiography, but the story of St Colman is so delightful that it is worth recounting, and readers may believe or disbelieve as they think fit.

St Colman lived in an oratory in the mountains with a cockerel to call him to devotions, a mouse to nibble his ear if he fell asleep while praying or studying, and a pet fly that would move along the page as he read to keep his place. One Easter Day Colman ended a year-long fast and prayed for sustenance. At that moment the silver dishes prepared for a banquet for King Guaire at his palace 8km away rose into the air and flew out of the windows of the banqueting hall. The king and his courtiers mounted their horses and pursued this flying banquet and came upon the saint surrounded by the dishes which had come to rest in his cell. There and then the king gave the saint the lands necessary for the building of his monastery. No list of bishops is preserved earlier than the Synod of Ráith Bressail, but why let the facts spoil a charming story! Colman is said to have died c.632, and his feast-day is 29 October.

1. *The Cathedral*

The present cruciform cathedral, 29.2m long and 6.8m wide, is the result of a 14th/15th-century rebuilding of a much earlier cathedral which must have been a very plain and

severe building. Some early cyclopean blocks of stone can be seen beside hammer-dressed stones of later centuries, and the structure is an unharmonious mixture of Romanesque, Gothic and Tudor.

The west wall of the nave is 11th or 12th century but incorporates a blocked 10th-century doorway below a three-light Tudor window, one of the reveal stones of which shows zig-zag carving. The rest of the nave was built in the 12th century when the cathedral was enlarged. The south wall has a Romanesque lancet, a Gothic arch leading to the south transept, a small lancet window and a low Gothic entrance door. The north wall has a blocked flat-arch early doorway. The Gothic archway leading to the north transept has been blocked up but contains a small round-headed doorway.

A high Romanesque arch leads to the late 13th- or early 14th-century chancel, which has an Early English east window replacing a blocked Romanesque window. The south wall also has a replacement Gothic window, next to which is a doorway leading to what may have been a sacristy. It has one round-arched window in the south gable. The north wall of the chancel has a plaque bearing the inscription 'PRAY FOR THE SOULE OF IAME SMULANE AND HIS WIFE SARA LAUGHNANE WHO MADE THIS TOMBE FOR THEM AND THEIR POSTER[ITY]. 1709'.

The cathedral gained its present cruciform shape when the transepts were added early in the 14th and 15th centuries. The 15th-century south transept (7.6m long and 6.8m wide) has Gothic windows in the south and east walls. The north transept is probably 14th-century; its entry arch is more crude in its construction, and was walled off from the nave in the 17th century with the exception of a small Gothic-style doorway. It has square Tudor windows in the east and west walls and a narrow window in the north wall. It contains the tombs, dating from the 16th to the 18th centuries, of the O'Shaughnessy family, who were lay patrons of the cathedral, and is sometimes known as the O'Shaughnessy Chapel. The 16th-century wall tomb is that of Sir Dermot O'Shaughnessy of Gort.

2. *The Round Tower*

The 'Leaning Tower of Kilmacduagh' is 34.28m high, making it the tallest surviving Round Tower in Ireland. Built of local limestone, it leans 38.3cm to the south-west and is twice as old as its more famous counterpart in Pisa. The cap collapsed c.1859 and was rebuilt as part of a general restoration of the site in 1878–9. Its irregular and battered appearance is partly due to the repairs undertaken at that time. It was repointed in 1971. There are no floors or ladders, and the doorway is 7.92m above ground.

3. *Church of St John the Baptist*

The primitive 10th-century Church of St John the Baptist, lying to the north of the cathedral, has rounded and pointed windows and a much later chancel, but little of it is left. Parts of the north and south walls of the chancel adjacent to the chancel arch are 2.5–3m in height. The west and north walls are only 1m in height. The church measured 22.5m long by 6.7m wide.

disappeared by 1893, and moss-covered mounds marked the site.

6. *The Augustinian Church (O'Heyne's Church)*

This nave and chancel church was built in the 13th century by Owen O'Heyne (d.1253), the local chieftain, as part of a monastery for Augustinian canons, and it was used as the mausoleum for the O'Heynes, chieftains of the Uí Fiachrach

Kilmacduagh: the Round Tower and the cathedral

4. *Church of St Mary*

The Church of St Mary, built *c.* 1200, is a single-chamber church with a wide-splay, round-headed single lancet in the east wall and a south doorway inserted into its present position in the 15th century. The church measures 12.6m long by 5.7m wide. The little that remains is situated against the wall of a road that was driven through the site in the 18th century.

5. *Church of St Colman*

A church of this name is supposed to have stood about 91m to the south-west of the cathedral. It had completely

Aidni whose territory was coextensive with the diocese of Kilmacduagh. The site shows evidence of earlier buildings.

The chancel has a double-light Romanesque east window of limestone, with two widely splayed slender lancets 2.4m in height and 15.2cm wide. The stonework here is among the finest in Connacht and is comparable with the east window at Clonfert. There is a single lancet on the south wall, below which is an unusual projecting piscina. The chancel arch, also of limestone, is of the same period and style and has decorated capitals and clustered columns. The arch itself has gone and only the piers remain. When the north wall of the nave collapsed, probably in the 14th or 15th centuries, a new wall was built inside incorporating the original north door-way. Part of the old north wall remains, leaning out at an angle. Much of the west wall was rebuilt at the same time.

Remains of a building attached to the south side of the church include a barrel-vaulted chamber lit by a single east lancet. It is thought to have been the monastic treasury.

7. *Unidentified building*

On the west side of O'Heyne's Church are the remains of a building of uncertain date, but with a 15th-century window and a square-headed doorway set in the west wall, which is all that remains to any height.

8. *Glebe House*

There is also a two-storey 13th-century fortified house to the north-east of the cathedral which may have been the dwelling of the abbot or bishop.

The destruction of Kilmacduagh Cathedral and its attendant churches can probably be dated to the religious troubles of the mid-16th century. When Bishop Roland Lynch arrived to take charge of the see at the beginning of 1587, he found 'all the Buildings thereof spoiled and wasted by the Rebellion of the traitor Mahown O Brien of Cloghannaine whereby the said Bishoppricke was then worth yearlie but twenty poundes'.[2] The diocese of Kilmacduagh was very small, being about 28.9km long and 19.3km wide, and Bishop Lynch was doubtless glad to be given the diocese of Clonfert as well in 1602. He went to live at Clonfert and was the last separate Bishop of Kilmacduagh, the two dioceses remaining united.

In 1647, during the course of the rebellion of the Confederate war, the cathedral, which had been roofless and disused for some twenty or thirty years previously, was repossessed by Hugh de Burke, the Roman Catholic Bishop of Kilmacduagh (1647-*c.* 1654). He began the work of re-roofing the cathedral, and it was virtually complete by 1649. However, the new lease of life given to Kilmacduagh Cathedral was brief, for shortly afterwards the Confederation was crushed by Cromwell's armies, and the cathedral was again allowed to fall into ruin.

The parish church of Gort was subsequently used as the Church of Ireland cathedral church and fitted up accordingly. But attachment to the historic cathedral lingered on well into the 19th century. When he was installed in 1874, the new dean recorded that he 'had to sit upon a tombstone amid a luxuriant crop of stinging-nettles, within the precincts of the roofless cathedral'.[3] The church at Gort was built in 1820 with a loan of £1,292 6s 1³/₄d from the Board of First-Fruits. It is now a public library, and there are no longer any Church of Ireland places of worship in the diocese of Kilmacduagh.

References

1 *The Parliamentary Gazetteer of Ireland* (Dublin, 1844–6), iii, 496.
2 P. K. Egan, 'The Royal Visitation of Clonfert and Kilmacduagh, 1615' in *Journal of the Galway Archaeological and Historical Society*, xxxv (1976), p. 74.
3 T. M. Fallow, *The cathedral churches of Ireland* (London, 1894), p. 92.

KILMORE

The Cathedral Church of St Fethlimidh

Diocese of Kilmore (Church of Ireland)

KILMORE (*Cill mór* – big church) is in Co. Cavan and lies on a hillside site 5km west of Cavan itself. An early tradition says that a church was founded here by St Fethlemidh (Phelim) (feast-day 9 August) in the 6th century, but there is no mention of a church at Kilmore, Co. Cavan, in the monastic annals; they refer only to the burning of a church at Kilmore, Co. Armagh, in 749. The early history of Kilmore and the diocese which bears its name is very confusing, and the location of the see before the mid-15th century is a matter of speculation.

The territory covered by the diocese of Kilmore is roughly co-terminous with the ancient kingdom of Breifne, the territory of the Uí Briúin. The Synod of Ráith Bressail in 1111 included the kingdom in the diocese of Ardagh, but the Synod of Kells–Mellifont in 1152 designated Kells as the episcopal see for Breifne. After the Anglo-Norman settlement of the northern part of Co. Meath, this part of the diocese was absorbed into the diocese of Meath. A Cistercian bishop was expelled from Kells *c.*1185, and the episcopal status of the monastery had been abolished by by Bishop Simon Rochfort of Meath (1192–1224) by 1216. The rest of the kingdom of Breifne was left without a see, and the division of the territory in the 13th century between the two rival lordships of O'Rourke and O'Reilly compounded the difficulties.

A succession of bishops, styled Bishops of Breifne or Tír mBriúin, are known from the beginning of the 12th century and papal documents refer to a diocese of Triburnensis, but the location of the episcopal see is uncertain. A list of suffragan sees to Armagh compiled by the papal legate to the Synod of Kells–Mellifont includes the name Darnth, and it is thought that this is a corruption of the name *Dair-inis* (island of oaks), which was the name of the island in Lough Oughter later called Trinity Island, about 4.8km from Kilmore.

The present 19th-century cathedral incorporates a fine 12th-century doorway which was moved from the Premonstratensian priory on Trinity Island in Lough Oughter; the priory buildings, however are 13th century, which suggests that there was an important church, perhaps a cathedral, on the island before the arrival of the Premonstratensians in 1237. It has been suggested that after the arrival of the canons on Trinity Island the see was moved c.1250 to Slanore on the mainland 3.2km south-west of Kilmore; but nothing remains to be seen at this site.

The see was finally settled at Kilmore on the border between the rival lordships of O'Rourke and O'Reilly in either 1453

The cathedral was again in a ruinous condition when Bishop Bedell arrived in 1629. William Bedell (Bishop of Kilmore and Ardagh 1629–42), famous for translating the Bible into Irish, and who spent the last months of his life in the custody of the rebels, wrote to Archbishop Laud in 1630 shortly after his appointment to the diocese: 'The church here, built, but without Bell or Steeple, Font or Chalice.'[1] It was a small building, only 21.3m long and 7.3m wide. It was certainly in ruins by 1739, when an eye-witness recorded that 'there are now neither Cathedral, Chapter, Canons or Prebendaries

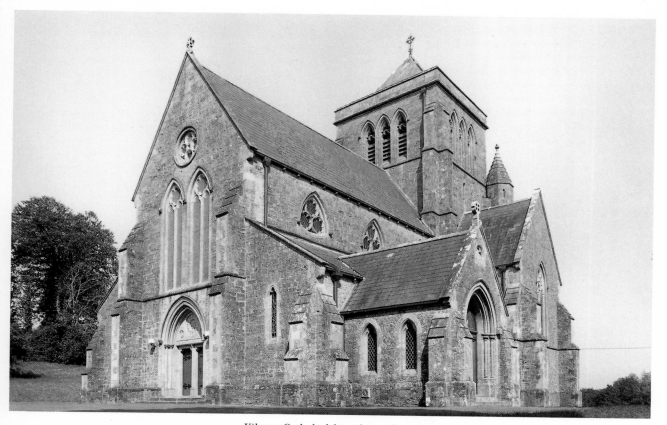

Kilmore Cathedral from the south-west

or 1454. If the see had been at Slanore, then it was abandoned by Bishop Andrew MacBrady (1445–55), who obtained the consent of Pope Nicholas V to raise the parish church of St Fethlimidh, Kilmore, 5km west of Cavan, to the status of a cathedral church.

The medieval church used by Bishop MacBrady had been built c.1400 and may have been intended to replace a building that was either ruinous or too small. This cathedral itself appears to have been ruinous or dilapidated at the time of the Reformation, and it was substantially repaired and altered.

belonging to the See. A small church at Kilmore, contiguous to the Episcopal House, is a Parish Church but serves for a Cathedral.'[2]

The remains of the old cathedral are to the north-west of the present cathedral and churchyard. It has been re-roofed and is now used as the Parochial Hall. Apart from the old churchyard on the south side and some medieval masonry, there is no inidication of its former status. Bishop Bedell is buried in the churchyard.

The present cathedral was built as a result of the efforts of

Bishop Marcus Gervais Beresford (1854–62). It was designed by William Slater, a London architect, in the fashionable Gothic Revival style at a cost of £6,000. The foundation stone was laid on 19 May 1858, and the cathedral was consecrated on 17 July 1860. It was conceived as a memorial to Bishop Bedell and is also known as the Bedell Memorial Church. The cathedral is attractively set on a hillside amid a landscape that in another place might have been the work of 'Capability' Brown.

The shape is cruciform, with a central tower capped by a short spire. An external octagonal stair-turret at the angle formed by the chancel and the south transept gives access to the bell-chamber. The aisled nave of three bays has a clerestory and is divided from its aisles by pointed arcades resting on clustered columns. The convex triangular clerestory windows have hexafoil tracery. The cathedral is comparatively modest in size. It seats about 500 people, and the internal length is only 32.9m. 'The interior is cozy and yet dignified, nothing more. It is small . . . Yet the effect is very expansive if lop-sided, because the crossing is given over to the stalls. This means that much more than half the length of the cathedral is taken up by the choir and clergy.'[3]

The oak stalls for the Dean and Chapter are on the south side of the crossing, with the throne at the south east corner. The organ is in the north transept. All the windows have stained glass added at different periods since construction. The east window, depicting the parables of the Ten Virgins, the Good Samaritan and the Prodigal Son, was a gift from Bishop Hamilton Verschoyle (1862–70). The chancel floor is tiled, and the walls have stencil decoration. The sanctuary is tiled and walled in red and green marble. The reredos is a representation of the Last Supper painted on Caen stone with red pilasters of Kilkenny and Galway marble.

The fine 12th-century Romanesque doorway is incorporated into the north wall of the cathedral. It was transferred from Trinity Island to the mainland cathedral at Kilmore in the 17th century and duly transferred again to the present cathedral in the 19th century. Some of the stones have been incorrectly placed, but no matter; in all the uncertain peripatetic wanderings of the episcopal see of this diocese since the 12th century, the abiding presence of this doorway is the one constant factor.

The Bishop's Palace, now called the See House, near the cathedral, is a three-storey Grecian-style building of 1834.

The Dioceses of Elphin and Ardagh were added to Kilmore in 1841.

References

1 T. M. Fallow, *The cathedral churches of Ireland* (London, 1894), p. 16.
2 Ibid.
3 D. S. Richardson, *Gothic Revival architecture in Ireland* (New York, 1983), ii, 578–79.

Kilmore: the Romanesque north doorway

LEIGHLIN

The Cathedral Church of St Laserian

Diocese of Leighlin (Church of Ireland)

OLD Leighlin (pronounced 'Lock-lin' and derived from *Leath gleann* — half-glen) is set in a quiet and secluded hollow in the Carlow Hills 14.4km south of Carlow on the main road to Waterford. This ancient monastic site is now little more than a small village. But this remote and isolated place is the proud possessor of a largely unknown medieval cathedral of great charm. Old Leighlin was once populous, and sent two members to the Irish parliament until 1801. In 1181 Hugh de Lacy built a castle 3km to the west, to command a crossing over the River Barrow. The castle stood on the edge of the Pale and offered some degree of security in times of civil strife. Gradually the population moved away to the town, known as Leighlinbridge, which grew up around the castle, 'until, at length in the seventeenth century, [Old Leighlin] was but a sorry village'.[1]

A visitor in 1860 described Old Leighlin as 'an assemblage of poverty-stricken cabins',[2] In 1894 it was described as 'a poor hamlet with a few wretched cabins',[3] and 'there is scarcely anyone to attend the services'.[4] In 1932 it was 'a tiny village with a few cottages clustered about the gateway of the cathedral'.[5] Old Leighlin was still the same in 1991 – the cathedral and a few houses.

St Gobban (feast-day 23 May) founded a monastery at Leighlin ('Old' Leighlin is a much later designation) at the end of the 6th century. It became famous during the rule of his successor, St Laserian (also known as Molaise), a Scot of noble birth and the nephew of Saints Blane of Dunblane and Cathan of Kilcathan. Laserian spent fourteen years studying in Rome with Pope Gregory the Great, who ordained him priest. At the Synod of Mag Léne in 630 the Irish Church decided to abandon its own method of calculating the date of Easter, and follow that of Rome. Trained in Rome and acting as papal legate, Laserian spoke out strongly in favour of the Roman observance, and the synod followed his lead.

Laserian visited Rome again after the synod and was consecrated bishop by Pope Honorius I. In *c.*632 St Gobban, with some of his contemporaries, retired to found a monastery at Killamery in Ossory, leaving Laserian to be Abbot of Leighlin. The abbey flourished under his rule, and at one time the community was said to number 1,500 monks. He died in 639 or 641 and was buried in his church at Leighlin. His feast-day is 18 April.

Leighlin was raided by the Vikings in 859 and 916, and was totally destroyed by fire in 1060. The Synod of Ráith Bressail in 1111 established Leighlin as one of the five dioceses for Leinster. The present cathedral was begun by Bishop Donatus (Dúngal Ua Cáellaide) (1152–81) and completed by the end of the 13th century.

The cathedral consists of a plain aisleless 13th-century nave and chancel with a 16th-century tower between them. Two transepts were added to the nave later in the 13th century, but the north transept is now roofless, and the south transept was demolished long ago. They are entered through arches with shafted responds of granite. A large Lady Chapel, later used as a chapter house, and almost as long as the chancel itself, was built on to the north side of the chancel in the 16th century. The 16th-century alterations, including the rebuilding of the north and south chancel walls, were done during the episcopate of Matthew Sanders (1527–49), whose tomb is near the sanctuary. Bishop Thomas O'Fihely (1555–67) is buried in the same grave.

Bishop Sanders succeeded Bishop Maurice Doran (1524–5) 'an eloquent preacher and man of unsullied life', who was murdered by his archdeacon, Maurice Kavanagh, whom he had reproved for misconduct. Kavanagh and his accomplices were hanged on the site of the murder. The bishop was buried in his cathedral church, and during repairs in 1848 his skull, with a piece missing from the left side, was discovered. A large floor slab in the chancel marks the site of the grave.

A print of 1792 shows the tower with 'a mean sort of slated spire on the top; which, from its pigmy size, and general unsuitableness to the building on which it is erected, has the worst possible effect'.[6] The Chapter House is also shown roofless, and the cathedral is generally covered with ivy. It is probable that the north transept was also ruined by the end of the 18th century; its windows are now blocked. A general restoration took place in the mid-19th century, including the removal of the despised spire. A report in the *Irish Ecclesiastical Gazette* for 19 December 1865 described the Chapter House as 'newly roofed' at the expense of Henry Scott Stopford, the then Archdeacon of Leighlin. The same article mentioned that a fund had been started to re-roof the north transept. Since the transept remains roofless at the time of writing, it is reasonable to assume that the fund never reached the required sum.

position *c.*1890 in an alcove on the north wall of the chancel created from part of the Chapter House. The chapter stalls are sited below the tower vaulting.

Leighlin Cathedral from the south-west

The exterior walls are rendered. The nave is 25.6m in length and 18.3m high, and the chancel 18.3m in length. The tower is 18.2m high. The nave has no windows in its north and south walls, the only light coming from a window above the west door and four small skylights of more recent date in the roof. This gives it a rather gloomy and cavernous appearance, slightly relieved by whitewashed plastered walls. There are two altar tombs – one with a large floriated cross, the tomb of William O'Brin, who died in 1569. There are also two 19th-century floor memorials to members of the Vigors family at the west end. A screen of pine and glass separates the chancel from the nave, which is no longer used.

The tower vaulting is a good example of lierne vaulting – with intricate ribs but no bosses. It is an exact copy on a smaller scale of the tower vaulting at St Canice's Cathedral, Kilkenny. The organ, by Messrs Browne & Son, was installed under the tower in August 1880. It was moved to its present

In 1926 the walls of the chancel were stripped of the rough plaster which had covered them. In this case the removal of the plaster was a successful exercise, revealing a very beautiful silver-grey stone which is now one of the most striking features of the interior. Funds permitting, the same might be done to the nave at a future date. The wooden ceiling was inserted in 1899. The chancel has a unique and very fine four-seat sedilia on the south side of the sanctuary, with trefoil heads and shafts. Above the sedilia are two windows of three lights each. One of the lights in the westernmost window is blocked by an exterior buttress which also seems to have caused the blocking up of an internal semicircular recess which may have been a wall tomb. This buttress, together with that at the external north-west angle of the nave, were erected in the 17th century.

The masonry of the east window is of crude workmanship and unlike the two windows in the south wall and the flamboyant tracery of the east window of the Chapter House. It has four lights, crossed by a transom, with plain uncusped intersecting tracery. The stained glass of rich deep colours depicts Christ with Saints Moling, Brigid, Fiacc, Canice, Patrick, John, Paul and Laserian; the glass is by Catherine O'Brien and was given in memory of Mary Louisa Helen Vigors (1851–1933).

There are many memorials to members of the Vigors family, who did much to restore the cathedral in the 19th century and were descendants of Bartholomew Vigors, Bishop of Ferns and Leighlin 1691–1722. In fact the twenty or so memorials are a chronicle of the Vigors family from the 18th to the 20th centuries. The earliest memorial is to Urban Vigors, High Sheriff of Co. Carlow in 1700, who died in 1718; his descendant, Edward Cliffe Vigors (1879–1945), was High Sheriff in 1916. The altar candles are the most recent memorial – to Ludlow Ashmead Cliffe Vigors (1884–1969).

buried John the dumb son of William, son of David Roe O'Brien, and his wife Mabel Cavanagh daughter of Wilbmona, on whose souls may God have mercy. Amen. In the years of our Lord 1555. O all you who pass by, remember us, I beseech you. We were what you are; and what we now are you will sometime be.'

In 1916 four steps of black Kilkenny marble were laid leading up to the altar, the sanctuary was paved with grey Cork marble, and the altar was raised upon a marble footpace. A new bishop's throne was provided on a dais of Kilkenny marble, replacing a large throne of the 'family pew' type with a flat tester for a canopy above. The black marble font, possibly dating from the 11th century, was placed on a dais of Kilkenny marble beneath the western arch of the tower. Another and more richly carved font dating from 1225 stands in the nave by the south door. It was brought here from St Mary's Church, Gowran.

The chancel of Leighlin Cathedral looking east

The nave of Leighlin Cathedral looking west

On the floor of the chancel before the sanctuary steps is a tablet bearing the following inscription: 'I.H.S. Here lies

The pulpit is a memorial to John Finlay, Dean of Leighlin 1895–1912. On his retirement in 1912 he went to live at

Bawnboy in Co. Cavan, where, on 12 June 1921, at the age of seventy-nine, he was murdered and his house burnt, during the disturbances resulting in the partition of Ireland. The Dean Finlay Memorial Scholarship, awarded by the Diocesan Council, was founded in his memory. He presented to the cathedral parish a plot of land adjoining the cathedral and known as the Dean's Field. A part of this field was subsequently enclosed as an addition to the graveyard.

To the west of the cathedral is St Laserian's Well, formerly a place of pilgrimage. The visitor may experience some confusion in discovering it since a sign in the village points to 'St Molaise's Well', while the site itself is signposted 'St Laserian's Well'. In the mid-19th century it was 'almost choked up with mud, and scarcely distinguishable from the expanse of marsh which surrounds it'[7] but it is now covered over, apart from a small manhole, and surrounded by an unsightly wall. Near the well stands St Laserian's Cross, a 1.5m-high plain Celtic cross which may date from the time of the saint.

St Laserian's Cathedral is a delightful and unspoiled treat, grey and bluff and with all the atmosphere of a 13th-century fortress church. 'The whole edifice is in the plainest Gothic style, at once church and castle, being designed not only for worship, but also, and perhaps quite as much, for protection from the attacks of "the wild Irish", who dwelt all around.'[8] This picture is confirmed by Pope Innocent IV in February 1248 when he wrote to the Archbishop of Dublin saying that the Bishop of Leighlin and his chapter had proposed that the see should be moved to some more convenient and accessible site, since the cathedral was 'situated in the midst of a wicked and perverse nation, at the far boundaries of the diocese, in a mountainous, inconvenient and barren place'.[9]

The cathedral has neither grandeur nor architectural sophistication, but it retains a strong medieval atmosphere. Peering up out of the hollow in which it was built, it presents a stern and frowning countenance, as if looking at its visitors suspiciously and defensively, blinking with surprise that anyone should want to pay it a visit. The casual visitor will be equally surprised. St Laserian's Cathedral is hidden away down so many twisting lanes that the likelihood of a chance visit is remote. The interested visitor will have to make a determined effort to get here, and the effort will be well rewarded.

A charming image of life in Leighlin at the end of the 15th century is given by a description of Bishop Nicholas Maguire (1490-c.1512). He 'studied at Oxford, although it was but 2 years and 3 months, yet he profited so much in logik, philosophie, the seven liberall sciences and divinitie that in his latter days he seemed to excel'; and he 'was noted for his hospitality and the number of cows that he was able to graze without loss (so well was he beloved) upon the woods and mountains of Knockbraanen, Cumnatally, Aghcarew and Moilglas.'[10]

The diocese of Leighlin was united to Ferns on the death of Bishop Richard Meredith (1589–1597). Further amalgamations have made it part of the united dioceses of Cashel, Waterford, Lismore, Ossory, Ferns and Leighlin. In the Roman Catholic arrangement Leighlin is united to Kildare, and the cathedral is at Carlow.

References

1 'Among the graves, pt II: Old Leighlin' in *Irish Ecclesiastical Record*, 3rd ser., vi (1885), p. 288.
2 Mackenzie Walcott, *The cathedrals of the United Kingdom* (London, 1860), p. 318.
3 T. M. Fallow, *The cathedral churches of Ireland* (London, 1894), p. 33.
4 J. G. F. Day and H. E. Patton, *The cathedrals of the Church of Ireland* (London, 1932), p. 120.
5 R. W. Jackson, *Cathedrals of the Church of Ireland* (Dublin, 1971), p. 85.
6 *The Parliamentary Gazetteer of Ireland* (Dublin, 1844–6), ii, p. 601.
7 Ibid.
8 'Among the graves', p. 288.
9 Aubrey Gwynn and R. N. Hadcock, *Medieval religious houses: Ireland* (Dublin, 1970), p. 89.
10 Ibid., pp 89–90.

LETTERKENNY

The Cathedral Church of St Eunan and St Columba

Diocese of Raphoe (Roman Catholic)

LETTERKENNY (*Leitir Ceanainn* – hillside of the O'Cannons) is a town of about 6,500 inhabitants in Co. Donegal near the head of Lough Swilly, 37km west of Derry. It is the centre for consumer durables for most of northern Donegal and is the largest town in the county. The cathedral, the only building of note, is a noble and handsome structure, with all the advantages of a splendidly prominent site. Dominating this hillside town, it captures the gaze at first sight when driving down into the town on the road from Derry.

The population and prosperity of Letterkenny grew rapidly in the second half of the 19th century; during the same period thought was given to the provision of a cathedral church for the Roman Catholic diocese of Raphoe, and Letterkenny was the obvious choice. A church, used as a pro-cathedral, had been built on the site of the present cathedral in the 1830s. Letterkenny also had the advantage of being close to the ancient see town of Raphoe.

Letterkenny Cathedral looking east

Bishop Daniel McGettigan (1861–70) drew up plans for the construction of a cathedral. But, in reverse of the traditional construction process, the bishop had the unusual and interesting idea of beginning with construction of the tower, the idea being that the sight of this lofty tower would then stimulate the further donations necessary to complete the cathedral. McGettigan left Letterkenny in 1870 to become Archbishop of Armagh before any building work had begun. His departure ended the tower plan, but his successors, Bishops James McDevitt (1871–9) and Michael Logue (1879–87), kept the project alive by continuing to raise funds.

Despite the relative prosperity of the area, construction was delayed for some time by lack of funds. Only with the arrival of Bishop Patrick O'Donnell (1888–1922) was it felt possible to begin construction. Discussing the dedication of the new cathedral, the *Irish Monthly* observed: 'Work has already begun in spite of hard times, or rather on account of the hard times, in order to give as much employment as possible to the impoverished people.'[1] The foundation stone was laid on 6 September 1891, and the completed cathedral was consecrated on 16 June 1901. The total cost was more than £300,000.

The cathedral was designed by the Dublin firm of Hague & McNamara. After the death of William Hague in 1899, supervision of construction was continued by his partner T. F. McNamara. The cathedral was designed in the slightly restrained style of late 13th-century French Gothic: less elaborate than the 14th-century French Gothic of Monaghan Cathedral and the remarkable Cathedral of St Finn Barre in Cork. The exterior was cleaned and restored in 1985 at a cost of £500,000.

The basic building material is Mountcharles sandstone with a slightly pinkish tinge; the walls are square, coursed rubble, and the tracery and quoins are smooth-faced; there are bands of green slate at window level. The spire rises from an intricate base of arcaded recesses and corner turrets with crocketed spirelets. It has lucarnes in the lower half and decorative bands pointed with gargoyles above.

The west front has three deeply recessed Gothic doorways and four small turrets and crocketed spirelets; the two larger turrets rise from the junctions of the nave with its aisles; the two smaller turrets, surmounting the north and south angles of the nave aisles, are linked to the nave turrets by flying buttresses. The nave aisle windows are single lights without tracery; the clerestory windows have simple geometrical tracery. The transepts have large wheel windows with very systematic geometrical tracery, and Romanesque doorways below.

Letterkenny Cathedral: detail of the chancel arch

The plan is cruciform: a five-bay nave with aisles and clerestory, two-bay transepts, a polygonal chancel, ambulatory and Lady Chapel, and an offset tower and spire to the south. Because of the awkwardness of the hillside site, the cathedral had to be built in north–south alignment along the hill rather than the traditional east–west. But to give the correct geographical references of various parts of the cathedral would be pointless and unnecessary. The traditional image of the altar at the 'east' end is a perfectly adequate system of reference and too deeply ingrained to allow slavish obedience to the points of the compass.

The internal measurements of the cathedral are 52m in length, 30m in width at the transepts; the nave is 22m high to the apex of the roof. The tower, surmounted by an octagonal spire, stands at the south-east corner of the apse and rises to a height of 73m. The nave, aisles and transepts have lierne vaulting, and the crossing has a pendant star vault. The nave arcades rest on clustered columns which continue around the apse in shorter form. The nave is lit by brass standard electroliers. The organ, originally by Telford & Telford of Dublin and restored in 1986 by Kenneth Jones of Bray, is in a gallery high in the south transept.

The great arch at the junction of the nave and the crossing, by Purdy & Millard of Belfast, is covered with a profusion of carvings linked by a carved rope border. The respond on the north shows scenes from the life of St Columba; the respond on the south, the life of St Eunan. The arch itself depicts a variety of episodes from Irish ecclesiastical history, with a representation of the Blessed Trinity at the top.

The pulpit by Pearse of Dublin is an exquisite piece of work, mainly of Sicilian marble, with a base of granite and elements of Connemara, Midleton and Carrara marble, and an elaborately carved canopy. The altar rails are also by Pearse.

The richly painted gold and dark-green ceiling of the chancel is by Amici of Rome. The carved busts at the springing of the arches depict the patron saints of the parishes of Donegal. The spandrels contain arabesques of angels, birds and vine leaves on a gold ground. A very successful reordering of the sanctuary was undertaken in 1985 by Barry Feely of Roscommon. The guiding principles were taste and discretion. 'Great care was taken to preserve the style and materials of the original altar in the new pieces.'[2] The altar and celebrant's chair incorporate the styles and materials of the former high altar, especially the original altar piece, an Irish carving of Leonardo da Vinci's Last Supper. Although the cathedral has now been adapted for the liturgy introduced by the Second Vatican Council, the remodelling of the cathedral has been undertaken with such taste and discretion that the visual harmony of the building remains unimpaired, and the cathedral sanctuary appears much as it did when completed in 1901. The old high altar reredos remains in position. The bishop's throne is on the north side.

The chancel ends in a polygonal apse surrounded by an ambulatory. The walls of the ambulatory and the adjacent transepts have vesical paintings by Richard King (1907–74) on the theme of the Mysteries of the Rosary. The ambulatory leads to a small Lady Chapel behind the reredos. The entrance arch and string course have intricate carving. There are two paintings by Harry Clarke (1889–1931). The former baptistery, in the base of the tower, opens off the south side of the ambulatory and contains the altar from the old pro-cathedral which occupied the site of the present building.

To the north and south of the chancel are the Chapels of the Blessed Sacrament and St Columba with painted ceilings by Amici. The ceiling in St Columba's Chapel shows representations of the saints of Donegal. The chapel is now used as the baptistery. The octagonal marble font is supported by eight green marble colonettes with an oak dome cover. The ceiling in the Blessed Sacrament Chapel shows angels singing and playing music in honour of the sacrament.

The stained glass in the sanctuary and south aisle is by Meyer & Co. of Munich. But Irish craftsmanship is well represented by An Túr Gloine (the Tower of Glass), the Celtic Revival stained-glass studio founded in Dublin by Sarah Purser in 1903. The clerestory glass is by Harry Clarke (1889–1931) and was installed in 1928–9. The north transept was filled with glass by artists from the studio in the years 1910–11: Michael Healy (1873–1941) was responsible for the rose window depicting the life of St Columba and other windows in the north transept; the work of A. E. Childe, Beatrice Elvery and Catherine O'Brien are also represented. The work of the studio, represented by Ethel Rhind and Michael Healy, can also be seen in the south transept.

References

1 *Irish Monthly*, xix, (7 Sept. 1891), p. 495.
2 Graham Harrison, *St Eunan's Cathedral, Letterkenny* (Dublin, 1989), p. 11.

LIMERICK

The Cathedral Church of St Mary

Diocese of Limerick (Church of Ireland)

LIMERICK (*Luimneach* – bare land) stands mainly on the south bank of the River Shannon just above its estuary. It is the fourth largest city in Ireland (after Dublin, Belfast and Cork), and has two fine cathedrals. St Mary's Cathedral, standing on the site of the palace of the Kings of Munster, is the finest of the medieval cathedrals of southwest Ireland. The city grew from the work of St Munchin (feast-day 2 January), who founded a monastery at Inis Ibhton in the River Shannon in the 6th or 7th century. The city became a centre of Dalcassian power after its capture from the Vikings by Brian Boru, and the presidency of Bishop Gilbert of Limerick (1107–40) as papal legate at the Synod of Ráith Bressail in 1111 ensured its place as the see of a new territorial diocese.

The nucleus of the cathedral, which stands in Nicholas Street to the east of Matthew Bridge, was built 1168–1207 under the direction of Domnall Mór O'Brien, King of Thomond, with most construction being done in the period 1180–95. The king was an indefatigable church-builder and at least five abbeys are credited to his efforts. The lid of his coffin can be seen in the chancel. The cathedral was built on the site of his palace which he donated to the church, and the Romanesque west doorway is alleged to have come from the palace, though there is no firm evidence for this. The doorway was heavily restored in 1895, and only the hood and the innermost of its four orders are original.

The length of the cathedral from east to west is about 51.8m, and the width, 27.4m from north to south through the transepts. Stepped battlements, so typical of Irish architec-

St Mary's Cathedral, Limerick: the Tower

ture, crown the tower, the west front and the aisles of the nave. The 14th-century west tower is 36.5m high; the upper part was restored after the siege of 1691. It contains a peal of bells, some of which date from 1678.

The design of the cathedral was strongly influenced by Cistercian architecture, especially noticeable in the stern simplicity of the massive square 12th-century nave piers, 1.7m thick and without chamfering or moulding. The round-headed clerestory windows have narrow galleries beneath in the thickness of the walls. The barrel-vaulted roof is of Cratloe oak from Co. Clare.

The 12th-century cathedral was oblong in shape with a four-bay aisled nave. The north and south transepts were added in the 13th century, and a number of chapels were added to the north and south nave aisles in the 14th and 15th centuries, extending the north and south walls beyond the walls of the end of the transepts and obscuring the original outline of the building.

At the north-west was the Creagh Chapel, later a baptistery and now temporarily used as the cathedral appeal office. To the east of the Creagh Chapel is the Chapel of St Mark, sometimes known as the O'Brien Chapel, with a roof of lierne vaulting. Many of the Kings of Thomond and their descendants are buried under these chapels; among them was Murrough of the Burnings, the warrior Earl of Inchiquin, who died in 1674.

To the east of the Chapel of St Mark is the Chapel of St Nicholas, originally divided into the Chapel of St Catherine to the west and the Chapel of St Nicholas to the east. It is also known as the Jebb Chapel and formerly the Arthur Chapel. John Jebb was Bishop of Limerick 1823–33 and anticipated certain of the doctrinal emphases of the Oxford Movement which began in England in 1833. He was highly regarded by John Henry Newman, the most prominent figure in the movement at that time. The chapel was restored in 1869 and contains an 1836 statue of Jebb by Edward Hodges Baily (1788–1867). It also contains segments of a floriated Gothic tomb of the 15th century. The window has stained glass depicting St Nicholas as 'Santa Claus' and St Catherine with her wheel of torture. It was given in 1961 and designed by the Harry Clarke Studios in Dublin.

To the east of the Chapel of St Nicholas is the north transept, now the Chapel of the Holy Spirit. It contains two wall tombs and a modern triptych of paint and mosaic in front of the organ case. Beside the organ is a rectangular hole in the wall known as the 'Lepers' squint'. Any sufferer from leprosy would come and peer through this hole to watch the celebration of mass and to receive communion from the priest. Adjacent to this chapel is a Caen stone pulpit of 1860.

The Chapel of St James and St Mary Magdalene is located in the original south transept. After many years of other uses, including service as a choir room, it was restored to its ancient use and designation in 1962. The east and south walls were rebuilt in the 16th and 17th centuries. The Gothic arches and the sedilia of c.1400 are the only remaining medieval features. The altar in this chapel incorporates a massive medieval altar slab which mercifully survived the Reformation. It is made of a single piece of limestone 3.9m long and weighs over 3 tons.

To the west of this chapel are two bays which were at one time chapels but are now empty; the dividing walls had been removed by the end of the 19th century. The first was the Chapel of St Anne, and the second was the Sexton Chapel, named after a famous Limerick family. The Chapels were later used as the consistory court. The next bay leads to the south-west entrance porch, and then, at the south-west corner, the former Chapel of St George, now containing tombs and memorials of members of the Pery family. William Cecil Pery (1721–92) was Bishop of Killala 1781–84 and Bishop of Limerick 1784–94. He was created Baron Glentworth in 1790 and his eldest son Edmond (1758–1844) was created Viscount Limerick in 1800 and Earl of Limerick in 1803.

The cathedral was heavily restored in 1660 because of damage during the Cromwellian period, when horses were said to have stabled in the cathedral. This is a common story about many cathedrals during the rule of Cromwell; but there is corroboration at Limerick where a contemporary document speaks of 'providing fodder for the same'.[1] The restoration lengthened the ritual choir westwards to take in the whole of the first bay of the nave with returned stalls for the Dean and Chapter.

Further restoration in 1759 included the introduction of some Classical furnishings, which incurred severe disapproval from visitors at the end of the 18th century. 'The introduction of Grecian architecture has ruined many a noble Gothic edifice. The pillars that surround the Communion Table and bishop's throne are Corinthian; it must have been owing to a want of taste that they ever found a place here. Indeed, the modern sashes in the choir and blocking angles in the nave have greatly diminished that magnificence, that awe with which ancient churches strike a sentimental mind and at once inspire respect and devotion.'[2]

In 1860, with the craze for Gothic Revival reaching its high peak, the *Dublin Builder* vented its hatred of the 18th-century work, calling it the result of 'perverted taste'. 'Most of the arches were filled up with brick or woodwork, one-third of the church was cut off by a huge glazed wooden screen, over which the organ was placed, galleries were erected in the transepts and . . . all that depraved taste and ignorance could do was done to change and disfigure its original beauty.'[3] The nave of the cathedral was disused after the erection of the screen, since the journal also reported that the clerestory windows in the nave were open 'and being without sashes, through them a constant stream of cold air passed into the outer part of the church'.[4]

St Mary's Cathedral, Limerick: the restored Romanesque west doorway

A substantial Gothicising restoration took place in 1859–68 under the supervision of William Slater of London. The mistake of extending the ritual choir into the nave in the 17th century was remedied by removing the chapter stalls to the north and south sides of the chancel. Galleries had been erected in both transepts at the beginning of the 19th century to accommodate the military and the city corporation; they were removed in 1859, as was a low plaster whitewashed ceiling which concealed the oak roof and the clerestory. The perpendicular-style east window, a 17th- or 18th-century insertion, was removed in 1866 and replaced by the present triple-light Early English window with glass by Clayton & Bell. A new pine roof was erected over the chancel, and the organ gallery at the west end of the chancel was removed to the north transept. The chancel arches, which had been blocked up with brickwork, were reopened, and the cathedral's box

pews were removed and replaced with open pews. The total cost of the reordering was £4,000. The 18th-century eagle lectern and the three massive brass chandeliers, two in the nave and one in the chancel, are the only remaining evidence of the mid-18th-century work. They were made by Daniel Crosby of Dublin in 1758 and installed in the cathedral the following year.

The shortening of the chancel was completed in the early 20th century, and when a stone screen was erected in 1921 to divide the chancel from the nave. It was given as a memorial to Edmund, Viscount Glentworth (1894–1918), and his sister, Lady Victoria Brady (1893–1918), by their father, the 4th Earl of Limerick, and his American son-in-law, John Brady. Bronze gates were added to the screen in 1929 in memory of Dean Thomas Aylmer Pearson Hackett (1913–29), to a design by R. Caulfield Orpen.

The chancel contains twenty three fine black oak misericord seats, unique to Ireland, ornamented with angels, birds and semi-mythical creatures. They date from the period 1480–1500. The bishop's throne occupies the traditional site on the south side of the chancel; it was designed by James Pain in 1831. Eastwards of the throne is a canopied pew assigned to the Earl of Limerick as 'Prior of St Mary's'. In 1538 Henry VIII granted to Edmund Sexton, then Mayor of Limerick, the title and rights of prior in the cathedral. This title has ever since been held by the Earls of Limerick. The carvings on the back of the prior's stall were added in 1860.

The altar reredos, carved by Michael Pearse of Dublin, was erected in 1907 during the incumbency of Lucius O'Brien, Dean of Limerick 1905–13, in memory of several members of the O'Brien family. To the left of the altar is a memorial to Donough, Earl of Thomond, who died in 1624, and his wife Elizabeth. Below this memorial is the coffin lid of Domnall Mór O'Brien, founder of the cathedral.

St Mary's Cathedral is a curious mixture of styles of architecture and stained glass, giving it the appearance of a collection of unrelated segments which have been thrown together. The interior is dark and jumbled, but not unattractive, and the whole peculiar mix of the building makes it an interesting place to explore. Thackeray thought it 'a barbarous old turreted edifice',[5] while another contemporary dismissed its 'heavy lumpish exterior' and 'time-worn, neglected and dilapidated interior'.[6] Carlyle described it as a 'big dark brown hulk of an edifice' sarcastically adding 'what they call Cathedral'.[7] Prince von Pueckler-Muskau, visiting Limerick in 1828, thought it 'more in the style of a fortress than a church, the architecture solid and rude, but imposing by its massiveness'.[8] A kinder assessment from the late 18th century, with a feel for its Cistercian origins, spoke of 'a degree of solemnity, bordering on sadness, about this church, which must be attributed to a kind of stupendous simplicity which pervades the whole'.[9]

A detailed description of the interior would be unfair at the time of writing. A major restoration plan, costing £2,500,000, began in April 1990; there is little to be seen of the work in the interior beyond the fact that the walls were completely stripped of plaster in 1991. It is too soon to judge the full effect of this work, but it will presumably give the interior of St Mary's an appearance not unlike that of Killarney Cathedral. On an encouraging note, Jeremiah Newman, the Roman Catholic Bishop of Limerick, preached in St Mary's on 23 January 1989 and, on behalf of his people, warmly supported the appeal.

References

1 H. E. Day and J. G. F. Patton, *The cathedrals of the Church of Ireland* (London, 1932), p. 156.
2 John Ferrar, *The history of Limerick* (Limerick, 1787), p. 152.
3 *Dublin Builder*, 1 Dec. 1860, p. 378.
4 Ibid., 15 Sept. 1861, p. 633.
5 W. M. Thackeray, *The Irish sketch-book*, (London, 1843), i, 263.
6 *The Parliamentary Gazetteer of Ireland* (Dublin, 1844–6), ii, 634.
7 Thomas Carlyle, *Reminiscences of my Irish journey in 1849* (London, 1889), p. 170.
8 Prince H. L. H. von Pueckler-Muskau, *Tour in England, Ireland and france, in the years 1826, 1827, 1828 and 1829* (Zurich, 1949), p. 299.
9 George Holmes, *Sketches of some of the southern counties of Ireland, collected during a tour in the autumn if 1797, in a series of letters* (London, 1801), p. 66.

LIMERICK

The Cathedral Church of St John the Baptist

Diocese of Limerick (Roman Catholic)

THE history of a church or chapel in Limerick dedicated to St John can be traced to medieval times. The medieval church of that dedication was demolished in 1852 and replaced by the (now closed) Church of Ireland parish church. The first post-Reformation Roman Catholic church of St John was in existence in the Gallows Green area of the city by 1704. A new church was built near St John's Gate on the site of the car park of the present cathedral *c.*1706. In about 1730 it replaced the old chapel at Gallows Green which had fallen into disrepair.

By 1753 the new church was itself 'tottering to the ground'.[1] It was replaced by a simple church, typical of its date, with a bell-turret above the west gable. It became the bishop's parish in 1754 and was used as a diocesan church from that date

onwards. A visitor to the church in 1852 described it as being crammed with people in every passage and doorway.[2] It was too small for the Catholic population of the parish which numbered 12,000–15,000, and its replacement by a larger church was only a matter of time. It was demolished in 1861 after the construction of the cathedral.

In the early 1850s Bishop John Ryan (1828–64) visited England and the continent to examine the pattern of church-building with a view to building a cathedral for Limerick. He was for long uncertain about the viability of the project, but as it became increasingly clear that the old St John's Church was in need of major restoration, a decision was made to proceed with a new church. The first major public meeting was called on 27 January 1856, and Bishop Ryan launched an appeal for funds. A competition was announced to find a suitable architect, and the winner was Philip Charles Hardwicke (1820–82), a young Englishman. Some disquiet was caused among Irish entrants to the competition by the choice of an English architect, and there were protests in the press. But Hardwicke belonged to a distinguished architectural dynasty and had an established track record. He worked in Ireland as well as England from 1851 to 1866 and had completed Adare Manor for the Earl of Dunraven, and the restoration of the Augustinian abbey at Adare. He had also designed a number of Roman Catholic parish churches, as well as the Hall and Library of Lincoln's Inn in London.

Hardwicke's brief was to build a large plain church capable of serving the needs of the 15,000 Catholics in St John's parish. He produced a design in the Gothic Revival building of the Early English phase, with its typical narrow lancet windows. The design was inspired by Salisbury Cathedral but was intended to resemble Pugin's great cathedral at Killarney. St John's Cathedral has some points of similarity with Salisbury Cathedral, though the size, detail and ornamentation of Salisbury is on a very different scale, and the tower and spire are central at Salisbury.

When the appeal was launched in January 1856, the new building was still regarded as being no more than a parish church. But the widespread response to the appeal, among parishioners and beyond, indicated to Bishop Ryan that he should make St John's his new cathedral; the splendour of Hardwicke's design may also have been instrumental. The first printed public reference to the upgraded status of the church was an article in the *Munster News* on 5 April 1856. An announcement of the date of the laying of the foundation stone was headed 'The Cathedral of St John's'.

The foundation stone was laid on 1 May 1856, and the cathedral was formally opened on 25 July 1861 with the consecration of George Butler as coadjutor bishop. He succeeded Bishop Ryan in 1864 and remained Bishop of Limerick until his death in 1886. The tower was built to a height of about 20m before work stopped in 1862. Tower and spire

St John's Cathedral, Limerick: the east end

were completed in 1878–82 to a design by Maurice Hennessy that was taller and more elaborate than that intended by Hardwicke. A 5m cross of galvanised iron was erected at the summit of the spire on 27 September 1882, only to collapse three days later during a storm, falling on the roof of the cathedral. Damage and injury were mercifully slight, and after renovation a new cross was erected in September 1883. The total height is now 93m, making it the highest spire in Ireland and among the tallest in the world.

The cathedral is built of blue Limerick limestone and measures 51m in length and 36m in width at the transepts. The internal height of the nave is 24m. The nave is of five bays with aisles and a clerestory. The tower nestles in the angle formed by the nave and the north transept. The chancel has a fine very tall east window of five stepped lancets, 11m high and 5m wide, a feature repeated in both transepts. The windows of the north and south transepts and the Chapel of St Vincent de Paul have glass by Meyer of Munich. The walls of the chancel are lined with green Galway marble and red Cork marble to a height of 4m. The aisle floors are mosaic. There are pine confessional boxes along the walls of the north and south nave aisles.

The chancel is flanked by four chapels, two on each side. All four have rose windows. Those leading off the north transept are dedicated to St Joseph and the Blessed Sacrament, and those from the south transept to the Blessed Virgin Mary and St Vincent de Paul. The Lady Chapel has a fine statue of the Virgin by Giovanni Benzoni. The Blessed Sacrament Chapel now incorporates parts of the former bishop's throne, carved from Riga oak in Munich in 1894, over the tabernacle.

Ten years after the completion of the tower and spire St John's Cathedral was in need of major restoration. 'For some time the interior has been presenting a wornout decaying appearance. The white lime-washed walls of the nave and aisle were marked by patches of damp-stained colour, and were depressingly melancholy; the mural decorations around the altars had almost faded out; and on wet days, particularly, the flagged passages in the aisles and transepts were very greasy and cold looking.'[3] Bishop Edward O'Dwyer (1886–1917) decided to restore the cathedral before proceeding to a solemn consecration. The flagstones were replaced by tiles, and sanctuary was raised 1m in height. A throne and prebendal stalls made of Riga oak were added, and the interior was repainted. Consecration took place on 21 June 1894 in the presence of the Archbishops of Armagh, Tuam and Cashel and eleven bishops.

No building of this size is ever free from the continual need for maintenance. Further restoration was undertaken in 1920–23 under the supervision of Ashlin & Coleman. The main work involved the repointing of the exterior and the repainting of the interior. In 1950–56, under the supervision of Andrew Devane of the Dublin architects Robinson, Keefe &

Devane, the cathedral was completely re-roofed, the old roof of Killaloe slate being replaced by a new roof of copper, and the interior was replastered; the total cost was £60,000.

The latest restoration, in accordance with the requirements of the Second Vatican Council, took place in 1977–86 at a cost of £300,000. The architect was Patrick Sheehan of Limerick. The sanctuary floor was lowered to its original level, and the altar was separated from the reredos and moved forward. It was also tastefully enlarged by the use of carefully selected matching marble from Italy. The bishop's throne of 1894 was placed against the reredos, while the back and

St John's Cathedral, Limerick: the tower and spire

canopy of the throne were moved to the Blessed Sacrament Chapel to form a new backing for the tabernacle. The interior was completely repainted.

There is nothing very remarkable about the exterior of St John's Cathedral, with the exception of the gables over the aisles, and the tower and spire, which is reckoned to be one of the most beautiful in Ireland. But the interior has an attractive quality which is difficult to define. The loftiness, the dark-grey stone of the arcades and piers, and the dark oak ceiling, contrasts pleasantly with the white plaster walls. Somehow these features combine to give the building a feeling of being much older than it actually is.

References

1 John Fleming, *St John's Cathedral, Limerick* (Dublin, 1987), p. 35.
2 Ibid., p. 43.
3 Ibid., p. 73.

LISBURN

The Cathedral of Christ Church

Diocese of Connor (Church of Ireland)

*L*ISBURN is a manufacturing and commercial town of about 40,000 inhabitants, in Co. Antrim, 12.8km south-west of Belfast. Once known as Lisnagarvey, meaning 'ring fort of the gamblers', its present name translates as 'ring fort of the spring'; it came into use in January 1662 for reasons which have been forgotten.

Lisburn Cathedral stands on the highest point in the town on a cramped site surrounded by houses except for the gardens to the east. The first church was built here in 1623 by Sir Fulke Conway, who had been granted the territory around Lisnagarvey by the crown *c.*1609. He constructed a castle in the gardens adjacent to the present cathedral, and the church, dedicated to St Thomas, was a chapel of ease to the castle. The church was 24.3m long and 7.6m wide and may have had a tower and spire. As the town of Lisnagarvey began to grow up around the castle, the church ceased to be a private chapel and became the parish church of the district. Town, castle and church were destroyed during the Confederate war of the 1640s. The church was later rebuilt, probably much on the same lines as before, and a gallery was added in 1674.

Connor Cathedral was almost entirely destroyed in the same rebellion and, as Downpatrick Cathedral was also in ruins, and both dioceses shared the same bishop, the parish church of Lisburn was constituted the cathedral church for the Dioceses of Connor and Down by royal charter on 27 October 1662. 'Whereas the Church of Lisburne alias Lisnagarvie, in our county of Antrim and diocese of Down, being situate near the middle of the diocese aforesaid, and now united, can more conveniently serve as a Cathedral Church for the Bishoprics aforesaid . . . we have erected, created, founded, ordained, made, constituted and established the said Church, to be forever hereafter the Cathedral Church and the afore-

said seat of the aforesaid several bishoprics of Down and Connor and to continue for ever in all future times.'[1]

The bishop at the time was the saintly Jeremy Taylor, Bishop of Down and Connor and administrator of Dromore 1661–7 ('the immortal Jeremy' as Browning calls him). He died at Lisburn, but was buried at his own request at Dromore Cathedral. A memorial to his memory was erected in an 1827; it bears the following inscription: 'Reader, though it fall not to thy lot to attain to the intellectual greatness of this master in Israel, yet thou mayest rival him in that which was the highest scope even of his ambition, an honest conscience and a Christian life.'

Lisburn Cathedral from the south

On Sunday 20 April 1707 a disastrous fire broke out in the cathedral during divine service, and town, castle and cathedral were again destroyed. The castle was not rebuilt, but the foundation stone of the new cathedral was laid on 20 August 1708, funds being raised in part by a tax on the inhabitants of the parish. The work of construction took several years to complete; building was still in progress in 1714.

The plan of the rebuilt church was an aisleless nave of four bays with a tower at the west end. The division between the bays is indicated externally by buttresses. The tower, whose external appearance resembles a jigsaw, is slightly inset at each of its four floors and has a very slight batter. The slender octagonal spire was added in 1804. A photograph of the interior in 1885 shows north and south galleries, a Perpendicular east window, a centrally placed wooden pulpit, gas lighting and stoves. The galleries, including the west gallery, were erected about 1824; no doubt of great practical use, the galleries unfortunately bisect the windows and crowd and darken the interior.

The existing two-bay chancel was added to the cathedral in 1889. The sanctuary has typical Victorian Gothic wooden panelling, and, as is so often the case, the central part behind the altar makes the mistake of rising above the window-sill. Some reordering took place in 1950, when the east window, with geometrical Decorated tracery, was filled with stained glass presented by Sir John Milne Barbour in memory of his wife and son. In the same year, after managing without them since 1662, the cathedral was presented with a set of chapter stalls and a throne for the bishop as a Second World War memorial.

A bequest to the Dean and Chapter enabled the chancel to be re-ordered in 1990–91. The purpose was to provide more space in the area around the altar and improve the rather congested situation during Communion services. The re-ordering involved the removal of the elaborate Victorian octagonal stone and marble pulpit, which looked out of place, and its replacement by a new wooden pulpit; the existing altar rails were removed, and the altar was brought away from the east wall on to a new dais and surrounded by new simpler rails; the chapter stalls on the north and south walls were left in position, but the bishop's throne was moved further east and sited in the new sanctuary area; the existing choir stalls were removed and replaced by new chairs on a new dais below the chancel steps; the gallery fronts were lightened to harmonise with the new pews.

In 1952, owing to suggested doubts as to whether Lisburn was in fact a cathedral church, a bill of the General Synod of the Church of Ireland recognised it as the cathedral church of the diocese of Connor. The doubts were of a formal and technical nature, revolving around suggestions that the charter of Charles II had never been made effective, neither had it received the sanction of parliament nor the royal seal.

The interior of Lisburn Cathedral looking east in 1989

The organisation of the hierarchy of Lisburn Cathedral is a little confused. The building is, principally, a parish church, with a rector and select vestry who effectively manage and maintain it. Yet there is a passing nod to its cathedral status in the form of a Dean and Chapter. As with every other Church of Ireland diocese, the members of the chapter are parish priests in the diocese. The offices of Dean of Connor and Rector of Christ Church are usually separate, the title of dean being an honorific appointment given to a long-serving priest in the diocese. The Chapter has the odd, if historic, style of 'The Dean and Chapter of St Saviour, Connor, in the Cathedral of Christ Church, Lisburn'. The whole cathedral hierarchy seems to sit lightly on the shoulders of Christ Church, which is really little more than a parish church providing shelter for a homeless chapter.

Since the rebuilding of Downpatrick Cathedral at the beginning of the 19th century, and the separation of the diocese of Connor from the dioceses of Down and Dromore in 1944, Lisburn Cathedral is now the cathedral church of the diocese of Connor alone. In the Roman Catholic arrangement, the diocese of Connor is held with Down, and the cathedral is at Belfast.

In size and architecture, Lisburn Cathedral is a small and unremarkable parish church. With the growth of Belfast in the 19th century, the Dean and Chapter began to think of building a new cathedral in Belfast (see BELFAST). The *Irish Ecclesiastical Gazette* reported of Lisburn Cathedral in 1861 that 'neither its situation, nor its size, nor yet the style of its architecture, is suitable for a cathedral church'.[2] Some observers within the diocese have thought that the massive structure of St Anne's Cathedral in Belfast would be a more appropriate cathedral for the diocese.

References

1 R. W. Jackson, *Cathedrals of the Church of Ireland* (Dublin, 1971), p. 29.
2 *Irish Ecclesiastical Gazette*, 15 Nov. 1861, p.323.

LISMORE

The Cathedral Church of St Carthage

Diocese of Lismore (Church of Ireland)

LISMORE (*Lios mór* – great ring-fort) is a village of 900 inhabitants 24km west of Dungarvan and 25.6km east of Fermoy in Co. Waterford. Its cathedral enjoys a most beautiful setting in the valley of the River Blackwater, famous for its trout and salmon. 'In its setting of trees, river and mountain it has a very special old-fashioned charm.'[1] 'Mountain and glen, the lovely Blackwater and the wooding of a great demense, conspire to make Lismore one of the fairest

places which may entrance a visitor to Ireland.'[2] The town is best approached along a winding road through the Knockmealdown Mountains which crosses the ancient track from Lismore to Cashel – now a green highway sweeping down to Cashel on the Plain of Tipperary, covered with gold flowering gorse and purple rhododendrons.

The east window of Lismore Cathedral

Natural beauty as well as remoteness was often an important factor in determining the site of a Celtic monastery, and to this remote and beautiful place came St Carthage *c.*636. With several of his fellow monks, Carthage (also known as Mo Chutu or Mochuda) had been expelled from the monastery at Rahan (Rathain) in Co. Offaly, which he had founded *c.*596. His foundation at Rahan had enlarged to a community of 867 monks, causing concern to Clonard, Clonmacnoise and older and more well established houses. Carthage was 'prevailed upon' to leave Rahan and return to his native Munster. He founded a new monastery at Lismore which became a great centre of learning and retreat, and one of the most richly endowed and frequented monastic schools of Ireland. In the life of St Carthage, Lismore is described as 'a famous and holy city, into the half of which (there being an asylum) no women dare enter. It is filled with cells and holy monasteries, and a number of holy men are always in it. The religious flow to it from every part of Ireland, England, and Britain [*sic*], anxious to remove thence to Christ.'[3]

Carthage (feast-day 14 May) died in 637 or 639, shortly after his arrival, but the monastery continued to flourish and reached the zenith of its renown at the beginning of the 8th century. The test of the strength of any monastic community is whether it can survive the death or departure of its founder, and Lismore was successful. It suffered more than the usual degree of attention from the Vikings, as a result of its proximity to Waterford, and seven burnings and ten plunderings are recorded between 812 and 1207, but it still survived.

As early as 1096 the Viking city of Waterford had been established as a suffragan see of Canterbury. In 1111 the Synod of Ráith Bressail set up a diocese for the neighbouring kingdom of the Déise, leaving a choice between Waterford and Lismore for the episcopal see. The Synod of Kells–Mellifont settled the matter by establishing two territorial dioceses, Waterford and Lismore. Waterford was always a small diocese, Lismore taking in most of the present-day county of Waterford. Disputes between the two dioceses were common in the early 12th century, escalating into personal violence between individual bishops (see WATERFORD).

On 31 July 1327 Pope John XXII decreed the amalgamation of the dioceses of Waterford and Lismore. As always there was a long delay between the pope issuing a decree far away in Rome and the implementation of that decree in a local situation; one doubts whether medieval popes ever really knew the extent and depth of conflicting local interests. In 1355 Innocent VI confirmed the union of Waterford and Lismore, and on 18 November 1356 Edward III ordered the temporalities of Lismore, then vacant, to be delivered to Roger Cradock, Bishop of Waterford (1350–61). But in 1358 Innocent appointed Thomas le Reve as Bishop of Lismore. After Cradock's translation from Waterford to Llandaff in 1361, a decree from Urban V finally effected the delayed union, and the two dioceses have remained united in both the Church of Ireland and the Roman Catholic hierarchies.

Lismore Cathedral is an aisleless cruciform church with tower and spire at the west end, mainly the result of a substantial rebuilding of the 17th century. A round arch in the nave survives from that period, together with five inscribed grave slabs, set in the west wall, each carrying an incised cross and dating from the 9th to 11th centuries. The stones were placed here in the mid-19th century. The fine altar tomb in the north-west corner of the nave was erected in 1548 for John and Catherine Magrath. It bears a relief of St Gregory the Great wearing the triple crown.

The north and south transept arches date from the 13th century, as do the clustered columns at the intersection of the south transept, as well as the basement moulding on the outside of the south wall of the chancel, and the remains of the shafts of the columns resting on that moulding.

The medieval cathedral was almost entirely destroyed *c*.1600 by the rebellious Edmund Fitzgibbon (d.1608), who bore the quaint and romantic hereditary title of 'The White Knight'.[4] Referring to the White Knight, the Earl of Cork thought that 'a more faythless liar never lived upon the earthe'.[5]

The south doorway of Lismore Cathedral

The notorious Miler Magrath, Archbishop of Cashel (see CASHEL), was Bishop of Lismore at the time and granted a lease on the bishop's palace and estates to Sir Walter Raleigh in 1589. Raleigh in turn sold the property to Richard Boyle, 1st Earl of Cork (1566–1643), who made considerable efforts to restore the cathedral. He wrote on 10 January 1633: 'God bless my good intendments and endeavours in this work. This day, I resolved, with the assistance of my good God, to re-edifie the ancient Cathedral church of Lismore wch was demolished by Edmund Fitzgibbon – and other traitors in the late rebellion of Mownster. The choir of wh Ch, I did at my own charges of £CCXVI [*216*] 13 & 9d. rebuyld, & put a new Rooff, covered with slatt, and plaistered and glazed: then furnishing it with seated pews and pulpit: And now have given order to have the ruyns of the boddie and Ile of that Church cleered, & to have the same new built and re-edified, as fair, or fairer than ever it was before.'

The chancel was re-roofed, but despite the Earl's expressed intention, nothing was done to the nave and transepts. Five years later, on 9 April 1638, he wrote: 'God bless my good intencions. I this day began to enter on the puling down of the Ruyns of the old defaced Chapels[6] of Lismore wh was so ordered to be done by an act of the Bp Dean and Chap: with a godly resolucion to rebuyld the demolished Cath Ch: of Lismore, & mansion for the 5 vicars choral at my own charges.'[7] Because of the deteriorating political climate and the earl's death in 1643, these resolutions were not put into effect.

The rebuilding of the nave and transepts was delayed until after the Restoration. In 1679 the Dean and Chapter declared their intention to restore the remainder of the cathedral and invited Sir William Robinson (c.1643–1712), Surveyor General of Works in Ireland, to be the architect. Robinson is best known for the Royal Hospital at Kilmainham. The work was carried out in the years 1679–87 at a cost of £1,600. The nave and transepts were roofed, a tower and cupola were erected at the crossing, and a Chapter House was built onto the north wall of the chancel. Because of alterations in the 18th and 19th centuries, the only surviving parts of his work are the transept roofs and the Chapter House.

In 1726 the chapter decided to spend 45 on internal alterations to the stalls and galleries, and in building and 'adorning' a seat[8] for the 4th Earl of Cork (1695–1753), who presented the South Mall to the cathedral in that year. In 1738 it was ordered that the 'cupilow' should be rebuilt, and a drawing of 1739 shows a short octagonal tower and spire at the crossing with quoins at the angles. The 'cupilow' had been demolished by 1774, when a contemporary drawing shows the cathedral without a tower but with a small bell-cote surmounting the west gable.

By the beginning of the 19th century the south wall of the chancel was leaning out at a angle and had to be supported by buttresses. The Dean and Chapter consulted the architect Sir Richard Morrison, who advised that the south and east walls be rebuilt. The work began about 1811 and continued for many years. The Gothic plasterwork of the ceiling with its elaborate roof bosses, the wall arcades and the windows all date from this time. The wall plaques, which contain the titles of the cathedral dignitaries and prebendaries, also date from the period. The gate piers, formed by clustered columns with gadrooned tops, and the wrought-iron entrance gates also date from 1811, The cobblestone path and lime trees are mid-18th century.

In 1827 a tower and spire were erected to a design by J. and G.R. Pain at a cost of £3,500. Because their Gothic Revival design contrasted with the Classical style of the remainder of the cathedral, the nave was given a fan-vaulted ceiling and the nave windows were given pointed arches.

In 1851 Henry Cotton, Archdeacon of Lismore, built and furnished the Cathedral Library. It can be seen, built onto the north wall of the chancel between the Chapter House and the north transept. Cotton was a great book-collector and had been assistant librarian at the Bodleian Library in Oxford in his younger days. His major work, *Fasti Ecclesiae Hiberniae* (1845–60), was the first modern study of the subject.

The interior has been as heavily remodelled as the exterior. The nave was formerly full of large box pews, probably like those which still exist at Killala Cathedral, and the crossing was empty except for the font. An organ of 1775 was placed on top of the solid stone choir screen which divided the chancel from the crossing.

Some internal reordering took place in the years 1877–8 owing to the generosity of the Duke of Devonshire. Galleries in the chancel were removed. The stone screen was demolished and an organ chamber made on the south side of the chancel. The chapter stalls and bishop's throne were removed, the latter being placed in the nave of Youghal church. The font was moved to the south side of the west door, and the crossing, transepts and nave were filled with pews. A three-decker pulpit was removed from the nave; the upper part went to Tullow church and can now be seen in Knockmealden church. An oak screen, adapted from the west gallery of St Olaf's Church, Waterford, was placed in the choir about 6m from the east wall, behind a small tiled sanctuary. The screen seems to have functioned as a reredos, and no use was made of the area behind. The present pulpit of Caen stone with coloured marble colonettes was erected in 1877 and is typical of its date.

Some alterations were made in 1913; the chancel floor was laid with encaustic tiles, and the semicircular 1815 altar rails were moved to the west end of the nave to stand around the font which then stood there.

Further alterations were made in 1963 during the incumbency of Dean Gilbert Mayes (1961–87). The 1878 screen was removed from the choir and placed at the entrance to the north transept, which was converted into a chapel dedicated to St Columba. The round-arched doorway in the north wall of the transept was built up and now forms a reredos to the altar, which, with the 18th-century rails, came from the disused chapel at Villierstown. The altar was moved into the centre of an enlarged sanctuary, and a piscina and aumbry were created in a built-up doorway. A bishop's throne was created, using the canopy and pulpit from the Villierstown chapel, the first provision of a throne since the alterations of 1877–8. The nave and transepts were cleared of pews, and the font was moved to the south transept, given a cover, and flanked by portions of the 1815 altar rails.

The latest addition to the cathedral is an oak pulpit of 1733 from the (now redundant) church of St Olaf, Waterford, which was placed in the nave in 1984. The main altar, rails and sanctuary floor are also from St Olaf's. In recent years the nave and chancel have been re-roofed, and the vaulting ribs and bosses of the chancel ceiling have been coloured. The chancel has a large clear-glass east window with external iron fretwork, formed to resemble stone tracery.

The seating of the dignitaries and prebendaries of Lismore Cathedral is unusual in the fact that the labelling bears no relation to the seating. The labelling consists of black lettering on a gold shield-shaped field, within quatrefoil frames, themselves set within recessed roundels in the north and south walls of the chancel, adjacent to the crossing. Rearrangement of the seating in the chancel has removed the Gothic stalls from below the wall plaques which bear the titles of the prebendaries and dignitaries.

The churchyard is a most tranquil place surrounded by an ivy-covered wall and planted with a variety of shrubs and trees – so many, in fact, that photographing the entire cathedral from any angle on the ground is now impossible because it is so well hidden. The only evidence for its existence is the slender tapering spire which, now and then, suddenly appears through gaps in the trees.

Because of the raising of the level of the surrounding ground over the centuries, the external proportions of Lismore Cathedral seem modest and belie its internal height. It seems to snuggle in amongst the enveloping trees and bushes of its churchyard. This is of no consequence because there are no striking architectural features to catch the eye. But the location, on an eminence 28m above the south bank of the Blackwater, is delightful. That stern and cynical critic, W. M. Thackeray, visited Lismore in 1842 and was charmed by what he saw. 'The graceful spire of Lismore, the prettiest I have seen in, or I think out of, Ireland.'[9] 'The church, with the handsome spire that looks so graceful among the trees, is a cathedral church, and one of the neatest and prettiest edifices I have seen in Ireland.'[10]

Lismore Castle, originally a 12th-century structure, was the residence of the Bishop of Lismore until Bishop Miler Magrath (who was also Archbishop of Cashel) gave it to Sir Walter Raleigh in 1589. In the possession of the Earls of Cork from 1602 to 1753, it then passed by marriage to the Dukes of Devonshire, in whose ownership it still remains. Some medieval work remains, but the castle was largely rebuilt in 1812–21 and remodelled in 1850–58. Two treasures from the greatness of medieval Lismore were found in the castle in 1814; the 'Lismore Crozier' (c.1100) and the Book of Lismore, a 15th-century manuscript collection of the lives of Irish saints as well as some secular material.

References

1 R. W. Jackson, *Cathedrals of the Church of Ireland* (Dublin, 1971), p. 75.
2 H. E. Day and J. G. F. Patton, *The cathedrals of the Church of Ireland* (London, 1932), pp 31–32.
3 Ibid., p. 129.
4 Together with the Knight of Glin and Knight of Kerry, the White Knight was an hereditary Irish title originating with the FitzGerald family in the 14th century. The first two titles survive, but the title of White Knight has been dormant since the early 17th century.
5 T. M. Fallow, *The cathedral churches of Ireland* (London, 1894), p. 67.
6 Lord Cork's use of the plural 'chapels' may be explained by the presence of two small Romanesque churches beside the cathedral. They were demolished in 1680, probably to be used as stone quarries for the rebuilding of the cathedral.
7 Fallow, *Cathedral churches of Ireland*, p. 67.
8 A gesture not dissimilar to the provision of a seat for Henry Roe among the Chapter Stalls at Christ Church Cathedral in Dublin.
9 W. M. Thackeray, *The Irish sketch-book* (London, 1843), i, 93.
10 Ibid., p. 96.

LONGFORD

The Cathedral Church of St Mel

Dioceses of Ardagh and Clonmacnoise (Roman Catholic)

LONGFORD (*Longphort* — fortress) is 122km north west of Dublin via Mullingar and is situated on the Camlin, a tributary of the Shannon. The Roman Catholic cathedral of the diocese of Ardagh and Clonmacnoise was established here in 1838. The Bishops of Ardagh and Clonmacnoise had formerly resided at Ballymahon from 1788, and the church there (predecessor of the present building) functioned as the pro-cathedral of the diocese.

The idea of a purpose-built cathedral was conceived by Bishop William O'Higgins (1829–53) a man of extravagant taste. He chose the town of Longford a few kilometres to the northwest of the ancient see of Ardagh. The project was launched at a meeting on 6 May 1838, and the foundation stone, taken from 'St Mel's Cathedral' at Ardagh, was laid on 8 May 1840. Because of the distress of the Great Famine, work was stopped in 1846 after the walls and columns had been completed. The poplulation of Co. Longford fell between 1846 and 1853 from 115,000 to 82,000. Bishop O'Higgins was disappointed that the building work had to be deferred, but there was no other option, and nothing further was done before his death in January 1853.

He was succeeded by John Kilduff (1853–67), at thirty-three probably the youngest Roman Catholic bishop in Ireland at the time. Bishop Kilduff began construction again, and in 1856 the cathedral was substantially complete and was dedicated and opened in the presence of the Archbishops of Armagh and Dublin and a congregation of 18,000 on 24 September of that year. He also saw the completion of the tower *c.* 1860 before his death from typhoid at the early age of forty-seven.

The last phase of building saw the construction of the portico in the years 1889–93 under Bishop Bartholomew Woodlock (1879–94). In 1940, nearly fifty years later, there were still some alive who remembered the building of the portico. 'Great cylinders of granite, weighing many tons, began to arrive from the Ross quarries near Finea, in 1889. Gradually the six gargantuan pillars . . . rose higher and higher, were crowned with their capitals, and then received the entablature.'[1] The construction of the portico completed the cathedral, and it was solemnly consecrated on 23 May 1893 at a ceremony lasting six hours.

The cathedral was officially designed by Joseph B. Kearne, but if one account is to be believed, Bishop O'Higgins gave Kearne a fairly clear brief of the grandiose building that he required. 'The great bishop is said to have conceived his plan partly according to the Madeleine Church in Paris, partly according to the Pantheon, Rome....and partly from St John Lateran.'[2] John Burke designed the tower, and the portico is the work of G. C. Ashlin. Not everybody liked it; Pugin crossly described it as 'a bad copy of that wretched compound of pagan and Protestant architecture, St Pancras New Church in London.'[3] But then, Pugin died in 1852 and never saw the cathedral in its completed state.

Longford Cathedral is an impressive building in the Greek revival style, constructed of grey marble and limestone. The west front has a portico of six bays divided by Ionic granite piers and crowned by a tympanum of Knockcroghery limestone. The piers are 11.2m high, and the total height of the portico is 18.8m from the top step to the apex of the tympanum. The carvings in the tympanum are by George Smyth and depict the enthronement of St Mel as Bishop of Ardagh by St Patrick. Smyth was also responsible for the 3.2m-high statue of Christ over the pediment. Statue and tympanum are carved in Portland stone. The cathedral measures 62m in length and 38.4m wide at the transepts. The front is 26m wide.

The Corinthian style campanile is 57m high and was designed by John Bourke. It has three stages: the first is octagonal and deeply recessed on four faces containing niches for four figures of the Evangelists, together with a stature of St Mel; the second is a couple-columned temple containing a belfry; the third is a drum crowned by a dome and pierced with circular and rectangular openings. The whole is surmounted by an open lantern and a gilt bronze cross.

The interior is in the Italian Renaissance style. The nave is connected with the side aisles by arcades resting on Ionic columns of grey marble. The theme of the columns is continued around the apse by six pilasters. There are twenty-four clerestory windows over the colonnade arches. A moulded cornice runs under the window sills, and a highly ornamented cornice runs around the whole circuit of nave and apse. The walls of the aisles have high semi-circular round-arched niches containing statuary, and these alternate with windows. The transepts are each 36m square and contain chapels with good Celtic Revival stained glass from the Harry Clarke studios. The semi-cylindrical ceiling is divided into double-recessed coffers by arcs doubleaux, the lower portion being pierced by Diocletian windows lighting the nave. The ceiling is of plaster of Paris, and the general décor is pink and grey. The organ gallery at the west end is a recent addition and blends reasonably well, with the exception of the two additional pillars needed to support its weight.

The interior of Longford Cathedral looking east

The apse has suffered rather badly from the post-Vatican II reordering in 1976 by Richard Hurley and Wilfrid Cantwell with furnishings by Ray Carroll. A long narrow tapestry depicting the Second Coming hangs in between and in front of the two central pilasters behind the bishop's throne. The new altar, ambo and bishop's chair and the semi-circular row of canons' seats are made of limestone, and are good examples of their type, but no attempt seems to have been made to secure harmony with the building. As usual, the building wins, and here the altar looks quite insignificant. A further tapestry by Imogen Stuart depicting the Holy Ghost is on a pillar above the limestone font. The Chapel of the Blessed Sacrament on the south side of the sanctuary has a painting by Ray Carroll depicting the Supper at Emmaus. The new sanctuary arrangements were dedicated on 17 July 1977.

The foundations of the building spread far beyond the external walls and consist of a complex series of reversed arches supporting each of the twenty-eight Ionic columns which in turn support the roof, as well as the the six piers which support the portico entablature. The thirty-nine pilasters which reinforce the exterior walls rest on a similar series of arches.[4]

Bishop O'Higgins's plans also extended to the provision of an astonishing episcopal residence built on to the east end of the cathedral and inspired by the papal palace attached to St John Lateran in Rome. 'His design was fully accomplished alas! But no bishop would live there. Hence arises the one and only criticism against the plan of the great bishop. The cost and space lavished on a useless project would have increased enormously the magnitude of the cathedral. The elimination of that palace would solve the whole problem of light to the whole width of the sanctuary. We can only faintly imagine what seven windows on the north end might add to the beauty and glory of this wondrous edifice.'[5] This odd excrescence to the cathedral still exists, but now houses a museum and choir rooms.

The modern presbytery to the north of the cathedral was constructed in 1967 to replace an older building.

Built on a slight incline, Longford Cathedral is a fine building of its type and dominates the surrounding town. But it looks as though it was put here by mistake. Rome would be a natural setting for this building, which sits a little uncomfortably in Longford.

References

1   M. J. Masterson, 'Centenary of St Mel's Cathedral, 1840-1940" in *Ardagh and Clonmacnoise Antiquarian Society Journal*, ii, no. 7 (1940), p. 60.
2   Ibid., p. 57.
3   Michael, Lord Killanin, and Michael Duignan, *The Shell Guide to Ireland* (Dublin, 1962; revised ed. by Peter Harbison, London & Dublin, 1989), p. 237.
4   Masterson, 'Centenary of St Mel's Cathedral, 1840–1940', p. 57.
5   Ibid.

LOUGHREA

The Cathedral Church of St Brendan

Diocese of Clonfert (Roman Catholic)

LOUGHREA (*Loch riabhach* — grey lake) is a market town of about 3,400 inhabitants in Co. Galway, situated 35.2km east of Galway and 30.4km south-west of Ballinasloe. Lying on the north bank of Lough Rea, it was the centre of the medieval de Burgo lordship of Connacht and has the ruins of a Carmelite friary and castle, both built *c.* 1300 by Richard de Burgo. It lies at the western extremity of the Roman Catholic diocese of Clonfert, but was chosen as the see because it was the largest centre of population within the diocesan boundaries.

The construction of a cathedral for the diocese of Clonfert was delayed for various reasons until the end of the 19th century, during the episcopate of John Healy (coadjutor bishop 1884–96, diocesan bishop 1896–1903). The foundation stone was laid on 10 October 1897, and the cathedral was completed in 1902.

Loughrea Cathedral is a comparatively small building standing in pleasant grounds which slope gently towards the lake beyond the east end. It was designed by William Byrne in an unremarkable style of Gothic and is not externally impressive. 'One is at best pleased rather than stirred. The building, one feels, is the work of an accomplished craftsman rather than a passionately inventive creative artist. As it stands, Loughrea Cathedral is a tasteful piece of modern Gothic, but hardly more than that.'[1]

The cathedral consists of an aisled nave of five bays, clerestory, shallow transepts, an apsidal sanctuary with flanking chapels, and a north-west tower surmounted by an octagonal broach spire with lucarnes. The nave aisles are lit by twin single-light windows in each bay, while the clerestory bays above have twin hexafoil windows set within deep Gothic reveals on the interior. The transepts have three single-light windows in each bay, with three small quatrefoil windows below. The nave piers are of polished granite, and the floor of the central aisle has polychromatic tilework. The nave aisles and chancel are walled and paved in different marbles. The cathedral is not as large as Byrne intended. He designed a two-bay chancel, to which Bishop Healy initially agreed. But the bishop changed his mind, and construction was stopped almost as soon as it began, leaving the present shallow apse.

The glory of Loughrea Cathedral is the adornment of the interior, which is a positive treasury of the Celtic Revival. Because its construction was delayed until the end of the

19th century, the cathedral was fortuitously contemporary with a major renaissance of Irish arts and crafts, of which it became a major patron. Sculpture, woodcarving, metalwork,

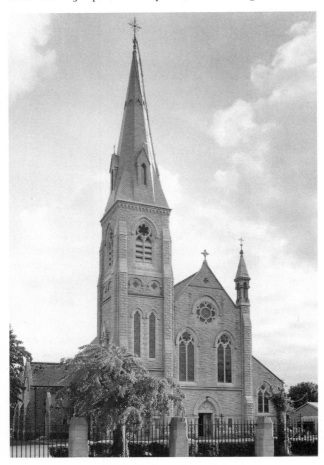

The west front of Loughrea Cathedral

textiles and stained glass from the Celtic Revival school are all represented at Loughrea.

Sculpture is represented by the work of Michael Shortall in the high altar, the carved capitals of the nave columns and the transepts, and the corbels in the clerestory. The table of the high altar (1903–5) rests on a marble six-bay Romanesque arcade. The sixteen corbels (1901) display animals, birds and fish intertwined with foliate decoration, a reference to the Creation. The capitals in the transept and the nave were carved *c.* 1924. Those in the transepts depict incidents from the history of the diocese of Clonfert, and those in the nave episodes in the life and legendary voyage of St Brendan.

The cathedral's stained glass is a fascinating array of work from the artists of An Túr Gloine (The Tower of Glass), the studio founded by Sarah Purser in 1903. Seven different artists working for An Túr Gloine were responsible for the

glazing of the cathedral between 1903 and 1950. The Ascension window in the west transept, designed by Michael Healy in 1936, is perhaps the finest. The Stations of the Cross in *opus sectile* with inscriptions in Irish are by Ethel Mary Rhind, also of An Túr Gloine, and were made between 1928 and 1933.

The post-Vatican II sanctuary arrangements are well made and include a bishop's throne, ambo, altar and bench made of wood to designs by the church artist, Ray Carroll, and are good additions to this treasury of Irish art. The altar has a delightful representation of St Brendan in a ship. The new arrangements have not required the removal, alteration or destruction of the high altar and reredos; it would be as unthinkable to remove Michael Shortall's altar as it would be to remove one of the An Túr Gloine windows.

Loughrea Cathedral is a delight to visit. The exterior is bland and unpromising Gothic Revival, but the visitor who is willing patiently to explore the interior, and who is desirous of learning something of the 20th-century history of Irish art, will be delighted by the richness of its decoration and furnishing.

References

1   Thomas MacGreevy, 'St Brendan's Cathedral, Loughrea, 1897–1947' in *Capuchin Annual* (1946–7), p. 355.

LOUTH

The Cathedral Church of St Mary

LOUTH is the smallest county in Ireland and takes its name from a small village 11.25km south-west of Dundalk and 8km north of Ardee. The site is said to have been a druidic centre; this possibly accounts for the name Louth (*Lúbhadh* in modern Irish), which has been variously derived from the name of the Celtic god Lugh or from *luibh* (herb). A monastery was founded here by St Mochta who died *c.* 535. Nothing for certain is known about Mochta, although it has been claimed that he was a Briton. Stories that he lived to be 300 and had a court of 200 bishops and 300 priests are poetic fables. His feast-day is 19 August.

Louth achieved temporary prominence in the 12th century, when for a few decades it became the see of the diocese of Clogher. Clogher was established as a territorial diocese at the Synod of Ráith Bressail, but unlike other Irish dioceses it was not co-terminous with a distinct tribal area; it was simply the small territory of Clogher with a small part of the present Co. Fermanagh. The diocese lay within the domains of Donnchad Ua Cerbaill (O'Carroll), King of Airgialla (Oriel), whose kingdom also included Monaghan and Louth, both in the archdiocese of Armagh. The king was at the height of his power in the early 12th century, and by his wish Monaghan and Louth were surrendered by the Archbishop of Armagh to the Bishop of Clogher whose diocese was thereby extended to cover the whole of the Oirghiallan kingdom. Some bishops in the the 12th century were styled Bishops of Airgialla. Either Bishop Gilla Críst Ua Morgair (1135–8) or Bishop Áed Ua Cáellaide (1138–78) then moved the see c.1138 from Clogher to Louth. The monastery was burned in 1148 (and again in 1152, 1160 and 1166) and refounded in the same year as an Augustinian priory under the dedication of St Mary; the priors were mitred and sat in parliament.

By the end of the 12th century the power of the kingdom of Oriel was waning. Louth was reincorporated into the archdiocese of Armagh, probably at the Synod of Dublin in 1192, and the see was returned to Clogher. Though its days as a cathedral church were over, Louth continued as an Augustinian priory until the dissolution of the monasteries in the 16th century. The only disaster that punctuated its later history was the destruction of the priory by fire in 1312; the surviving church is largely an early 14th-century post-fire rebuilding. Since a general chapter of Augustinian Canons was held at Louth in 1325, it seems reasonable to assume that the church was complete by that date.

Mochta's House, everything else has disappeared. The presence of two castles in such a place sound unlikely, but if they did exist, one at least may have stood on the Anglo-Norman motte which overlooks the graveyard in the centre of the village.

The ruined church stands adjacent to a derelict graveyard which contains what may be an ancient oratory, subsequently used as a tomb. The church is long and narrow, measuring 46.9m by 4.9m, and was divided into a nave and chancel by a crossing wall of which a fragment remains; the chancel is 26.9m long. It has recently been suggested that this crossing wall may in fact be the remains of a slender tower.[1] The east, west and and south walls of the church are intact, but less than a quarter of the original north wall remains, the rest being the result of rebuilding after the church had fallen into ruin. The original section in the chancel contains a blocked doorway with a rounded internal masonry arch; presumably it led to the monastic buildings which have gone. To the east are the remains of two windows. One was rectangular and small; only the wide internal masonry arch remains of the other.

The east wall has a large pointed window, partly blocked, with several vertical lights and the remains of complex trac-

Louth: St Mochta's House and the priory church

At the dissolution of the monasteries Louth was found to have a priory, rectory, church, two castles, hall, bake-house, pigeon-house and granary. With the exception of the church and the 'pigeon-house' which is probably a misnomer for St

ery. The window is crowned by a higher and wider arch with a drip-moulding on the inner face. The internal ashlar arch and the exterior masonry arch are clearly visible. A finely carved though weathered head sporting a smile can be seen at the northern end of the drip-moulding. This moulding may have acted as a surround for a number of narrow lancets; alternatively, this intention may have been cancelled in favour of the present window during the course of construction. The west wall has a pointed window set fairly high in the gable.

The south wall of the nave has an open square-headed door at the west end. High up in the wall are some apparently dressed blocks of limestone which may have come from a Romanesque window. The south wall of the chancel has four windows, most partly blocked. The windows are basically 15th century, though the eastern window is Decorated. A narrow squint and a niche for an elaborate wall tomb can also be seen.

A small restored oratory known as St Mochta's House stands in the middle of a field about one hundred metres west of the church. It dates from the 12th century and belongs to the category which includes St Kevin's Church at Glendalough, St Flannan's Oratory at Killaloe, and St Columba's House at Kells, though the roof is not pitched so steeply as those at Glendalough and Kells. The house is a single cell with a vaulted roof, above which is a croft with a pointed vault. Its external measurements are 6.2m by 5.1m, and the apex of the roof is 7.1m above ground. The croft is lit by a small window and reached by narrow stairs. The protecting wall was built in 1906, and the door and windows are modern, probably dating from the restoration of 1934.

Thackeray visited Louth in the 1840s and thought it 'a fine ruin, the windows of a good style, the tracings of carvings on many of them'. But the place had a creepy atmosphere. 'A great number of stones and ornaments were removed formerly to build farm-buildings withal, and the place is now as rank and ruinous as the generality of Irish burying places seem to be. Skulls lie in clusters amongst nettle beds by the abbey-walls; graves are only partially covered with rude stones; a fresh coffin was lying broken in pieces, within the abbey; and the surgeon of the dispensary hard by might procure subjects here, almost without grave-breaking.'[2]

The priory church must have been an impressive building in its day, but it now looks rather gaunt and tragic.

References

1   Peter Harbison, 'New light on St Mary's "Abbey", Louth' *in County Louth Archaeological and Historical Society Journal*, xviii, no. 1 (1973), p. 40.

2   W. M. Thackeray, *The Irish sketch-book* (London, 1843), ii, 204.

MAGHERA

The Cathedral Church of the Blessed Virgin Mary

*M*AGHERA (*Machaire rátha* – plain of the ring-fort) is a small town of about 2,000 inhabitants in Co. Londonderry, 62.4km north-west of Belfast and 56km south-east of Derry. A church was founded here by St Lurach (Lowry), probably in the 6th century. His burial place is said to be on a little knoll about 35m west of the cathedral in the old graveyard; a small rough pillar-stone marks the alleged grave.

Maghera was the episcopal see of the diocese of Derry for a century after the Synod of Kells–Mellifont. The synod's choice of this obscure site was motivated partly by Bishop Mauricius Ua Cobthaig (1152–73), who had strong family connections with Maghera, and partly by a desire for an episcopal see which would not be overshadowed by the great Columban church of Derry, whose abbot was given mitred status in 1158. In 1247 Bishop Germanus Ó Cerbailláin (*c*.1230–79) petitioned the pope to transfer the see to Derry; a decision to this effect was confirmed on 31 May 1247 and finally made effective in 1254.

The last echo of Maghera's association with the episcopate occurred on 3 April 1471 when Thomas Ingleby, an absentee English adventurer, secured provision to the extinct see from Pope Paul II. He appears as a suffragan bishop in the diocese of Lincoln on 1 February 1475, and again in London on 25 April 1491. Nothing further is known of him.

The ruined cathedral church stands at the eastern end of the town on the south side of the main Belfast–Derry road in a walled and overgrown graveyard. After the removal of the see to Derry in 1254 Maghera became a parish church and was taxed as such in 1306. In 1622 it was 'repayred', burnt in 1641, damaged by fighting in 1688, and repaired again in

1693. It was reported to be in good repair in 1768, but was abandoned in 1819.

The cathedral is built of rubble and dates from several different periods. The nave is 10th century and is built of very large irregularly sized stones. It represents the original church, which was a simple rectangle measuring 11.5m long by 6.4m wide. A chancel and an elaborate west doorway were added after Maghera became the see of the diocese. The chancel is 8.8m long by 6.4m wide, and there are remaining fragments of the chancel arch. The west wall, much of the north wall and about half of the south wall remain. The east wall, including an aumbry base with grooved decoration, stands less than 1m high. There is no surviving window tracery, though the centre window on the south wall has traces of a 17th-century sandstone side mullion. A large and ugly early 19th-century tomb of the Hamilton family occupies about half of the south side of the nave.

the cross kneels Longinus with his spear and the sponge-bearing soldier. The sculptor has carved in relief the drops of blood which spurt from Christ's wound onto Longinus. Eleven standing figures represent the Apostles, each with an identifiable symbol, though all are very weathered. The door jambs and frames are carved with chequers, interlace, plant and animal patterns. The figure on the right at the top of the frame is a bishop, wearing mitre and vestments and carrying a crozier. The door is now sheltered by the tower, which was added in the 17th century.

Extensive renovations to the cathedral were completed in 1984 and included the provision of a roof, doors and windows for the tower to give the Romanesque doorway a dry environment. The tower originally had four floors indicated by external banding and is inset at each floor. The lower part of a sheela-na-gig is built into the north side of the tower about 6m from the ground.

Maghera Cathedral from the north-west

The architectural gem of Maghera is the Romanesque west doorway, which has a semi-circular arch within but is square-headed outside with inclined jambs. The lintel is a block of hewn stone, 1.6m long and 0.6m deep, carved with a curious representation of the Crucifixion, which is the most detailed treatment of the subject in early Irish art. The cross is almost a 'T' and is barely higher than the figure of Christ. Beneath

The cathedral was abandoned in 1819 when a new parish church was built across the road. Dedicated to St Lurach, it is a First-Fruits Gothic church of 1819, built to a standard design by John Bowden. The tower is tapered in three stages and has large pinnacles. The chancel, of basalt rubble, was added in 1864 to designs by Welland & Gillespie.

Maghera: the Early Christian door lintel

MAYO

The Cathedral Church of St Michael

*M*AYO (*Magh eo* – plain of the yew trees) is about 4km south-east of Eyrecourt in Co. Mayo. The Celtic monastery at Mayo was founded in the second half of the 7th century by St Colman of Lindisfarne. Colman was chosen as third Abbot-Bishop of Lindisfarne, but his reluctance to accept the Roman traditions prescribed for England at the Synod of Whitby in 664 led him to withdraw with about thirty of his monks to Ireland. In 668 he founded an abbey on Inishbofin, an island off the coast of Co. Galway with a group of Irish and Anglo-Saxon monks. Within three years disputes arose between the two races, and Colman founded Mayo for the Anglo-Saxon monks, ruling both monasteries until his death in 674 or 676. His feast-day is 18 February. He was succeeded by St Gerald, who died in 732.

The foundation at Mayo became known as Magh Eo na Sacsain and retained its English character for some considerable time. As late as 1380 a decision was made that no Irishman was to be professed here. The monastery was famed throughout Europe as a centre of learning and was praised by St Bede the Venerable. A legend tells that Alfred the Great studied here.

A diocese of Mayo was established at the Synod of Kells–Mellifont in 1152, but it lasted only fifty years before being amalgamated with Tuam in 1202 by John of Salerno, the papal legate, when he installed a new archbishop. The extent of the diocese is not known, but it was probably coterminous with the later deanery of Mayo in one of the wildest and poorest parts of the diocese of Tuam. The existence of the dioceses of Mayo and Annaghdown at the end of the 12th century would have reduced the diocese of Tuam to a very small area, and it was inevitable that the Archbishops of Tuam would seek to annex one or other; eventually they annexed both.

It is possible that Bishop Céle Ua Dubthaig (?–1210), the last substantive Bishop of Mayo, was a rival candidate for the archbishopric who was expelled by the legate, and that the see of Mayo was being used as a backdoor to ensure eventual succession to the archbishopric by members of the Ua Dubthaig family.

Archbishop Eugenius of Armagh revoked the legate's decision *c.*1215 and claimed Mayo for the province of Armagh. The case was brought before Pope Innocent III, who gave judgement in favour of Tuam. Not content with the ruling of one pope, the archbishop raised the matter with Innocent's successor Pope Honorius III, claiming that John of Salerno had been deceived. The pope ordered an inquiry in November 1217, and a legate, James of St Victor, was appointed to examine the case. The legate, who visited Ireland in 1221, pronounced against Armagh and upheld the claims of Tuam, and his judgement was maintained by Pope Gregory IX on 3 July 1240.

After the suppression of the diocese the abbey church became a secular collegiate church until *c.*1370, when Archbishop John O'Grady of Tuam (1364–71) converted it into an Augustinian abbey with an abbot and five or six Canons Regular — a decision confirmed by the pope on 8 November 1411.

A completely muddled succession of titular, non-resident Bishops of Mayo appeared from 1428 onwards. Two Franciscans were appointed in 1428 and 1430; William Prendergast was deprived in 1430 'for not having expedited his letters of provision'[1], another way of saying that he had not visited his diocese; his successor, Brother Nicholas, declined the honour. A Dutch Cistercian, Martin Campania, was appointed in 1432, and acted as a suffragan in Holland for the next twenty-five years. During his time Abbot Hugh O'Higgins obtained provision to the see in 1439, but was deprived after an appeal to the pope in 1447, when instructions were given to reduce the church to its former status. Martin Campania died in 1457, but was replaced by a German friar, Simon de Düren, who acted as a suffragan in Worms. In his petition to Pope Calixtus III he sought a dispensation to hold benefices in Germany, since Mayo was situated *in partibus infidelium*, and its fruits were in the possession of infidels and enemies of the Christian name. An Englishman, John Bell, was appointed in 1493 and acted as a suffragan in England 1493–*c.* 1530. Nothing is known of his activities and he died in 1541. Eugene MacBrehon was Bishop of Mayo from 1541 to *c.*1559, but the see was effectively held by Archbishop Bodkin of Tuam (1537–72). Two friars were appointed during the reign of Elizabeth I; Dermot O'Dwyer (or O'Clery) in 1574 and Patrick O'Healy in 1576. Bishop O'Healy attempted to take possession of his see in 1579, but was caught and hanged by the English. The last known papal appointment was Adam Magauran in 1585.

Absentee bishops of minor or dissolved Irish dioceses were quite common in the 15th century. Since many of the candidates were from the religious life, procurement of provision to a diocese, whether it was vacant or not, even when it had ceased to have true canonical existence, may have been a means of escaping from the duties of the religious life. Individual popes would have had only slight knowledge of affairs in Ireland, and appointments to dioceses alleged still to exist may have been easy to purchase from an unscrupulous papal courtier.

There is no real evidence that these fragmentary walls are remnants of the abbey church, but the structure is in east-west alignment with the disused church. Further support for the theory might be found in the hypothesis that after the dissolution of the monasteries the church continued to be used as such, though for a parochial congregation, and generally long outlasted the domestic buildings.

Mayo Abbey and its possessions were granted to John Rawson in 1594. But it would be reasonable to assume that at least

Mayo: the ruined Church of Ireland parish church

Mayo Abbey was a great monastic site in its day, but only fragments now remain. An unidentifiable west-gable wall covered with ivy, with north and south walls attached, constitutes the only substantial structure. There is a low doorway in the west wall, a blocked window in the north wall, and the remains of a barrel vault on the exterior of the south wall. Traces of the domestic buildings and the circular enclosure wall can be seen to the south of the churchyard. On 17 December 1411 a papal indulgence was granted for the completion of the newly built church and monastery; this would date these surviving fragments to the early 15th century. A now disused Roman Catholic church was built on part of the site of the abbey church in the 19th century; it was replaced by a new church built in recent years in the centre of Mayo.

part of the church continued to be used (as at Ardmore and Duleek) for the few members of the Church of Ireland in the vicinity. This would have continued until the building of a new parish church in 1811. This church can be seen on a hill further to the south. It was built with the help of a loan of 553 16s 11d from the Board of First-Fruits and looks lovely as a romantic ruin set on a low wooded hill in the middle distance. A closer inspection reveals a disappointingly small, plain, hall-and-tower church of the dreariest kind, typical of the First-Fruits Gothic style that was mass-produced by the board in the early 19th century. One strongly suspects that it looks better as a ruin than it did in its fully functioning days.

Mayo: the ruins of the 15th century abbey church with the disused 19th century Roman Catholic church beyond

The church was built for a relatively low sum and could seat no more than a hundred people, but it is a wonder that it was built at all. In 1834, twenty-three years after its construction, the population of Mayo comprised 37 members of the Church of Ireland and 3,312 Roman Catholics. In 1844 the usual attendance at the parish church was reckoned to be between twelve and thirty. In the light of such statistics, it is not surprising that its active life was short. The last known marriage at the church took place in 1862 and the last burial in 1875. The last incumbent died on 29 June 1876, and Mayo last appears in the Irish Church Directory for that year. It seems reasonable, therefore, to infer that the church was closed in 1876. Permission was given to demolish the building in June 1912, but, though now roofless, it is still standing.

References

1   W. H. Grattan Flood, 'The diocese and abbey of Mayo' in *Irish Ecclesiastical Record*, 4th ser., xxi (1907), p. 607.

MONAGHAN

The Cathedral Church of St Macartan

Diocese of Clogher (Roman Catholic)

THE town of Monaghan (*Muineachán* – place of the thickets) lies 129km to the north-west of Dublin and 24km south-east of Clogher. It stands at the crossroads of the north–south road between Derry and Dublin, and the east–west road between Belfast and Galway. It was the historic capital of the MacMahons, Kings of Oriel, but there is now little sign of antiquity beyond a few fragments of the friary for Conventual Franciscans founded by Felim MacMahon in 1462. The friary survived beyond the Reformation, becoming Observant in 1567, until 1588 or 1589, when the Guardian and five friars were put to death. Sir Edward Blayney, governor of Co. Monaghan during the reign of James I, built a 'plantation castle' (at Castleblayney, 24km south-east of Monaghan) using the stonework of the friary.

Monaghan Cathedral stands on a hill in Castleblayney Road on the edge of the town, at the summit of series of terraces; the site has points of similarity with the Roman Catholic

178

cathedral at Armagh, but at Monaghan the climb is shorter and the gradient is less steep, and the slopes are attractively ornamented and landscaped.

Monaghan has been the seat of the Roman Catholic Bishops of Clogher since Bishop Charles McNally (1844–64) came to live here in 1851. Clogher itself is about 32km to the north-east. Monaghan was chosen as the see for the diocese because it was a growing county town with a substantial Catholic population in the mid-19th century. Adopting the usual format, Bishop McNally called a public meeting of the Catholic people of the vicinity, on Sunday 3 January 1858. The meeting resolved to build a new Catholic Church at Monaghan, and the present eight acre site was purchased by the bishop for 800 from Humphrey Jones of Clontibret. The commission to design the cathedral went to J. J. McCarthy, 'Ireland's Pugin' and the leading Irish Catholic architect of the 19th century.

The west front of Monaghan Cathedral

Bishop McNally laid the foundation stone on 18 June 1861, and construction began in April 1862. McNally was succeeded by Bishop James Donnelly (1865–93), who saw the dedication of the cathedral on 21 August 1892 before his death in the following year. McCarthy himself died in 1882 and was succeeded by William Hague of Cavan, who designed the spire and the gate lodge. The spire was completed on 5 March 1884. Bishop Eugene O'Callaghan (1943–69) was responsible for the front entrance and the landscaping of the grounds on the west side in 1948, and the cathedral was solemnly consecrated in that year. The Bishop's House, to the east of the cathedral, was completed in 1901. It contains two windows of 1911–12 by Michael Healy of An Túr Gloine depicting Saints Macartan and Brigid and Saints Patrick and Damhnat.

Dedicated to St Macartan, the historic patron of the diocese of Clogher, McCarthy's design was in the style of 14th-century French Gothic, with a large rose window in the west front, transepts set in pointed frames, numerous turrets and pinnacles and thick stepped buttresses separating the bays, and a tower and spire elegantly attached to the south transept. The north and south transepts have pointed arcades filled with carved figures. The Chapter House and sacristies are at the north-east corner.

The exterior is rich in statuary carving. The niches on either side of the main west door, constructed in 1945, contain statues of Saints Peter and Paul in white Carrara marble, the work of Pietro Lazzerini, one of a family of prolific artist-masons at Massa Carrara in Italy who exported large quantities of Catholic statuary. The tympanum contains a high-relief carving of Christ giving the keys to St Peter. The north and south transept gables have seven-niche arcades. Those in the north transept contain statues of various figures from the Old Testament, though the last two are St Anne and St Joachim, the parents of the Blessed Virgin Mary; the statue of St Joachim bears the likeness of Pope Leo XIII (1878–1903). The statues in the south transept gable represent various Bishops of Clogher, with the exception of St Dympna of Gheel. The gallery begins with St Tiarnach, successor of St Macartan and second Bishop of Clogher, and concludes with Bishop Donnelly.

Monaghan Cathedral is cruciform, 53.9m long, 21.9m wide in the nave and 33.5m wide at the transepts. The tower and spire on the south side is 74.6m high. The nave, with aisles and a clerestory, is only five bays long (seven were planned), and the former baptistery opens off the north aisle. The chancel has a polygonal apse and double aisles to the north and south. The basic building materials are grey and cream Dungannon limestone with facings of Armagh limestone.

The nave has a hammer-beam roof with carved angel terminals resting on corbels with carved naturalistic heads; the chancel has a roof of simple ribbing. The arches, with a sky-blue and beige painted border, rest on cylindrical piers whose capitals are carved with stylised foliage. The nave is divided from its aisles by pine balustrades; there are standard nine-light brass electroliers of foliate design in each bay. A

The interior of Monaghan Cathedral looking east

THE CATHEDRALS OF IRELAND

single window in each bay of the nave aisles is matched by two windows in the clerestory above. The former baptistery, opening off the westernmost bay of the north nave aisle, contains a modern bronze Pietà. The organ gallery at the west end is supported by eight columns of polished red Aberdeen granite and was added by Hague. The decoratively painted organ pipes indicate something of the style and furnishing of the cathedral before the reordering of 1973.

The cathedral's stained glass was inserted between 1884 and 1892 and is the work of the three different companies; Meyer & Co. of Munich, Earley & Powell of Dublin, and Cox & Buckley of Youghal; none of them found favour with Bishop Donnelly. The great rose windows in the transept are filled with clear glass and shed brilliant light on to the new sanctuary arrangements at the crossing.

In 1973 the cathedral was reordered in line with the decrees of the Second Vatican Council. For the purposes of record, the pre-1973 arrangements were as follows: there was an Italian marble high altar with tabernacle set deep into the apse, backed by a tall reredos; inside the sanctuary were the canons' stalls in two rows facing each other; the altar was covered by a baldachino of slightly oriental appearance resting on four columns; the Bishop's throne on the north side of the sanctuary and the 10.6m-high pulpit at the south-west corner of the crossing were covered by gilded wooden canopies resting on marble columns; the side chapels were divided by iron grilles. All these furnishings were personally commissioned by Bishop Donnelly in Naples and Carrara.

These arrangements were entirely swept away in a re-ordering that is radical and interesting, but not altogether successful. Some reorderings of the Catholic cathedrals of Ireland have been nothing short of disastrous to architectural harmony; Killarney, Letterkenny, Limerick, Mullingar and Skibbereen are notable exceptions. The reordering at Monaghan, executed in marble and granite, is comparable to that of the Catholic Cathedral at Armagh in its harsh contrast with the surrounding 19th-century Gothic Revival. The architect was Michael Biggs, who was also responsible for the work in the side chapels, which are equally radical but somehow more successful.

The Chapels of the Blessed Sacrament and of Reconciliation are on the south side of the chancel. The baptistery and the Chapel of the Holy Oils are on the north side. The tabernacle in the Chapel of the Blessed Sacrament is of silver plate and sculpted bronze and carved in the unusual form of a tent, the symbolic dwelling-place of the Lord in the Old Testament. The tabernacle is encircled by the words 'SOLAS DÉ' (light of God) and was designed by Richard King.

The Chapel of Reconciliation contains a most unusual confessional or reconciliation room which echoes the beehive hut design of monasteries in Early Christian Ireland. It was designed by Michael Biggs and constructed of solid unpolished blocks of travertine marble. The Irish inscription is a translation of Mark 6:50–51: 'Jesus said to them: It is I. Do not be afraid. Then he got into the boat with them, and the wind dropped.' The room is quite incongruous in this setting, but it has appeal.

The font in the baptistery is set in a symbolic pool, a circle of dark-green tiling with a white marble border. The aumbry in the Chapel of the Holy Oils to the north of the baptistery is recessed in the east wall. It contains three pewter jars containing the Oil of Catechumens, the Oil of the Sick and the Oil of Chrism. The aumbry gates, locks and bolts were designed by Michael Biggs and executed in bronze by Michael Leonard.

A central granite throne, flanked by curved benches for concelebrants, now stands at the east end of a long dais of travertine marble which sweeps down to the crossing. Ten steps up from the floor of the nave, the throne is higher than the new altar and has a cold and bare look. A circular brass plaque set in the back of the throne bears the inscription 'HAEC EST SEDES EPISCOPALIS CLOGHERENSIS' (This is the seat of the Bishop of Clogher). The new altar is a single piece of South Dublin granite weighing six tons and hand-carved in the shape of a *tau*-cross. The ambo and cantor's lectern, both also of granite, are sited on curved platforms to the north and south of the altar respectively. Three vividly coloured tapestries representing Baptism, St Macartan and the Eucharist (in the baptistery, sanctuary and Chapel of the Blessed Sacrament, all designed by Frances Biggs) do little to make the scene any less cheerless; they only compete for attention with the tall east windows.

There are two problems with this otherwise interesting arrangement: firstly, there is the common though not universal feature of post-Vatican II reorderings, namely a deliberate attempt to make a total break with the architectural style of the host building; secondly, the arrangements at Monaghan convey a impression of total emptiness. The new arrangement probably works very well indeed during the celebration of mass, at least when the throne and benches are occupied by the bishop and concelebrants. When mass is not being concelebrated by a large number of priests and the cathedral is empty, then this expanse of plain granite and marble seems remorselessly to declare and to emphasise the emptiness. Apart from the presence of the Blessed Sacrament, now out of immediate sight in a side chapel, there is nothing at the east end to attract and hold the attention of those who come individually for quiet prayer and meditation. In a great Gothic church of this kind, the eye is naturally drawn towards the east, to the presence of the Blessed Sacrament enthroned on the altar, visible from every seat in the nave. Now the eye is allowed to rest on a set of empty seats which, by virtue of their unoccupied state, loudly proclaim not a presence but an absence.

MULLINGAR

The Cathedral Church of Christ the King

Diocese of Meath (Roman Catholic)

MULLINGAR (*Muileann cearr* – wry or left-handed mill), 79km west of Dublin and 38.4km east of Longford, is the county town of Co. Westmeath and the market centre of a cattle-rearing district.

Two early Celtic saints are associated with Mullingar. St Loman, a disciple and alleged nephew of St Patrick, built a

father. Not having enough, his father sent Colman to the mill with a sack of barley seed. Colman found the king's wheat being put under the mill. He asked for the mill to be stopped because he was in a hurry. The steward refused, so they put their loads in on different sides. Colman put his hand against the wheel and turned it to the left, so giving Mullingar its name. By a miracle the wheat and barley were reversed, so Colman left with the wheat, and the steward with the barley.

The site of Colman's foundation is to be seen 4.8km south-west of Mullingar near the north-east corner of Lough Ennell. The fragmentary remains of Lynn church mark the site of his monastery. The monastery, church and shrine, together

Mullingar Cathedral from the north-west

monastery at Port Lomáin, 8km to the north-west on the shore of Lough Owel, and is said to have been the first Bishop of Trim; he died *c.* 450. The site contains the remains of a medieval church, called Portloman 'Abbey', founded on the site of the monastery. There is a decorated medieval gravestone in the cemetery.

St Colman of Lynn, who was born *c.* 600, was baptised at Port Lomáin. In his youth the steward of the King of Meath went to demand three hundred cakes of wheaten meal of Colman's

with the saint's relics, were destroyed in 1394 by Muircheartach Óg Mac Eochagáin.

After the Anglo-Norman invasion Mullingar was a manor granted by Hugh de Lacy to William le Petit. Ralph Petit, Bishop of Meath 1227–30 founded an Augustinian priory at Mullingar *c.* 1227 which flourished until until the dissolution of the monasteries in 1539.

During the penal years mass was celebrated in the open at

what was then called the Mass Bush. The site in Violetstown is marked by the Mass Bush Memorial. When the penal laws were relaxed in the 18th century, mass was celebrated regularly in the town in the drying-room of a tannery belonging to the Dowdall family. The first purpose-built Catholic church after the Reformation was a modest chapel built in 1730 near the site of the present cathedral. It was replaced in 1831–6 by a cathedral church dedicated to St Mary, a Gothic Revival building with four octagonal turrets on the west front, of which the clock survives in its new location at the Ennis Pro-Cathedral.

'classical' and 'modernized renaissance', has a successful style of its own which is reminiscent of the work of Sir Edwin Lutyens in Delhi: square banded towers rise from the roof of the narthex and become more ornate towards their tops, which finish in small domes. The clerestory stage pushes its way out between the towers like a train emerging from a station. The tympanum contains a frieze in Portland stone by Albert Power showing the Blessed Virgin Mary giving a model of the old cathedral into the care of Christ the King.

The interior of Mullingar Cathedral looking east

St Mary's Cathedral was replaced by the present cathedral, built during the episcopate of Bishop Thomas Mulvany (1929–43), which stands on the site of its predecessor. The dedication of the new cathedral, to Christ the King, was made at the request Pope Pius XI. The foundation stone was laid on 6 August 1933, and the dedication service was held on 6 September 1936. The consecration took place on 4 September 1939. The total cost was approximately £250,000.

The cathedral, which seats about 1,800 people, was designed in the classical style by Ralph Byrne and takes the form of a Roman basilica with twin west towers, 42.6m high, and a dome at the crossing. The exterior, variously described as

The nave is 36.5m long and 15.2m wide and follows the pattern of the great Roman basilicas such as St Paul's-Without-the-Walls, to which it bears a resemblance by its forest of columns. It has a flat coffered ceiling and is separated from the side aisles by colonnades of Rochambeau marble Doric columns with caps and bases of Irish marble. The Stations of the Cross between the arches of the nave columns are in *opus sectile* and mosaic. The baptistery on the right of the main door has a marble font and bronze gates and railings. The pulpit, of white marble, has carvings depicting the Sermon on the Mount, St John the Baptist and St Patrick.

The cathedral has seven chapels. The Chapel of St Therese of Lisieux, Patroness of Foreign Missions, has a mosaic over the altar representing the conversion of many different races to Christianity.

The Chapel of St Anne has a mosaic executed by Boris Anrep in 1954. It depicts the Presentation of the Blessed Virgin Mary in the Temple by her mother, St Anne. She is accompanied by St Joachim, and on the temple steps the high priest is waiting to receive her. The mosaic above depicts the glorification of the Blessed Virgin Mary and her coronation in heaven.

The Mortuary Chapel has a fresco by Fr Aengus Buckley, O.P., depicting the Resurrection of Christ from the dead, and the new hope among those detained in limbo.

The Lady Chapel is dedicated to Our Lady of Lourdes, the subject of the marble group behind the altar.

The altar in the Chapel of the Blessed Sacrament stands against a background of marble and gold mosaic, enshrining the Saints of the Blessed Sacrament in *opus sectile*.

The Chapel of St Patrick is embellished with mosaics, again by Boris Anrep. It was executed in 1948 and shows St Patrick lighting the Paschal Fire on the Hill of Slane in 433. The logs of the fire take the form of a Christogram signifying the symbolical importance of the fire. Lightning from the throne of Christ in heaven destroys a pagan idol, and beneath the pedestal the banished snakes creep away.

The Chapel of St Joseph and the Holy Family contains a marble group of the Holy Family by Early of Dublin. The mosaics depict the life of St Joseph.

The chancel and sanctuary contain an impressive array of coloured marbles used to magnificent effect. The mosaic in the apse represents the Ascension of Christ into Heaven. The altar rails are of white marble with panels of lapis lazuli and gold. The chancel floor is made of a variety of marbles, mostly Irish, and contains mosaics of St Loman, St Columba, St Finian and St Oliver Plunkett, saints of the diocese of Meath. The cathedra and choir stalls are of Irish oak and were carved in Waterford.

It has been reordered in accordance with the requirements of Vatican II, but with such care and taste that the difference is hardly noticeable, and the harmony of the building is preserved. The high altar, which has been moved forward, is of white, green and variegated marbles, with a central panel of green onyx with jasper markings. The door of the tabernacle formerly on the high altar was coated with 22 carat gold and ornamented with rich jewels in a Celtic design.

The interior of Mullingar Cathedral was designed as an elegant Renaissance basilica and, like Longford Cathedral, has little reference to any traditional Irish architectural styles. But the interior is a very impressive sight of its kind, and

Mullingar has a good claim to be one of the most stylishly triumphant Irish cathedrals. Passing through the west narthex into the nave for the first time is an overwhelming experience, and visitors might imagine themselves to be in a basilica in the heart of Rome.

The cathedral is adjoined on the right by Cathedral House, the residence of the parochial clergy, built in 1873, and on the left by St Mary's National Schools, built in 1958–9, and St Mary's College, built in 1858.

NEWRY

The Cathedral Church of St Patrick and St Colman

Diocese of Dromore (Roman Catholic)

NEWRY (*An iubhar* – the yew tree), fringed by hills, is an old border town and seaport in Co. Down on the main Dublin–Belfast road. Belfast is 60.8km to the north, and Dublin is 104km to the south. The name of the town is said to derive from a yew tree planted by St Patrick beside a church that he founded. Others consider that there was no monastery here before the foundation of a Benedictine abbey in 1144 by St Malachy and Donnchad Ua Cerbaill, King of Oriel. The abbey adopted the Cistercian rule in 1153. After the dissolution the site of the abbey was given to Sir Nicholas Bagnall in 1552; there is no surviving trace.

Newry became the *de facto* seat of the Roman Catholic Bishops of Dromore in the time of Bishop Anthony O'Garvey (1747–66). A small house built in 1740 served as a chapel until the construction of St Mary's Church in Chapel Street in 1789. St Mary's was used as the pro-cathedral for about thirty years until, in turn, it became too small to hold the congregation and was superseded by the construction of the present cathedral in Hill Street.

The initiative for building a cathedral came from Hugh O'Kelly, Bishop of Dromore 1820–25, who inaugurated plans soon after his appointment. A building committee was formed, and the search for a suitable site began. The Marquess of Downshire was approached, but either had nothing available and suitable or was not disposed to grant their request since two and half years passed before 'the swamp beside the Mill Race, known as Seymour's Green' was purchased from John Johnson and James Coulter on 20 September 1823.[1]

Bishop O'Kelly had the satisfaction of laying the foundation stone of his cathedral church on 8 June 1825, two months before his death. Construction lasted four years, and the dedication service on 6 May 1829 was the first of a Roman Catholic cathedral in Ireland after the passage of the Roman Catholic Relief Act which removed virtually all civil disabilities.

The architect was Thomas Duff, and he designed a cathedral in the Perpendicular Gothic style. His success at Newry probably led to the commission to design the cathedral at Armagh in 1840. Duff's design consisted of a single nave-chancel with aisles and clerestory, probably of seven bays, without

structural division, 36.5m long and 21.3m wide. Later additions have extended the length to nearly 58m and the width to 41m; the nave is 14m high.

The usual lack of funds postponed interior decoration, and when Thackeray visited Newry in 1841 he remarked sarcastically: 'The Cathedral is a fine building, but . . . the interior is quite unfinished and already so ruinous that one would think a kind of genius for dilapidation must have been exercised to bring it into its present condition.' But he thought the church 'noble and simple in style, and one cannot but grieve to see a fine work of art that might have done good in the country so defaced and ruined as it is'.[2] The interior was decorated in 1851, but because of extensions to the cathedral, and the passage of time, nothing remains of this work.

The second phase of building in the 1888–90 was stimulated by the visit of a papal envoy to Ireland. The envoy, Archbishop Persico of Damietta, rather unkindly told the elderly Bishop John Leahy of Dromore (1860–90) that his cathedral was not in keeping with the dignity of the diocese. The bishop was too old to act in obedience to the implications of the envoy's remarks and charged his coadjutor and succes-

Newry Cathedral from the south-west

sor, Thomas McGivern (Bishop of Dromore 1890–1900) with the task of improving the standard of the cathedral. Two transepts were added in 1888, a tower was added at the north side, sacristies to the rear, and a new porch at the front, at a total cost of £12,000.

The third and final stage of building, in 1904–9, was due to the efforts of Bishop Henry O'Neill (1901–15). The supervising architect was G. C. Ashlin, who had designed the spectacularly sited cathedral at Cobh. The sacristy at the rear of the sanctuary was dismantled and rebuilt to allow for a 9m extension to the sanctuary. The shallow square sanctuary with a single Perpendicular window was replaced by a deeper polygonal apse with five windows. The cathedral was extended 12m to the west by the addition of a further bay, but the west front was taken down and rebuilt in its original form. The entire interior decoration in mosaic, by Oppenheimer of Manchester, was also executed in the 1904–9 phase.

Known since its construction as St Patrick's Pro-Cathedral, it was raised to the status of a full cathedral church on 7 March 1919, and the name of St Colman was added to the dedication. With all the debts cleared and the purchase of the ground rents secured, the cathedral was solemnly consecrated by Bishop Edward Mulhern (1916–43) on 21 July 1925.

The cathedral as completed in 1909 is what the visitor sees today, and, despite the various dates of construction, it achieves a remarkable harmony of appearance. It is a handsome and romantic crisp little castle that might well have come from a film-set about jousting knights and chivalrous deeds in the Middle Ages. It is built of coursed, roughdressed or wrought granite, which was cleaned by sandblasting in 1970. The west front, approached by an expansive terrace of five granite steps, has a deeply receding and highly ornamented central Norman doorway flanked by twin octagonal Norman turrets. The walls are crowned by a wonderfully medieval-looking crenellated parapet. Slender buttresses indicate the bays of the aisles, and pinnacled pilasters with decorative arches and finials, some 21m above the ground, fulfil the same function for the clerestory.

The chief attraction of the exterior of Newry Cathedral is the 42.6m tower, which is plain for most of its height but becomes increasingly elaborate towards the top. The upper part of the tower has tall, unglazed, balconied and recessed Perpendicular windows on each face. The windows are flanked by ornamented pilasters and crowned with blind arcades. Above the arcades the tower suddenly transforms itself into an astonishing sight which carries the romanticism of the cathedral below to new heights. A balustrade joins four elaborate pierced square corner turrets of three storeys with battlements, pinnacles and richly crocketed spirelets, and four smaller ornamented towers and spirelets at the mid-point on

each side, to form a perfectly detailed and quite delightful miniature fantasy castle.

The tower was entirely the work of local sculptors, and its summit is matched only by the tower of St Patrick's Church in Dundalk. Thomas Duff was the architect at Dundalk, which was built in 1835–47, and the tower at Newry is almost a duplicate of that at Dundalk. It is possible that, although the Newry tower was completed long after Duff's death, he had himself sketched out the design for it, copying his work at Dundalk. Alternatively, it may be that a later architect simply reproduced the Dundalk tower at Newry.

The nave has a rib-vaulted ceiling and is separated from the aisles by a lofty arcade of obtuse-angled arches springing from granite clustered columns. Over the arcade and round the clerestory windows are found the names of the parishes of the diocese worked in Gothic lettering on shields, between floral designs and medallions with busts of saints. Along the walls of the aisles are ogee-headed mosaic cartouches with portraits of saints, also by Oppenheimer. The Stations of the Cross are executed in terra-cotta. Almost every wall surface is covered with mosaic, which gives the interior the effect of a splendidly wall-papered Edwardian drawing-room. It must have been an immense labour, but the result is a beautiful and permanent strength of decoration that will save the cathedral authorities the periodic agony of replastering and repainting. The hanging lantern lights were installed in 1950.

The clustered columns supporting the chancel arch and the other sanctuary columns are of polished Newry grey and Balmoral red granite. The sanctuary steps are of polished Peterhead red granite. Despite their names, Balmoral red and Peterhead red come from Finland – the Scottish names are only for trade purposes.

The sanctuary and side chapels are beautifully decorated in a variety of Italian marbles. The lower part of the sanctuary walls are panelled in Levanto red, Porta Santa and Paonazzo marbles, and the upper part is finished in gold and coloured mosaics. The sanctuary windows are by Messrs Oppenheimer of Manchester and were inserted in the years 1908–14.

For several years after the Second Vatican Council a temporary wooden altar and lectern were in use at the front of the sanctuary. Functional as they were, their quality and appearance were not in keeping with the style and beauty of the cathedral. A permanent reordering of the sanctuary and chapels and a thorough cleaning of the interior of the cathedral took place in 1989–90, in accordance with the decrees of the Council. The sanctuary arrangements in place before 1989 were as follows. The high altar (erected in 1891 as a memorial to bishop Leahy) was constructed in white Carrara and statuary marble, with columns of Siena and Verdi Alpi, and small panels of Porta Santa, the whole backed by an elegant turreted reredos. The front panel was a carving in Sicilian marble of Leonardo da Vinci's Last Supper. The altar rails enclosing the sanctuary and side chapels were of white Carrara marble with colonettes of red Cork marble. The sanctuary was divided from the side chapels by carved screens of Carrara marble. The bishop's throne, also of Carrara marble and turreted to harmonise with the high altar, was on the south side of the sanctuary.

The reordering at Newry has been performed with considerable thought, care and taste, and deserves warm congratulations. This is possibly the most successful reordering of a Roman Catholic Cathedral in Ireland. Being one of the more recent of cathedral reorderings, it may indicate that lessons have been learned from disastrous mistakes made elsewhere.

The former sanctuary has been extended to cover the crossing area. Because of the widespread use of mosaic in the cathedral, it was decided that, despite the expense, mosaic would be used throughout for the flooring in the new sanctuary area and the transepts. Whereas the existing mosaic floor was of ceramic material, the new floors, designed and laid by Centro Domus Dei of Rome, are of natural marble. The new sanctuary steps are of Botticino marble. The 1891 altar rails have mostly been removed, though two small sections remain on the north and south sides for the benefit of those who still wish to receive communion kneeling.

The new altar, placed in the centre of the crossing, consists of a large slab of white Carrara marble resting on rectangular pillars inset with Breccia Pernice marble. The front panel, a representation of Leonardo da Vinci's Last Supper, was taken from the former high altar of 1891. The side panels depict the Crown of Thorns and Nails of Crucifixion, and the Bird and Grape, symbolic of the sacrificial character of the Mass. The altar contains relics of St Felicissimus, St Virginia and St Columbanus, placed in the old high altar at the consecration in 1925, and St Oliver Plunkett and St Malachy.

The white marble pulpit, dating from the alterations of 1888–90, has a front panel depicting the Sermon on the Mount. Under the new arrangements, it has been kept in position as the ambo or lectern.

The bishop's throne has been retained and is now positioned against a cluster of columns at the north-east of the crossing. A new panel at the back of the throne depicts the 14th-century seal of the Bishops of Dromore.

The area occupied by the 1891 high altar has been imaginatively reconstructed instead of being allowed to remain vacant as an embarrassing retrochoir. The turreted reredos has been divided into three sections. The central portion forms a backdrop to the tabernacle, which now rests on a plinth of white Carrara marble with panels of Breccia Pernice between columns of Rosso Verona marble. The two side portions, of white Carrara and statuary marble with columns of green Siena and Verdi Alpi marble and small panels of Porta Santa

marble, are fronted by similar plinths to that supporting the tabernacle. The north portion of the reredos carries a sculpture of the Nativity, and the south portion a sculpture of Christ commissioning his Apostles. To the north and south are marble seraphs, which formerly flanked the old altar, now symbolically guarding the Blessed Sacrament.

The Chapel of the Blessed Virgin on the north side of the chancel is now used as a Marian shrine. Invocations from the Litany of the Blessed Virgin, all worked in mosaic, can be seen on the walls around the altar. The altar itself is of Carrara marble with columns of Siena and Rosso Corallo with small panels in Levanto red. The marble statue above the tabernacle is of Our Lady of Lourdes. The two small panels in the marble reredos present the Annunciation and the Coronation of the Virgin. The sanctuary lamp was presented in 1925 to mark the centenary of the consecration.

The former Chapel of St Joseph on the south side of the chancel has an altar of Carrara marble with columns in Siena and Porta Santa presented in 1908. A gilt door, centred by red onyx columns, encloses the tabernacle, over which stands a statue of St Joseph. In the marble reredos are panels showing the betrothal of Joseph and Mary, and the Holy Family in their workshop at Nazareth. The sanctuary wall contains a number of invocations in mosaic to St Joseph. The sanctuary lamp was a gift in 1925.

This chapel is now used as the baptistery. The font was formerly located in a small mosaic alcove in the entrance porch below the cathedral tower. Because of inadequate accommodation when several baptisms were taking place, and also because of the draughtiness of the area, the font was moved to St Joseph's Chapel.

In the north transept is the shrine of the Sacred Heart. The altar is of Carrara marble with panels in Rosso Amiato. The columns in the reredos are in Rosso Corallo, the others in Verde Serpentino and Siena. The upper panels to the side of the reredos are in Paonazzo. Over the altar is a shrine portraying Christ revealing his sorrows to St Margaret Mary.

Newry Cathedral has not escaped the troubles of Northern Ireland in recent years. On 9 August 1971 the front windows were shattered by the blast of a bomb which had been placed outside the front door of the Allied Irish Bank facing the cathedral. Several stained-glass windows were shattered on 20 July 1972 by the explosion of a bomb placed in the post office in Hill Street.

References

1   Edward Campbell, *Cathedral of Saints Patrick and Colman, Newry* (Newry, 1948; revised ed. by Anthony Davies, Newry, 1979), p. 7.

2   W. M. Thackeray, *The Irish sketch-book* (London, 1843), ii, 213.

RAPHOE

The Cathedral Church of St Eunan

Diocese of Raphoe (Church of Ireland)

RAPHOE, a village of about 1,000 inhabitants in Co. Donegal, is 11.2km north-west of Strabane and 25.6km south-west of Derry. The name Raphoe derives from *Ráith both,* meaning 'ring-fort of the huts', and is presumably an allusion to the earliest form of Irish monastery – beehive huts clustering around a church.

The early history of Raphoe is very obscure. A monastery is said to have been founded here in the 6th century by St Columba. But the cathedral is dedicated to St Adamnan or Eunan (*c.* 625–704), an Irishman who became ninth Abbot of Iona in 679. He is said to have zealously advocated the Roman observance of Easter, which his own abbey did not adopt. He is best remembered as the author of a life of his kinsman St Columba. His feast-day is 23 September.

The names of the first three territorial Bishops of Raphoe are known only from a 17th-century catalogue, but their dates are unknown, and no Bishop of Raphoe was present at the Synod of Kells–Mellifont in 1152. The diocese began to take shape in the late 12th century and was well established by the end of the 13th century.

The small and comfortable cathedral is rather difficult to date with any precision. It contains medieval elements, but substantial rebuilding and restoration on several occasions has left it as an essentially 17th/19th-century structure. Only the sedilia, the range of lancet windows in the south wall and the fragments of a piscina are visible remnants of the medieval fabric. If there is anything else, it remains well hidden.

When Bishop Andrew Knox (1611–33) first arrived at Raphoe, he found the cathedral, then a simple rectangle, 'ruinated and decayed' and spent several years rebuilding it. In 1738–40 two transepts, the tower and the south-west Galilee porch were added to the cathedral as the result of a generous bequest from John Pooley (Bishop of Raphoe 1702–12). The transepts were probably quite small; one was used as a vestry and the other for the pews of the bishop and the dean.

In 1876 the cathedral was described as 'the most neglected church in the diocese though situated in the richest part of Donegal'.[1] A further restoration took place in 1892–3 under the direction of Thomas Drew and was paid for by descendants of Bishop Andrew Knox. Drew's guiding principle was the recovery of the outline of the medieval cathedral. He initially proposed to screen the transepts, but eventually decided to demolish them, leaving the building in its present shape, a long (36.9m) narrow building with a tower at the west end.

The external appearance of Raphoe Cathedral is that of a nave-and-chancel church. The visitor enters through the base of the tall, square, crenellated tower, which is built of coursed rubble, inset at each of its four floors. The tower has aged well and acquired a greater appearance of antiquity than it deserves. The tower has a late 19th-century clock on the second floor, and the remains of an early 18th-century clock on the first floor.

The strikingly elaborate doors were carved by a Mrs McQuaide in 1907 and restored in 1968. The Gaelic inscription around the doors reads: 'The household of God, the Church of the

Raphoe Cathedral from the south

living God, the pillar and foundation of the truth.' (1 Tim. 3:15). Passing through the doors, the visitor has to brave a windowless, murky and most uninviting vestibule. It houses part of an interesting 9th-century door lintel on which is carved a representation of the Arrest in the Garden. Pieces from the remainder of the lintel are embedded in the exterior of the north wall.

Beyond is an inner vestibule which is really the first 4.2m of the west end of the 17th-century nave. It has a vestry on the south side and a well-preserved consistory court on the north. These courts once sat regularly to grant probate and licences for marriage, but much of their importance was lost when their jurisdiction in these matters was removed in 1857. The well of the court is now used as a baptistery. The font is a sixteen-sided alabaster bowl on a circular shaft and was presented by Bishop Pooley in 1706.

and bold east gable. The beginning of the liturgical chancel is indicated by a step well beyond the arch. Here are the nondescript choir stalls and the pulpit, a late 19th-century white stone octagon with colonettes. The organ is an electric instrument by Hammond.

On the south wall are the three visible remnants of the medieval cathedral. A range of low and narrow lancets with wide internal splays reminiscent of a cloister, and the 12th-century stone triple sedilia, adjacent to the arcade, has an unusual design of shamrocks carved on the capitals of its pillars. It was discovered behind lath and plaster in the 1893 restoration and now provides stalls for the dean and two of the canons. Facing the sedilia, on the north wall, are three Jacobean wooden stalls which accommodate the archdeacon and the other two canons. An oak chair of 1665, used as the bishop's throne, is set in a window bay inside the sanctuary

Raphoe: Part of a 9th century door lintel

The cathedral is a double-chamber church with a triple-lancet east window. The double-chamfered chancel arch supported by responds can deceive the visitor into thinking of it as a nave-and-chancel church, but the pews sweep through the arch to the level of the old transepts occupying roughly half the area of the 'chancel'. The nave west of the arch is well lit by two clear glass windows, one each on the north and south walls. A door in the south wall at the west end gives access to the Galilee porch, which was the main entrance to the cathedral from 1740 to 1893. The porch has scroll carving and is possibly the earliest example of this south Italian style in the British Isles. The nave aisle floor and the chancel and sanctuary floors are covered with polychromatic tilework.

The section beyond the chancel arch is much darker than the nave and looks larger because of its higher-pitched roof

rails on the north side adjacent to the Jacobean stalls. The medieval piscina is on the south wall of the sanctuary.

Until the present century the bishop's throne was of the large family pew type, designed to accommodate not only the bishop but also his wife and children – leading to the assumption that his entire family exercised episcopal jurisdiction! A visitor to Raphoe Cathedral in about c.1890 observed a harmonium and some benches in the bishop's 'throne' and was told that it was used to hold a Sunday-school class. This throne was consigned to the former consistory court in 1962, but has since been removed.

The altar is raised up on four steps against the wooden panelled east wall. The central part of the panelling, behind the altar, has some carving and rises above the sill obscuring part of the triple-light east window. This only serves to darken the east end of the cathedral, which is an unwelcome sight after the visitor has braved the darkness of the porch.

The former Bishop's Palace stands on a hill to the east of the cathedral. Construction was begun in 1635 during the episcopate of Bishop John Leslie (1633–61). The palace is a fortified house with square corner towers originally of two storeys. A third storey was added in the late 18th century. Like most episcopal palaces of the Church of Ireland, it was much larger than the cathedral. It measures 14m square and the walls of coursed rubble are more than 1m thick. The palace was occupied until the union of Raphoe with Derry in 1834, then it was abandoned. It was accidentally burnt in 1839 and is now a sinister-looking ruin.

A Round Tower was demolished on the orders of Bishop Leslie to provide stones for his new palace. The traditional site is along a lane to the north-west of the cathedral. The wall of a farmyard in the vicinity may include stones from the tower.

The last separate Bishop of Raphoe was William Bissett (1822–34). On his death the diocese was united to Derry. Raphoe remains a separate diocese in the Roman Catholic arrangement, and the cathedral is at Letterkenny.

References

1   Alistair Rowan *North-west Ulster* (London, 1979), p. 468.

ROSCREA

The Cathedral Church of St Cronan

*R*OSCREA (*Ros Cré* – Cré's wood) is a prosperous market town of about 4,200 inhabitants in Co. Tipperary, situated on the Dublin–Limerick road about 72km north-west of Limerick. A monastery was founded here by St Cronan, who was born in Munster and founded several religious houses in various parts of Ireland. Cronan died *c.* 626, and his feast-day is 28 April.

An attempt was made to establish Roscrea as an independent diocese in a period of confusion after the Synod of Ráith Bressail in 1111. No Bishop of Roscrea was present at the Synod of Kells–Mellifont in 1152, but it was subsequently listed as a suffragan see of Cashel in Cardinal Paparo's list of the same year; it would be reasonable to assume that the synod established Roscrea as a diocese at that time, at the expense of Killaloe. Isaac Ua Cuanáin died as Bishop of Éile and Roscrea in 1161, but no more is heard of the diocese after that date. Whatever independent existence it might

have enjoyed was ended by the rising power of Domnall Mór O'Brien, King of Thomond 1168–94, who secured the reunion of Roscrea and Scattery Island with his diocese of Killaloe. There were Augustinian canons at Roscrea in 1173, but the church reverted to parochial status on the demise of the diocese.

Roscrea: the west front of the 12th century Augustinian priory church

The present Church of Ireland parish church in Church Street, built in 1812, is dedicated to St Cronan. The entrance to the church grounds is formed by the Romanesque west front of the church founded in 1100 on the site of Cronan's monastery. The rest of the church was demolished in 1812. The wall has antae, and the arch of the doorway is of three orders, the two inner ones with chevron work, springing from four shafts. Above is a tall triangular pediment not unlike the west door at Clonfert, but nowhere near so elaborate. The hood-moulding above the round-headed and much-weathered Romanesque doorway encloses the figure of an abbot or bishop (possibly St Cronan), and the doorway is flanked on either side by a series of blind arcades.

One suspects that the front survived the destruction of 1812 only because those responsible felt that it would form a 'nice' gateway to the new church. The 1812 church is a pleasant oblong building of ten bays formed by clustered wooden columns and galleries on three sides. A square, battlemented and pinnacled tower rises out of the west end. It may have been partly constructed with stones from the priory, but this is no compensation for its loss.

A decorated but mutilated and weathered High Cross of the 12th century can be seen to the south of the façade. It shows a Crucifixion on one side and St Cronan on the other.

There is also a Round Tower of coursed limestone with a level top. Now 20m high, it was reduced by about 6.6m in 1798 to make it suitable for a canon emplacement after an English sentinel had been shot by a sniper. About 7.6m up the tower there is a relief of a ship inside a window. It was inhabited until 1815. Its appearance is spoilt by a collection of run-down corrugated shacks which cluster around it.

The modern Dublin–Limerick road cuts straight through the site of the ancient monastery, leaving the Round Tower on one side and the west facade of the priory on the other. 'Every articulated truck from Dublin to Limerick thunders and belches within feet of it.'[1] The road runs perilously close to the soft sandstone façade, which is deteriorating, and there is an even chance that a heavy vehicle will collide with it sooner or later.

References

1 Maurice Craig, *The architecture of Ireland from the earliest times to 1880* (London & Dublin, 1982), p. 44.

ROSSCARBERY

The Cathedral Church of St Fachtna

Diocese of Ross (Church of Ireland)

ROSSCARBERY (the name derives from *Ros O gCairbre* – an ancient sept) is a small village above the shore of a narrow bay in Co. Cork on the south coast of Ireland, 74.5m south-west of Cork itself, and was once thought to rival Lismore for the beauty of its surroundings. 'The little town, half hidden in wood, and with its cathedral church encircled with trees, and close to the narrow inlet of the sea, presents a striking and exceedingly picturesque effect.'[1] 'In its grove of trees and in its quiet seclusion this is a cathedral of rustic charm and of devotional atmosphere.'[2] Although the latter comment was written only in 1971, the trees seem to have gone, houses now press against the walls of the cathedral churchyard, and the site is not quite so arboreal and secluded as it was in former times.

A monastic settlement, then known as *Ros Ailithir* meaning 'wood of the pilgrims', was founded at Rosscarbery in the late 6th century by St Fachtna, who had been Abbot of Molana in Co. Waterford. Fachtna (*alias* Fachnan, Fachan, Fachanan, Facthnan, Faughan or Faughnan – there are many variations in spelling) is said to have died *c.* 600 at the age of forty-six. He may be identified with the St Fachanan who founded Kilfenora; the similarity of their names and the fact

that they are commemorated on the same day (14 August) are adduced to support the theory.

Ross was not chosen to be a diocesan see at the Synod of Ráith Bressail in 1111, and no Bishop of Ross was present at the Synod of Kells–Mellifont in 1152 although it appears in Cardinal Paparo's list of the same year. The first named Bishop of Ross was Nechtan Mac Necthain, who died in 1160. There was a vacancy in the see *c.*1195–8, when two rival candidates, Daniel and Florentius, went to Rome to plead their cause before Pope Innocent III. Charges were laid, many later proved false, about the theft of holy oils and books.

On the resignation of Bishop John Edmund de Courcy (1494–1517), an inquiry into the state of the diocese, on the order of Pope Leo X, described Ross as a walled city of two hundred houses with the cathedral in the centre. 'The Church is built of cut stone and in the form of a cross. It has two doors, one in front and the other in the side. It is covered with slate. The floor is unpaved. It has a choir and nave – the latter separated from the former by pillars. To the left of the choir is the sacristy, which is well supplied with all necessaries for a Cathedral Church, viz: Mitre, pectoral staff, etc. On the right hand side is the belfry tower and bell . . . Low Mass is offered up daily – on Festival days Solemn Mass is sung. The Bishop lives on the seashore about half a mile distant from the city.'[3]

The diocese was so far from Dublin that no Bishop of Ross was appointed by the crown until 1582, and a succession of papal appointees seem to have had possession of the see until that year. But distance was no shield for Rosscarbery and its cathedral from the strife that swept Ireland during the 16th century. The cathedral was wrecked during the Desmond rebellions, and when William Lyon arrived as Bishop of Ross in 1582 he spoke unflatteringly of his see town as being 'in so desolate and barbarous a place as it is not fit for an Englishman, especially one of his sort, to live in'. But he set work to build 'a fine school and a fair bridge' and also 'erected a proper church and a fair house in the wildest part of Munster'.[4] Bishop Lyon's cathedral was begun in 1589 and finished in 1612, five years before his death.

Bishop Lyon's 'proper church' was not destined to last long; it was wrecked during the rebellion of 1641. The nave and tower were destroyed, but the chancel and two chapels, dedicated to the Blessed Virgin Mary and St Fachtna, remained standing and were used as a slaughterhouse. Bishop Lyon's 'fair house' was burnt, and his deaf and dumb daughter, Elizabeth, who had survived him by twenty-five years, died in the fire.

The history of the cathedral during the following half-century is a mystery. The rebuilding of the cathedral began towards the end of the 17th century and may have involved partial demolition of what remained of the medieval masonry. The Dean and Chapter gave orders in 1696 for the building of the tower; presumably the nave had already been built, probably at some date after the restoration in 1660. The 17th-century spire was removed in 1785 and replaced in 1806, at a cost of £964, with the present octagonal limestone spire. The upper 2.7m of the spire has twice been blown down by storms, in the winter of 1886 and in February 1923, and restored on each occasion; in 1923 the cost was £206.

The present cathedral, an aisleless cruciform church with a western tower rising from the roof of the nave, is an odd

The east window was given a wooden casement in 1718, and the present stone mullions in 1877, but there are traces of 13th-century work, and a certain amount remains in the north transept. The round-headed arch standing isolated in the churchyard on the south side of the cathedral is probably a relic of the medieval cathedral, though of what part is impossible to say. The 16th-century west window may either be a remnant of the medieval cathedral or of Bishop Lyon's 'proper church'.

Roscarbery Cathedral from the east

collection of architectural bits and pieces. Repeated destruction and rebuilding has left only a slight sense of antiquity. It incorporates a little medieval work, but the rest is a mixture of architectural styles. The window styles, some Gothic, some Georgian, and wooden casements with stone lintelled heads, echo the general confusion.

The nave has been divided roughly in half by the erection of a wall to create a large narthex 11.6m long and 8.3m wide. The wall was inserted possibly before 1829, to judge from the date of a memorial. The narthex contains an ancient font from the prebendal church of Inchidoney, which has been in ruins since 1642. A projecting head above the inner arch of the tower is supposed to represent St Fachtna. There are several memorials to members of the Hungerford family, and a large wall tablet eulogising John, 6th Baron Carbery (1765–1845), whose title was added to the ancient name of the town. The tablet was brought from Rathbarry church in 1927 (after the closure of that church) to accompany the marble statue of the peer already at the cathedral. The visitor is left with a slight feeling that the virtuous character of Lord Carbery is to be clearly understood before entering the house of God. The Carberys lived formerly at Castle Freke near Rosscarbery, but the house was sold after World War I by John, 10th Lord Carbery (1892–1970), and was dismantled in 1952.

The remainder of the nave, together with the chancel, has been transformed into a choir 22.3m long, with return chapter stalls against the west partition wall.

There are some references to galleries in the cathedral during the 19th century. The 'Dean's Gallery' was on the south side, and a new gallery was built in 1812 on the north side by Lord Carbery at his own expense, in consideration for having given up his seat in the west gallery to accommodate the organ. This west gallery, above the present chapter stalls, was entered by staircases in the narthex which led to a door above the present entrance. The galleries were removed in 1892.

The chancel is very shallow, and the crossing has been fitted up as a ritual choir and paved in red and white marble. The north transept now serves as the vestry and chapter room. The south transept is shallow and may be a truncated form of the full structure.

Much of the present internal appearance and furnishing of the cathedral dates from the incumbency of the Isaac Morgan Reeves (Dean of Ross 1876–1905). His plans for restoration are alleged to have been predicated on either the belief or the hope that the diocese of Ross would be separated from Cork and Cloyne and resume its independence.[5] The work done during his time was as follows:

The limestone pulpit resting on four colonettes of red Cork marble was erected in 1876 in memory of Prebendary Horatio Townsend. The work on the east window in 1877 has already been noted; the stained glass in the window was inserted in 1907 in memory of Dean Reeves, by his widow and children. The brass eagle lectern was presented in 1878. The white marble font was presented in 1886 by Margaret Hungerford the authoress. The heavy wooden roof of 1889, resting on floriated corbels, was an unwise attempt to Gothicise an essentially 17th-century interior, and the result is oppressive. The bishop's throne, on the south side of the nave, immediately west of the crossing, was presented in 1895 by the dean. The sanctuary was paved with white mosaic and the altar set up on two steps of white marble in

1895, and the oak chapter stalls were erected in 1896. The oak panelling in the sanctuary was erected in 1896 in memory of Margaret Hungerford by her husband and children. A peal of five bells was installed in 1897; the dean contributed to the cost of four of them, and his sister paid for the fifth.

Of all the additions to the cathedral during Reeves's ministry, the Romanesque-style west doorway below the tower is the most incongruous. It was built in 1895 to a design based on a doorway in Cormac's Chapel on the Rock of Cashel, in memory of William Somerville of Farley.

Rosscarbery Cathedral has been described as 'a comely, but small building' which 'presents no features of much interest at the present day.'[6] It is a modest little cathedral standing on high ground and enjoying good views of the bay. A grey and weatherbeaten 17th-century structure, its graceful Georgian spire sits oddly on the simple cathedral below, perhaps suggesting an unnecessary striving towards architectural elegance in this part of south-west Ireland.

The slight remains of an early 12th-century Augustinian priory are to be seen on a promontory in a graveyard to the south of the cathedral. In 1541 there was a church, hall, buttery, kitchen and other houses 'very ruinous and decayed'.[7] Only the rough unhewn stone north and south walls of the church remain. In 1576 Elizabeth I granted it to James Gowle of Cork, in 1580 to Sir Oliver Lambert, and in 1602 there is a grant of the late priory of Ross 'Hillarie' to Robert Morgan.

The diocese of Ross is quite small, little more, in fact, than forty miles of coastline from Ballydehob to Courtmacsherry, and the Church of Ireland diocese has only four benefices. With the exception of the sea to the south, Ross is surrounded by the diocese of Cork, and the amalgamation of the two was inevitable. In the Church of Ireland arrangement, Ross has been held with Cork since 1583, Bishop Lyon being appointed additionally to Cork in the year after his arrival at Ross. The diocese of Cloyne was added to Cork and Ross in 1835.

References

1 T. M. Fallow, *The cathedral churches of Ireland* (London, 1894), p. 68
2 R. W. Jackson, *Cathedrals of the Church of Ireland* (Dublin, 1971), p. 83.
3 W. R. Holland, *History of West Cork and the diocese of Ross* (Skibbereen, 1949), p. 302.
4 Jackson, *Cathedrals of the Church of Ireland*, p. 83.
5 C. A. Webster, *The diocese of Ross*, (Cork, 1924), p. 47.
6 Fallow, *Cathedral churches of Ireland*, p. 69.
7 Holland, *History of West Cork and the diocese of Ross*, p. 306.

SCATTERY ISLAND

Scattery Island Cathedral

SCATTERY Island is a deserted little island of about 40 hectares at the mouth of the Shannon estuary, about 2.8km south-west of Kilrush, Co. Clare, and 1.2km from the pier at Cappagh, from where it can be reached by boat at high tide. It is a desolate, lonely and beautiful place.

A monastery was founded here by St Senan. But even the century in which he lived is uncertain, since his death is not recorded in any of the monastic annals, and the first mention of an Abbot of Scattery occurs in 797. One authority states that Senan died *c*. 540, but the only reliable statement that can be made about him is that certain legends, some of them half-pagan in origin, have gathered around the memory of a saint from an early and misty period in Irish Celtic Christianity in a remote part of Ireland. His feast-day is 8 March.

The name Iniscattery (*Inis Cathaigh* – Cata's island) is the first indication of the type of legend that has stuck to St Senan. Cata was allegedly a dreadful monster who was defeated and killed by St Senan, who then established a monastery on the island. Senan was born at Moylougha, 7km east of Kilrush, where a lake and a ruined church mark the site. He made Scattery an important centre of learning, and among his pupils was St Kieran of Clonmacnoise. St Senan, like St Kevin of Glendalough, excluded all women from his retreat. Like many holy men, he attracted the devoted attentions of women, and of a St Cannera in particular. Cannera wished to share the island retreat with him, but, unlike St Kevin's admirer, she obediently returned to the mainland at the saint's express command! She lived as a recluse near Bantry and died *c*. 530; her feast-day is 28 January.

The island site ensured that the monastery was the first prize available to the Vikings as they sailed up the Shannon estuary. It was twice plundered, in 816 and 835, and was probably occupied by the Vikings in 972–5 until they were driven out by Brian Boru (High King of Ireland 1002–14).

The diocese of Scattery Island was set up at the Synod of Kells–Mellifont at the expense of Killaloe, Ardfert and Limerick, to represent the interests of two tribes in west Clare and west Limerick. No bishop did fealty to Henry II in 1172, and the island was sacked and burnt by Normans from Limerick in 1176. A further devastation took place in 1178 under William Hoel, a Norman knight. A Bishop of Scattery Island named Áed Ua Bécháin died in 1188, and the diocese had been suppressed by the end of the 12th century and incorporated into Limerick.

After the dissolution of the diocese the cathedral became a collegiate church with a prior and twenty-four perpetual chaplains, but maintained traditional rights over certain churches on both banks of the Shannon and enjoyed a period of importance in the 14th and 15th centuries. A coarb, prior and others were still in residence in 1579, and the death of Calbhach, 'Coarb of Senan' is recorded in 1581. The island's churches probably ceased to function in the reign of Queen Elizabeth I and fell steadily into ruin thereafter.

A series of mostly non-resident titular bishops are recorded in the 14th and 15th centuries. Pope Innocent VI began the line in 1360 by appointing Thomas MacMahon, an Irish Friar Minor from Nenagh who fooled the pope with forged letters. Bishop MacMahon did eventually take possession of his ill-gotten diocese, but complained to the pope in 1361 that he was hindered from exercising his functions and from receiving revenues and rents by the Bishops of Limerick, Ardfert and Killaloe.[1] The complaints of these bishops seem to have reached Rome, and in 1366 Pope Urban V declared MacMahon's appointment null and void, and no more is heard of him. In 1414 Richard Belmer, an English Dominican friar, was appointed to the see and was translated to Achonry in 1424; he was an absentee, acting as a suffragan in England from 1414 to 1433. A Bishop Dionysius, of doubtful authenticity, resigned before 1447. He was succeeded by John Grene, an Augustinian friar, formerly former Prior of Leighs in Essex, who was a suffragan in York and Canterbury in the period 1452–1467.

The monastic site on the island contains the cathedral, the Round Tower, and the usual constellation of churches so typical of Celtic foundations. John Lloyd, who visited Scattery in 1780 during the course of a tour of Co. Clare, noted that the island had five or six churches. The cathedral and five churches remain to this day.

1. *The Round Tower*

The most notable feature on the island is the Round Tower, with its marked orange colour due to lichen growth. Its height is often stated to be 120ft (36.58m), which would make it the tallest of the Round Towers in Ireland. This was an 18th-century guess, however, and its true height is about 26m. John Lloyd called it 'perhaps, the loftiest old steeple in the kingdom'.[2] Both he and his contemporaries long perpetuated the myth of its height. A safer claim would be that it is probably one of the oldest surviving Round Towers in Ireland. Unusually, the entrance door is at ground level, allowing the visitor to walk in and gaze up the full height of the tower into the cap, with light peering in through the small windows. The cap appears complete from the inside

original structure. The upper part of the west gable and the windows in the south and east walls are constructed of flagstones and date from the rebuilding. There is a single window in the east wall and doors in the north and south walls. The east window is 15th century; it had two trefoil-headed lights with a quatrefoil above, but the shaft has fallen. Windows in the south wall have been replaced, probably in the 15th century, by trefoil-headed slits. A door in the north wall at the east end opens into a sacristy which is not bonded to the cathedral wall; it measures 8m by 3m. The remains of a

Scattery Island: the Round Tower and the cathedral

but truncated from the outside, probably because the exterior was never completed. Together with the rugged masonry, small windows and total absence of decoration, the ground-floor round-arched doorway could indicate a very early date before the merits of raised doorways were appreciated. Most Round Tower doorways are raised 1.5m to 4.5m from the ground.

2. The Cathedral

The cathedral, standing 23.7m to the east of the Round Tower is a 9th/10th-century building which was altered in the 13th/14th centuries; it measures 20.7m long by 8.2m wide. The lower part of the west wall with antae, the west door with lintel and inclined jambs and other sections of the walls display large uneven masonry which dates from the

porch can be seen outside the west door, and the east wall is buttressed. There are primitive guttering holes along the base of the parapet.

3. Unidentified church

There is a small nave and chancel church 1.5m to the north of the cathedral. The nave measures 7.1m by 3.9m, and the chancel 2.6m by 3.2m. The chancel had been levelled before 1878. but was partly rebuilt by the Board of Works. Excavations of the site disclosed the base of a rich Romanesque chancel arch of *c.* 1100 with clustered pillars and chevrons.

4. Well

To the south of the tower is a sunken walled well entered by steps and still filled with water.

5. *The Church of the Hill of the Angels*

Standing on a ridge to the south-west of the cathedral are the fragmentary remains of a very early church known as the Church of the Hill of the Angels (*Teampall Aird na nAingeal*). St Senan is alleged to have been placed here by an angel before he defeated the monster. Only the foundations and the south wall survive, including a window and the remains of two doorways, together with a stump of the north wall. The church measures 12.3m by 5m. There was a later building measuring 10.9m by 4.5m attached to the south-east of the church, but this has now completely disappeared.

6. *The Church of St Senan*

To the north of the Round Tower is the much-rebuilt Church of St Senan, reputed to be the saint's burial place. It is entered by a Gothic south door and was divided in the 12th century by a chancel arch with clustered pillars, vestiges of which can still be seen. The nave measures 7.2m by 5.1m, and the chancel 3.3m by 3.2m.

7. *Unidentified oratory*

The oratory that stands close to the west gable of the Church of St Senan reputedly contains Senan's tomb. It has a south door, south window and east window and measures 6.6m by 3.4m. It is built of flagstones, and the walls are less than 2m high. Part of an Ogham inscription can be seen on a stone outside which now forms a bench. A cross-inscribed slab nearby asks for a prayer for Moenach, teacher of Mogron.

8. *The Church of the Dead*

Near the east shore, close to the landing place is a cemetery containing the ruined 14th/15th-century Church of the Dead. The church is a rectangle measuring 20.6m by 5.6m. There are slight remains of a later north aisle entered from the main body of the church by a once external doorway and two later pointed archways, one now blocked. The east window is 2.6m high and has moulded inner jambs, but the shaft has gone. The main entrance was through a door in the north wall at the west end. The east wall has large stepped buttresses, and the original stone guttering is intact. The cemetery was used for interments until recent years, and the church was probably the last on the island to be used.

9. *The Castle*

A small castle was built close to the quay in 1577. It was a flat-topped tower several storeys high in 1681, but only a featureless lower vault remains.

10. *Quayside houses*

The island had a population of about a hundred at the end of the 18th century and remained inhabited until the 1970s. The ruins of cottages can be seen along the shore facing Cappagh. Their collapsed roofs, empty doorways and win-

dows and ghostly skeletal gables silhouetted against the sky are an eerie sight. Some of them may have been constructed with stones from the island's churches. The last inhabitant left in the late 1970s and was killed in a traffic accident on the mainland shortly afterwards.

In 1780 John Lloyd found Scattery to have 'a noted and excellent Harbour for large and small vessels'.[3] George Holmes visited the island in 1797 and found 'the soil good: well stocked with cattle, and abounding with rabbits and wild fowl'.[4] They were rare and determined visitors. Because of its remoteness and the difficulty of access, not many people find their way to Scattery, and the island has been spared the mass invasion of tourism which has done so much to spoil the atmosphere of Clonmacnoise and Glendalough. Apart from a lighthouse at the far end of the island, thankfully distant from the monastic ruins, and the occasional appearance of a surprised and inquisitive goat, Scattery is now a wild and deserted place, covered with brambles, irises and bulrushes, its ancient walled pathways mostly overgrown. But that is the principal charm of this quiet and lonely island. The desolation of the ruins and the general and profound silence evoke a magical atmosphere. Carlisle was right when he called it 'the rich and beautiful little island of Iniscathrie'.[5]

References

1 John Begley, *The diocese of Limerick* (Dublin, 1906), p. 389.
2 John Lloyd, *A short tour: or an impartial and accurate description of the county of Clare, with some particular and historical observations* (Ennis, 1780), p. 21.
3 Ibid.
4 George Holmes, *Sketches of some of the southern counties of Ireland, colllected during a tour in the autumn, 1797, in a series of letters* (London, 1801), p. 94.
5 Nicholas Carlisle, *A topographical dictionary of Ireland* (London, 1810), p. 191.

SKIBBEREEN

The Cathedral Church of St Patrick

Diocese of Ross (Roman Catholic)

*S*KIBBEREEN (*Sciobairín* – place of little boats) is a small market town 92km south-west of Cork. It stands on the River Ilen where it widens to form a creek and unites with an inlet on Baltimore Bay. The town is the location of the cathedral church of the small Roman Catholic diocese of Ross. Although there is some evidence of a 13th-century Cistercian house on the site, the present town developed on the estate of Sir Walter Coppinger, a Cork merchant who acquired property in the area at the end of the 16th century. In 1615 Coppinger secured the right to hold a fair in connection with the former MacCarthy Reagh castle of Gortnaclohy, which stood to the east of the present town. After the Confederate war of the 1640s Coppinger's estate was forfeited, and granted to two Englishmen named Prigg and Hall, who called the growing town New Stapleton. Meanwhile another small settlement was growing up beyond the Kiel stream that flowed into the Ilen. The union of the two settlements, by Bridge Street, has created the present town of Skibbereen.

The diocese of Ross was administered by the Bishops of Cork and Cloyne from 1693 until 1747, when Pope Benedict XIV decreed its amalgamation with the diocese of Cloyne. The two dioceses remained united until 1850, when a recommendation to separate was made to the Synod of Thurles by Bishop Timothy Murphy of Cloyne and Ross (1849–1849). There is evidence that separation was urged by Archbishop Paul Cullen (of Armagh 1849–1852, of Dublin 1852–78) who wished to place his own nominees in vacant bishoprics. One author has written that 'The separation was apparently unexpected.'[1] This may refer to local feeling within the dioceses of Cloyne and Ross; but it appears to have been anything but unexpected at a higher level.

The synod accepted the recommendation and separated Cloyne and Ross on 24 November 1850. Bishop Murphy remained Bishop of Cloyne alone thereafter (1850–56). On 2 February 1851 William Keane, parish priest of Midleton, was consecrated Bishop of Ross and the diocese resumed its independence.

The antiquity of Ross as a 12th-century diocese based on the 6th-century monastic foundation of St Fachtna was beyond dispute, but maintaining a diocesan structure for such a small area cannot have been easy. Skibbereen had been recognised as a mensal parish from the time of Bishop Michael Collins (1831–2); Bishop Keane came to live in Skibbereen after his consecration, and appears to have used the parish church as his pro-cathedral thereafter.

There may have been a feeling in some quarters that the parish church in Rosscarbery should become the cathedral church for the diocese; since Rosscarbery was the historic see of Ross diocese, consideration of the possibility was natural. But Rosscarbery was only a small village when compared with the town of Skibbereen, and the parish church there was never raised to cathedral status. The church at Rosscarbery was built in 1820 to replace a chapel from the penal days. It was repaired and decorated in the late 1870s and consecrated on 15 August 1880. An article in the *Cork Examiner* in June 1880 implied that it would subsequently be the cathedral church of the diocese,[2] but this was never the case. The church at Rosscarbery was renovated and extended eastwards during the incumbency of the Fr P. Hennessy (1921–39).

Skibbereen Cathedral was built in the 1820s as a parish church within the diocese of Cloyne and Ross, at the end of the long episcopate of Bishop William Coppinger (1791–1831). The site was purchased from William (later Sir William) Wrixon-Becher (1780–1850) in 1822. Wrixon-Becher, a local landowner and member of parliament for Mallow 1818–26, was created a baronet in 1831. The initiative for building a new parish church came from Fr Michael Collins, parish priest of Skibbereen 1814–27. The scheme was the usual one of replacing a small, humble 'mass-house' built in the penal times. Building work was in progress in 1824, and was complete by 1826. Collins was much regarded by his fellow clergy, and in 1827 he was elected coadjutor bishop. He succeeded Bishop Coppinger in 1831, but his tenure of the see was short; he died from the effects of a stroke on 8 December 1832.

Skibbereen Cathedral from the south-east

Skibbereen Cathedral is a plain pre-Emancipation Greek Revival building with transepts, erected in 1824–6 at a cost of £3,000. Set in the west gable is a plaque with following inscription: 'DEO OPT MAX ET BEATO PATRITIO PAROCHUS POPULUSQUE EXTRUERE. A.D.1826 VENITE ADOREMUS ET PROCIDAMUS ANTE DEUM.' (To the glory of Almighty God the greatest and the best and to St Patrick, the parish priest and people [caused this church] to be built. A.D.1826 Come let us adore and fall down before God.)

The cathedral is built of greenish-coloured coursed rubble, and is alleged, at least in part, to incorporate stonework from the now vanished 13th-century castle of Dunagoul (Dún na nGall) at Ringarogy.[3] A small empty Italianate bell-cote, probably added in 1835, perches precariously on the west gable and is the only notable external feature. The bell fell down in 1987 and is now to be seen inside the cathedral, on a plinth in the north-west corner of the nave, bearing the inscription 'The Cathedral Bell 1835–1987'. The west door has red marble stoups supported by polished granite columns with limestone bases.

The cathedral was described in 1837 as 'a spacious and handsome edifice in the Grecian style. . . The interior is fitted up with great taste, and the altar, which is ornamented with a painting of the Crucifixion, is very chaste.'[4] Little remains of this description, with the exception of the spacious nave.

The nave, with pine pews, is quite plain, apart from a coffered ceiling. The north and south walls each have three tall round-arched windows, framed with egg-and-dart moulding; the stained glass was inserted *c.* 1920. There is an organ gallery at the west end supported by four columns of marblelised iron; two are fluted and have Corinthian capitals. The gallery obscures the two west windows. The Stations of the Cross are of painted plaster set in grained Gothic frames.

The galleried transepts are each separated from the nave by two round arches resting on large cylindrical piers of polished brown granite. The disused Mortuary Chapel is off the east side of the south transept.

The real delight of this cathedral is the shallow chancel and sanctuary, elegantly decorated in gold, pink and white. The chancel is separated from the nave by three round arches which rest on piers of polished brown granite with elaborately carved white stone capitals. There are decorated panels in the spandrels. The white marble altar rail has wrought iron screening between its brown marble piers. The floor beyond is covered with polychromatic tilework. The chancel finishes in an apse, which has a mural of angel musicians and singers, crowned with the motto 'IN CONSPECTU ANGELORUM PSALLAM TIBI DEUS MEUS' (In the sight

The interior of Skibbereen Cathedral looking east

There are memorials to three former bishops on the south wall. The most important is that to Bishop Michael Collins of Cloyne and Ross (coadjutor bishop 1827–31, diocesan bishop 1831–32). The work of John Hogan (1800–58), and executed in marble, it shows an allegorical personification of religion (with her attribute the Cross) seated on a cube beside which are a mitre and an open book, gazing at an oval cameo relief of the deceased bishop. There are also memorials to Bishop Michael O'Hea of Ross (1858–76) and Bishop Denis Kelly of Ross (1897–1924).

of the angels I will sing to you my God — Psalm 137:1 — Vulgate). Six angels are playing musical instruments. The two central angels are reading scrolls and are flanked by two further angels in a state of adoration. The apse and sanctuary windows have intricate stencil decoration in the reveals.

The high altar is of white marble with pink marble colonettes, but of a more chaste and classical design than many others of its type. The circular tabernacle is surmounted by a domed cupola. A new altar at the top of the sanctuary steps is in harmony with the general design of its surroundings. The simplicity of the nave is more than compensated by this small chancel and sanctuary, which is neither noble nor striking nor majestic, but very beautiful.

The pulpit and the throne are on the north side. The pulpit is of polished white marble with red marble colonettes and richly decorated panels of mosaic. The centre panel bears the date 1950 and the inscription 'ANNO JUBILATE'.

The high altar is flanked by the Chapel of the Sacred Heart, and the Chapel of the Blessed Virgin Mary, the latter of which is now used as the baptistery.

The small size of the diocese of Ross has probably always caused debate at one level or another about its separate existence. There was an interregnum of more than two years between the death of Bishop Denis Kelly on 18 April 1924, and the consecration of his successor, Bishop James Roche, on 30 May 1926. When Bishop Roche was appointed Bishop of Cloyne in 1931, he was appointed Apostolic Administrator of Ross,[5] and remained so until the appointment of Bishop Patrick Casey (1935–40). This might indicate that a renewal of the union between Cloyne and Ross was contemplated in those years.

The present position and status of the diocese of Ross and Skibbereen Cathedral is a little unclear. Skibbereen had pro-cathedral status for many years, until it was declared to have full cathedral status in 1951. This declaration was made by Bishop Denis Moynihan (1941–53) on his return from a visit to Rome. On 10 February 1953 Bishop Moynihan was translated to the Diocese of Kerry. After a vacancy lasting nearly year, Bishop Cornelius Lucey of Cork was appointed Apostolic Administrator of Ross by the papal nuncio in Ireland, in February 1954. So the situation continued until 19 April 1958, when a papal bull formally united the dioceses of Cork and Ross 'in an equally principal manner'. Despite this provision, the two dioceses are still listed separately in the *Irish Catholic Directory*, but there is no mention of a cathedral at Skibbereen. The bull cited, among other reasons, that the diocese 'lacks a cathedral church' — a statement which contradicts Bishop Moynihan's declaration in 1951.

The 1958 bull spoke flatteringly of Ross as 'illustrious in its antiquity and glory', before listing 'small boundaries', a decreasing population, and other drawbacks to its continued independence. Ross is a very small diocese, containing only eleven parishes (the Church of Ireland diocese of Ross contains only four benefices), and a case can be made for its union with Cork. But Skibbereen Cathedral has been included in this book because it is still known and styled locally as St Patrick's Cathedral, and the diocese of Ross still seems to enjoy a semi-autonomous existence. When Bishop Michael Murphy succeeded as Bishop of Cork and Ross in 1980, he was enthroned in the Cathedral of St Mary and St Anne at

Cork, but then visited Skibbereen shortly afterwards and read his brief of appointment to the assembled clergy.

To the north of the cathedral is the chapel for the Convent of the Sisters of Mercy, built in 1867–8 to designs by Pugin and Ashlin.

References

1 W. R. Holland, *History of West Cork and the diocese of Ross* (Skibbereen, 1949), p. 421.
2 Ibid., p. 305.
3 Ibid., p. 241.
4 Samuel Lewis, *A topographical dictionary of Ireland* (Dublin, 1837; repr. Washington, 1970), ii, 558.
5 Holland, *History of West Cork and the diocese of Ross*, p. 425.

SLIGO

The Cathedral Church of St Mary the Virgin and St John the Baptist

Dioceses of Elphin and Ardagh (Church of Ireland)

SLIGO (*Sligeach* – shelly river), with a population of 17,000, is the second largest town in Connacht and lies in the centre of a wooded plain mainly on the south bank of the River Garavogue, which connects Lough Gill with the sea. It has two cathedrals — Church of Ireland and Roman Catholic — of very different styles, which are adjacent to each other.

Sligo is first mentioned in 537 as the scene of a battle between the men of Connacht and those of the north. It was plundered by the Vikings in 807, and in 1245 it became important as the residence of Maurice FitzGerald, Earl of Kildare. FitzGerald built a castle here in 1245 and founded a Dominican friary in 1253, and Sligo has remained an important town since that time. All trace of the castle has disappeared, but there are substantial remains of the friary which mostly date from the 15th century, though there is also some 13th-century work.

The Cathedral Church of St Mary the Virgin and St John the Baptist in John Street is one of the two cathedrals of the united dioceses of Kilmore, Elphin and Ardagh, and serves as the cathedral church for Elphin and Ardagh. Elphin Cathedral was wrecked in a storm in 1957 and abandoned. Ardagh Cathedral was ruined in the rebellion of 1641.

To replace Elphin Cathedral, the parish church of St John the Baptist, Sligo, became the cathedral church of St Mary the Virgin and St John the Baptist on 26 October 1961, taking on the dedication of Elphin. In deference to history and tradition, the dean of the cathedral is styled 'Dean of Elphin and Ardagh'.

The first church in Sligo dedicated to St John was built in the early 14th century, but nothing remains of this building and hardly anything is known of its history or appearance. A royal visitation early in the 17th century found the church 'recently repaired', but in 1641 it was used as the headquarters of insurgent forces at the outbreak of the rising.[1] The church was probably repaired after the Restoration, but by the early 18th century the population of Sligo was increasing rapidly. In 1659 the population was 488, of whom 130 belonged to the Church of Ireland. By 1739 the total population had risen to about 1800 of whom about 400 belonged to the Church of Ireland. The increase in Sligo's population was probably instrumental in causing the demolition of the medieval church in the 1730s, though the state of the fabric of the medieval church may have been a factor.

Owen Wynne. A collaboration between Ormsby, Wynne and Cassel led to the beginnings of the present cathedral.

Cassel is better remembered for his country houses than for the cathedral; Powerscourt, Carton, Leinster House in Dublin (now the meeting-place of the Oireachtas), as well as the Printing House and Dining Hall of Trinity College, are all to his credit. Only three churches in Ireland are known to have been designed by him, the other two being Knockbreda parish church in Belfast and Castlebar parish church (now demolished) in the diocese of Tuam.

In its way Cassel's design was far ahead of its time. He provided a large central chamber in which the congregation would gather around the altar, shallow transepts, an apse at the east end and a massive tower at the west. The west tower may include some 13th-century work. It contains the mutilated mensa of the (1637) tomb of Sir Roger Jones, a rich merchant and governor of Sligo; it has effigies of Sir Roger

Sligo: the Cathedral of St Mary the Virgin and St John the Baptist from the south-east

In 1730 Eubule Ormsby arrived in Sligo to be Rector of St John's. In the following year Richard Cassel, a German-born Dublin architect, came to Sligo, to build Hazlewood, a large Palladian house on a peninsula in Lough Gill, for Colonel

and his wife. A brass plaque on the wall close by describing Jones as the builder of the first church on the site in 1622 is incorrect. When the chancel was constructed in 1883, a burial chamber was found on the site containing the remains of a man and a woman. These are believed to be those of Sir Roger and his wife. The chamber may have been the remnant of a chapel erected for the family at the east end of the 13th-century church. There are galleries resting on clustered columns at the west end and in both transepts. Those in the transepts bisect the windows.

The nave and transepts have pine pews, now black from repeated varnishing. The original box pews were removed in 1860. Most of the windows have stained glass, pleasant to the eye but nothing remarkable. The north transept has a tablet to the memory of Susan Mary Yeats, mother of the poet, W. B. Yeats, and another to his uncle. There is a memorial window to his grandfather and grandmother, and the brass altar rails were given also in memory of his uncle.

Cassel's design was substantially altered in the 19th century with the remodelling of the exterior and the addition of a chancel. In 1812 battlements were added to the walls, and small towers to the corners of each transept, with the result that the cathedral now resembles a small castle. Its large central space would make it ideal for present liturgical practices, but Cassel's square design was spoilt in 1883, when the craze for Gothic was well under way; the apse was demolished and replaced by a chancel.

The chancel is an odd Gothic excrescence on an 18th-century church. It has two small projecting transepts and an arched oak ceiling, in contrast to the ribbed curves of the 18th-century plaster ceiling in the nave. The chancel steps are made from slate. At the north end of the steps is a typical late 19th-century pulpit; at the south end, two stalls and a reading-desk, all of Bath stone and dark red marble. The chancel floor is tiled.

The former choir stalls were removed from the chancel to the nave in 1961 to make way for the new bishop's throne and chapter stalls. They were designed by Donal O'Dwyer of Dublin and made by Hearne of Waterford from Belize mahogany.

The sanctuary was walled with a blind Gothic arcade c.1930; the panels, of reddish-brown onyx, are separated by colonettes of red marble. The reredos picture of "Creation" was painted by Percy Francis Gethin (1874–1916) in memory of his brother Reginald, who was killed in 1899 in the South African War. Gethin was himself killed in the First World War.

The cathedral is basically no more than a plain 18th-century town church. The bishop's throne and chapter stalls are the only indication of its cathedral status. It would be easy to criticise the incongruous Gothic additions and furnishings, but, despite this clash of styles, the interior is homely and inviting.

References

1   Charles Tyndall, *The ancient parish church of St John the Baptist, Sligo, from the early times to Disestablishment* (Dublin, 1962), pp 8–9.

SLIGO

The Cathedral Church of the Immaculate Conception of the Blessed Virgin Mary

Diocese of Elphin (Roman Catholic)

THIS lofty and impressive cathedral, built in 1869–74, is a striking and interesting 19th-century exercise in Romanesque Revival. At the time of its construction Gothic was still the favoured and dominant architectural style, and the Cathedral of the Immaculate Conception at Sligo is the only example of Romanesque Revival among the 19th- and 20th-century Irish cathedrals.

Bishop Laurence Gillooly was the prime inspiration behind the establishment of Sligo as the see for the Roman Catholic diocese of Elphin and the construction of a cathedral. He was appointed coadjutor bishop in 1856 at the age of only thirty-seven, and succeeded as diocesan bishop in 1858 on the death of Bishop George Browne; he remained there until his death in 1895. 'He was one of the outstanding figures at the First Vatican Council and spoke in support of Papal Infallibility there. A man of genius, with a legal and orderly mind, he brought much-needed discipline and organisation to the Diocese. . . Bishop Gillooly took complete charge of the building of the Cathedral. He had an amazing knowledge of building construction in all its aspects. He was meticulous about every detail at every stage of the building and was seen on the site almost every day.'[1] The cathedral was completed within five years and was consecrated on 26 July 1874.

The cathedral was designed by an English Catholic architect, George Goldie of London, and was built of cut limestone. Goldie designed the cathedral in the form of a basilica with a square pyramid-capped tower and supporting turrets at the west end. Contemporaries called his design 'Norman', but it is a round-arched style that contains elements of English, German and Irish Romanesque. 'The plan of the north end might be French in inspiration but the stiffness and height seem Germanic, while the Lady Chapel is as English as Reckett's Crown at Canterbury — which is French.'[2]

The cathedral is 69m long, 20m wide at the nave and aisles, 35m wide at the transepts, and 19m high to the apex of the nave roof. The aisled nave has a triforium and clerestory, and the aisles continue to form an ambulatory around the apse. The triforium continues around the apse above the ambulatory. The walls have pine wainscoting. The round piers in the nave are of finely chiselled dark-grey limestone and have simply ornamented capitals. The roof has simple quadripartite ribbed vaulting. The vaulting shafts, also of dark-grey limestone, descend through the triforium to rest on corbels in the spandrels of the nave arcades. The aisle roofs have simple groining.

There is a fine carved wooden statue of St Assicus, the first Bishop of Elphin, at the west end of the nave. It was discovered by a Catholic priest in an antique shop in London and acquired by the cathedral in 1962. The dedication of the cathedral might have been either to St Assicus or to St Patrick, who founded the see. But the ancient cathedral at Elphin was dedicated to St Mary the Virgin, and its successor at Sligo follows the theme and is dedicated to the Immaculate Conception.

The apse has five lancet windows above the triforium. The stained glass here and throughout the cathedral is by Loblin of Tours in France. The choice of Loblin instead of the generally preferred Meyer of Munich was almost certainly influenced by Bishop Gillooly himself. He had studied at the Irish College in Paris, and at Geneva and Montpelier, and was fluent in French. The circular baptistery at the rear of the apse is lit by a lantern window. Designed as a mortuary chapel but never used as such, it was converted into a baptistery during the reordering of 1975, in accordance with the new liturgy which requires the font to be sited near the altar. The font is surrounded by a new floor of Carraig stone.

The transepts contain altars to the Sacred Heart and to St Joseph, but these are now disused.

The reordering of the cathedral, in accordance with the requirements of Vatican II, involved a total and very successful renovation in 1975. The architects were William H. Byrne & Son, and Patrick Rooney & Associates (for the sanctuary). Most of the original furnishings have been retained, though the pulpit and altar rails were unfortunate losses. The cathedral was reconsecrated on 7 December 1975 and solemnly reopened on the following day.

The old timber floor was removed and replaced by iroko parquet tiles, and the walls were painted a soft cream colour relieved by arches and ribs in white. The congregational seats are of mahogany and date from the restoration.

The former high altar thankfully remains in position. It is an interesting piece of work, unlike the usual late 19th-century Gothic creations in white Carrara marble. The altar has a mensa of white marble and stands on a plinth of red marble; the front and sides have carved alabaster panels, framed by veined onyx colonettes with gilt brass capitals and bases. The tabernacle is gilt brass with colonettes of dark-red marble, embellished with panels of polychrome champlevé enamel and coloured glass. The baldachino, of beaten brass, is supported by polished granite columns with capitals and bases clad in brass, standing on red marble plinths. A brass screen now fills the space between the front two pillars of the baldachino. This has been worked in quatrefoil pattern and allows a good view of the old high altar behind, preserving both altar and baldachino, which are important and integral features of the cathedral. The wide use of brass honours the memory of St Assicus, a metal-worker.

In many cases high altars have either been stripped of their furnishings and pointedly ignored, or they have been removed altogether; here is a good example of an imaginative change which preserves and transforms. The old altar has carefully been separated from the new altar by the screen. Yet this glittering screen somehow enhances the status of the old high altar, without detracting from the new, by partially shielding it from irreverent gaze and giving it the air of important mystery, thus creating a *sancta sanctorum*. This is quite appropriate, since the Blessed Sacrament is still reserved here in the great brass tabernacle.

Sligo: the Cathedral of the Immaculate Conception from the south

Standing in a niche above the tabernacle is the alabaster statue of the Immaculate Conception placed here by Bishop Gillooly during the dedication in 1874. It is of French design and shows the Virgin in an attitude of prayer, crowned by a garland of roses and crushing the head of a serpent.

The new altar occupies a central position on a raised dais. It is formed of two solid blocks of Ballinasloe limestone, the upper honed with chiselled edges and an engraved central cross resting on a smaller block with bush-hammered facing. The table contains a relic of St Oliver Plunkett, who was canonised in 1975, and Celestine, an early Christian martyr. The bishop's throne is on the south side of the new sanctuary area.

The Cathedral Church of the Immaculate Conception is the only example of a Romanesque-style cathedral built in the 19th century, when the craze for Gothic was at its height. George Goldie deserves praise for not being swept along by the tide, and for producing a building which is a joy to visit.

References

1 Cyril Haran, *Sligo Cathedral, 1875–1975* (Sligo, 1975), p. 37.
2 D. S. Richardson, *Gothic Revival architecture in Ireland* (New York, 1983), ii, 506.

THURLES

The Cathedral Church of the Assumption of the Blessed Virgin Mary

Diocese of Cashel and Emly (Roman Catholic)

THURLES (*Durlas Éile* – Éile's strong fort) is a sugar-manufacturing and market town of about 7,000 inhabitants in Co. Tipperary, 20.8km north of Cashel. A Carmelite friary was founded here by the Butler family at the end of 13th century. The friary was never very large, and when it was dissolved on 28 March 1540, it consisted of a church, chapter house, three chambers, a stable and two gardens, all in a ruinous state. The friary was granted to Thomas, Earl of Ormond and Ossory, in 1557, but the Carmelites appear to have maintained a presence in Thurles or its neighbourhood and 'Thurlusiae' was listed among Carmelite houses *c.*1737.

About 1730 a large thatched chapel was erected near the ruins of the friary with the help of the Mathew family, and became known as the 'Old Chapel' or the 'Mathew Chapel'. After the Reformation, when the cathedral on the Rock of Cashel passed to the Church of Ireland archbishops, the Roman Catholic archbishops of Cashel and Emly led a wandering existence, often in exile, until the mid-18th century. In the early 1750s Archbishop James Butler I (coadjutor 1750–57 and archbishop 1757–74) came to reside in a

thatched house near the Mathew Chapel, beginning the tradition of archiepiscopal residence at Thurles. There are no known illustrations of the Mathew Chapel; the Archbishop's House now stands on the site.

With the relaxation of the penal laws in the second half of the 18th century, it became possible to build churches on a more elaborate scale to replace the humble thatched buildings of earlier years. Archbishop Thomas Bray (1792–1820) constructed a new church, dedicated in 1809, to replace the Mathew Chapel. It was a cruciform building incorporating the sacristy and 30m-high tower of the old friary. The interior was T-shaped, 36.5m long, 36.5m wide at the transepts, and 10.3 high; known as the 'Big Chapel', it was regarded as one of the finest Catholic churches in Ireland at the time. At the time of the Synod of Thurles in 1850 it was decribed by the *Illustrated London News*: 'The Cathedral is, in ornament, within nearly as plain as without, save and except the high altar, which is rich and florid in the extreme; but what is of more importance, the buildings are large and convenient, and were, upon this occasion, fitted up with much care and costly taste.' An illustration of the interior of the chapel shows a sarcophagus-shaped altar set against a Classical reredos with fluted Corinthian columns.

Though nothing remains of the Big Chapel, it occupied roughly the area of the nave (without the aisles), crossing and transepts of the present cathedral.

In September 1862 Archbishop Patrick Leahy (1857–75) announced plans for extensive renovation of the Big Chapel in order to provide a cathedral church for the archdiocese. It was an ambitious plan: Ireland was still in the throes of post-Famine economic depression; the situation in Thurles had been exacerbated by the failure of a local bank in 1856; and the 1860s were a period of large scale emigration. Strenuous efforts were made to raise funds abroad. Priests were sent to England, Spain, Canada and the United States to solicit funds, but with little result; of the total cost of £45,000, only £2,000 was raised abroad.

Nevertheless, work began in 1865 and continued uninterruptedly until the building was substantially complete in 1872. Because of the remaining decorative work and paying off debts, the solemn consecration ceremony was delayed until 21 June 1879. The appointed architect was J. J. McCarthy, the 'Irish Pugin'. The work began as renovation and extension, and Archbishop Leahy optimistically expected it to be complete within a year. But the design of the new enlarged cathedral required a total rebuilding, and nothing of the structure of the Big Chapel now remains. McCarthy modelled his design for Thurles on the cathedral of Pisa with elements of Irish Romanesque, and the hybrid Lombardic–Romanesque style that was the result is a startling sight in Co. Tipperary. It is unlikely that the design originated entirely with McCarthy; Decorated Gothic would have been his natural choice. The likely explanation is that Archbishop Leahy, who had something of a taste for things Italian, wanted a Classical building and McCarthy obliged but produced one in a medieval style.[1]

The predominant building material is blue-grey Glenbane limestone with some imported Aberdeen granite and Portland stone. The west front has three storeys of blind arcading with pillars of red Cork marble and a colonnade of green Galway marble, surmounted by a stylised rose window with glass by Meyer of Munich. Statues of the Blessed Virgin Mary, St Patrick and St Albert stand on the cornice. Similar statues of Christ, St Peter and St Paul stand on the gable of the east transept, and of St Augustine, St Ursula and St Brigid on the west transept.

On the north side is a massive four-storey 38m-high rectangular bell-tower; its clock was the gift of Archbishop Thomas Croke (1875–1902) on the occasion of his silver jubilee as a bishop in July 1895. On the south side is a Byzantine-style circular domed baptistery, with a copper roof of 1927 surmounted by a gilt metropolitan cross. The present font in the baptistery was originally part of a fountain; the basin is supported by three sea-horses and has four intertwined serpents carved in relief above its upper rim. Both the baptistery and the campanile continue the Romanesque theme of blind arcading. A statue of Archbishop Leahy by Pietro Lazzarini of Carrara was erected in the forecourt in 1911. Lazzarini's work can also be seen at Armagh and Monaghan.

Immediately inside the central entrance porch is a stoup carved in the shape of a shell of Griotte de Flandres marble resting on two columns of polished grey Aberdeen granite. Its age and origin are unknown; it was purchased for the newly built cathedral from Boucneau, a London marble merchant, and was then considered to be 'an ancient font'. Two further stoups are set in recesses on either side of the entrance porch inside the cathedral; together they formed the font of the Big Chapel.

The cruciform cathedral is aligned north–south rather than east–west, but the traditional points of the compass are used in the description of the building. The interior is basilical, with an aisled nave of four bays with high round arches and a clerestory. The nave is separated from the aisles by massive columns of red Cork marble with bases and capitals of Caen stone, standing on plinths of Leugh limestone; the capitals were carved by different sculptors, and no two are alike. The hoods above the clerestory windows rest on vaulting shafts of white, red and green marble, which in turn rest on a gallery of carved saints' heads. The nave and transept walls have a rather garish mosaic dado. The hexagonal pulpit is situated in the penultimate bay on the south side of the nave and has carved representations of Christ and the four Evangelists in its panels. It was erected in 1878, but is now rarely used; in accordance with the requirements of the new liturgy, the ambo in the new sanctuary area is used instead.

The altars in the west and east transepts are are of marble and are modelled on the high altar. The west transept is a Sacred Heart shrine, and the large statue of the Sacred Heart in Parian marble is by Benzoni. The tabernacle door bears the letters **IHS** on the centre and fishes on the side worked in lapis lazuli and malachite; the structure incorporates eight columns of giallo antico, a rich yellow marble. The shrine of Our Lady in the east transept contains a statue of the Blessed Virgin, also by Benzoni. The tabernacle is inlaid with lapis lazuli, agate and other precious stones and incorporates pillars of tinted onyx; those supporting the domes are miniature replicas of the columns which support the canopy over the high altar in the basilica of St Paul's-Without-the-Walls in Rome.

The apsidal chancel is separated from its ambulatory by an arcade of nine bays. The ambulatory itself has a polychromatic tiled floor, but the ambulatory wall is well worth seeing. Arranged in thirty-seven panels, the wall constitutes an astonishingly rich art gallery of the widest variety of marbles. The former mortuary chapel, now called the Croke Chapel in memory of Archbishop Croke, is on the north side of the ambulatory; its floor level has been raised to the level of the cathedral, and the dividing ornamental screen has been removed.

The high altar is splendid and unusually large, measuring 3.3m by 2.1m. It is made of white marble inlaid with precious stones (malachite, lapis lazuli, rosso, agate and others) and a variety of other marbles, some donated by Pope Pius IX. Sixteen colonettes — six of yellow Siena marble, six of Griotte and four of vert campan — with bases and capitals of bronze support the table of the altar, which rests on solid masonry with a veneer of precious marbles. The altar was made to be set on the topmost of a number of steps at a distance and looks somewhat uncomfortable in its post-Vatican II position since 1979, but its preservation and continued use is something for which to be thankful. The stained glass tends towards garishness in the sanctuary, but is more restrained elsewhere.

The altar was made to match the great tabernacle which stood on it until 1979; it now stands on a separate marble plinth at the rear at the rear of the chancel. Rising to a height of 2.4m, it is believed to be the work of Giacomo della Porta (1537–1602), one of the architects of St Peter's Basilica in Rome and a pupil of Michelangelo. It was made for the Church of Gesù, the Jesuit church in Rome, and remained there for 300 years. During the 19th-century renovation of the Gesù the tabernacle was discarded and purchased by Archbishop Leahy, while in Rome for the First Vatican Council (1869–70), 'for the sake of the antique marbles composing it'. The back was originally of a soft stone called tuffo, but the archbishop, who had something of a taste for marble, had it remodelled on the design of the front. He was unable to procure any verde antico marble, but used green Conne-

Thurles: The Cathedral Church

mara marble instead. The doorway at the back is closed by a slab of oriental alabaster in which a large cross of lapis lazuli is inlaid; this was said to have been done by the archbishop himself. The front door is of bronze with a silver host bearing the letters IHS over three nails. The tabernacle also uses giallo antico, rosso antico and africano marbles.

The arrival of the tabernacle in 1871 caused something of a misunderstanding between the archbishop and the *Irish Builder*. The periodical immediately presumed the tabernacle to be newly made and condemned the importation of a foreign work of art into Ireland as an offence to Irish craftsmen. 'Ireland or Irish art cannot afford to suffer in this ignoble manner.' Archbishop Leahy wrote an angry letter to the editor saying that such remarks were actionable and demanding to know the identity of the author of the article. An apology was subsequently published, but the *Irish Builder* criticised the archbishop for responding in such an intemperate and unchristian way and reminded him that the church should never be above criticism.[2]

The chapter stalls of Roman Catholic cathedrals have often been the unremembered victims of post-Vatican II reorderings. Here at Thurles Cathedral is the unique instance of chapter stalls being allowed to remain in position on the north and south sides of the sanctuary. The carved oak throne of the Archbishop of Cashel and Emly also remains, but it was moved from the north east to the south west of the sanctuary.

The interior of the cathedral was thoroughly redecorated and reordered in 1979 to mark the centenary of its consecration and to introduce a permanent sanctuary arrangement that would be in accordance with Vatican II. Apart from the obvious move of the altar and the addition of an ambo to replace the hexagonal pulpit of 1878, which still remains in position, many other alterations were effected: the old mortuary chapel was renamed the Croke Memorial Chapel, and the dividing screen was removed; the woodwork between the nave and aisles was removed; the Stations of the Cross were repainted; the Victorian floral pattern stencil work which covered the ceiling was painted over on the grounds that the interior would be brighter, and that future heavy expenditure would be avoided, and that it was 'in keeping with the modern trend'. The reordered cathedral was reconsecrated on 21 June 1979.

The style of Thurles Cathedral is unusual for its date, but Ireland already has enough 19th-century Gothic Revival, and Thurles is a refreshing change. It speaks of a love for papal and Renaissance Italy and says as much about the Italianate tastes and egotism of Archbishop Leahy as it does about the need for a cathedral church for the diocese of Cashel and Emly. Its hybrid architecture has incurred some disfavour, but it is imaginative and attractive, and Thurles provokes curiosity and interest rather than the yawning dismissiveness which greets many of its Gothic Revival contemporaries. It is an extraordinary building to find in Co. Tipperary and an amazing design for an Irish cathedral. Without doubt it is a unique and valued addition to the architectural heritage of Ireland.

In the Roman Catholic arrangement, the diocese of Emly was incorporated in the diocese of Cashel on 10 May 1718 by decree of Pope Clement XI.

References

1 Jeanne Sheehy, *J. J. McCarthy and the Gothic Revival in Ireland* (Dublin, 1977), p. 25.
2 *Irish Builder*, xiii, no. 287 (1871), p. 307.

TRIM

The Cathedral Church of St Peter and St Paul

TRIM (*Áth truim* – ford of the elder-trees) is the county town of Co. Meath, with a population of 2,150, and lies on the River Boyne about 18km north of Dublin. A monastery was founded here by St Patrick *c.* 433,

Trim: the Cathedral of St Peter and St Paul

who placed St Loman in charge and departed further into Meath. Loman is said to have been a nephew of St Patrick and his feast-day is on 17 February. Trim was of no great note as a monastic school, and it was always overshadowed by fame of the neighbouring centres of Clonard and Clonmacnoise. The church at Trim maintained a continuous existence, though owing to its proximity to the east coast it often attracted the attentions of the Vikings. The monastic foundation was on the site now occupied by the so-called Yellow Steeple.

1368, with its east wall buttressed by remaining fragments of the south and north walls. The rest of the abbey was blown up in 1649 to prevent occupation by Cromwellian troops.

The Synod of Ráith Bressail decided that the see of the new diocese for the territory of Meath should be at Clonard, and it remained there until the beginning of the 13th century. The move from Clonard to Trim took place within the context of the Anglo–Norman control of Meath. The policy of the invaders was to replace Irish bishops with Anglo–Normans

Trim: the Yellow Steeple

The Yellow Steeple is all that remains of an abbey constructed for Canons Regular of St Augustine by Hugh de Lacy in the late 12th century. The de Lacy family was one of the most powerful families in Ireland during the 13th century, and their territory, stretching from the Shannon to the Irish Sea, was virtually co-terminous with the diocese of Meath.

The steeple, 38.1m high, stands in the Porchfields on a ridge on the north bank of the Boyne directly opposite Trim Castle. Its name is a misnomer acquired because of its colour in the setting sun. It is a lofty and gaunt ruined tower, dating from

as part of a strategy of extending Anglo–Norman rule further into Ireland. In 1192 Simon Rochfort became the first Anglo–Norman Bishop of Meath, and because of its distance from the military centre at Trim, the days of Clonard as the see of the diocese were numbered. It was also on the edge of the Pale and, being subject to periodic raiding, was not the safest place for an Anglo–Norman bishop.

In 1202 Rochfort (who was bishop until his death in 1224) obtained permission from the papal legate to move the see from Clonard to the Anglo–Norman centre of Trim. He brought the Augustinian Congregation of St Victor of Paris here in 1206 and gave them a site on the banks of the Boyne at Newtown Trim, 1.6km east of Trim itself. The priory church, dedicated to St Peter and St Paul became the cathedral church of the diocese of Meath and remained so until the Reformation. An attempt to substitute secular priests for the Augustinian canons in 1397 was unsuccessful. A faculty to build a new cathedral had been granted by Pope Alexander IV in the middle of the 13th century, but the project never materialised.

The extensive and impressive remains of the priory and its church lie on the north bank of the River Boyne. The Cathedral Church of St Peter and St Paul was a massive building and must have been one of the largest churches in Ireland in its day.

The cathedral measures 41.4m long by 9.1m wide. The north and south walls are 12.1m high and 1.6m thick. It was cruciform, consisting of an aisled nave, chancel and two transepts, with ribbed vaulting over the chancel. Remains of the Caen stone springing of the vaulting can be seen on the south wall of the nave. Only the chancel walls and parts of the nave walls remain. The nave was reduced by 24.3m in length in the later Middle Ages, when, apparently, the transepts and nave aisles were removed. The present west wall, which is 16.7m high, was built at that time. It has a small pointed doorway and two windows above in succession. The east window is now only a gaping hole 8.2m high and 3m wide. The effigy of an unknown 13th-century ecclesiastic can be seen in a niche in the north wall of the chancel. It is said to be a representation of Bishop Simon Rochfort, who is buried under the high altar of the cathedral. A large part of the south wall collapsed in a storm in 1839; there is a double-arched recess in the remaining portion.

Of the claustral buildings which were situated to the south-west on lower ground sloping to the bank of the River Boyne, little more than the south and west walls of the refectory remain. There are the remnants of a fine 13th-century doorway near a stile at a point where the east wall of the cloister stood. It was the doorway of the chapter house. The kitchen at the west end of the cloister, near the refectory, was built in the 15th or 16th century. The refectory measures approximately 24m by 9m, and the kitchen 12m by 9m.

The priory was dissolved in 1536, and the buildings subsequently fell into ruin. The Church of Ireland diocese of Meath had no cathedral church from that time until the elevation of St Patrick's Church in Trim in 1955.

The remains of the small medieval parish church lie 90m to the east of the cathedral. The church contains the much-weathered 1586 altar tomb of Sir Luke Dillon of Moymet and his wife, Jane Bathe, who are represented by recumbent effigies. Sir Luke's effigy has Renaissance armour.

On the other side of the river are the remains of the Friary and Hospital of St John the Baptist; the east end of the church is 13th century, and the tower to the west is 15th century.

TRIM

The Cathedral Church of St Patrick

Diocese of Meath (Church of Ireland)

T HE Church of Ireland diocese of Meath had no cathedral church from the suppression of the monasteries in the 16th century until 1955. In that year the parish church of St Patrick, Trim, was made the cathedral church of the diocese. The move to provide Meath with a cathedral began with Bishop James McCann (1945–59). After careful examination of all options, the location and antiquity of St Patrick's Church made it the most popular choice. Permission was sought from the General Synod in 1954, and on St Patrick's Day 1955 the Archbishop of Armagh hallowed the building as the cathedral church of the diocese of Meath.

The church allegedly stands on the first church built in the area by St Patrick, but no part of the present structure is earlier than the 15th century. The building has three distinct sections: the tower, built in 1449; the nave and chancel of 1802–3; and the mid-15th-century ruined chancel.

The fine battlemented tower, more than 18m high, is attached to the north-west corner of the nave. It has six storeys, two of which are vaulted. The tower has a clock with one face on the south side. It was made in 1863 by Patrick Donegan of 32 Dame Street, Dublin, to commemorate Richard Butler, Rector of St Patrick's 1819–61 and Dean of Clonmacnoise 1847–61. A plate set in the wall above the clock face, proudly proclaims it to be 'THE DEANS CLOCK'.

The church was sacked and burned in the rebellion of 1641 and the chancel has remained roofless since that time. The nave with a much shorter chancel was rebuilt c.1660 by the Corporation of Trim and again in 1802–3 by Bishop Thomas Lewis O'Beirne (1798–1823) at a cost of £738, but substantial traces of medieval masonry remain. The presence of the ruined medieval chancel indicates that the original length of the cathedral was 45.4m. The present length is 26.5m. The width of the medieval building was 16.4m, but this was reduced in the rebuilding of 1802–3 to 10m. In the medieval period there were four chantry chapels, dedicated to St Laurence, St Mary, St Patrick and the Rood. Masonry projecting from the east wall of the tower indicates either a north aisle or a much wider nave at one time, and the chapels may have been located here.

Entering Trim Cathedral through the ground floor of the 15th-century tower with its fireplace and medieval memorials, the visitor might expect to see a clash on moving into the 19th-century nave; in fact the join is scarcely noticeable, and the unplastered interior walls have mellowed well. A gallery was added at the west end in 1827 with the help of £350 from the Board of First-Fruits, and a reference to the removal of galleries in 1869 probably indicates the presence of additional galleries on the north and south walls. There are two clear-glass windows on each of the north and south walls of the nave, and stained glass windows in the east and west walls. The rebuilt chancel is small and has plastered walls; this could be removed in some future redecoration. The chancel arch is painted grey and rests on short responds with elaborate capitals and foliated terminals. The lower part of the sanctuary wall is walled with a brown-veined marble overlaid with a Gothic frieze. The stained glass in the east window is a memorial of c.1902 and replaces memorial glass of 1869, now transferred to the west window.

marble. Because of flaking stone, both pieces were, unwisely, coated c.1985 with white paint which has splashed onto the marble columns in places. A clear stone preservative would have been more suitable. The 1868 stone font standing on a single column of red Cork marble has also been painted. The brass eagle lectern of c.1901 is typical of its kind. A 15th-century piscina bears the royal arms, the arms of Richard Plantangenet, Duke of York, and James Butler, Earl of Ormonde.

The bishop's throne and chapter stalls, all of pine, were acquired from Elphin Cathedral, which was wrecked in a storm in 1957 and deconsecrated in 1958. They were rededicated for use at Trim on 25 October 1960.

The ruined chancel stands 2–3m east of the cathedral's present east wall. Only the north and south walls remain, and there is a square mid-15th-century window in south wall, comprising three ogee lights. The carved head on the west-

Trim: the cathedral of St Patrick from the south-east

ern side, wearing a ducal coronet, corresponds with a feature of the tower — the armorial shield of Richard, Duke of York, Lord Lieutenant of Ireland 1447–60, who made Trim his headquarters. A bishop's head is on the corresponding position on the east side. A blocked doorway can be seen in the north wall.

Ardbraccan, the former palace of the Bishops of Meath, is a great country mansion at Navan built on the site of the old castle where the Bishops of Meath lived from the 14th century. It was begun c. 1734 by Bishop Arthur Price and completed c. 1780 by Bishop Henry Maxwell. Bishop Maxwell boasted that he would build a palace so grand that no scholar or tutor would dare to live in it. None but the very wealthy could afford to live there now. The centre block is a simple and dignified two-storey grey stone house of seven bays, joined by curved sweeps to the two original wings, both of two storeys and five bays. Lord Plunket (Bishop of Meath 1876–84) was the last to live in the palace. For some years Ardbraccan Rectory served as the episcopal residence and

Trim: the 15th century tower of the cathedral of St Patrick

The pulpit and reading-desk were installed in memory of Charles J. Bayley, Vicar of Trim, who died in 1869. Both are of stone with columns of green Connemara and red Cork

was called Bishopscourt. By the early 1960s the residence had moved to Bishop's House, Killucan, Co. Westmeath, and then to the Ivy House, Leixlip, Co. Kildare. A new house was built at Moyglare, near Maynooth, in 1991.

TUAM

The Cathedral Church of St Mary

Diocese of Tuam (Church of Ireland)

TUAM (*Tuaim* – grave mound) is a town of about 4,350 inhabitants in the northern part of Co. Galway, 33km directly north of Galway itself, and is the ecclesiastical capital of the province of Connacht.

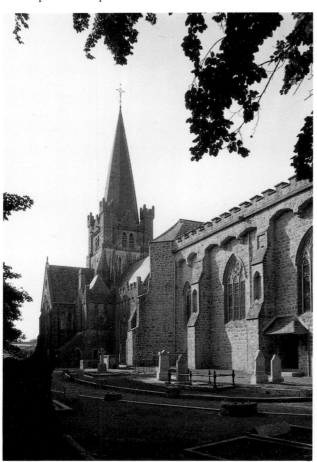

Tuam: St Mary's Cathedral from the south-east

A monastic house was founded here by St Jarlath, whose feast-day is kept on 6 June. Jarlath is not mentioned in the monastic annals, but is said to have died *c.* 550. No account of his life, trustworthy or otherwise, has been discovered, but there are isolated references to him in the lives of other saints. The generally accepted story of the origins of the foundation at Tuam is as charming as any other. Searching for an idea or inspiration about where to establish his monastery, St Jarlath was told by St Brendan of Clonfert to drive his chariot until the wheel broke, and there to build his abbey; the wheel broke at Tuam *c.* 520. To the north-west of St Mary's Cathedral there stands the remains of a medieval church dating from *c.* 1360, which is known as Teampall Iarlaithe (Jarlath). Conceivably it stands on the site of Jarlath's foundation.

The diocese of Tuam was established at the Synod of Ráith Bressail in 1111, being one of the five dioceses established for Connacht. Three further dioceses, Achonry, Kilmacduagh and Mayo, were added to Connacht at the Synod of Kells–Mellifont in 1152, and Tuam was made an archbishopric and given metropolitan rights over the province of Connacht at Kells–Mellifont. In the Roman Catholic arrangement, Tuam remains an archiepiscopal see. In the Church of Ireland arrangement, Tuam was reduced to the rank of a bishopric in 1839 on the death of the Hon. Power Le Poer Trench (archbishop 1819–39), and its metropolitan rights were annexed to Armagh. The dioceses of Killala and Achonry, united in 1622, were united to Tuam on 13 April 1834.

In 1123 a magnificent processional cross, enshrining a piece of the True Cross, was presented to the church at Tuam by Turlough O'Connor, King of Connacht. It still exists, in the care of the National Museum of Ireland. The king rebuilt the church in 1152, the year in which the bishop became an archbishop and received the pallium from the papal legate. The church was simple, consisting of a nave and square chancel and the 4.5m square barrel-vaulted chancel still exists, sandwiched between much larger 14th- and 19th-century additions, and its great arch matches the west doorway of Clonfert Cathedral as one of the finest examples of Hiberno–Romanesque architecture in existence.

The arch was constructed *c.* 1165–73 and has a huge span of 6.8m and a height of 4.8m, making its construction an impressive feat of technical skill. It consists of six semicircular concentric and recessed arches rising from five pillars. There is no keystone, and so the responds have a slight inward inclination to bear the great weight of the structure. 'The shafts of the columns . . . are unornamented, but their capitals which are rectangular on a semicircular torus are very richly sculptured, chiefly with a variety of inerlaced traceries, and in two instances, those of the jambs, with grotesque human heads. The arch mouldings consist of the rebule, diamond fretta, and varieties of the chevron, the execution of which is remarkable for its beauty.'[1]

The fate of the Romanesque nave is something of a mystery. In 1184, it collapsed, 'both roof and stone'. But the small chancel would have been quite insufficient to serve alone as the cathedral, and the nave was presumably repaired and used until the early 14th century or later. the work of Archbishop de Bermingham was designed as the first stage of a complete rebuilding, and the Romanesque probably fell into disuse at some later date. Its remains had disappeared by the 19th century.

During his episcopate Archbishop William de Bermingham (1289–1312) inaugurated a scheme to rebuild the cathedral. The work began with the construction of a new chancel, built to the east of the Romanesque chancel. It was intended to be only the first stage of a larger building, because after de Bermingham's death funds were solicited for the 'rebuilding of the church of Tuam begun by the late Archbishop William and continued by Dean Philip who petitions for and to complete it'.[2] No further building work took place, and so the great red sandstone chancel arch became the main entrance to the cathedral, the 12th-century square chancel and sanctuary became the entrance porch, and the new chancel became the nave, chancel and sanctuary. The arch was blocked up, and a door in the centre became the main entrance to the cathedral. For six hundred years the 14th-century chancel served as the cathedral church, the great arch being exposed to the onslaught of the weather. Repairs were undertaken in 1688 and again about 1787 after damage by fire.

The 14th-century chancel is a plain rectangular building measuring 21.6m long by 8.2m wide. The walls are crowned by an arcaded corbel course topped by a 19th-century parapet, supported by buttresses with trefoil-headed niches. The east window has five lights, and there are three windows with Decorated tracery on each of the north and south walls. There is nothing of note internally beyond a beautiful but mutilated piscina in the south wall. The only addition to this building was a slender 15th-century tower with crenellations, which had acquired a squat spire by the beginning of the 19th century.

In the ten years from 1851 to 1861 the Anglican population of Tuam had grown from 310 to 640, and the Revd C. Seymour, Vicar and Provost of Tuam, decided to embark on the ambitious programme of providing the city with a larger and more impressive cathedral.[3] In 1861 Sir Thomas Deane was commissioned to design a new cathedral with the proviso that he should incorporate the existing 12th- and 14th-century buildings into his design. The work lasted for seventeen years, and the extended cathedral was consecrated on 9 October 1878.

Tuam: the 12th century arch and sanctuary with the 14th century cathedral beyond

Deane's intention was to complete, to his own designs, the work begun by Archbishop de Bermingham. He constructed, to the west of the 12th-century chancel, a choir, north and south transepts, a massive central tower and spire, and an aisled nave of five bays with clerestory; his design makes many references to St Canice's Cathedral, Kilkenny, an obvious inspiration. The nave and choir have a stepped and machiolated parapet. The west door is surmounted by an arcade of seven equal trefoil-headed windows, the centre window commemorating Deane; the windows on either side of Deane, appropriately, commemorate King Solomon and Ezra, two prominent Old Testament figures concerned with the building and rebuilding of the Temple. The seven-light window above contains memorial glass of c. 1912 and is flanked on each side by side by three side lights stepping up to the central light. The aisle windows are coupled lancets. Each transept has a stepped five-light window similar to the west window. The choir is lit by four lancets on the north wall and two on the south wall.

Tuam: the bishop's throne

Deane's 19th-century building is 46m long and 23m wide at the transepts; the tower and spire are 55m high. The walls of the nave are of limestone from Kilroe in Co. Galway, but lined inside with red sandstone from near Castlebar, Co.

Mayo, to match the great arch. A space of 5cm was left between the outer limestone wall and the inner sandstone lining to prevent the penetration of damp. The octagonal nave piers and the mouldings of the chancel are of blue-grey limestone. The transepts are brilliantly lit by five-light windows in their north and south walls. Deane, as he had been instructed, retained the 12th- and 14th-century buildings, but the 15th-century tower was demolished. He added a parapet to the 14th-century chancel.

Deane took care to use red sandstone to harmonise the new cathedral with the Romanesque chancel. The great arch is now surmounted by an blind arcade of six trefoil-headed arches resting colonettes. The bishop's throne and chapter stalls are unfortunate and ostentatious additions, and not of Deane's choosing. Made from Caen stone and Irish marble, they were donated by Thomas, Lord Plunket (Bishop of Tuam 1839–66). Curious, inelegant and ungainly structures, the stalls are unharmonious additions to the deep red sandstone around them. In front of each stall is a small stone lectern supported by a single coloured marble column; the stall of the dean has a larger desk of the same materials. The bishop's throne boasts a stone desk supported by a 'pelican in her piety' and a grotesque stone canopy attached to the wall behind, which has no visible supports to bear its weight. The lecterns are notable for their impracticality; they are barely large enough to hold a single book. There is nothing in their material or design to enhance the beauty of Deane's cathedral. 'All this costly marble and stonework is ugly and most unsuitable. The appearance of the choir would be enormously improved were it furnished in dark oak.'[4]

The 12th-century chancel, long used as a porch, has now been restored to its original function as the sanctuary of the cathedral. The three windows in its east wall have been filled with glass, and the 14th-century chancel can be seen beyond. The building has had a variety of functions since it ceased to be used as the cathedral in 1868. It has been used as a chapter house and library and synod hall and, after restoration in 1987, as a general community centre. It formerly housed a collection of twenty-eight 18th-century Piedmontese Renaissance stalls of mahogany, maple and walnut inlaid with richly elaborate marquetry decoration of ivory and mother-of-pearl. They were made in 1740 for a Piedmontese monastery later destroyed by Napoleon c. 1790. Hidden in a Turin cellar for fifty years, they were purchased for the chapel of Markree Castle at Collooney, in Co. Sligo, by Edward Cooper, who bought then in Nice for £3000. His daughter presented them to the cathedral in 1882. They were sold in 1984 and returned to Italy.

Deane's separation of the outer and inner walls to prevent the penetration of damp was to no avail, and the cathedral has always suffered badly. In 1886, only seven years after the consecration, the organist addressed a letter to the select vestry complaining of the damp state of the organ loft and warning of serious damage to the organ if it was left un-treated. The vestry authorised the purchase of a small oil stove at a cost of £1, deeming that to be sufficient. But by the following year the organ was in a 'lamentable' state and the vestry decided to raise money to have it thoroughly repaired. The response indicates the extent of the problem: one month after the launch of the appeal the honorary secretary of the organ fund reported that 'no one would subscribe until something was done to stop the leakage in the cathedral and prevent the damp from coming in contact with the organ'. The result was disappointing, and a new organ was not installed until after 1913. But the cathedral continued to suffer badly from damp, and in 1924 two electric heaters were installed in the organ loft in order to keep that part of the cathedral as dry as possible.[5]

St Mary's Cathedral is presently in a sad state. As the congregation has dwindled, so the cathedral has fallen into disrepair and the fabric has deteriorated. Stalactites drip from the capitals of the nave piers, and the blue-grey limestone mouldings have a bloom of green mould. The average Sunday morning congregation, when a service is held, numbers about twelve people, and the maintenance of the building is far beyond their resources. The cathedral desperately needs the help of a wider constituency.

There are encouraging signs: the 14th-century chancel has been restored for use as a community centre, and work has begun on a restoration of the 19th-century cathedral at an estimated cost of £200,000. But its long-term future as a centre of worship for a Church of Ireland congregation is less easy to predict.

Near the west-door is the shaft of a 12th-century High Cross with the following inscription: OR[OIT] DON RIG DO THA[I]RDELBUCH Ú CHONCHOBAIR OR[OIT] DON THAER DO GILLU C[H]R[IST] U THUATHAI[L]. (A prayer for the king, Turloch O'Connor. A prayer for the craftsman, Giolla-Críst O'Toole); and OR[OIT] DO CHOMARBA IARLAITHE .I. DO AED U OSSIN [LAS]IN DERNAD AN CHROS-SA. (A prayer for the successor of Jarlath, i.e. for Áedh O Hession for whom this cross was made). O'Hession was Abbot of Tuam 1126–51 and Archbishop of Tuam 1152–61.

Tuam Palace was constructed between 1716 and 1741 by Archbishop Edward Synge. In 1787 it was described as old-fashioned and ill-contrived. Improvements were carried out early in the 19th century and completed by 1823, so that the palace was described in 1837 as 'large and handsomely built, though not possessing much architectural embellishment'.[6] It was later sold, and the Bishop of Tuam, Killala and Achonry now lives at Knockglass, a two-storey, five-bay Georgian house, formerly the seat of the Paget family.

References

1 H. E. Day and J. G. F. Patton, *The cathedrals of the Church of Ireland* (London, 1932), p.68.
2 Brian De Breffny and George Mott, *The churches and abbeys of Ireland* (London, 1976), p. 84.
3 T. M. Fallow, *The cathedral churches of Ireland* (London, 1894), p. 95.
4 Day and Patton, *Cathedrals of the Church of Ireland*, p. 70.
5 W. H. Grindle, *Irish cathedral music* (Belfast, 1989), pp 151–152.
6 Mark Bence Jones, *A guide to Irish country houses* (originally published London, 1978, as *Burke's guide to country houses*, Vol. I: *Ireland*; revised ed. London, 1988), p. 276.

TUAM

The Cathedral Church of the Assumption of the Blessed Virgin Mary

Diocese of Tuam (Roman Catholic)

THE Cathedral of the Assumption was built through the efforts of Archbishop Oliver Kelly (1815–34), who called a meeting on 18 March 1827 to discuss the possibility of building a new cathedral for the diocese. The meeting was held in Tuam's first post-Reformation Catholic church, an irregular structure with transepts built in 1783, and the decision was taken to build a cathedral. 'It is the unanimous and decided opinion of the meeting that the erection of a spacious and commodious Catholic Cathedral in the Metropolitan See of Tuam is expedient and necessary, not only as a tribute justly due to our religion, but also with a view to the comfort and convenience as well as of the parishioners as the numerous strangers who occasionally attend at the celebration of the Divine Mysteries in this town.'[1]

The site was obtained, initially on a rental basis, from William Henry Handcock of Carrintrily, and on 10 February 1830 he agreed to a lease at a yearly rent of one shilling. The lease was to run for the lives of Josephine Handcock, daughter of William Henry; Lord Altamont, eldest son of the Marquess of Sligo; and Geoffrey Dominick Browne, eldest son of Dominick Geoffrey Browne of Castle Magarrett, Co. Mayo, whichever of the three survived longest, or for a period of thirty-one years.

The original architect was Dominic Madden, who also designed the cathedrals at Ballina and Ennis. The foundation stone was laid on 30 April 1827, but work came to a halt for some while because of lack of funds. Archbishop Kelly called another meeting on 14 May 1830 to consider a proposal to obtain a loan of £2,000 to finish the cathedral. It was agreed that loans for £100, £50 and £25 should be obtained at 5 per cent to the total amount of £2,000. With some foresight, Archbishop Kelly and those with him, insured the lives of Miss Handcock, Lord Altamont and Mr Browne for £3,000 with the

European Insurance company. This ensured some security until the Company went bankrupt in 1872. But the Archbishop need not have worried. One of the three was still alive in 1897, but the terms of the lease had by then ceased to apply. In 1895 Captain Quintin Dick of 12 Grosvenor Crescent, London, acquired the Handcock property and on 7 August 1897 he handed over the cathedral and its grounds to Archbishop

the diocese were paying 1 each per year, which paid off the interest on the loans but nothing more.

Archbishop Kelly took a keen interest in the work of building the cathedral, and although he was forced through ill-health to spend some time in Leamington in the summer of 1828, he still felt responsible for the project. 'Notwithstanding my

Tuam: the Cathedral of the Assumption for the south-west

John McEvilly (1881–1902) and his successors for ever for a nominal annual rent of one shilling.

Finance was a constant problem, and the loans raised in 1830 had still not been paid off in 1928. At that date the priests of

distance from the new Cathedral, my thoughts were often turned towards it; and you will be pleased to mention to the Committee that I have great reliance on their exertions during my absence. For my part, I will, God willing, work double tides on my return.'[2]

Madden abruptly left the project in 1829 after being told that his planned chancel would have to be reduced in size because of lack of money. For a while the cathedral committee themselves supervised the building works until the appointment of Marcus Murray, and the cathedral was completed to his revised plan. Murray's son William was responsible for the tower, the high altar and the gateway. The glazing of the cathedral was in progress in March 1832, and Archbishop Kelly had employed Michael O'Connor of 80 Dame Street, Dublin, 'to prepare a beautiful stained-glass eastern window, which will cost £240'.[3]

Archbishop Kelly lived to see the cathedral roofed and all but finished by the time of his death in 1834. Because it was still not ready for use, Archbishop John MacHale (1834–81) was enthroned in the old pro-cathedral. He supervised the construction of the tower and dedicated the completed cathedral on 18 August 1837. The cost, at the end of December 1837, was the very low figure of £14,204 0s 5d, due to 'minute attention to economy'.

The cathedral was beset by trouble in its earliest days, and economy, though necessary, might not have been the best guiding principle. When Caesar Otway was touring Connacht in the late 1830s, he went to Tuam and found that the isolated site of the cathedral had exposed it to blustering winds, apparently severely damaging the O'Connor window. The winds 'hurtled furiously up against [the east] window from the north-east — and so now it is all broken — the stained glass has mighty gaps in it, and these gaps . . are filled up with uncouth boards instead of being properly restored'.[4] The unfinished west tower was in an even worse state: 'The foundation has given way, an awful settlement has bent out of line the courses of the masonry, crushed the magnificent western doorway, so that its strong jambs have cracked and split, and splintered, as if this had been so many laths. And there they have come to a stop, and now they dare not go up higher, they tremble lest it should all come down.'[5] These defects incline one to believe that the cathedral was built on a limited budget and in a hurry.

The Cathedral of the Assumption is built of limestone in the style of Decorated Gothic. Standing in isolated grandeur at the end of a wide mall, it measures 53m in length, 42m in width at the transepts, and 14.6m high at the apex of the nave. The three-storey west tower is 43m high and surmounted by eight richly crocketed pinnacles rising above the parapet which is enriched by open tracery. The tower has crenellated turrets emerging from its north-west and south-west corners, square at the base, becoming octagonal above. The tower clock was installed in 1859. There are six square turrets at the angles of the Cathedral each rising above the parapets in octagonal form and terminating in eight octagonal spirelets. When Thomas Carlyle visited the cathedral in 1849 he described these turrets as being 'like pots with many ladles'.[6]

Internally, the cathedral is very similar to Madden's cathedral at Ballina, though the east window is much larger and the ceiling bosses are more elaborate. The aisled nave of five bays is 20m wide. The aisles are divided from the nave by octagonal limestone columns which support a rib-vaulted plaster ceiling with elaborate floriated bosses and giant heads. Because nearly all the roof timbers were affected by death-watch beetle, the original ceiling was taken down in 1929–31 as part of a major restoration costing £20,000 and replaced by the present plaster-vaulted ceiling which copies the design of its predecessor. In 1933 the woodwork of the cathedral organ (purchased in 1870 from Bevingtons of London) was also found to be riddled with death-watch beetle. A new electric organ, incorporating parts of the original instrument was built and installed by Compton of London.

The large east window is nearly 13m high and 5.4m wide and may be a relic of Madden's design for a much longer chancel. The O'Connor glass depicts the Blessed Virgin Mary and the four Evangelists. O'Connor moved to London in 1845 and became prominent in the revival of stained glass in Victorian England. There are also two good windows by Richard King inserted in 1961. The fourth window of the north aisle shows St Jarlath founding his cell beside the broken chariot wheel. The opposite window depicts St Patrick. The Stations of the Cross, with the exception of the eighth, which is not original and noticeably of poorer workmanship, are oil paintings purchased by Archbishop MacHale in 1861 at a cost of £200. They were restored in the 1920s by a Dutchman, van Alan, who gave his opinion that they were the work of Eustace La Soeur who died in 1655. This is difficult to accept, since the style of painting is very much of the 19th century, not of the 17th century. A painting of the Assumption of the Blessed Virgin Mary was presented to the cathedral in 1881 and hangs in the south transept. It is the work of Carlo Maratta, an Italian artist who belonged to a school that flourished c.1690.

The initial reordering of the chancel and sanctuary in accordance with the decrees of Vatican II took place in 1969, at the very end of the episcopate of Archbishop Walsh (1940–69). The Italianate baldachino over the high altar, the two transept altars, the pulpit and the communion rails were removed. The marble high altar (designed, with the baldachino and the tabernacle, by Leonardi of Rome) was moved to a dais at the centre of the crossing, and the baptistery was transferred to the shallow chancel at the rear. A new bishop's throne by the local craftsman Al O'Dea was installed. The Blessed Sacrament was reserved in a new aumbry in the east wall of the south transept, facing the south nave aisle. The aumbry, of gilt brass, was set in a slab of salmon-pink marble with a border of fluted grey granite.

In more recent years the exterior has been sandblasted and siliconed.

Further reordering took place in the early months of 1992. The entire cathedral was repainted and rewired, and the sanctuary area reordered. A new wooden screen with chevron patterning was erected behind the altar, turning the truncated chancel into a sacristy. O'Connor's great east window is now partly obscured by the screen. A new dais of limestone was created, to provide a focus for the new barrel-shaped granite altar. The Blessed Sacrament is now reserved in the gilt brass tabernacle which now rests on a free-standing cylindrical granite plinth. The structure is now sheltered by a fine wooden baldachino.

References

1   E. D. D'Alton, *History of the archdiocese of Tuam* (Dublin, 1928), i, 357.
2   Caesar Otway, *A tour of Connaught* (Dublin, 1839), p. 183.
3   Bernard O'Reilly, *Life of John McHale, Archbishop of Tuam* (New York, 1890), i, p. 196.
4   Otway, *Tour of Connaught*, p. 184.
5   D'Alton, *History of the archdiocese of Tuam*, i, 359.
6   Thomas Carlyle, *Reminiscences of my Irish journey in 1849* (London, 1882), p. 195.

WATERFORD

The Cathedral Church of the Blessed Trinity

(commonly called Christ Church)

Diocese of Waterford (Church of Ireland)

WHEN the Vikings first arrived in Ireland, they came as pirates and marauders. But from the middle of the 9th century they began to establish permanent settlements along the Irish coast; Dublin, Wicklow, Waterford and Wexford are all Danish foundations. A Viking settlement is known to have existed on the banks of the River Suir, close to the south coast of Ireland, in 914. The Vikings called their settlement Vadre Fjord (the River of the Father, i.e. Odin). The present city of Waterford, regional capital of south-east Ireland, is the direct descendant of the 10th-century Viking settlement.

These permanent settlements inevitably absorbed something of the religion and culture of the surrounding Irish. Inter-marriage between the Vikings and the Irish became commonplace, and the former soon absorbed the Christianity of the latter. Two churches in Waterford stand on the site of Viking foundations: St Olaf's and Christ Church. St Olaf's was allegedly a 9th-century foundation, but was reconstructed

by the Normans and substantially rebuilt in 1734. The building, which was in the possession of the Church of Ireland, was closed in recent years and is now a youth centre.

The date of the foundation of the cathedral is uncertain. Some authorities say that it was founded by Reginald, son of Sigtryg, c.1050; others that it was the work of Malchus (Máel Ísu Ua hAinmere), a monk of Winchester who was consecrated first Bishop of Waterford in 1096 by St Anselm (Archbishop of Canterbury 1093–1114). Both accounts agree that it was dedicated to the Blessed Trinity. The name 'Christ Church' is a surviving Scandinavian term for 'head church' or cathedral.

Malchus was listed as Archbishop of Cashel at the Synod of Ráith Bressail in 1111, but seems to have resigned that office, since he died as Bishop of Waterford in 1135. Close links between Waterford and Canterbury seem to have been ended at Ráith Bressail when Waterford was fully incorporated into the new Irish diocesan structure.

After the conquest of Waterford by the Anglo–Normans Richard FitzGilbert de Clare, Earl of Pembroke (better known as Strongbow) and leader of the invading forces, was married to Eva, daughter of King Dermot of Leinster, in a politically convenient ceremony at the cathedral in 1170.

Between 1200 and 1223 the diocese of Waterford was held in succession by a Norman bishop named Robert, a Welshman named David, and a second Norman bishop named Robert. The period was one of vicious dispute between Waterford and the neighbouring diocese of Lismore, still held by an Irish bishop. Bishop Robert I of Waterford pursued a policy of direct annexation of Lismore, encountering the fierce resistance of Bishop Felix of Lismore (1179–1202) and by his successor, Malachias, a Cistercian monk. Bishop Robert I was excommunicated in 1203 by Pope Innocent III, who often intervened on the side of Lismore. His successor, Bishop David, pursued the attempt to annex Lismore until he was himself murdered by Irishmen in 1209. In 1211 Pope Innocent gave final judgement in favour of the independence of Lismore, but the violence continued. Bishop Robert II of Waterford seized Bishop Malachias of Lismore and himself fastened shackles on his prisoner. For his actions against Lismore he was, like his namesake, excommunicated by the pope. Innocent III gave a further decision in favour of Lismore in 1215, and the decision was confirmed by Pope Honorius III in 1219. A Norman bishop was consecrated to Lismore in 1219, and the two sees lived in peace from that date until they were formally united in 1363.

The 13th century cathedral consisted of a nave and chancel (added in 1220) with side aisles but without transepts. There was no structural division between the nave and the chancel, which were separated only by a screen. The total length was more than 40m, and the nave was 14m wide. The nave was separated from the aisles by an arcade of eight pointed arches on each side, supported on clustered columns, surmounted by a clerestory. Behind the high altar was a large Lady Chapel which after the Reformation became a parish church under the name of Trinity. It had ceased to be used before the demolition of the cathedral in the 18th century. At about the half-way point on the north side of the cathedral was a large square tower with typically Irish stepped battlements, surmounted by a low pyramidal spire.

From time to time chapels were added to the cathedral by the prosperous merchants and citizens of Waterford. Among them was the Chapel of St James the Elder and St Catherine, 6.7m square on the north side. It was built in 1482 by one James Rice, who was Mayor of Waterford on eleven occasions between 1468 and 1489 and enjoyed great popularity in the city. Eventually it became known as Rice's Chapel. Because of his popularity, Rice was concerned that the townsfolk should not imagine him to have some kind of immortality. He therefore ordered that a year after his death his grave should be opened and the people of Waterford allowed to see his body in a state of physical decay. In case this one viewing were insufficient, his memorial takes the form of a recumbent effigy in semi-skeletal condition with vermin, including a frog or toad, crawling in and out of the ribs. 'There is no mistake at all about his dissolution.'[1] The inscription includes the line 'It is our fate to pass through the gates of death.' The origin of the monument is not entirely clear; one account says that it was carved on the orders of Rice during his lifetime; another, that it in a genuine representation of the state of his body twelve months after his death. It is now thought that Rice ordered it to be made during his lifetime. The monument is somewhat weathered; it was removed from the medieval cathedral before its demolition in 1773 and stood in the burial ground opposite the west door until 1880, when it was placed inside the present cathedral.

Rice's Chapel was flanked by another chapel to the east and the Chapter House to the west. All three were demolished in the 18th century to allow the churchyard to be enlarged. There were other chapels, dedicated to Our Lady, St Saviour, St John the Evangelist, St Nicholas, St Katherine and St Anne. An arched or vaulted ceiling was added to the Lady Chapel and chancel by Bishop Nicholas Comyn (1519–51).

To judge from the representations which appear in 18th-century paintings and engravings, Christ Church Cathedral had developed into an unusual and interesting collection of buildings, and its demolition in the 18th century was a very sad loss. The ground plan and the bases of many of the piers of this building remain about 2m below the floor of the present cathedral. They are now inaccessible, and the passageways between them have been bricked up. But the stump of one pier of clustered columns can still be seen on the south side of the nave by lifting a grate in the floor.

During the 18th century consideration was given to replacing this cathedral with a new structure, and in 1739 William Halfpenny, an architect with Bristol connections, was invited to submit plans for rebuilding the cathedral. The plans were never implemented, but his drawings are still preserved.[2]

Waterford: Christ Church Cathedral from the south-west

In 1773 Thomas Ivory, a Dublin architect, was invited to present a report on the condition of the cathedral; he recommended that the cathedral be rebuilt. On 14 July 1773 it was decided at a meeting of a committee appointed by the City Council, assisted by the bishop and the dean, to follow the recommendation and demolish the cathedral on the ground that it was decayed and unsafe. This view seems to be contradicted by the report of an eye-witness who saw 'the extreme difficulty which the workmen experienced in effecting the demolition'.[3] In fact the walls were so strong that explosives had to be used for demolition. 'It is a matter of sincere regret to many who recollect the ancient edifice, that the profane hands of the last generation should have violated this beautiful remnant of antiquity.'[4]

217

A (perhaps legendary) story records that the desire to demolish the medieval cathedral originated with the Dean and Chapter, but that Bishop Richard Chenevix (1746–79) was less than enthusiastic. 'Dr Chenevix did not easily fall in with the profane idea, but to bring the logic of facts to bear upon him it was regulated that as he passed through the church one morning a quantity of dust and rubbish should drop at the right time, which brought him to his "right" senses, and caused him to believe that the church was falling.'[5]

A sum of £4,000 was proposed for demolition and for the construction of a new cathedral. The total cost was £5,397 including a sum of £150 for demolition. Work began in 1774, and body of the cathedral was finished by 1779. Subscriptions were invited in 1783 for the construction of the tower and spire, which may not have been part of the original design, and the whole cathedral was completed by about 1792. During the demolition of the cathedral a set of 15th-century vestments was found in the crypt; as the two Bishops of Waterford (Church of Ireland and Roman Catholic) were on good terms with each other, the Church of Ireland bishop presented them to his Catholic counterpart.

The new cathedral was designed by John Roberts (1714–96), a local architect whose Welsh grandfather had settled in Waterford c.1680. Roberts was well known in Waterford and Bishop Chenevix had employed him to complete the Bishop's Palace. He fathered twenty one children, eight of whom survived to adult life, and one of his great-grandsons was Field-Marshal Earl Roberts (1832–1914) who was Commander-in-Chief of the forces in Ireland from 1895 to 1899. It is nice to record on a happy ecumenical note that such was his standing and reputation that he was invited to design the Roman Catholic cathedral in Waterford as the Church of Ireland cathedral was being completed.

Roberts's design is typical of the 18th century's liking for the lightness and elegance of the Classical style. He designed the cathedral as an aisled rectangle 51.8m long and 17.6m wide, and 12.1m high, with a shallow chancel and seating for 1,100. The west entrance is through a portico supported by four Corinthian columns from which rises a heavy grey tower surmounted by an octagonal spire with banding, 58.8m high. The tower has a collection of Corinthian columns, pilasters, blind balustrades and empty niches on each face. 'The tower and spire suffer a little from the relative triviality of their architectural embellishments which emerge incompletely and with difficulty from the over-heavy mass of the tower.'[6] The exterior walls of the cathedral have been painted white, with the exception of the quoin stones.

Roberts appears to have had a liking for Baroque architecture and the interior is similar to some of Wren's London churches, built almost a century earlier. The 'nave' uses the five eastern bays, the three western bays being empty. The aisles are divided by a double row of columns which support the galleries on each side. At the west end is a lofty and spacious vestibule. On either side are vestries for the clergy and choir. Roberts included north, south and west galleries in his design and a high central carved oak 'wine-glass' pulpit with tester above. The columns are stone Corinthian pillars with richly carved capitals and entablature and red marble plinths.

On 25 October 1815 the cathedral was badly damaged by a fire which burnt much of the woodwork and destroyed most of the ceiling and the organ. The fire broke out in the organ loft, and 'had not the weather been calm, and the hour favourable for exertion, the fire would have reduced the entire pile to ruin.'[7] Restoration took three years, and the cathedral was opened for worship again on 10 May 1818. The new ceiling was a more ornate version than its predecessor, with foliage enrichment of the arches. The ceiling is profusely decorated with applied plaster garlands of leaves and flowers. The ceiling of the vestibule is original; the rest of the cathedral is post-fire.

A new ring of eight bells was installed in the tower in 1872, and two years later the 18th-century spire was demolished because of structural instability; there is no evidence of any connection. In 1878 the *Irish Builder* carried a short note referring to a proposal to 're-erect the spire' at a cost of about £2,000, of which £800 had already been raised. Raising sufficient funds took several years, and a new spire was not erected until 1880; the work was carried out by a local firm, Ryan & Son of William Street.

As the 19th century progressed it was clear that the internal ordering of the cathedral was no longer satisfactory to the changing view of liturgy and worship. James Godkin remarked in 1867, in his usual sarcastic style: 'It is quite evident that those by whom the internal arrangements were planned were not High Churchmen; for nothing could be more offensive to the taste of such men than the way in which the altar is overshadowed by an immense pulpit and reading-desk, standing right in front of it, and obstructing the view of the worshipper.'[8]

A thorough remodelling of the interior took place in 1885–91 under the direction of Sir Thomas Drew. The galleries were removed, the lower nave windows were bricked up, the box pews were replaced and the vestibule thrown open to the nave by the erection of a beautiful arch of Caen stone. The organ, formerly in the west gallery, was removed to the north side of the chancel. The pulpit (Caen stone with red marble columns) which had been erected in the centre of the church in memory of Bishop Robert Daly (1843–72), was moved to the north side and reduced in height; Drew was reported to have had 'a most difficult task in adapting the pulpit to the new arrangements'.[9] A new brass double-sided lectern was presented in 1891.

The cathedral library, housed in a room in the north-west corner of the cathedral, has a good collection of 16th- and

Waterford: the interior of Christ Church Cathedral looking east

17th-century bibles and prayer books, including a 'Breeches Bible' of 1599.

There is also a memorial to Henry O'Hara, Bishop of Cashel, Emly, Waterford and Lismore 1900–19. Not a popular or successful bishop in the south of Ireland, he is remembered elsewhere for conceiving the idea of building St Anne's Cathedral in Belfast.

The nave, aisle and chancel floors are of black and white marble checks, and the walls have a pine wainscoting; the pews are also of pine. The chancel screen has a base and pillars of stone with festooned corbels, panels of red marble, and a top of black Kilkenny marble. The chapter and choir stalls are of oak, and were designed by Drew to harmonise with the architecture of the cathedral. The organ case on the north side of the chancel is of mahogany.

The sanctuary steps are of white marble, and the sanctuary floor (the work of Drew) is covered with floral-patterned mosaic set between narrow bands of black marble. The ceiling has a modillion cornice. The north and south walls have a dado of red marble panels. The oak altar was presented in 1924 by the Goff family. There is no east window, the wall being covered with plaster decoration; three panels below an architectural pediment are framed by egg-and-dart moulding and include a mitre and a mortar board; the sunburst at the centre of the reredos enshrines the word YAHWEH, the Hebrew name for the deity.

A small chapel, dedicated to St Nicholas, was created in the south chancel aisle in 1944.

Judging its appearance by contemporary prints, the medieval cathedral was a curious and fascinating structure. The decision to demolish was, in the judgement of many, an act of wanton destruction, worse than the unroofing and abandonment of Cashel Cathedral in 1748. From that standpoint the first reaction is anger followed by sadness and regret, and a feeling that the present building is scant compensation. However, it is easy to formulate an opinion and deliver a judgement on little more than a love of medieval architecture. It is also easy to criticise decisions taken more than two centuries ago, without detailed information about the state of the medieval cathedral and the problems of maintaining the structure.

Before the bishop and the Dean and Chapter of the day are condemned for an act of gross vandalism, they deserve consideration for providing Waterford with a light, airy and elegant Classical cathedral, which is only a product of the aspirations of its age. Godkin damned it with faint praise in 1867, likening it to 'a good large old parish church in a third-rate English town'; but even though he was often sarcastic of Irish ecclesiastical architecture, Godkin was prepared to admit that Christ Church Cathedral was 'commodious and cheerful'.[10] Other observers have been more generous; for example, Day and Patton commented: 'It is of its type a noble building, and is by no means to be despised. It cannot aspire to the solemn majesty of a great Gothic church, but it is of fine proportions and considerable dignity, a worthy House of God.'[11]

The former Bishop's Palace, on the south side of the cathedral, is one of the largest and finest episcopal residences in Ireland. The palace is a seven-bay, three-storey house of limestone ashlar begun in 1741 by Bishop Charles Este and still incomplete at the time of his death in 1745. It has been attributed to Richard Cassels, but was certainly by John Roberts. The palace was sold *c.* 1920, and was then used as the Bishop Foy School until *c.* 1965. After restoration by the Corporation of Waterford in 1975 it now houses the City Engineering Department.

To the north-east of the cathedral is the 18th-century former Deanery, also now restored by the Corporation for their own use. It has a 13th/15th-century undercroft which may have been part of the cathedral or may have had secular uses.

The diocese of Waterford was always very small, the neighbouring diocese of Lismore, covering most of what is now Co. Waterford, and part of Co. Tipperary. In the Church of Ireland arrangement, Waterford and Lismore, which had been united since 1363, were added to Cashel and Emly in 1833. In 1976 Emly was detached, and Cashel, Waterford and Lismore were joined to Ossory, Ferns and Leighlin. The bishop is usually styled Bishop of Cashel and Ossory.

References

1 H. E. Day and J. G. F Patton, *The cathedrals of the Church of Ireland* (London, 1932), p. 126.
2 In the Drawings Collection of the Royal Institute of British Architects in London.
3 T. M. Fallow, *The cathedral churches of Ireland* (London, 1894), p. 74.
4 Ibid.
5 P. M. Egan, *History, guide and directory of the county and city of Waterford*, (Kilkenny, 1895), pp 481–2.
6 Maurice Craig, *The architecture of Ireland from the earliest times to 1880* (London & Dublin, 1982), p. 209.
7 *The Parliamentary Gazetteer of Ireland* (Dublin, 1844–6), iii, 492.
8 James Godkin, *Ireland and her churches* (London, 1867), p. 323.
9 *Irish Builder*, xxxiii, no. 745 (1891), p. 11.
10 Ibid.
11 Day and Patton, *Cathedrals of the Church of Ireland*, p. 129.

WATERFORD

The Cathedral Church of the Holy Trinity

Dioceses of Waterford and Lismore (Roman Catholic)

HOLY Trinity Cathedral fronts on to Barron Strand Street, a busy main street leading down to the river, and is hemmed in by buildings; only the west front is entirely visible. It was built at the instigation of Thomas Hearn (Dean 1772–1810). The Roman Catholic community petitioned the City Corporation to build a chapel in 1700 on the site of the present cathedral. It was an undistinguished building, and, considering the date of its erection, it was not surprising that the old chapel should have been concealed from public gaze by houses fronting on to Barron Strand Street; entry at that time was from Conduit Lane by a long narrow passage.

John Roberts (1714–96), the architect who had designed Waterford's Church of Ireland cathedral in 1773, was invited twenty years later to design the city's Roman Catholic cathedral as well. It was built in 1793–6 during the episcopate of Bishop William Egan (1775–96) and is the oldest Roman Catholic cathedral in Ireland. The total cost was about £20,000. Unusually, it bears the same dedication as the Church of Ireland cathedral, a practice not always followed in later years. Roberts was over eighty when he designed it. His custom was to rise at 6 a.m. to superintend the workmen. One morning he rose by mistake at 3 a.m.and found the cathedral empty. He sat down in it, fell asleep and caught a chill from which he died. His appointment as designing architect was a tribute to his reputation, and this is obvious in his ability to design two completely different cathedrals, both with their respective denominations very much in mind. 'The Protestant cathedral is cool and northern, redolent of lawn sleeves and the communion service; the Catholic cathedral with its forest of huge Corinthian columns, is warm, luscious and Mediterranean.'[1]

The Classical-style cathedral is basically a rectangle with an apsidal east end. Shallow four-bay recesses on the north and south sides may be taken as the architectural descendants of transepts. The sanctuary was extended during the years 1829–37. Thackeray visited the cathedral during a tour of Ireland early in the 1840s and did not like it, calling it 'a large, dingy . . . chapel, of some pretensions within; but, as usual, there had been a failure for want of money, and the front of the chapel was unfinished, presenting the butt end of a portico, and walls on which the stone coating was to be laid.'[2]

The apse was added in 1854, and it was also intended to erect the portico at the same date. The bases of the columns with short sections of the shafts were in position when it was discovered that the foundations, standing on the bed of a reclaimed creek, would not bear the weight, and the west front was not completed until 1893. Extensive repairs were undertaken at the same time, and the cathedral was finally consecrated on 24 September 1893.

The marble high altar and reredos date from 1881, though the altar incorporates the front of its predecessor of 1854. It is roofed by a baldachino supported by five Corinthian columns with gilt capitals, white marble shafts and square red marble bases. The high altar is now partly obscured by the new carved oak altar in keeping with Baroque style of the cathedral. The sanctuary area is lit by a circular roof window.

The Baroque style is continued in the bishop's throne, the choir and chapter stalls, and the very high oak pulpit. There are disused side altars, and the bishop's throne is on the north side. There is a memorial to Thomas Hussey, first Roman Catholic Bishop of Waterford (1797–1803) to live in the city since the Reformation. The organ is in a bow-fronted gallery over the west entrance, and the 'transepts' have bow-fronted galleries of grained pine supported by fluted Ionic pine columns. The pews are also of pine. The roof is supported by large Corinthian columns set in groups of four, which lean alarmingly out of the perpendicular. With dark-blue shafts and white and gilt capitals, they present a somewhat garish appearance. The Stations of the Cross, which adorn the nave columns, are unframed and varnished 19th-century oil paintings on canvas by Alcan of Paris; some were restored by A. Hodgkinson of Limerick in 1978.

The cathedral is criss-crossed by electrical conduits which move from column to column at capital level. The cathedral was completely renovated in 1978. Eight large Waterford glass chandeliers were added in 1979 as a gift from Waterford Crystal. With its Ionic stone west front facing on to a busy street, and surrounded by buildings on three sides, Holy Trinity Cathedral has a dark and sultry atmosphere, but there is no feeling of oppressiveness, only a welcome refuge from the crowded clamour of the city outside.

References

1 Mark Girouard, 'City of Waterford, Ireland' in *Country Life*, 15 Dec. 1966, p. 1628.
2 W. M. Thackeray, *The Irish sketch-book* (London, 1843), i, 82–3.

Waterford: the west front of Holy Trinity Cathedral

BIBLIOGRAPHY

ADDLESHAW, G.W.O., and ETCHELLS, Frederick, *The architectural setting of Anglican worship* (London, 1948).

ALLEN, J.R., 'Notes on the antiquities in Co. Kerry' in *Journal of the Royal Society of the Antiquaries of Ireland*, 5th ser. ii; consecutive ser. xxii (1892), pp 158–66.

ANDERSON, William, and HICKS, Clive, *Cathedrals in Britain and Ireland* (London, 1978).

ANREP, Boris, and ALLEN, Máirín, *The Mullingar mosaics* (Mullingar, n.d.)

ARCHDALL, Mervyn, *Monasticon Hibernicum* (London, 1786).

ATKINSON, E. D., *Dromore: an Ulster Diocese* (Dundalk, 1925).

BARROW, G. L., *Glendalough and Saint Kevin* (Dundalk, 1972).

——, *Irish Round Towers* (Dublin, 1976).

——, *The Round Towers of Ireland* (Dublin, 1979).

BAYLY, Henry, *A topographical and historical account of Lisburn* (Belfast, 1834).

BECKETT, J. C., *The making of modern Ireland, 1603–1923* (London, 1966).

BEGLEY, John, *The diocese of Limerick, ancient and mediaeval* (Dublin, 1906).

BENCE-JONES, Mark, *A guide to Irish country houses* (London, 1978; revised ed., London, 1988).

BERNARD, J. H., *A history of St Patrick's Cathedral Dublin* (Dublin, 1903; revised ed. by J. E. L. Oulton, Dublin, 1940).

BOLSTER, M. A. *Cathedral of St Mary and St Anne* (Cork, n.d.).

——, *The North Parish* (Cork, n.d.).

BRADY, W. M., *Clerical and parochial records of Cork, Cloyne and Ross*, (3 vols, London, 1864).

BRASH, R. R., *The ecclesiastical architecture of Ireland* (Dublin, 1875).

BRETT, C. E. B., *Buildings of Belfast, 1700–1914* (Belfast, 1966; revised ed., Belfast, 1985).

BREWER, J.N., *The beauties of Ireland* (2 vols, London, 1825–6).

BRISLANE, B. A., *St Mary's Cathedral, Limerick. the organ. a short history with specifications*, (2nd ed., Limerick, 1971).

BROPHY, Edward, *Carlow Cathedral, 1833–1983* (Carlow, 1983).

BROWNE, Michael, *Galway Cathedral* (Galway, 1967).

BUTLER, William, *Christ Church Cathedral, Dublin* (Dublin, 1874).

——, *The Cathedral Church of the Holy Trinity Dublin* (London, 1901).

CAMPBELL, Edward, *Cathedral of SS. Patrick and Colman. Newry* (Newry, 1948; revised ed. by Anthony Davies, Newry, 1979).

CANBY, Courtlandt, *A guide to the archaeological sites of the British Isles* (New York, 1988).

Capuchin Annual (1941), pp 241–304. (Photographs of the bishops and cathedrals of the Roman Catholic Church in Ireland.)

CAREY, Maurice, *Saint Fin Barre's Cathedral* (Cork, 1984).

CARLISLE, Nicholas, *A topographical dictionary of Ireland* (London, 1810).

CARLYLE, Thomas, *Reminiscences of my Irish journey in 1849* (London, 1882).

CARMODY, W. P., *Lisburn Cathedral and its past rectors* (Belfast, 1926).

CARPENTER, S. C., *Church and people, 1789–1889* (London, 1933).

CARRIGAN, William, *The history and antiquities of the diocese of Ossory*, 4 volumes (Dublin, 1905).

CASSIDY, Herbert, *St Patrick's Cathedral, Armagh* (Derby, 1991).

——, *The Cathedral Church of St Fethlimidh, Kilmore* (Kilmore, n.d.).

The Cathedral Church of Christ Church the Redeemer, Dromore (Dromore, n.d.).

The Cathedral of Christ Church, Lisburn: a short guide for visitors (repr., 1965).

Cathedral of the Assumption, Thurles, 1879–1979 (Thurles, 1979).

CAULFIELD, Richard, *A lecture on the history of the Bishops of Cork and Cathedral of St Fin Barre* (Cork, 1864).

——, *Annals of St Fin Barre's Cathedral, Cork* (Cork, 1871).

——, *Annals of the Cathedral of St Coleman, Cloyne* (Cork, 1882).

CHADWICK, Owen, *The Victorian church*, (2 vols. London, 1966; revised ed., London, 1971).

CHART, D. A. (ed.), *A preliminary survey of the ancient monuments of Northern Ireland* (Belfast, 1940).

CLAFFEY, J. A., *The Cathedral of the Assumption, Tuam* (Tuam, 1986).

——, *St Mary's Cathedral, Tuam, Co. Galway* (Tuam, n.d.).

CLAPHAM, A. W., 'Some Minor Irish Cathedrals' in *Archaeological Journal of the Royal Archaeological Institute for Great Britain and Ireland*, (1949) (Supplement Memorial Volume to Sir Alfred Clapham).

CLARKE, B. F. L., *Church builders of the nineteenth century* (London, 1938).

COEN, Martin, *The wardenship of Galway* (Galway, 1984).

COGAN, Anthony, *The diocese of Meath, ancient and modern* (3 vols, Dublin, 1862).

COLE, J. H., *Church and parish records of the united dioceses of Cork, Cloyne and Ross* (Cork, 1903).

CORISH, P. J., *A history of Irish Catholicism* (Dublin, 1967–).

COSTELLO, Peter, *Dublin churches* (Dublin, 1989).

COTTON, Henry, *Fasti Ecclesiae Hiberniae*, (5 vols, Dublin, 1845–60).

COWELL, G. Y., 'St Brigid and the Cathedral Church of Kildare' in *Journal of the Co. Kildare Archaeological Society*, ii (1896–9), pp 235–52.

CRAIG, H. N., *Some notes on the Cathedral of St Brigid, Kildare* (Dublin, 1931).

CRAIG, Maurice, *The architecture of Ireland from the earliest times to 1880* (London & Dublin, 1982).

CROOK, J. M., *William Burges and the high Victorian dream* (Chicago, 1981).

CROOKS, Samuel, *Belfast Cathedral* (Belfast, 1985).

CURL, J. S., *Classical churches in Ulster* (1980).

D'ALTON, E. D., *History of the archdiocese of Tuam*, (2 vols, Dublin, 1928).

DAVIES, Oliver, 'Old Churches in County Louth – the barony of Louth' in *County Louth Archaeological and Historical Society Journal*, x, no. 2 (1942), pp 101–7.

DAY, J. G. F. and PATTON, H. E., *The cathedrals of the Church of Ireland* (London, 1932).

DE BREFFNY, Brian, and MOTT, George, *The churches and abbeys of Ireland* (London, 1976).

DONOHOE, B., 'Galway's New Cathedral' in *Capuchin Annual* (1966), pp 399–407.

DOWD, James, *History of St Mary's Cathedral, Limerick* (Limerick, 1899).

DOWN CATHEDRAL RESTORATION COMMITTEE, *The Cathedral of the Holy Trinity of Down: restoration, 1952* (Down, 1952).

DOWNING, D., 'The Pro-Cathedral, Marlborough Street, Dublin: Its story and associations' in *Irish Ecclesiastical Record*, 5th ser., ix (1917), pp 455–62.

DUHIG, Thomas, *St Ailbe's Church, Emly, 1882–1982* (Emly, 1982).

DUIGNAN, Michael, 'Clonfert Cathedral: a note' in *Journal of the Galway Archaeological and Historical Society*, xxix, (1954–5), p. 29.

DUNNE, John, *Shrines of Ireland* (Dublin, 1989).

DWYER, Philip, *The diocese of Killaloe from the Reformation to the close of the eighteenth century* (Dublin, 1878).

EGAN, P. K., 'The royal visitation of Clonfert and Kilmacduagh, 1615' in *Journal of the Galway Archaeological and Historical Society*, xxxv (1976), pp 67–76.

——, *St Brendan's Cathedral. Loughrea* (Dublin, 1986).

EGAN, P.M., *History, guide and directory of the county and city of Waterford* (Kilkenny, 1895).

EMERSON, N. D., 'Donnchadh Ua Cerbhaill' in *County Louth Archaeological and Historical Society Journal*, vi, no. 1 (1925), pp 16–23.

EMPEY, Adrian (ed.), *A worthy foundation: the Cathedral Church of St Canice Kilkenny* (Portlaoise, 1985).

FAHEY, Jerome, 'The diocese of Annaghdown' in *Journal of the Galway Archaeological and Historical Society*, iii, (1903–4), pp 102–13.

——, *The history and antiquities of the diocese of Kilmacduagh* (Dublin, 1893).

FALLOW, T. M., *The cathedral churches of Ireland* (London 1894).

FERRAR, John, *The history of Limerick* (Limerick, 1787).

FERREY, Benjamin, *Recollections of A. N. Welby Pugin and his father, Augustus Pugin* (London, 1861).

FLEMING, H. T., 'Some of the history of the castell and see demesne of Cloyne' in *Journal of the Cork Historical and Archaeological Society*, ix (1903), pp 209–23.

FLEMING, John, *St John's Cathedral, Limerick* (Dublin, 1987).

FLOOD, W. H. Grattan, 'The diocese and abbey of Mayo' in *Irish Ecclesiastical Record*, 4th ser., xxi (1907), pp 603–9.

FRENCH, N. E., *Trim places and traces* (Trim, 1988).

FROST, James, *History and topography of County Clare* (Dublin, 1893).

FRY, Peter and F.S., *A history of Ireland* (London, 1988).

FRYDE, E. B., GREENWAY, D. E., PORTER, S., and ROY, I., *Handbook of British Chronology* (3rd ed. London, 1986).

GALLOWAY, P. J., *The Order of St Patrick 1783–1983* (Chichester, 1983).

GARNER, William, *Carlow: architectural heritage* (Dublin, 1980).

——, *Cóbh: architectural heritage* (Dublin, 1979).

——, *Ennis: architectural heritage* (Dublin, 1981).

——, *Galway: architectural heritage* (Dublin, 1985).

GIFF, W. L. M., *The Story of St Patrick's Cathedral, Trim* (Trim, 1959).

GIROUARD, Mark, 'City of Waterford, Ireland' 3 pts in *Country Life*, 8 Dec. 1966, pp 1560–63; 15 Dec. 1966, pp 1626–9; 22 Dec. 1966 pp 1695–8.

GODKIN, James, *Ireland and her churches* (London, 1867).

GOGAN, L.S., 'The name of Louth' in *County Louth Archaelogical and Historical Society Journal*, xiii, no. 1 (1953), pp 5–7.

GOGARTY, T., 'St Mary's Abbey, Louth' in *County Louth Archaeological and Historical Society Journal*, iv, no. 2 (1917), pp 169–89.

GRAVES, James and PRIM, J. G. A., *The history, architecture and antiquities of the Cathedral Church of St Canice, Kilkenny* (Dublin, 1857).

GREER, James, *The windings of the Moy* (Dublin, 1924).

GRINDLE, W.H., *Irish cathedral music* (Belfast, 1989).

A guide to St Macartan's Cathedral, Monaghan (Monaghan, 1987).

A guide to the Cathedral Church of Saint Eunan, Raphoe (Raphoe, n.d.).

GUNNIS, Rupert, *Dictionary of British Sculptors 1660–1851* (London, 1951).

GWYNN, Aubrey, 'The Twelfth-Century Reform' in *A History of Irish Catholicism* (ed. P. J. Corish), ii, 1 (Dublin, 1968).

——, and GLEESON, D. F., *A history of the diocese of Killaloe* (Dublin, 1962).

——, and HADCOCK, R. N., *Medieval religious houses: Ireland* (Dublin, 1970).

H.M.S.O., *Report of Her Majesty's Commissioners on the Revenues and Condition of the Established Church (Ireland)*, 1868.

——, *Ancient monuments in Northern Ireland, vol. i: In state care*, (4th ed., Belfast, 1962).

——, *An archaeological survey of County Down* (1966).

HANDLEY-READ, Charles, 'St Fin Barre's Cathedral' in *Architectural Review*, cxi, no. 844, (June 1967), pp 423–30.

HARAN, Cyril (ed.), *Sligo Cathedral, 1875–1975* (Sligo, 1975).

HARBISON, Peter, *Guide to the national monuments in the Republic of Ireland* (Dublin, 1970).

——, 'New Light on St. Mary's "Abbey", Louth' in *County Louth Archaeological and Historical Society Journal*, xviii, no. 1 (1973), pp 39–42.

HARRIS, John, and LEVER, Jill, *Illustrated Glossary of Architecture 850–1830* (New York, 1966).

HARRISON, Graham, *St Eunan's Cathedral, Letterkenny* (Dublin, 1988).

HARTNETT, P. J., *Cork city: its history and architecture* (Cork, 1943).

HARVEY, Patrick, *A guide to the Cathedral Church of St Mary the Virgin, Limerick* (Limerick, 1990).

HAYES, R. J., *Sources for the History of Irish Civilization* (9 vols. Boston, 1970).

HAYWARD, Richard, *Munster and the city of Cork* (London, 1964).

HAYDN, J. A., *Misericords in St Mary's Cathedral, Limerick* (Limerick, 1963).

HEALY, John, *Insula sanctorum et doctorum; or Ireland's ancient schools and scholars* (Dublin and London, 1890).

——, *History of the diocese of Meath*, (2 vols. Dublin, 1908).

——, *Historical guide to Kells (Ceanannus Mor), County Meath* (Dublin, 1930).

HICKEY, Elizabeth, 'Arms of the Earls of March and Ulster on the tower of the Cathedral of Trim, Ireland' in *Coat of Arms*, v (1983), pp 148–52.

HILL, Arthur, *Ardfert Cathedral* (Cork, 1870).

HOLLAND, W. R., *History of west Cork and the diocese of Ross* (Skibbereen, 1949).

HOLMES, George, *Sketches of some of the southern counties of Ireland, collected during a tour in the autumn, 1797, in a series of letters* (London, 1801).

HUGHES, Kathleen, and HAMLIN, A. E., *The modern traveller to the early Irish Church* (London, 1977).

HUNT, St L., *Cashel and its abbeys* (Dublin, 1952).

HYNES, J. P., *A short guide to Kilmacduagh* (1986).

The Irish Builder (*the Dublin Builder* until 1866)

vol. ii, no. 18 (1860), p. 277 (Carlow).

vol. ii, no. 20 (1860), p. 313 (Longford).

vol. ii, no. 21 (1860), pp 325–6 (Dublin – St Patrick's).

vol. ii, no. 21 (1860), p. 327 (Ballaghaderreen)

vol. ii, no. 24 (1860), p. 378 (Limerick – St Mary's).

vol. iii, no. 37 (1861), p. 562 (Monaghan).

vol. iii, no. 42 (1861), p. 626 (Tuam – St Mary's).

vol. iii, no. 42 (1861), pp 633–4 (Limerick – St Mary's).

vol. iv, no. 51 (1862), p. 34 (Tuam – St Mary's and the Assumption).

vol. iv, no. 52 (1862), p. 40 (Tuam – St Mary's and the Assumption).

vol. iv, no. 68 (1862), p. 261 (Cork – St Mary and St Anne).

vol. vi, no. 109 (1864), p. 131 (Tuam – St Mary's; Kilkenny – St Canice's; Dublin – St Patrick's).

vol. vii, no. 121 (1865), p. 9 (Cork – St Fin Barre's).

vol. vii, no. 123 (1865), p. 34 (Tuam – St Mary's).

vol. viii, no. 165 (1866), pp 258–9 (Kilkenny – St Mary's).

vol. ix, no. 189 (1867), pp 282–4 and 287 (Cobh).

vol. ix, no. 219 (1869), pp 36–7 (Cobh).

vol. xi, no. 234 (1869), pp 210 and 213 (Cork – St Mary and St Anne).

vol. xii, no. 257 (1870), p. 211 (Ardfert).

vol. xiii, no. 286 (1871), p. 291 (Kildare).

vol. xiii, no. 287 (1871), p. 307 (Thurles).

vol. xv, no. 316 (1873), p. 47 (Derry – St Eugene's).

vol. xv, no. 329 (1873), p. 329 (Armagh – St Patrick's – RC).

vol. xvi, no. 351 (1874), p. 218 (Sligo – Immaculate Conception)
vol. xvii, no. 373 (1875), pp 190–3 (Kilkenny – St Canices's).
vol. xvii, no. 377 (1875), p. 248 (Kildare)
vol. xvii, no. 379 (1875), pp 276–8 (Kildare).
vol. xviii, no. 388 (1876), p. 388 (Limerick – St Mary's).
vol. xix, no. 425 (1877), p. 255 (Thurles).
vol. xx, no. 434 (1878), p. 29 (Kilmacduagh – Gort).
vol. xx, no. 443 (1878), p. 163 (Cork).
vol. xx, no. 449 (1878), pp 254–6 (Kilkenny – St Canice's).
vol. xx, no. 452 (1878), p. 305 (St Mary's, Tuam).
vol. xx, no. 455 (1878), p. 353 (Waterford – Christ Church). vol. xxi, no. 463 (1879), p. 99 (Kilkenny – St Canice's).
vol. xxi, no. 477 (1879), p. 344 (Limerick – St John's).
vol. xxii, no. 498 (1880), p. 263 (Leighlin).
vol. xxix, no. 658 (1887), p. 134 (Killaloe).
vol. xxxiii, no. 745 (1891), pp 11–2 (Christ Church, Waterford). vol. xxxiii, no. 755 (1891), p. 130 (Letterkenny).
vol. xxxiii, no. 761 (1891), p. 195 (Leighlin).
vol. xxxiv, no. 779 (1892), p. 124 (Belfast – St Anne's).
vol. xxxv, no. 802 (1893), p. 122 (Cloyne).
Irish Monthly, xix (7 Sept. 1891), pp 495–7 (short note on the dedication of Letterkenny Cathedral).
J. C., 'St Colman of Cloyne' in *Journal of the Cork Historical and Archaeological Society*, xvi (1910), pp 132–42.
JACKSON, R. W., *Cathedrals of the Church of Ireland* (Dublin, 1971).
JACKSON, Victor, *St Patrick's Cathedral, Dublin* (Dublin, 1976).
JENNETT, Seán, *Cork and Kerry* (London, 1977).
JOHNSTON, E. M., *Ireland in the 18th century* (Dublin, 1974).
JOHNSTON, Jack, *St Macartan's Cathedral, Clogher* (Clogher, 1989).
JONES, Cheslyn, et al, *The study of liturgy* (London, 1978).
KENNEDY, T. P., 'Church Building' in *A History of Irish Catholicism* (ed. P. J. Corish), v, 8 (Dublin, 1970).
KIERSE, Seán, *Historic Killaloe* (Killaloe, 1983).
KILLANIN, Lord, and DUIGNAN, M., *The Shell Guide to Ireland*, revised and updated by Peter Harbison (London, 1989).
KNOX, H. T., *Notes on the early history of the dioceses of Tuam, Killala and Achonry* (Dublin, 1904).
LANGRISHE, Richard, 'Clonfert Cathedral' in *Journal of the Royal Society of Antiquaries of Ireland*, ix (1899), p. 426.
——, *Handbook to the Cathedral Church of St Canice, Kilkenny* (Kilkenny, 1879).
LANIGAN, Katherine, and TYLER, Gerald, *Kilkenny: its architecture and history* (Belfast, 1977).
LAWLOR, H. J., *The Reformation and the Irish episcopate* (2nd ed. London, 1932).
LEASK, H.G., *St Patrick's Rock, Cashel* (Dublin, n.d.).
——, *Glendalough* (Dublin, n.d.).
——, 'The Restoration of St Mochta's House' in *County Louth Archaeological and Historical Society Journal*, ix, no. 1 (1937), pp 32–5.
——, *Irish churches and monastic buildings*, (3 vols, Dundalk, 1955–1960).
LESLIE, J.B., *Ardfert and Aghadoe clergy and parishes* (Dublin, 1940)
——, *Armagh clergy and parishes* (Dundalk, 1911).
——, *Clogher clergy and parishes* (Enniskillen, 1929).
——, *Derry clergy and parishes* (Enniskillen, 1937).
——, *Ferns clergy and parishes* (Dublin, 1936).
——, *Ossory clergy and parishes* (Enniskillen, 1933).
——, *Raphoe clergy and parishes* (Enniskillen, 1940).
LEWIS, Samuel, *A Topographical Dictionary of Ireland*, (2 vols, London, 1837; repr. Washington, 1970).
LEWIS-CROSBY, E. H., *A short history of Christ Church Cathedral* (Dublin, 1949).

LINCOLN, Colm, *Steps and Steeples: Cork at the turn of the century* (Dublin, 1980).
LLOYD, John, *A short tour: or, an impartial and accurate description of the county of Clare, with some particular and historical observations* (Ennis, 1780).
LOEBER, Rolf, *A biographical dictionary of architects in Ireland 1600–1720* (London, 1981).
LUCE, A. A., *The life of George Berkeley, Bishop of Cloyne* (Dublin, 1949).
LYNCH, John, *The portrait of a pius bishop; or the life and death of the Most Rev. Francis Kirwan, Bishop of Killala, with introduction and notes by C. P. Meehan* (Dublin, 1864).
McCARTHY, Dermod, *St Mary's Pro-Cathedral, Dublin* (Dublin, 1988).
MacCURTAIN, Margaret, *Tudor and Stuart Ireland* (Dublin, 1972).
MacDONAGH, Michael, *Bishop Doyle 'J.K.L.' a biographical and historical study* (London & Dublin, 1896).
McDONNELL, Thomas, *The diocese of Killala from its inception to the end of penal times* (Killala, 1976).
McFALL, T. H. C., *An account of the history of Ferns Cathedral Church* (Dublin, 1954).
MacGOWAN, Kenneth, *Clonmacnoise* (Dublin, 1985).
MacGREEVY, Thomas, 'St Brendan's Cathedral, Loughrea 1897–1947' in *Capuchin Annual* (1946–7). pp 353–73.
McGUIRE, James, *Steeple and people. The Story of Ballina and its Cathedral* (Ballina, 1991).
MacKENNA, J., et al., *St Mary's Cathedral. Killarney* (Tralee, 1973).
McNAMARA, T.F., 'The Architecture of Cork 1700–1900' in *Royal Institute of Architects of Ireland, Year Book, 1960*, pp 15–39.
——, *Portrait of Cork* (Cork, 1981).
MacNAMEE, J.J., 'Lecture on the history of Ardagh' in *Ardagh and Clonmacnoise Antiquarian Society Journal*, ii, no. 7 (1940), pp 3–20.
——, *History of the Diocese of Ardagh* (Dublin, 1954).
McPARLAND, Edward, 'A bibliography of Irish architectural history' in *Irish Historical Studies*, xxvi, no. 102 (Nov. 1988), pp 161–212.
MANT, W. B., *Memoirs of the Rt Rev. Richard Mant, Lord Bishop of Down and Connor, and of Dromore* (Dublin, 1857).
MASON, W. M., *The history and antiquities of the Collegiate and Cathedral Church of St. Patrick, near Dublin* (Dublin, 1820).
MASTERSON, M. J., 'Centenary of St Mel's Cathedral 1840–1940' in *Ardagh and Clonmacnoise Antiquarian Society Journal*, vol. ii, no. 7 (1940), pp 45–62.
MAYES, Gilbert, *Saint Carthagh's Cathedral, Lismore* (Lismore, c. 1986).
MONTAGUE, H. P., *The saints and martyrs of Ireland* (Gerrards Cross, 1981).
MOODY, T. W., MARTIN, F. X. and BYRNE, F. J., et al. (ed.), *A New History of Ireland*, (9 vols. Oxford, 1976– , in progress).
MOONEY, Canice, 'The church in Gaelic Ireland' in *A History of Irish Catholicism* (ed. P. J. Corish), ii, 5 (Dublin, 1969).
MOYLAN, Francis, *Pastoral instruction to the Roman Catholics of the diocese of Cork* (Dublin, 1798).
——, *Doctor Francis Moylan to the lower order of the Roman Catholic inhabitants of the Diocese of Cork* (Cork, 1799).
MURPHY, Ignatius, 'The Cathedral of SS Peter and Paul, Ennis in *Ennis 750*, ed. by Gerry O'Connell (Ennis,
MURRAY, L., 'Monasteries of Louth, Pt I: Pre-Norman' in *County Louth Archaeological and Historical Society Journal*, vol. i, no.1 (1904), pp 21–36.
NELSON, R. G., *St Macartin's Cathedral, Enniskillen* (Enniskillen, 1990).
Notes on Cloyne Cathedral (Cloyne, n.d.).
O'BOYLE, Enda, *A history of Duleek* (Duleek, 1989).
Ó CAOIMH, Tomás, *Killarney Cathedral* (Dublin, 1990).
O'CONNELL, James, *The meaning of Irish place names* (Belfast, 1978).

O'CONNELL, Philip, *The diocese of Kilmore: its history and antiquities* (Dublin, 1937).

O'DONNELL, Augustine, *St Patrick's Rock*, (2nd ed., Thurles, 1963).

O'DONOVAN, Timothy, *Another frame-up in Ross Diocese* (Baltimore, 1988).

——, *The bag of tricks on Ross Diocese* (Baltimore, 1988).

——, *Drama on Ross Diocese. "actors" and "actresses"* (Baltimore, 1989)

——, *Ross Diocese heavenly intervention* (Baltimore, 1990).

Ó FIAICH, Tomás, *St Patrick's Cathedral, Armagh* (Dublin, 1987).

O'HARA, Bernard (ed.), *Mayo: Aspects of its heritage* (Galway, 1982).

O'LAVERTY, James, *An historical account of the diocese of Down and Connor. ancient and modern* (Dublin, 1880).

O'NEILL, Michael, *Marks of unheeded dilapidation: the 19th and early 20th century restorations*, St Patrick's Cathedral 800 series, no. 3 (Dublin, 1991).

O'REILLY, Bernard, *Life of John MacHale, Archbishop of Tuam* (2 vols, New York, 1890).

OFFICE OF PUBLIC WORKS, *Exploring Glendalough valley* (Dublin, 1990).

One hundred and fifty years of St Mel's Cathedral, Longford, 1840–1990 (Longford, 1990).

OTWAY, Caesar, *A tour of Connaught* (Dublin, 1839).

OWEN, Edwin, *St Flannan's Cathedral, Killaloe: A guide for visitors* (Killaloe, n.d.).

PARKER, J. H., *A concise glossary of architectural terms* (Oxford, 1896, reprinted London, 1989).

PARKINSON, R. E., *The Cathedral Church of the Holy Trinity of Down, Downpatrick* (Downpatrick, n.d.).

The Parliamentary Gazetteer of Ireland, (3 vols. Dublin, 1844–6).

PATERSON, John, *Meath and Kildare: an historical guide* (Kingscourt, 1981).

——, *Kildare: the Cathedral Church of Saint Brigid* (1982).

PEACOCK, H. H. E., *St Laserian's Cathedral, Old Leighlin* (Leighlin, n.d.).

PHELAN, M., 'St Mary's Cathedral: a personal approach' in *Old Kilkenny Review*, no. 24 (1972), pp 4–17.

PHILLIPS, W. A. (ed.), *History of the Church of Ireland*, (3 vols. Dublin, 1933).

POTTERTON, Homan, *Irish church monuments 1570–1880* (Belfast 1975).

POWER, Patrick, *Waterford and Lismore: a compendious history of the united dioceses* (Cork, 1937).

PUECKLER-MUSKAU, Prince H. L. H. von, *Tour in England, Ireland and France, in the years 1826, 1827, 1828 and 1829* (Zurich, 1949).

PURCELL, Mary, *Dublin's Pro-Cathedral* (Dublin, 1975).

QUANE, Michael, 'Tour in Ireland by John Harden in 1797' in *Journal of the Cork Historical and Archaeological Society*, lviii, no. 187 (1953), pp 26–37; lviii, no. 188 (1953), pp 81–90; lx, no. 192 (1955), pp 80–7.

RANKIN, P. J., *Irish building ventures of the Earl-Bishop of Derry, 1730–1803* (Belfast, 1972).

RICHARDSON, D. S., *Gothic Revival architecture in Ireland* (2 vols, New York, 1983).

ROBERTSON, I., *Blue Guide: Ireland*, (5th ed. London, 1987).

ROBINSON, A. C., *St Fin Barre's Cathedral, Cork* (Cork, 1897).

ROGERS, Edward, *Memoir of the Armagh Cathedral, with an account of the ancient city* (Belfast, 1881).

ROWAN, Alistair, *North-west Ulster* (London, 1979).

ROYAL SOCIETY OF ANTIQUARIES OF IRELAND, *Journal* (1897), Proceedings, pp 261–86.

RYNNE, Edward, *North Munster studies* (Limerick, 1967).

ST AUGUSTINE'S ABBEY, RAMSGATE, *The book of saints: a dictionary of the servants of God canonized by the Catholic Church*, Compiled by the Benedictine monks of St Augustine's Abbey, Ramsgate (London, 1989).

St Brigid's Church, Ardagh – St Mel: Centenary Souvenir 1881–1981 (Ardagh, 1981).

ST MARY'S CATHEDRAL, TUAM, *St Mary's Cathedral, Tuam*, Guide leaflet no. 1 (Tuam, n.d.).

——, *The chancel arch, St Mary's Cathedral, Tuam*, Guide leaflet no. 3 (Tuam, n.d.).

——, *The Stained-glass windows of St Mary's Cathedral, Tuam*, Guide leaflet no. 5, (Tuam, n.d.).

SEYMOUR, Edward, *Christ Church Cathedral, Dublin* (Dublin, 1869).

SEYMOUR, St J. D., *The Diocese of Emly* (Dublin, 1913).

——, *The succession of parochial clergy in the United Dioceses of Cashel and Emly* (Dublin, 1844).

SHEARER, John, *A short guide to Belfast Cathedral – St Anne's* (Belfast, n.d.).

SHEEHY, Jeanne, *J. J. McCarthy and the Gothic Revival in Ireland* (Dublin, 1977).

SMART, S. M., *Muscular Churches* (Fayetteville, 1989).

SMITH, Charles, *The antient and present state of the county of Down* (Dublin, 1744).

——, *The ancient and present state of the county of Kerry* (Dublin, 1756).

——, *The ancient and present state of the county of Waterford*, (2nd ed. Dublin, 1774).

SMITH, J. T., 'Ardmore Cathedral' in *Journal of the Royal Society of Antiquaries of Ireland*, vol. 102, Part 1 (1972), pp 1–13.

STOKES, A. E., *Christ Church Cathedral, Dublin* (Dublin, 1978).

STORY, Joan, *St Macartan's Cathedral, Clogher* (Clogher, 1970).

STUART, James, *Historical memoirs of the city of Armagh* (revised ed. by Ambrose Coleman) (Dublin, 1900).

SWANZY, H. B., *Sucession lists of the diocese of Dromore* (Belfast, 1933).

SWINFEN, Averil, *Kilfenora Cathedral* (Ennis, 1986).

TALBOT, M. J., *A pictorial tour of Limerick Cathedral* (Limerick, c.1969).

THACKERAY, W. M., *The Irish sketch-book* (2 vols, London, 1843).

THOMPSON, Patrick, *Guide to St Colman's Cathedral, Cóbh* (Cóbh, n.d.).

TILLOTSON, Arthur (ed.), *The correspondence of Thomas Percy and Edmund Malone* (Louisiana, 1944).

TRIMBLE, W. C., *The history of Enniskillen*, (3 vols, Enniskillen, 1919–21).

TURPIN, John, *John Hogan: Irish neoclassical sculptor in Rome* (Dublin, 1982).

TYNDALL, Charles, *The ancient parish and church of St John the Baptist, Sligo, from the early times to Disestablishment* (Dublin, 1962).

WALCOTT, Mackenzie, *The cathedrals of the United Kingdom* (London, 1860).

WARD & LOCK, *Illustrated historical handbook to the Irish cathedrals* (London, 1889).

WATT, John, *The church in Medieval Ireland* (Dublin, 1972).

WEBB, Alfred, *A compendium of Irish biography* (Dublin, 1878).

WEBSTER, C. A., *The diocese of Cork* (Cork, 1920).

——, *The diocese of Ross* (Cork, 1924).

——, *The Cathedral Church of St Fachtna, Ross* (Cork, 1927).

——, 'The diocese of Ross and its ancient churches' in *Proceedings of the Royal Irish Academy*, xl, Sect. C (1931–2), pp 255–95.

WESTROPP, T. J., 'Killaloe: its ancient palaces and cathedrals', pt. II in , xxiii (1893), pp 187–201.

——, 'The Churches of County Clare, and the Origin of the Ecclesiastical Divisions in that County' in *Proceedings of the Royal Irish Academy*, 3rd ser., vi, no. 1 (Oct. 1900).

——, 'Notes on the Antiquities of Ardmore' in *Journal of the the Royal Society of Antiquaries of Ireland*, (1903), pp 353–81.

WHEELER, H. A. and CRAIG, M. J., *The Dublin city churches* (Dublin, 1948).

WILSON, D. F. R., *St Patrick's Cathedral Dublin* (Dublin, n.d.).

WINDELE, John, *Historical and descriptive notices of the city of Cork and its vicinity; Gougaun Barra, Glengariff and Killarney* (Dublin, 1840).

YOUNG, J.A., *Unfinished pilgrimage: the story of Belfast Cathedral* (Belfast, c.1960).

INDEX

DATE DUE